PLANETTERRA JOURNALS
VOLUME I

WET SEASON

by

RAVEN DAVIES

Copyright: 2007 Raven Davies

Publication Date: 2011

Publisher: Friction Fiction Books Inc.

ISBN No.:   978-0-9866742-1-1

Acknowledgements

Thank you to the many researchers who allowed me to use their experiences in Amazonia, and to the many newspapers that gave accurate reports to confirm my friends' knowledge and added more detail. Although a fictional gay romance, this story is based on known facts and statistics during the writing process.

Table of Contents

Prologue

Chapter I 1

Chapter II 12

Chapter III 19

Chapter IV 37

Chapter V 51

Chapter VI 63

Chapter VII.. 71

Chapter VIII 85

Chapter IX 101

Chapter X 116

Chapter XI 131

Chapter XII... 146

Chapter XIII.. 153

Chapter XIV.. 164

Chapter XV... 178

Chapter XVI.. 188

Chapter XVII 198

Chapter XVIII 211

Chapter XIX.. 228

Chapter XX... 239

Chapter XXI.. 254

Chapter XXII 264

Chapter XXIII 277

Chapter XXIV 292

Chapter XXV 305

About the Author 317

Other Publishing Credits... 318

Prologue

*"What we call the beginning is often the end,
And to make an end is to make a beginning.
The end is where we started."*

T. S. Eliot

Chapter I

Two aircraft headed for New York: a long international flight, the other a short domestic hop. Two men, traveling separate journeys, flew on the wings of different dreams and aspirations: one already in the throes of achievement, the other just beginning. Although having never met, and neither knowing if they would ever meet, their thoughts fused unbeknownst on a telepathic link. The older man slept in a memory of young lovers and the sweet delights they brought, as he floated above the clouds somewhere between Bangkok and his next destination, unaware that a much younger man gazed misty-eyed at the billows of endless white, while traveling at cruising altitude on a jet from Denver.

Separated from all he knew and had experienced, an innocent had left his adoptive parents and biological grandmother in tears, while he struggled to maintain a mature demeanor to prevent jumping out the aircraft window and running the distance home to Pueblo. His family refrained from further advice, applauding his decision and giving him the extra confidence needed to handle the trip and a new adventure--an adventure to rise up and live again--just as he once did a long ten years prior. Once aboard and in the air, young nerves vibrated in unison with the fine hummed movement of the fuselage that he leaned against. He shook from his tapping toes to quivering lips--beautiful lips, perfect lips, adorning a male face of exquisitely fragile detailing--the eye-catching, second-look variety. Shunning offers of food and beverages, his heart pounded harder with each utterance of the stranger walking up and down the narrow aisle; he started to hyperventilate.

"Excuse me, sir. Can I get you something? You have become extremely pale, and your face is damp with perspiration." Questioning from across two other passengers, the flight attendant studied the oddly beautiful creature shaking his head vehemently. "Flying frightens more than a few. I think you should use this brown bag to aid your breathing. Please, sir."

"Yes, ma'am."

"Nice and slow; ring for me if you need medical assistance. Here's some ice water and another blanket. Perhaps they will help."

"No, no thank you, only the blanket. Do you have a sealed bottle of water; one that no one has opened?"

"I'll check. Keep breathing into the bag, and I'll return shortly. Snuggle into this extra covering, until I locate some water and sufficient handi-wipes to freshen your face."

The young man said nothing, choking on a response of gratitude to the redheaded woman in the navy blue uniform. Wiping perspiration off his flushed face and examining the bottle handed him, he placed both the damp cloth, which smelled of decaying wildflowers, and the unopened frosted container into the back pocket of the seat in front of him. Impossible to swallow anything while experiencing a waking nightmare, his memory jolted him into a flashback of red hair, stiletto boots, and the putrid, rancid odor of overtly sweet perfume purchased at a cheap pharmacy. The scent had permeated his entire being when dragon-lady talons scratched deep, leaving the unfamiliar odor of female sexuality into his skin. Her fragrance of death had nearly suffocated him, unable to wash off the stench; his only reprieve came via a sudden inhale of remembered outdoor air mixed with the comforting scent of warm horses and fresh hay.

"Not thirsty? They usually don't carry the smaller bottles anymore." The elderly gentleman, in the seat next to him, attempted to catch his eye, seeing the shaking grow worse. His youthful neighbor, however, remained forever forward throughout the mini dialogue, but startled out of his fixation at the next question after deducing the impossibility of leaping out the tiny window. "Are you afraid of flying, son?"

"No, sir."

"Perhaps it's what awaits at the end of your journey."

"Partially."

"And the other partially part?" The silver-headed passenger, with cataracts turning his blue eyes paler, finally saw the full-face turn toward him, jolting him into silence at the stunning good looks and the bizarre reply of the young man.

"Redheaded women scare the hell out of me."

"Only redheads?"

"Yeah."

"This particular one seems nice enough, as is my daughter."

"Oh, I'm sorry."

"Not to worry, but don't let one heart breaker hinder your many choices."

"No, sir." The wondrous eyes blinked several times to refocus on the water bottle, which the young man reached for, opened, and downed completely.

Chuckling sympathetically, the older man refocused on his breakfast, leaving the frightened character to himself, as the domestic flight continued on course; while over the Atlantic, the morning sunrise continued to chase Trevor Sloane. The solar disk finally caught the man sleeping comfortably in a flat-bed seat provided in first class by British Airways. Coming around, he kept still, not wishing to miss a second of the feel-good stretch of his tall, muscular frame. The long journey had once been a back killer for a man of substantial size. Without a flick of an eyelid at the musical Irish voice waking his fellow flyers, he succumbed to the results of his wet dream without a moan or a movement, only smiling in awe at the fair-haired young men, skipping naked, hand-in-hand, down Broadway and through his head. Turning slightly to lie supine, he opened his eyes to a black void, while discreetly catching his excitement under the blankets.

"Wake up, Mr. Sloane. We shall be serving breakfast in a few minutes. I must get your bed into the chair position, in preparation for food service and landing."

"Winter in the land of the midnight sun from what I can see."

"No, sir. The sun is glowing orange behind us."

"Curse you, Baron von Richtohofen!"

"Sir?"

"The Red Baron? It's a saying, from the *Peanuts* cartoon!"

"Oh yes, the little dog."

"A little dog! He's not just a little dog, but a beagle--*the beagle--good* grief."

"Sorry, sir, but you Americans make a wee hunting dog into a hero. Perhaps, you should take off your mask and face the new day. I'll bring you a copy of yesterday's *Times*, so you can catch up on Snoopy's antics."

"Where are we, and what planet are you from?" Sloane slowly removed his eye mask to a giggling greeting by the cherubic face of the flight attendant. She had been toying with him; and he felt like pulling the blankets over his head for more sleep. Unfortunately, the devilish imp refused to let him get away with it.

"Planet Erin, Mr. Sloane. I believe you've been there; and we're approximately an hour and a half away from Kennedy."

"Kennedy? Oh yeah, usually land in Newark if passing through. Curse you again, Red Baron. Not home yet, Sloane." Rolling out of his snug position, he relented to her obligatory request, flexed the muscles he had worked on since his youth, and staggered to one of the lavatories to freshen up. His dreams had been delightful, and perhaps the hum of the jet caused the sensation of holding an anal vibrator, ready to insert gently into a willing, excited partner with an expectation of something increasingly stimulating.

Washed and freshly dressed, he always carried a set of clean clothes in case of a variety of potential mishaps, including losing your luggage and sleeping in a dorm-like room on an aircraft. Life was changing, and he felt ready for a new beginning, or at least a different direction. Trevor Sloane had more than fulfilled his expectations, becoming a world-renowned, multi-award-winning photographer. Few people grasped the meaning behind what he saw through his lens, but his images did touch the soft hearts and insightful minds of those who handed out the prestigious crystal honors; many, of which, sat on his mantle and in his trophy case. Returning from two assignments back-to-back, as personal favors (well paying favors), he looked forward to a little relaxation, after he developed and couriered the best images to the appropriate clients. Two months away from home, all in a day's work for a freelancer, one meeting awaited him in the large metropolis, and then home to the country. Upon debarkation, he readily spotted his well-traveled backpack, snatched it quickly off the carousal, and away from the strangely ominous circling of only black valises on wheels. With deliberation, he escaped through the airport glass doors, his camera equipment secured, and his New York attitude ready.

Yellow... yellow cabs appeared and disappeared before one could blink. Knowing the routine, he walked in front of the one being loaded, the one rudely stolen from him. He placed his bags gently to ground and suddenly hurled his very breakable body onto the hood of a passing empty yellow-checkered vehicle. Unscathed, he heard the familiar horns honking, brakes screeching, and all the four letter words, which he had learned the meaning of in college, sworn at him. With his gear and his now aching body safely inside, he ignored the cabby yelling obscenities. An address in Manhattan, shouted over the profanity, jump-started the symbolic car into the correct lane of traffic, finding a clear route to speed the distance. Seeing the blur of a familiar skyline through the frosted glass, Sloane shivered violently and sat back for the long ride, after demanding the heater be turned to maximum to stop his teeth from chattering. From tropical monsoons to Arctic blasts, the temperature change deemed difficult for his body to adapt to readily. Winter, in a city of glass, mirrors, and steel, was spectacular; a backdrop of white snow and shimmering ice crystals left only the cars and people to add color this time of day. Looking at his watch, he was running late, but who was ever on time in this frenzied city of paranoia. He wondered why all his clients were based in such a confining area and pined for the open deserts of his adopted second home of twenty years: New Mexico.

Ensuring he had his bags safely over his shoulder, he stepped onto the slippery sidewalk. Even with his tropical trekking boots with rubber soles, he carefully walked the twenty-odd treacherous feet to the entrance before looking up, and then further up at the gargantuan office tower, which accommodated his favorite patron. He breathed in a lungful of cold air that stung, the shock bringing him back into the real world of supposedly civilized man, including the elevator of glass that scared him witless as it crawled up the exterior wall to the thirty-fourth floor like a deranged spider. He pushed his back against what appeared the only solid unmoving wall, but it opened as well, causing him to fall backward into a reception area, one vastly different from what he expected. A familiar laugh greeted him when the publisher's assistant helped him to his feet. Feeling underdressed for the elegantly designed office, and after apologizing for his rude entry, he placed his luggage beside the statuesque beauty's opulent desk, raked his fingers through his disheveled graying hair, and straightened his hot weather apparel that was hidden under an army-green Arctic parka.

"He's waiting for you, Mr. Sloane." The haughty blonde winked at him. He returned the flirtatious gesture, and then gazed about the new décor, his eyes lingering on an intriguing new image and name.

"Nice logo, Gina."

"New beginnings."

"What was wrong with the old? You're not turning into a New Age mystic on me with that introduction?"

"Change is good for the mind, as well as the spirit. I think you'll approve of what Mr. Graham has done with our space and the new magazine."

"I heard he sold the rights to his other two. This must be a winner, if he's willing to risk highly respected and established publications." Trevor followed the elegant long legs down a wide corridor lined with closed wooden doors: tranquility prevailed. The feeling fit with Gina's new dialogue, or had she always been so wise?

"It's a chance that a select few of us were willing to take. We believe it time."

"Time for what? You truly are speaking in cryptic riddles of an old sage."

"You're still crazy; and I adore you. It's time to test freedom of the press without political boundaries. Mr. Graham will explain. This is it. Ready?" She laughed and winked at the handsome photographer who drew her in like a magnet. Off limits, she knew his preference, but he still made her tingle. A strikingly handsome man in his early-fifties, he turned heads with his good looks; his dark graying hair, habitually left longer than fashionable, framed the chiseled face and enhanced the brown eyes that warmed when they softened. A collegiate football player in his day, the powerfully built body could still star as Superman: an extremely tall Superman. "Good luck with the cappuccino waiting behind these double doors. His latest toy has twisted his non-mechanical mind, but it makes him laugh." Gina smiled broadly and opened the impressive portal in a grandiose gesture of welcome, allowing him entry before it closed quietly behind him.

"Sloane! Good to see you. You look terrible!"

"Love you too, Warren." Without looking at the major publishing mogul, Trevor gazed about the warm room of wood paneling, Persian carpets, and several important masterpieces hanging on the walls, not to mention a fireplace crackling merrily, intimately surrounded with lush leather furnishings, deep and comfortable. The décor invited one to talk as friends, rather than the intimidating separation of a monster desk, behind which the stocky man sat.

"So, what do you think? I grew tired of taupe (the color of road dust), and the look of a robot made of metal and glass, including my wardrobe."

"You've always been hard as steel and fragile as... Nope, solid metal and always will be. I do like the change, however, a rather countrified gentlemanly look, the squire sitting in his library. You've warmed up New York for me, although the chic competition will chide you forever, believing you've already lost your mind over your recent idiosyncratic behavior."

The publisher strolled, at his own leisurely pace, from behind the slab of wood covered neatly with papers, to clasp Sloane's large hand in both of his. "Good to see you, you son-of-a-bitch. Sorry to delay your upcoming plans, but I don't want to waste a second posing this question."

"Heard of a phone?"

Not put off by the weary traveler, Warren Graham invited him to sit by the fire. Quickly fixing two cappuccinos, he passed a filled mug to warm the cold hands of his returned friend. Those gifted hands captured amazing photographs the old fashioned way: waiting for the right moment for days, using special lenses and cameras you had to set the aperture manually, and then snapping dozens of images, hoping one out of fifty taken would be perfect.

"This may take some convincing. You can be a stubborn jackass, Sloane. Some things have to be screwed into you personally."

Raising an eyebrow and his eyes twinkling, Trevor made himself comfortable and retaliated. "Why Warren, you just spouted two of my favorite words. Although your invitation sounds appealing, you're..."

"...shut up. I forgot with whom I spoke, your lordship. Look at this layout of some old pictures you took when Bosnia was part of Yugoslavia, and the latest ones you took on your last commission. Read the text carefully." A large black binder was placed on his lap, and the urgency of Warren's voice had Sloane intrigued, but dubious.

"I'm excruciatingly tired, Sir Graham; Thailand isn't just across the street. Besides, I seldom, if ever, read what someone has written in your magazines. The text is always disappointing, not capturing the essence of what is visible; the written words have little to do with the pictures, only a boring caption--an insult to the photographer--and I happen to be that photographer! My feelings get hurt."

"Poor baby, but I trust you've read something for a comparison." Warren tapped his finger hard against the three-inch ringed binder, exchanging squint for squint with his perturbed friend. Out-stared, Sloane began, recognizing the images immediately, all carefully arranged within the text and no captions. More interest consumed him, comparing the past and current pictures of the once beautiful country to the one now dangerously pitted with land mines. Engrossed in the words interpreting the meaning within his photographs, as well as the unique layout leading you through the text, Trevor believed the piece to be an intensive collaboration between an extremely imaginative writer and an equally talented graphic artist. On his third cappuccino, he closed the loose-leaf to look into Graham's expectant face.

"It's good; excellent in fact. The author captured exactly what I saw through my camera lens, as if reading my mind and instinctively interpreting my wonderment in a different medium. It's damn frightening, Warren, considering I can't explain my own photographs, as they're a gut reaction for me. This writer sees and understands my intent with powerful words. I'm impressed, including the work of the layout artist."

The expression on Sloane's face had Warren chuckling, but the image-taker warranted his own commendations. "One and the same, Trevor, and your pictures make the article, instead of the other way around. Can we team you up with this writer?"

"By all means. Whoever this is can write the story behind whatever work you toss my way." Trevor put his feet on the coffee table in front of the fire, suddenly acknowledging the pins and needles in his thawing feet.

"Close to what I have in mind. As you noticed, and have probably heard, even in the bars of the Far East, we're building a new magazine. Cutting edge stuff only, the goal is to make people aware of global issues, but more importantly, to concern them enough to act more effectively." The publisher rubbed his hands together, growing more excited in the telling of his latest venture.

"Like to explain that, Mr. Graham? Remember, I'm a bit jet-lagged." Trevor rested his elbows on either side of the comfortable chair, brought his fingertips together, and brushed them gently back and forth across his lips: his thinking position.

"I want to hire you--fulltime--with this youngster writing only for you." The wheeler-dealer waited, praying his offer acceptable, keeping his fingers crossed for added security, while leaning forward nervously, in case additional coaxing was required.

"Fulltime? A team? A big change for a freelancer after too many years; so here's the only deal. I pick the subject matter and travel alone." The start of negotiations did not please Sloane, but permanent employment would lighten the load of the garbage sometimes thrust upon him. One seldom turned down a job in his profession, although he rarely suffered from the lack of a paying project.

"Captured your interest, have I? Subject matter is up to you and your new shadow, based on one factor." The executive took control. "Notice how the writer summed up the test piece."

"Yeah, pretty gutsy conclusions, plus a simple solution, possibly too simple. You'll be treading on thin ice, Warren, if this piece went to print."

"Every article will conclude on the premise of an innocent

youngster, cutting through the crap, using only known investigative facts, plus a layman's heartfelt and insightful reaction, with no fear of editorial cuts or censorship. Your work will examine world problems or unsolved ancient mysteries, which have been misinterpreted, mishandled, and mismanaged, resulting in unsubstantiated claims that appear senseless to the common man." The excited publisher's breathing grew heavier, his heart condition a troubling thought for his friend.

Sloane set his coffee cup down and sat upright, feet on the floor. "Sorry, man. As they say, been there, done that, got a closet full of..."

"...yeah, yeah, T-shirts, but none of them have Thornton-Jones' picture silk-screened on the front. Those one or two line endings are the simplest, most ingenious of answers. They will make people think, and with luck--react--or even act to solve the problem from a different perspective. This writer is such an innocent, the answers could be that simple; and if placed before the public in a grandiose fashion, the two of you could have an opportunity to rectify these monolithic disasters of governments, religions, ecologists, fanatics of any sort, whatever. Hell, I'm giving you free rein to go after anybody or anything, with this writer's simplistic look at it all."

"You're dreaming, Warren. People don't act; they just spout the same old rhetoric, do a lot of marching, write a few cheques to whatever the charity, while waving misspelled, home-made banners. Innocence doesn't make it in the real world and quickly dies in the knowing of it."

The man with the balding head refused to give up. His first call was correct; Sloane would always be a stubborn arse. "We can't change everything, but certain things we can stir into the soup. How about toppling a few governments, maybe even our own, considering how puritanical and paranoid we've all become, considering God is now in the guise of President Bush, or is it the other way around? Can't wait for the next election to boot him out permanently."

"Jesus, a dreamer and a troublemaker, that's just great. I'll paint a target on my back." Troubled over crossing too many boundaries, Sloane's own instincts ricocheted through his head, wondering just how much free speech those in control would allow before shutting the magazine down, particularly God, if what Graham said was true. He had his own ideas to eradicate the world of problems that he stumbled upon, just as he had done this last trip, secretly capturing a scandalous rendezvous on film, of two noteworthy figures in the world's political arena. Neither man should have been whispering and laughing with the other in an out-of-the-way Bangkok restaurant. With this very hot image in mind, Trevor believed that this particular writer, who could interpret his work, may be the person to verbally enhance the photograph, without insulting powerful people. Calm, liberal, literate, direct, discreet, with no hint of hatred, the journalist had a way with positive critiques, while offering solutions. Too much complaining, without alternatives, seemed prevalent in every social and political structure he encountered.

"Come on, Sloane, one story. Anything you want to try, but the little darling goes with you."

Trevor slowly stood, but leaned down to thumb through the binder a last time, paying more attention to the detail of the montage and rereading the last two lines. "So, who is this clever writer; not some flaming, arse-kicking, feminist yahoo with constant PMS to get in my way? You know the ones: straight hair, an attitude that eats into flesh like a piranha, seldom smiles, only smugness registered on her clenched collagen-filled lips when she's winning. I won't..."

"...Ouch! Harsh, very harsh. You watch too much television; and I won't tell my arse-kicking wife what you said. I never realized you disliked women that much."

"I adore women, in a refreshingly intellectual way, as well as being uproariously fun to be around. Just feel badly as to how they're portrayed in the entertainment industry, particularly dramatic roles; one reason I stopped watching television. Women aren't that cold-hearted or brainless; they're better than that. They're recent depictions in the media have become more stereotypical than the likes of me, for Christ's sake."

"You're hardly a stereotype, Sloane. Not even close." Graham smiled broadly, while turning his back and strolling toward his security monitor focused on reception. A black and white view popped up, as did the head of the photographer who gazed, with keen interest, over the shorter man's shoulder. Zooming in on the only other person in the room, besides the divine Gina, Graham pointed to a young man in unstylish, too tight, faded jeans with a crease, a light-colored turtleneck sweater, a dark blazer, and winter hiking boots. The kid sat like a lost shadow, a left fist to his mouth, and right fingers drumming the arm of the chair. A slow, appreciative whistle from Sloane made Warren laugh. He knew the famous Trevor Sloane well.

"Oh brother." The taller man immediately turned away to inhale deeply, as his friend laid a hand on his shoulder.

"Cute enough?"

"He's a baby! Goddamn it, Warren, I can't watch over him and do my job!" The photographer leaned against the oversized desk and crossed his arms in defiance.

"He's older than he looks; and I remember another talented baby who walked into my office eons ago. Forget that analogy; you were never a baby, but hatched fully grown from a prehistoric giant egg."

"Touché. You're a sweetheart." Sloane mischievously placed his hands on the chubby cheeks to plant a kiss on the baldhead. "So, for whom are we working?"

"The *PlanetTerra Journals* and he's not a present. Be nice to him."

"Nice? I'll be on my best behavior." Trevor returned to the monitor and scrutinized the nervous figure staring blindly forward, doing a remarkable imitation of a possum caught in the lights of a fast moving killing machine. "So little darling, we're going to save the planet on your recommendations. The idea scares the hell out of me too."

Chapter II

After a ten-minute introduction, a pep talk, and a shaking of hands, Warren had two strangers out of his office and on their way down the glass elevator. Trevor sucked in his breath and held it for the entire trip down the thirty-four floors; his back firmly braced against the metal door. He would be ready when the silent opening made its move. Unafraid of heights, he had scaled and repelled many a mountain cliff with heavy equipment in tow, but his hands and knowledge had checked the harnessing thoroughly, unlike the free-fall elevator mysteriously attached to the exterior surface of the looming tower. He never took his eyes off his new partner, a diversion to thwart the feeling of an impending crash.

An unusual young man in appearance and countenance, Phoenix Thornton-Jones had his gloved hands pressed against the see-through shell, enjoying the sensation of flying and the panoramic view he had never seen, except once on the way up. His naïve wonderment charmed Sloane, who watched the diminutive figure silently from the safest position, knowing a smile enhanced the remarkable face at the sight. Reaching ground, both men exited the building, the larger man heading toward traffic to engage in another altercation with a treacherous yellow vehicle. Feeling a presence behind him, he turned to see a befuddled kid looking up and down the street, and then down at his toes, mimicking a hapless tourist without a decent map in hand.

"What's up, kiddo? Did Graham give you the name of your hotel?"

"No, sir. Maybe you could recommend one. Don't know of any, or what I'm supposed to do. Thought we could go someplace and discuss our next step." The younger man did not look up to face the giant-sized man. He could not; he could not directly face anyone, but for a handful of very close friends.

"We'll wave down a cab, drop you off someplace respectable, and then I'll carry on to my apartment. While I sleep, you can settle in."

"Okay." Again, Thornton-Jones did not look up, but jumped to attention when asked to hail a taxi. Considering the items he carried, one arm seemed maneuverable enough to lift for attention, but he missed his first attempt. A second wave meant another miss, and he heard Sloane sigh heavily behind him.

"Step aside; you'll break trying this. I don't know if my own body can handle much more of New York's transportation system. Watch my bags, particularly the metal one." Trevor set his luggage at the edge of the curb, indicating to his new sidekick to move into position next to the distinctive case of valuable camera equipment, and to stand guard over his own costly gear. Tens of thousands of dollars now sat on the sidewalk for the taking, if not for the two men keeping an eye out as to their precise location. Phoenix stood exactly where told, his toes clinging to the edge of the cement rise, a good viewing point to watch a lunatic venture into bumper-car traffic.

Sloane picked his oncoming target, and as he had done at the airport, stopped the vehicle by slamming his upper body down hard against the hood from the side. Further frenzied insults peppered the unflappable photographer, while the younger man took the cue, opened the back door immediately, tossed in two backpacks, gently loading the three important cases of working gear, and then scrambled into the narrow remaining space. Without hesitation, but a little cursing over a possible rib injury, Trevor climbed into the front seat; an action seldom taken in the formidable city.

"Hey, man, what you doin'? You ain't s'posed to be sittin' next to me; 'sides, you could get yourself killed pullin' a stunt like that. Man, you are one crazy dude. You gotta be nuts." The cabby, in the Peruvian hat with ear warmers, gruffly snarled.

"I'm bolts; the one in back is nuts." Sloane's quick humor invoked a snicker from the rear, but the driver rolled his eyes and asked for a destination from Mr. Bolts.

"Mott Street, Chinatown, but we have to find Mr. Nuts a place to stay first. Hey, kiddo, did Graham give you expense money or a credit card?"

"No, I didn't think to ask." The voice sounded embarrassed. Obviously, the fledgling journalist had little business sense, and probably did not have the remotest idea regarding expense accounts, or even how much he would be earning.

"Do you have cash for a hotel, dinner, etc. etc. etc.?" Trevor tried to speed up the conversation with his best Yul Brenner imitation in *The King and I*, while praying, to the silver-clouded sun above, to speed him home and into bed.

"Some. Enough for..."

"...a burger and a scummy motel in another state. Shit. We're being played, my friend, or our publisher's becoming senile." Sloane leaned against the door of the cab, rubbing his temple on the right side.

"I'll be fine. You're tired and need rest. Just drop me off here." Rejection echoed in the soft, raspy voice; the hesitation accompanying it increased Trevor's bafflement.

The older man had lived on his own since sixteen, sent away to school and college by a caring, but antiquated English born and bred father. He had raised himself with little regard toward other's concerns, except for his small family and a few favorite lovers and friends. Drawing into himself only, today he needed to conjure up some honest compassion and quickly. With a lens between himself and Thornton-Jones, he would see the reasoning behind the man's nervousness and probably every detail of his life. A photographer was what he was and how he viewed the world--through his camera--to separate himself from the reality. "So, there's the rub, as Shakespeare wrote in *Hamlet*; I think. Okay, decision made; you'll come home with me, Warren's little darling; and we'll play his game of trick or treat. Once I've had my power nap, we'll get you sorted out."

"I can do this alone, Mr. Sloane. Truly, I can do this." The young man mustered his courage, while regretting the phrasing of an affirmation he often used in front of a mirror. Unable to readily communicate in a social or business environment, since the accident, he brushed off his stupidity as a rare encounter with strangers. He had to make a good, solid impression; but his inexperience created an error he could not retract without further explanation. Clenching his fabricated jaw, silence seemed the best choice.

"I'm sure you can, but we'll try again later. My studio has two large bedrooms, and to tell you the truth, I'm too damn tired and turned around to think."

Phoenix sat stone still; thankful Sloane did not catch the mistake. Nonetheless, weaving through late afternoon traffic to a stranger's home, in the middle of a place he had no escape from, had him wringing his gloved hands in terror. The shaking had stopped once off the plane, but the invitation hit him with a flashback so strong, he felt sick. His head yelled a series of negatives; his sad heart gave him hope to trust this man. Another memory, of a party held in an acquaintance's home, had him urgently demanding the cabby to stop. The man's invitation had been casual, as was Sloane's, to have a beer amongst fellow skiers in a condominium in a small resort town close to Telluride, where he customarily worked during Reading Week before

December examination finals. Usually a time to refresh his mind and body for the upcoming nail-biters, but the party took a horrible twist, turning the world of one seventeen-year-old upside down and backward. He thought the older man felt obligated to entertain his skiing instructor and had accepted, not thinking twice about asking if other coaches would be attending. Entering the door to meet the man's other guests, they were few but comfortable to speak with. One handed him a bottle of foreign brew, a bitter taste that trickled down his throat, causing numbness, and then nothing. Only later would he understand how long they had kept him, although what they had done was a lifetime too long.

Scrambling to open the backdoor, he hung his head out of the taxi to purge himself of the frightening nightmare. An extremely pale young man slowly returned to his position and apologized to the two startled men in front, neither of whom said a word, as he fumbled in his pocket for a stick of mint gum. The taste settled his stomach; the scent freshened his breath. Wiping his face with a neatly pressed handkerchief, he felt halfway normal, although he noted the photographer's worried expression. "Please, Mr. Sloane, I can find a hotel easily enough. I don't want to be a burden."

"No more mister or sir. The name is Trevor or Sloane. Okay, driver, directly to Mott Street." Contemplating the unnerving day heaped upon someone from who knows where, the older man left the sudden attack as stage fright; however, the unusual monogrammed handkerchief intrigued him. Seldom used in the age of disposable tissues, especially amongst the twenty-something crowd, the neatly folded item (with the embroidered initials TJ) seemed indispensable to the kid who tidied up and blew his nose. "Do you get car sick, and what was the name Graham called you? Sorry, I missed it when he shoved us out the door."

"Phoenix; and cars don't usually bother me. Just excited I guess."

Hearing the lie and wondering about a name different from the first initial, Sloane would figure it out. Time always exposed the truth, and the quiet young man in the sheepskin jacket was already turning into a mystery to be solved. The shock of snow-white hair, highlighted with the colors of a pastel rainbow, indicated something peculiar: perhaps hereditary, a trauma, or albino characteristics. The eyes, however, those eyes of violet invalidated the latter, and they had held Sloane's attention throughout the short conversation in the office. Not a co-incidence this partnership, the rider in the backseat had something important to offer the graying man in front, and vice versa. Any person who popped into your life had a purpose, according to his late grandmother, but Sloane continued to rub his aching temples, attempting not to think about it.

Home... Sloane stepped out of the cab slowly, and then assisted his new partner with the luggage. Although relieved, he still wished his journey had continued on to New Mexico, where winds blew to warm the soul, and the sun shone to elevate the spirit. New York was home away from home, for the last twenty-five years, thanks to a little inheritance money. He had invested the small bundle in a run-down building in Chinatown, before a developer gobbled it up to prey on the remaining community. Having traveled Asia throughout the beginning of his career, the ambiance and mystery of the Far East intrigued him; and he had to have a base in the Big Apple. The situation resulted in a hide-away on one of the busiest streets in the high-rise metropolis. Reconstruction, of the interior upper two floors into one, created a masterpiece of simplicity and elegance, incorporating his one-quarter Cherokee ancestral beginnings, Oriental influences, and his hidden side. He easily shut out a menacing, hurtful world, but allowed hopeful light to shine through the enormous floor to ceiling windows, which spanned the two full stories with five dramatic arches. To Sloane's advantage, you could see out, but no one could see in, and the soundproofing could not be matched.

Beneath his upper living area, he rented out the shops and the adjoining living facilities to the families who could have been displaced by his purchase. The design worked well for everyone. Just downstairs, he had a small grocery store and a laundry; neither family bothered him, paid their rent, and cared for their proprietor's suite when he traveled elsewhere. His favorite tenant tottered out of the store to greet him, attired in her winter gear, squealing his name, while her mother looked on.

"Hey, my little muffin, I've missed you! What a fluffy pink coat you're wearing? You look like a lovely strawberry today, good enough to eat!" Trevor had his luggage on the ground the moment she ran for him, and easily swung the three-year-old up for a baby's hug and kiss. "Best go with your mom. Looks like you two are heading someplace special."

"Nice to see you back, Mr. Sloane. I just told father of your return. Come along, Kimmie. We're off to a birthday party, and

Uncle Trevor has things to do."

"See you around, Sue Lin. Come on, Phoenix. That is such a bizarre name, sounds so Western."

"And Trevor doesn't?"

"Touché." Sloane unlocked the bright turquoise-colored door, embedded between the two shops; and both men headed up the steep straight stairwell that led to another entry, one more subdued and distinctly Asian in its fine lacquer and intricate symbols of gold against black. Once open and both inside, the younger man gazed at every detail, wandering how his new, or maybe only temporary, working partner had managed to keep this gem of New York under wraps from *Architectural Digest*. The legend's taste was impeccable and intriguing. Original artwork adorned the walls, sticking to an Asian theme, although incorporating everything from abstraction to pointillism. The large studio apartment warmed with exquisite furnishings of leather and wood, flat surfaces decorated with photographs by Trevor Sloane, and ones of him standing or sitting with the rich and important; the mix of décor came together with a dusty earth-tone palette. Five arched windows, scaled proportionately to the large area, spanned the distance from floor to ceiling, with everything in its appropriate place to produce a visually balanced effect. The ceiling stretched twenty feet high; and stairs (in twos, threes, and fours) led to different private quarters. Phoenix immediately clicked into the meditative ambiance of a masculine space--no women--not a picture, a painting, nor a likeness. Again, growing pale, he turned to face a statue in the foyer; two marble men embraced and entwined, forever united in the most erotic of fashion.

"Problem?" Trevor removed his warm outer garment and turned to see the expected disgust on his guest's face.

"No, sir, it's just... It's..." The young man, who appeared sculpted from the same white marble as the statue, tilted his head for a better study of the large *objet d'art*. Unlike the frozen duo that he reached out to examine, Thornton-Jones fevered with a blush. "You're gay!"

"Does that bother you?" Trevor hung his coat in a hidden closet, before casually returning to assist a curious new comrade with his gear.

"No, of course not. Just surprised how openly you display your sexuality." Without the hindrance of his pack, Phoenix shed his sheepskin coat along with his boots, unwilling to dirty the polished wooden floor and Tibetan rugs.

"Might as well lay the cards on the table. I'm gay and surround myself with gay friends. You'll meet some of them from time to time. Now, what about you? Girlfriend? Boyfriend? Both?"

"I don't know."

"You don't know what: whether you have someone in your life, or whether you're straight, gay, or something else?" Trevor stopped dead. Having skimmed over a brief resume, he did pick up two facts: Phoenix was no child, but a man of twenty-seven with large chunks of his life missing. Nevertheless, his sexual orientation had to be known in some physical manifestation.

"A long story you'll never hear, and as for you being gay, most of the people I love are so inclined; so please, go lie down before your knees give out. I'm happy just to sit and watch CNN. I promise not to touch anything, except for your television, keeping the volume very low. That is, if you don't mind?" Phoenix looked shaken and avoided the long story.

Too tired to persist with further questioning, Trevor bid his guest welcome, to make himself at home, and to turn the audio up as loud as he wanted. The photographer received a thank you, as he finally climbed the few steps to his private suite. Shutting the door behind him, he puzzled over Phoenix Thornton-Jones, the last name finally realized as the initials on the handkerchief. The only description of the young man was of someone scared to his grave. If homophobic, the kid did not register distaste and readily accepted to stay the afternoon, although some type of nervousness showed in his demeanor. Sloane shook off the serial killer paranoia rampantly spreading in many American minds, as the likelihood, of the extraordinarily pretty kid succeeding in butchering him, seemed slim. After all, the former university Tight End, a laughable position for a gay football player, weighed twice that of the journalist, not to mention standing a foot taller. With nothing to fear and a little humor of his past, Sloane smiled, remembering the sound and feel of the jet humming. Having slept only a few hours on his return journey, and even less the night before, the well muscled man stripped down to basic naked and slipped under the comforter in relief. His head hit the coolness of the pillow, and he fell into the softest cloud, sent adrift in special dreams for much longer than planned.

Chapter III

After four hours of a winter's deep sleep, a contented man yawned and stretched. Feeling refreshed upon waking in one of his beds and satisfied both paying tasks had gone well, Sloane could rest and work at the same time; always a treat to watch a perfect picture emerge under the eerie shadows of his darkroom. A whistling sound caught his ear; and he remembered his guest. Now early evening, the kid was probably ravenous but only finding the coffee at this late juncture. The high shriek of his screeching kettle alerted the big man to move. Sticking his head out the door, he smelled something wonderful and almost forgotten. "Hey kiddo, you still with me?"

"You insisted. Made dinner, and now that you're up, I'll finish it off."

"Dinner? Did you say dinner?"

"Thought you'd be hungry, and I didn't have much else to do."

"Where in the cosmos did Warren find you? New Yorkers don't cook; they eat out, or order in."

"Colorado, where we fend for ourselves. Besides, according to your lengthy bio, if you're not in New York, you reside somewhere east of Santa Fe." The astonishingly beautiful face turned and winked at the disheveled photographer.

"You're right; we'll do this Southwestern style. I'll take a shower and join you in ten." Trevor had eaten every type of food on the planet in his wanderings, and he laughed aloud while releasing his stiffness to the steam of a manufactured waterfall. Never had he foraged for food in the city of thousands of restaurants, which offered every type of cuisine for take-out, or dining-in by candlelight, any time of the night or day. He did know how to survive, however; his ancestral instincts and learned knowledge would kick in, enabling him to live off wild game, insects, reptiles, and fish, as well as discerning edible plants from those that could kill or give you stomach cramps for endless days. A home cooked meal would be a treat, something he loved about his late mother and grandmother. He missed them, particularly the latter, who enthralled him with the tales and rituals of the Cherokee. The old woman, in her silent way, taught him to observe the world in the smallest things, and in so doing, made him a master of his craft: the seeing of what lay beneath the surface.

Donned in his second set of fresh but warmer clothes for this cold day, Trevor emerged feeling better. His migraine induced melancholy disappeared upon finding a busy sprite stirring with one hand and controlling temperature gauges with the other. Continuing his subtle inspection, he noticed the backpacks rested side-by-side and out of the way, along with his camera case; a laptop computer sat on the coffee table, turned off; and a guitar, an expensive one on viewing the engraved leather case, leaned idly in the corner. "What have you concocted? Something smells delicious."

"I ventured downstairs and met Kimmie's grandfather. He told me what you usually purchased, and I picked up a few more things. Stew and biscuits okay with you? Please don't tell me you're a vegetarian!" The sudden realization he may have made a ghastly blunder showed in the violet eyes, which widened to their fullest.

Trevor had to chuckle, considering his muscles were protein based, never obtainable with celery sticks and grass. "Perfect, but I thought you only had a few dollars in those denims."

"You said it and assumed too much, not giving me the chance to tell you I have one of these." Phoenix pulled a card out of his wallet, flashed the platinum insignia at him, and laughed. "You really could have dropped me off at any hotel in town, Trevor."

"Shit! You're a rich little hustler!"

Phoenix's smile instantly disappeared, and he turned away. Another stream of emotions flooded over the sensitive man, remembering the name calling by the defense, as the district attorney retaliated as loudly. He dropped his wallet and put his hands over his ears to stop the racket in his head. Someone touched him, and he reeled around to push away the unwanted gesture from a man twice his size. "Stay away from me! Keep out of the kitchen when I'm cooking! Touch nothing!" In a dither and trying to determine where he was, the kid did accept the fallen wallet, but with a hand that shook so badly, he could barely replace it in his too tight back pocket.

"Whoa there, Phoenix. Easy son. I'll just set the table while you carry on with what you're doing." A little disturbed by the reaction to something he had said, Sloane stepped away and went about domestic business, quite a rarity for him; but the snapping turtle, on the far side of the island counter, had rocked him to the core.

The young man said nothing further, but quietly composed himself with deep breaths. Once again, he questioned why he had accepted the job of working with the intrepid Trevor Sloane and possibly traveling the world with him. His tight family of three attempted the giant task of reacquainting him with social niceties, as well as coaxing him off the ranch. Partially successful in his final year of college, he had driven solo back and forth every weekday to the University of Southern Colorado, from which he graduated at an accelerated rate, with resulting degrees in Journalism and Foreign Languages. In the latter, he had mastered fluency in eight, thanks to his grandmother; her gift of earphones and language tapes gave him something to do while recuperating. Achieving functionality in an academic environment encouraged him to apply for a position working with a legend, a job that promised a leap forward to another level of confidence. He had to prove himself capable of handling the world outside the ranch gates. The sweat slowly dried on his brow, until he noticed Sloane choosing a bottle of red wine from his large collection. Again, the journalist froze.

Trevor continued rummaging, finally setting a bottle on the counter, and then stepping toward the fridge to see what goodies they had for snacks. Master Chui would certainly send his favorites with the unnerving Mr. Thornton-Jones. Surprisingly, he found the oddest collection of one serving containers of milk, juices, and water, plus things he never purchased, fruits and vegetables, all neatly washed and bagged with one serving per package. The puzzle grew; Sloane started to think. Checking the overhead cupboards, he shook his head in wonder at the individual little boxes of cereal and single packets of nuts and raisins to add to the yogurt. Two items, he did spot, gave him hope that the young man retained some sanity. Obscure evidence presented itself with a full bag of Sloane's favorite Brazil nuts and a family-sized package of cookies. He startled out of his surrealistic trip through his own kitchen, when he heard a familiar compact disc switch on. One of his favorite songs, from a time long past and sung by an acquaintance, made his homecoming complete; Sting's sultry voice soothed him with the song *Fragile*. Perhaps the melancholy piece had been left on repeat by happenstance, particularly when he glimpsed the saddest eyes of one who could be the focal point of the haunting melody.

"I'm sorry, Mr. Sloane."

"Trevor."

"You welcome me into your home; and I go ballistic. Can't explain it, but it won't happen again. I'm scared, man, scared beyond any words I know; but I need this job; I need to repay everyone who put me back together. More than the million or so dollars medically, I owe them so much more. My success with this effort means everything."

"Slow down, kiddo, you're trying to tell me part of that long story, and maybe you should start from the beginning." Sloane reached for the wine and opener, only to remember the single serving drinks in the fridge. Carefully studying the unusual purple eyes, which apprehensively flickered over the bottle, he backed off. "Do you want me to open this Shiraz something or other, or do you wish to uncork it when dinner is ready? Perhaps you're not a connoisseur of red and would prefer another libation, alcoholic or not."

"Not much of a drinking man, a glass of red does sound tempting after my weird day. Hand me the bottle, and I'll open it over here. Would you like a glass now? The biscuits are almost done."

Relief clearly showed on the amazingly perfect face, convincing Sloane to set the expensive wine within the man's short reach. He scrutinized his troubling new partner who hustled to open the imported vino and pour two glasses half-full; one he handed to Trevor, the other he kept very close for himself, never putting it down or the container with the famous label. Seemingly caught in a conundrum, Phoenix did find a place for the bottle, assuredly out of the photographer's reach, permitting him to serve the salad and the stew in large bowls that he placed on the elegant dining table, along with the hot biscuits. Again, a sense of morbid fear overtook the young man; an expression noticed immediately by the photographer. Unfortunately, without a camera to capture Phoenix's terror of taking his eyes off the food, the bottle, and his glass, which all appeared in positions the kid could not possibly see at once, Trevor discreetly turned away, deciding on the expensive chinaware in the cabinet behind him, leaving his quirky guest to handle his curious dilemma. Quietly, he dressed the table, waiting for his next surprise, while Phoenix stood scrutinizing his every move. Both sat down at the same time and dinner commenced. Conversation was minimal, yet amicable, while feeling each other out and liking what they heard. Only the nervous journalist, with the look of a traumatized angel, touched the wine bottle and his own glass.

"Thanks, Phoenix. Dinner was tremendous, reminiscent of my grandmother's cooking."

"You have a grandmother as well?"

"We all have two at some point."

"Oh, I just meant..."

"Just joking, kiddo, considering I never met my paternal grandmother, and the one I loved passed away a number of years ago. A great lady, she taught me how to observe everything, catching the fine details." Finished with his second helping of everything, the man, with the bigger appetite, crossed his arms, leaned back to settle his overly full stomach, and gazed intently at his unusual guest sitting quietly in front of him. There was no doubt that Phoenix had the handsomest face he had ever seen, enhanced by the trendiest of hair fashion of wildly layered, white hair, which ended in defined triangles that brushed over his collar, and intricately highlighted with the faintest pastels. The unusual eye coloration, however, had him mesmerized. They were violet: not quite dark royal velvet, nor the light shade of lavender, but vibrantly rich purple with sparkles of lilac and rimmed in black. The long, thick, white lashes would have made the eyes overly large, but the dusting of a darker skin tone, which rimmed the eyelids, framed any expression exuded, doubling the effect. Succumbing to the exceedingly beautiful image, the photographer sucked in his breath, holding back a new fantasy and possible conquest. A sudden thought, Sloane smiled at the questioning face. "Can I take a picture of you, right now, in full light, just with a digital? I'd like to do a simple experiment."

"I guess so."

"Turn on my desk computer, while I grab my fun camera." The older man found his toy; Phoenix faced directly at the lens; and a shot was fired. Sitting down and plugging in the digital mechanism, Sloane brought the image up on the monitor and waved at his model to peer over his shoulder to share what he was creating. With lightning speed, he sized the picture, copied it, reversed the original, saved it as a second image, and then cut both in half. Adept at electronically enhanced imagery, the perfectionist used the new technology only as an artistic game, for he refused to allow a camera or a computer to enhance any of his professional pictures, except with a variety of filters. Carefully moving the images apart, he maneuvered the right halves together, and then the left ones. Shock registered immediately. "I'll be damned!"

"What's wrong?"

"I'm sure you're aware of this trick: two sides of a personality are exposed by flipping each side horizontally and splicing right to right and left to left. Well, that's what I've done. Look at them." Flabbergasted at what he had never seen, Sloane finally figured out the oddity of the extraordinary face, which could seduce anyone if placed on a billboard.

"I only see me, and both look the same. What's wrong with them, besides me looking like a girl?" Phoenix appeared a little disgruntled over the pictures. He could easily pass for a young woman; the unfortunate truth of the experiment as far as he was concerned.

"Can't you see it? This is amazing. The two pictures match exactly! The left and right sides of your face are symmetrical. It's as rare as finding two snowflakes alike. No wonder your face looks perfect. It is!"

Phoenix walked away from the man who continued to study the images. He should not have allowed the photograph--time to tell a little of his tale--*the accident story*. Starting to gather the dishes, he heard Trevor shut off the computer and walk over to help.

"I'll take care of tidying up, while you tell me things I need to know before hasty decisions are made. Sit down, sip the vino you've protected throughout dinner, and give me a little concrete information." Rolling up his sleeves, Sloane filled the dishwasher, set it to start in a few hours time, as not to interfere with one word that may come out of the younger man's mouth. Cleaning off the table with a damp cloth, he heard a soft voice start to drop bricks from the tall barrier behind which Phoenix hid. On hanging the tea towel on its peg, he ushered the man off a bar stool and directed him to sit in front of the fire, which had been started many hours earlier and occasionally stoked by either man to keep it ablaze.

"Ten years ago, just around this time of a cold late November, I had a really bad accident. If it weren't for my now adoptive parents, I would have died. Anyway, Caly and Twister found me, called the police and an air ambulance via their cell phone. I've spent most of those long years in a hospital. The face you see is new to me as well, created by a plastic surgeon, seemingly inclined toward feminine features. It took many years of surgeries and psychoanalysis to get me as far as your living room. I'm sorry, Trevor, but this is who I am: a man made of bits and pieces, bolts and screws, with a head full of phobias. You were right when you called me Mr. Nuts. I thought your statement very humorous in the cab, as well as the innuendo. Real cute, Sloane."

"So, you caught that. Hope you weren't insulted."

"Not me. I figure the acknowledgment of my presence a

compliment. I meant to thank you, and to tell you that I'm somewhat off-centered. Fighting fears, one at a time, I've conquered many, but not all. If you wish to discontinue this charade of saving the world, a ridiculous notion in the first place, just tell me. I'll return to Colorado tonight."

Trevor puzzled over the intent of his next remark, not wishing to disrupt the harmony slowly developing between the two men. Requesting the tightly secured bottle, he poured the remaining contents into his glass and motioned Thornton-Jones to take the seat beside him that had a direct view of the fire. An entrancing, heart-soothing sight, both men could gaze at the dancing flames and not look at each other. "First off, we all suffer from a variety of anxieties; and secondly, you do not look like a girl, although you're the best looking man I've ever seen, including your seductive little nose... a bit like Brad Pitt's."

"At least you didn't compare it to that of Francesca Annis who has the tiniest nose on the planet."

"Ms. Annis is one of the famed beauties of my generation, even in her sixties. I'm surprised you've heard of her."

"I'm into British miniseries, and she's been in a few. She stands out in my mind because of her resemblance to my grandmother."

"Your grandmother must be a knock-out."

"She is, as well as being tiny."

"So, you get your stature from your grandmother, and in an odd fashion, your face as well. Nothing wrong with either."

"Thanks, but it doesn't change the fact that I'm small and look like a girl. They didn't have much left to create stronger features."

"Your nose looks masculine enough, although very delicate; besides, I like your face. You're extremely handsome, Phoenix, so you can stop degrading something I admire. From what I've gathered so far, your adult life has been relatively isolated; and further, we'll have to get you over eating and drinking from single serving containers, or you'll starve on our trips. They don't have *Lean Cuisine* in the middle of the jungle; and I doubt if the Bedouins have bottled water to your taste. Am I right so far?"

"Yes, sir. Seems the plan is set. I'll call the airport right away." Phoenix could break a heart with those perfect lips for tasting, which turned downward, needing a kiss to stop the slight quiver.

"No you're not, but I need to know the facts before deciding how we can manage this. How strong are you? Healthy enough to trek long distances with heavy loads and quick enough to run like hell while dodging bullets?" Trevor staid his panic. A partner, who flipped out without warning, could jeopardize many a tightrope upon which they may balance. Unfortunately, he liked the young man, besides lusting over him, but if Phoenix had experienced a horrendous accident and a lengthy recovery, the long hours and hard journey could prove too difficult mentally and physically. He could not imagine the cause of such extreme trauma.

"Proportionally, I'm as strong as you, and I don't usually get sick. You appear to work out for muscle mass, while I've been in therapy, working in the gym to create endurance, speed, and flexibility. Does that mean you'll still consider me for the job? I'll follow orders to the letter." The violet eyes lit up and the long white eyelashes fluttered as natural washers to prevent the tap from dripping.

"So, you have a phobia of pre-opened containers, for whatever reason I can't deduce. You're rebuilt from top to bottom, but have no fear of further damage. Correct so far?" Trevor leaned forward, taking up his thinking position: his elbows on his knees, his palms pressed together, and his fingers against his lips.

"I'm fit enough to fight, and probably stronger and more daring in a combative scenario than when I competed. The container thing--I bet I can find *Coca Cola* anywhere--and bottled water." The younger voice sounded more enthusiastic, convincing the photographer that Thornton-Jones would willingly take on the challenges of a high-risk adventure.

"You're right about the coke, but no matter what, you have to eat whatever is placed in front of you, or what we scavenge. You would be considered rude, in most countries, if you didn't eat every morsel on your plate; and we wouldn't get anywhere in our search for whatever we're looking for. So, remember, eating is part of diplomacy." Growing stern, he turned to watch the paling face, while testing the young man's metal.

"Okay, starting now, you make the coffee. I'll drink it as it comes, as long as you have one with me and take the first sip. Oh, man, I already have my stomach in my mouth. One more thing, I'll probably be stopped by airport security, unless I carry current x-rays in my carry-on luggage. With most things replaced with new plastics, I still have a metallic plate securing my pelvic area, which may set off the alarms. I'm a candidate for creating more paranoia in airports."

"I can get you through security; and you'll learn how to handle such issues soon enough. Pelvis too, hunh? Shit, you must have been in pieces." Trevor again recognized a hint of fright, but rather than taking it further, he stood and sauntered over to make the suggested brew. His peripheral vision watched the still figure, as something caught the kid off guard, causing the beautiful eyes to glass over.

Bits and pieces: Phoenix cringed at how many. Twister called him his broken little doll whenever he could rub something not encased in acrylic or gauze wrapping. He felt nothing for months, only a memory of opening swollen eyes, seeing one or two cowboy hats hanging on the foot posts of the bed. His face softened, thinking about his adoptive parents, and how much they all needed each other. Having given him back his life, how many times in flashbacks and pain had he lashed out in hatred, wishing they had never found him, leaving him one spectacular sunrise as a last memory? No matter the anger, a Stetson always remained at the foot of his bed, while a soothing male voice comforted him with descriptions of mountains, meadows, and all the flowers in bloom, including those wriggled under his broken nose to heighten one of his senses.

"Here's your coffee. Take the time you need. It's black with no trimmings. Get used to it. Sugar and powdered cream are heavy luxury items on a long trek." Sitting beside his guest and daring to touch the accepting fingers gently on the pass over, he sensed a slight flinch, but Phoenix took the cup and held it away from him, as far as his arms allowed. "We'll exchange sip for sip; and you tell me why this is upsetting you."

"I can do this, really. Just a carry over, that's what the doctors call it, a reaction not pertaining to anything specific." Phoenix had become a competent liar. Trevor sensed it, as the kid brought the hot brew to his lips. A small sip, a deep breath, and the wildest-eyed expression swept over the beautiful face. Too much inhaling worried Sloane, but the determination persisted, as the perfect lips puckered to blow over the surface of the steaming liquid, cooling the coffee to a drinkable temperature. Both men sat in silence and drank the after dinner drink together. With every ounce of his courage and those eyelashes blinking back the mist of fear, Phoenix would take a sip, pause, and take one more. Having finished half the mug, he set it down, holding back the need to purge.

"Good job. You'll finish the next one tomorrow." Sloane picked up the ceramic vessel, perceiving it a threat to the unnerved man waiting for something to happen. Although Phoenix's willingness to please showed, the older man wished he could settle him with a tender hug and a delicious kiss to the coffee-flavored lips.

"I did it! Man, you accomplished something no other has been able to do. Thanks, I think. It will take a little time though."

"Changing habits always does." Trevor looked at the desk covered with mail, and then at the telephone flickering with too many messages. "Guess I have work tonight. Do you want to help?"

"Sure. What can I do?"

"I'll tackle the mail, if you handle the message machine, listing the caller, the date, and their number. Few people leave messages, making the contraption a modern day nuisance, right alongside spam."

"New technology helps but also hinders. I can relate to that. One thing we haven't discussed is what we're going to do. Where do we start? I made a list of things I'd like to investigate." Phoenix grabbed his pen from his computer case, an engraved silver ballpoint worth a great sum. A gift no doubt, Sloane started adding more pieces to the puzzle: the monogrammed handkerchiefs, a platinum Visa card, a silver pen, a Martin guitar, and the top of the line laptop computer--a Macintosh--with every conceivable publishing software program listed alphabetically on the desktop. The man had money, or a solid backing, but to ask outright was a subject taboo in polite society.

"Keep making a list, and we'll decide tomorrow. I've had three hints today, and if one more shows up, the subject may be attracting us both, as it should."

Trevor sat behind his opulent desk, while Phoenix curled up adjacent to the answering machine, quietly listening and jotting down the same names, numbers, and messages, with only different dates. Growing weary with one caller in particular, he wished the next message would not be a repeat. Nothing indicated any of Sloane's friends to be of a romantic nature, only a bevy of men who encircled his life. On the last call, he hit the erase button, climbed out of his comfortable position, and walked over to hand the messages to the attractive older man who wore reading glasses on the end of his slender, aristocratic nose. Phoenix liked Trevor Sloane and prayed this man would not deceive him.

"Finished? Let's see who's after me."

"Joey by the sounds of it."

The photographer looked up and over his wire-framed glasses, to study the face that registered a little sullenness. "Friends and lovers in our youth. You'll like him. None of us are sure of exactly what he does, but he occasionally writes investigative reports about the underbelly of the world: organized crime (international and domestic), serial killers, rapists, gang wars..." Again, the younger man became ashen gray and clasped the desk as support. "Jesus, what triggered that reaction? Come on, Nix, let's get you sitting down, and I'll bring you some water to open yourself."

"Never call me that! Ever! It's Phoenix, or Tyler, or TJ, but never Nix or X. I'm somebody, and don't you forget it!"

After another unwarranted outburst, the cool, tall dude had enough. Slamming the refrigerator door, gripping the water bottle tight enough to burst off the cap, Sloane marched over to the young man who immediately turned toward the fire, daring it to go out, while crossing his arms and clenching his face with a determined, belligerent attitude.

"Okay, Phoenix, one more raging fit, and you won't be coming with me to Costa Rica, Brazil, and a few other stops thereafter. Now, listen up, and answer me directly. You faced and endured some freakish accident, but you're alive, healthy, and currently kicking the shit out of me. First question, what's with the name thing and explain it to me thoroughly?" Sitting on the coffee table, blocking the kid's view of the flames, he handed over the water bottle, crossed his arms in equal defiance, and glared in a fashion only the darkest brown eyes could.

Thornton-Jones shuddered at the intensity of the stare. The orbs had been such a soft brown color, with a twinkling of amber, while they talked about trivial matters over dinner. Having come to believe he could trust this famous personage, things turned abruptly around, seeing another pair of dark crazed eyes. Shaking off the harsh scrutiny and the painful memory of another, Phoenix responded, "Look, Trevor, I lived in a plastic shell, unable to move or speak for nearly a year. When they found me, I had no identification, no clothing, no voice, no teeth, and no face for a picture. My parents had reported me missing, but the police did not connect my broken body to the missing kid from Evergreen. The hospital staff called me *Mr. X* and sometimes *Nix* to be cute. Unfortunately, that's exactly how I felt: a no one, alone, with no way to communicate my identity, if I actually was someone. It took forever, months and months, until they discovered a small tattoo of a cross on one crushed finger. A news bulletin went out; and my family showed up to identify me. After the doctors and police explained what had happened in detail, instead of relief that I'd been found alive, my birth parents accused me of many horrible things, blaming me for the

accident. That specific day nearly finished the job others had started.
A hideous scene unfolded, with me lying near comatose, unable to
defend myself, while medical staff, police officials, and strangers
looked on.   My righteous family shouted their grievances and
disowned me for doing nothing wrong, leaving me alone, penniless,
and with no one who cared. I forgot the cowboy hats always at the end
of my bed, and those soft voices convincing me to keep breathing.
That afternoon, my biological father's corporate lawyer showed up,
expunging me from the family.   He acted like some deranged
tyrannical dictator when he shoved the signed papers into the hospital
administrator's hand. My adoring family removed my name from their
health insurance policy, as well as every other document that indicated
I belonged to them. The hospital went nuts; the police didn't know
what to do either, because I was... Hell, the state couldn't afford the
bills I had already racked up!"

"Jesus, what kind of trouble were you in?   Did I trigger
something when I mentioned Joey's work?"

"Partly... a few things... but I just didn't want to hear the rest of
his gruesome investigations, including possible accidents like mine."
Phoenix grew calmer; speaking aloud stopped the flashbacks on
occasion, hiding his own grisly tale behind *the accident* scenario.

"So they disinherited you for what? Nothing could be that bad."

"Disowned, banished, discarded because I may cause them
shame amongst their influential friends and the church." The raspy,
hushed voice raised a pitch higher, announcing another barrier that
loomed over the young man.

"Then what happened?"

"Twister and Caly rescued me again."

"Your adoptive mom and dad?"

"No, my adoptive fathers. They're gay, Trevor. When I saw
your apartment and understood whom and what you were, I felt safe.
You remind me of them both in different ways, although only Twister
could possibly go head-to head with you in a confrontation." Phoenix
peeked through his fringe of white eyelashes, to watch the dark eyes
soften and the strong mouth muscles ease after such a surprise. He
sensed a kinship with this stranger, but not strong enough to divulge
such intimacies. A nervous talker, his chatter often escalated into
things that should be repressed.

"Caly and Twister are a male couple? Man, you hold one
surprise after another. I thought you took my sexuality lightly,

although yours concerns me."

"If you have to know, they have no name for people like me. Apparently, we don't exist, so I came up with the term *sexually inert*, although they have a new term now--asexual--which I don't like. In other words, I just don't care and have no desire to participate in any form of carnal activity."

"You are a loner. Good Lord, I hope you can satisfy yourself."

The shock in the older face hurt the kid. None of Sloane's business what he did or was, the truth could only ensure peace. "You weren't listening. I don't masturbate because I don't need to. The last time, I felt so inclined, was at the age of sixteen. Don't go crazy over this, just leave me be; and I'll leave you and Joey alone." Phoenix sniped back, again making a devastating error in communication.

"Is there some reason you keep bringing up Joey? He's a past love, only using each other after a long dry spell." Trevor mellowed, wondering about Thornton-Jones' statement. Catching him off stride, he would watch the man when he finally met the infamous Joey Calloway within the next couple of weeks. "Let's get back to Caly and Twister. Tell me about them. It takes courage for two men to adopt, particularly a teenager with severe and expensive problems. They sound like good people."

"They're the kindest, gentlest folk I know. Upon finding me close to death, they stuck by me through years of torment and suffered with equal intensity. A quick decision on their part, upon hearing the ruckus inside my hospital room, they called their lawyer immediately and had him investigate the legalities of adopting me. Although they couldn't write me into their health plan, due to the extreme expenses already incurred, which they actually paid, they still shyly asked of my desires. Considering the abhorrent behavior of my own family, and with no allies in my head, I agreed and was given a new name. With much confusion and emotion, I chose the last name the only way I could, by blinking my eyes. Since their names were Calvin Thornton and Raymond 'Twister' Jones, they hyphenated them for my last name. Twister wanted to call me Tyler, because the two met in Tyler, Texas, at a rodeo; and Caly suggested Phoenix, a special place they decided to collaborate romantically and depart from the hardships of the bone-jarring bronco and bull circuit. They both thought the name symbolic for me; which I guess is somewhat true, but rather embarrassing. According to Egyptian mythology, the phoenix was a bird of great beauty that lived for 600 years in the Arabian Desert, before consuming itself by fire, rising from its own ashes, young and beautiful to live through another cycle. With my heart breaking from sadness and joy, I became their son, Phoenix Tyler Thornton-Jones, which does not fit on a cheque." The young man finished and would spill no more of the story this night. He had exposed enough.

"Quite a tale and you are someone, particularly special to a couple of cowboys." Trevor finally relaxed and smiled. "You miss them badly, which is probably why you're experiencing these outbursts. Is this the first time you've been away, since they took you home?"

"The first night and it's hard. I'm sorry for the strife I've caused you, and all the jibber-jabber I'm spouting, which can't possibly interest you. Please, you talk for awhile, and I'll stop rambling. You mentioned you had a very small family with the passing of your mother and grandmother." Again, the head lowered, and the small hands played with the bottle of water. Praying for a change of topic, the stressed younger man only wished to hear the hushed, kind voice, instead of increasing the rawness of his own scratchy throat.

"I enjoy family stories, so let's continue. My remaining family, made up of cousins, uncles, and aunts, is scattered throughout the northwest. I have a sister in Australia whom I haven't seen in thirty years. She takes after my mother, a wild woman I loved, who was half Irish, half Cherokee. My father was an immigrant from the United Kingdom, while my maternal grandmother, the one I mentioned previously, was a Cherokee Medicine Woman. She told great stories and spoke wonderful words of wisdom. It would have been interesting putting you together to write about the old ways, testing your skill as a non-fiction writer interpreting the poetic abstraction of ancient native beliefs." Sloane arose to find a place more comfortable than his back to a scalding fire. The sofa seat beside his quieting guest seemed appropriate for the telling of family matters.

"My biological grandmother is a character as well, and she wants to meet you. As I mentioned, she's a tiny little thing, a box of dynamite sitting too close to a lighted match. Already blowing up several times with dire consequences for others, you wouldn't believe what she did after my disowning. Man, she wasn't a happy camper." Phoenix finally snickered and leaned back into the sofa padding, to be even with the bigger framed body, although the action prevented his feet from touching the floor.

"I'm waiting. Love feisty elderly women; they're the real arse-kickers in the world, everywhere in the world."

"Think you're right about that. Forget *Charlie's Angels* and *Bill's Viper Assassination Squad*, Granny could best any of them. She heard I had been found the same day, as did my birth parents, but arrived moments late to fight for my family status. Whipping into a whirlwind of activity, as the true holder of the wealth and the CEO of the family business, she hit Colorado Springs like a blizzard. Shouting orders at everyone for a bigger room, more equipment, specialists, truckloads of flowers, her concern focused on my well being, thinking of things I could do while recovering, not to mention falling in love with Caly and Twister who aided her with every decision. Her excitement over my survival, and then her rage at my banishment, turned her into a fire-breathing dragon scorching everyone. Quite funny, actually, considering I could only hear what was happening." Phoenix took a deep breath, issuing a wicked smile and a shake of his gorgeous head.

"Don't stop now; I like your Granny already." Trevor urged him on, seeing the change of a frightened kid into a man of courage. He avoided staring while listening, becoming increasingly bewitched by the sprite he had just met, and a definite replacement for one of his naked youths dancing down Broadway.

"Interrupting two attorneys arguing, she immediately fired her corporate lawyer, who represented the family and my birth father, who was the appointed president of the firm. Within seconds, she had her mind set, kissed my swollen eyelids, the only thing she could touch, promised to return with good news, while reassuring me I was still related to her in every way, even with my new name, something all thought a good idea as protection. Dear Granny waged war against her daughter, her son-in-law, and my unsupportive siblings by disinheriting them all, which shocked even me. She never looked back. With her security team in tow, she closed down the office the next day and called an emergency meeting of the Board of Directors. She's never said, but I think she had been planning this *coup de main* for some time, and I gave her the ultimate reason for her attack. Holding 65% of the stock, Granny had the power to do anything her little heart desired."

"Your Granny is a hell of an arse-kicker, Phoenix."

"No shit! On a calculated threat of selling the company, with or without shareholder approval, and no return on the 5% of non-family stock, she confiscated or purchased the outstanding shares. The family owned package of 30%, which my father thought secure under my mother's name, in reality showed Granny as co-holder, requiring her signature alone. My late grandfather was a cleverly devious man, hiding the fact he left the company solely to his wife, realizing something may go awry when my mother married a believer, a false Christian who my grandfather detested. His prediction came true. Granny also disliked my real father and took the opportunity to slam dunk him with no come back. I have no further knowledge of their status, except they sold the estate in Evergreen and moved into a dump of a condominium in Denver. Quite a come down. Currently, Granny is the sole owner of all holdings, but did give 5% of her shares to her house staff that now constitutes the Board. Shareholder meetings are radically fun, especially hearing the acute business smarts of the butler." The young man started to chuckle, with Trevor happily laughing with him. A gifted storyteller of life's tragedies, Phoenix smiled through it all, ingratiating himself further with his host who was fast becoming an ardent admirer.

Enjoying the moment of two new friends misadventures and family memories, Sloane suddenly alerted to a sound, hearing the giggling change dramatically to heart stabbing sobs. With great tenderness, not to startle the fragile being, he put his large arm around the heaving shoulders and held the young man. "Well, Mr. Thornton-Jones, you should write a biography about your grandmother. I bet your survival instincts come directly from her genes, plus the deep love Caly and Twister freely share with you. Why don't you phone them? They need to know you arrived and where you are. Go now; tell them you're safe, while I perk more Columbian. You do feel relatively secure here, don't you?" Sloane, through his chatter, eased the sorry heart, allowing the younger man to push away and regain control.

"Yeah, I'd like that, and I'm feeling better. Did I hear you mention Costa Rica and Brazil?" A squint from the damp purple eyes made Sloane laugh.

"No such thing as a coincidence, right?" He received a nod, while a small, well-manicured hand wiped away the residual salty water. "Think about this, although it's becoming a tedious subject; global warming is very real and escalating at cosmic proportions. Now, what do these mean to you? First, I found the nuts Master Chui orders for me, and beside it, an intriguing box. I snatched one of your cookies by the way; they're delicious. What's on the front of the packaging?" A twist of the head and an uplifted eyebrow posed the question.

"They're my favorite treat and easy to find because of the colorful hummingbird."

"A hummingbird against a backdrop of what, and the name of the cookies?"

"Rainforest! We're doing the article on the Brazilian rainforest? You've already taken countless pictures of the area."

"But not this specific. Two items had me wondering, and then you put on Sting's CD."

"And he heads the fight against deforestation."

"One of many people, but the man who brought it to world attention. While I was going through my mail, another arrow pointed in the same direction. I received an invitation from Elton, with tickets to his benefit concert last week. I'll have to send an apology and a rather large cheque for being absent."

"Elton, as in John! You know him?"

"I shot some private photographs of him and David before their marriage. This particular concert raised money for his AIDS charity, but Sting's cause is high on his priority list, and they perform for each other's benefits when available."

"A four arrow symbol pointing toward Brazil. It's on my list." Phoenix pondered the idea, knowing whom he would blame, but as a fledgling journalist, he had to uncover all the facts.

"Good, but it's not just Brazil. We're going to widen the scope to all woodlands in danger, as well as those currently being rectified. Your conclusions must encompass more than one country's trials."

"So, that means..."

"...North and South America, Africa, China, India, numerous other places that are endangered, as well as those surviving, thanks to quick action. We have a world in trouble, with unstable weather patterns and a host of villains in many arenas, so we had better get to work, as you said."

"The entire world, wow! It's something I've dreamed about, but are you sure you want to take me? I won't cry again; that was a onetime thing."

"I think you needed a spirit cleansing this evening. No one will hear of it. Now, go call your fathers and Granny. I look forward to meeting them."

Phoenix scrambled off the sofa, picked up the cordless phone, and found a private hideout for his conference call. Pushing himself up as well, the muscular man flexed his shoulder muscles, and strolled leisurely over to the kitchen for another coffee test for the delicious Mr. Thornton-Jones. Lustful thoughts notwithstanding, the trip would prove difficult, considering the mental frailty so far shown by his new partner; and worse, the gigantic logistics of time, distance, weather, and whom he had as contacts. The Northern Hemisphere first, winter chills left the trees dormant, but the people involved were easy to find and contact. Spring would be their best chance to enter Amazonia, the dry season much more manageable, although excessively hot, leaving the good work in Costa Rica to give people hope as their finale. He would leave the details to the oddest man he had ever met.

Chapter IV

The famous Manhattan skyline darkened quickly under twilight shadows, and the evening found Sloane in worry mode. With his heart as his only impetus, he would accept Phoenix as a working partner, but just one strange happening in another country, he would send the kid packing and call the job off. With one decision made and unintentionally having slept half the day, he caught up on the news and returned a few calls on his cellular telephone. Starting at the top of the list, which Phoenix compiled earlier, arrangements were made with a few friends for a one-night gathering. Seldom in town as a group, they finally found an opportunity, in mid December, to meet and rid their troubled minds of life's atrocities, calming their spirits to move forward, a form of therapy for them all. Wishing a good night to Joey, he turned to see his guest rubbing his eyes. "Guess we didn't get your accommodation sorted out. The room you just exited is yours. I suggest you go to bed; it's been a long day."

The red eyes burned into him, and an attempted smile faded on the perfect lips that Sloane longed to caress. "Yeah, guess I am tired. We get up early at the ranch and retire early as well." Thornton-Jones picked up his backpack, carried it into his designated quarters, and immediately observed the three cultures woven intrinsically throughout the décor: Cherokee, Asian, with a luxurious bathroom akin to Ancient Crete. The photographer did have remarkable taste, rather elegant compared to his own suite at the ranch, one filled with rustic western charm to hide the hospital paraphernalia. Returning to Sloane, he picked up his guitar before slumping down at right angles to the intimidating long-legged giant occupying the sofa. "Another coffee test, hunh? I'll be up all night."

"Don't think so, my friend. You look wasted. How's the family?"

"Fine. Although we're a strong group of individuals, some things hit the tear switch for us all. This morning was bad enough; but tonight, man, Twister mentioned Christmas, and swoosh, we were all babbling on a conference line." The small fingers raked through the pastel rainbow, and a groan of weariness, disguising the depression, brought the older man to attention.

"A special day for you?"

"I was raised Christian, even attended the Christian College in Denver before the accident. Some things make you relinquish certain beliefs. Faith in a single god force is still there, but I don't know what to call someone who doesn't believe in Christ the son."

"Jewish." Sloane immediately responded, always quick with a comeback. He delighted in hearing the chuckle so close to him and the younger man revealing an intimacy.

"Sorry, but I'm not waiting for a Messiah either." The young man chuckled.

"What? You don't believe in our President?" Trevor teased.

"Who? Oh, you mean God who doesn't recognize the effects of global warming and the peoples' right of choice."

"That's the one." Sloane laughed and gestured to his new partner to continue his thoughts.

"I chose a new path as I recuperated, enthralled by many different philosophies I had never heard of, and accepted many ideas that seemed plausible, deserving further study. Sounds easy, but discarding indoctrinated belief is difficult. Although I work on fitting each new piece into the puzzle, they sometimes don't mesh, and I fall into Christian ideology without realizing it, so my thoughts I keep hidden. Christmas festivities at the ranch became Freedom for Rights Day, with all the ribbons, lights, and trimmed trees. Caly and Twister go along with it, as they're not particularly spiritual but certainly spirited, only needing each other for support and to believe in. I'll miss watching their chemistry ignite when Twister flicks on the decorative lights strewn about the ranch; and it's just for Caly; for me too I guess. They both sounded upset about my absence this year, although very excited about my new job. Too bad holidays and work conflict."

"Maybe we can rectify that with some thought. It sounds like Caly's a romantic." Trevor enjoyed the sweet respite of trivial chitchat seldom experienced with his serious older friends, or the young, flighty, one-night stands without a gray cell amongst them. Having just met a vulnerable innocent, he pondered on the benefits of a committed relationship, one to entrap those perfect lips, claiming them forever as his alone. He shifted position to regain the momentum of the easy exchange of personal information.

"He's actually the hyperkinetic one, and Twister is the one who buys him presents, flowers, and the sweet kindnesses a carrying husband would do. A kid at heart, Caly loves surprises, sparkling lights, fireworks, and birthday cakes, which Twister plans meticulously, including the wildest birthday parties ever, even with only a handful of us to entertain. As I started to allow more people into my life, like the ranch hands and my only friend from Denver, his ideas grew grander, the last one a full-blown rodeo. Damn near killed me on one of those bucking bull machines."

"Must have been a special day, special people, and a special friend."

"Yeah, Rory. While attending the Christian College, I fell in lust with my straight roommate who kept my sexual orientation a secret; he liked me anyway. We were once skiers, competitive skiers at the collegiate level. I was an aerialist, just as the sport was gaining momentum, and Rory was one of the best technical downhill racers around, until he damaged his leg, which occurred after my incident. He stuck by me through dozens of excruciating operations, coming down from Denver to the hospital in Colorado Springs, where the paramedics had airlifted me. He kept a harder secret, even lying for me, informing mutual acquaintances that I had died from complications a year after the accident. I admire him for his courage, but he can't return love physically."

"So you are gay!" The easy admittance surprised Sloane, considering their earlier conversation. His attentiveness, to the odd creature, increased on hearing the death scenario.

"Once, I guess."

Trevor watched the melancholy grow and heard the soft strumming on the guitar. With the workload ahead, he had forgotten the holiday Phoenix pined for, one he never celebrated, although following his grandmother's Cherokee ways with lunar insights and ancient wisdom pre-European interference. "Sorry, but only your voice can come with us. Do you know how to play? Apparently, someone in the family knows guitars, as this one looks handmade specifically for you. Haven't seen another like it, but it's undeniably a Martin: very distinctive."

"A present from my fathers when my fingers became more agile. Quite phenomenal really, you get a sensual feeling when you run your hands along the fingerboard, over the frets, and trace the curves of the soundboard. I cried when they handed me this baby, never believing I would play again. The artisans at Martin spent months figuring out what would be the best fit for my recovering hands, how I could hold it, etc. etc. etc. as you said this morning. I can play and sing when my throat's strong enough, even compose if in the mood. Didn't know what to expect or bring with me, so I have very little; but whatever happens here, right now, this guitar will keep me company. Guess you'll be the entertainment when we begin our journey."

"How could I possibly entertain you? Opera is my choice, but singing... well, let's just say I attempt to keep up with Placido Domingo on a CD turned several notches higher than most people can tolerate, and only in the shower. How about playing something for me?"

"Opera? I can't accommodate you there, considering my voice is so weak." Phoenix looked up, closed his eyes, balanced himself in a comfortable position, and quietly strummed the expensive acoustic guitar. The harmonic vibrations sent shivers up Sloane's spine, as an unknown melody emerged, accompanied by a raspy, beautiful voice. The music and clarity, reminiscent of the late John Denver with a touch of Rod Stewart on a mellow day, painted images of silver-leafed aspens, mountain trails, and mirrored sparkling streams. Showing more than just writing talent, the kid was a singer and a skilled musician. The hauntingly dulcet riff relaxed the photographer to near comatose, listening to a musical style seldom heard over the electronic buzz--folk music--a memory of enchanted long-ago days of wearing flowers in waist-length hair and painting raindrops on the serenest of faces. His eyes closed, and a beguiling smile continued long after the song faded into the night.

"You're a talent, Phoenix. You can play or sing anytime you wish; and I'll just float away on the sweet breezes of your guitar."

"Thanks, but I can't let you do that, Trev, with so much work to do." Phoenix finally smiled shyly, hearing the compliment from the man for whom he would willingly serenade until he dropped off himself.

"Trev, now? I can live with that, and yes, we have much ahead of us. Here's the plan. You start researching tomorrow, while I finish these last two jobs, and then I'll join you to help seek out further details on the surviving rainforests and those in jeopardy. Investigate all large woodlands of any kind, anywhere." Sloane's experience filled him with grandiose ideas, but his methodical nature accomplished only what proved necessary.

"Besides the forests, we have to investigate the people, organizations, governments, all the administrative rubbish, and where the money comes from, where it sits, and where it goes." Artistically blessed, Phoenix also had a keen eye for business, policy-making, and legalities; they intrigued him, challenging his resourcefulness to summate a qualified answer quickly, while eliminating the usual bickering that common sense often initiated.

Impressed, Trevor wondered just how far this young mind leaned toward the logical and issued the first challenge. "We'll start our trip sometime before the New Year, beginning with the closest target in the Northern Hemisphere. Our best bet lies in the heavily forested and utilized areas of the Northwestern United States and Western Canada, moving eastward until reaching China. Once we establish the regions to visit, we lay out a route. Can you find an online international travel agency that fits our needs? No need for cheap travel when we may have to cancel and rebook. We'll need open tickets with easy changes of destination."

"Oh sure, I'll give the globe a spin and see which airlines offer open tickets to anywhere. You're a dreamer, Sloane, since Internet booking and scheduling can be a nightmare of cosmic proportions. You need to be a member of most websites, and the personal information they require is absurd." Another laugh, Phoenix felt better after the heartbreaking experience of disconnecting with his family, and then returning to hear Trevor whisper a beautiful good night to Joey Calloway. A strange feeling he had felt only once, he wondered if the giddiness would happen again, but a sudden surge of anger stabbed between his shoulder blades. At odds with Sloane, he had quickly leapt from fright to trusting this new acquaintance. The intrigues of life fascinated him, but paradoxes had him baffled. He believed himself one, pushing his desires further away and out of his reach, while desperately wishing to conquer his fears to regain normalcy. Shaking his head, he cleared his mind to listen to the seductive baritone voice.

"A dreamer always; and I would say that you've spent considerable time wishing on stars as well. Now, if we gather enough information and complete preparatory work before December 23, and if you can find those elusive tickets, making the first stop Denver on that date, perhaps, we (if you invite me) can spend Christmas in Colorado with your family, and then venture onward after the holiday. What do you say, or have I made myself the fool wanting to meet your fathers and grandmother?" Trevor's suggestion received the broadest smile of full lips ready for tasting; he knew he would have this man one day. Someone who fell in love at first sight, he had jumped off a high cliff for Phoenix Thornton-Jones. It would take time and probably more patience than he had, but this beautiful man would be his, with all the idiosyncrasies that came with the package. He could wait, before moving on to another who caught his frivolous fancy.

"Yeah, that would be fantastic! Your dream of a round the world ticket is unlikely; meaning we'll have to go with the flow, wherever the route takes us. Remember someone called Phileas Fogg? An uncharted course sounds exciting enough, especially starting at the ranch. Everyone will be thrilled to meet you; and I insist you call Granny just that, for she'll never mistakenly say her name because of my status. So, to work." Phoenix set his guitar back in its corner and headed for his computer, when a large hand stopped him.

"Status? Sounds ominous."

"My birth family, and 99.9% of the world, believes my original persona's dead and cremated, thanks to the police who duly notified them of my demise. My grandmother keeps us all hidden, so it's just Granny to everyone. A little mystery, Trev." Phoenix winked at him, although unable to disguise the nervousness of revealing too much.

"Fine for now, but I'll want details in the future. Now, I suggest you find your bed and start in the morning. I'll be working diligently in the darkroom, since I slept a good part of the day. Off you go. Good night, Phoenix." Sloane smiled, hiding his overwhelming curiosity, while gently shoving his houseguest toward the second bedroom, ensuring the young man found his way, and cautioning him about the stairs when exiting.

"See you in the morning then. Good night." The puzzling white-haired man slipped into the room and sighed, while listening to the photographer's whispered sentiment, sending him into an enchanted land where beautiful dreams dwelt. He would never forget how seductive it sounded, even better than Joey's gift of a breathless kiss through cyberspace. Suddenly very sullen, he wished upon one of Trevor's stars that he could feel the satisfying urge again; but deep within, he knew the treasure was lost. He had to find contentment with a man who could love without physical contact. He doubted such a person existed; the thought broke his heart. His head twisted in another misguided direction, making him feel sick from the resulting dizziness.

Sloane worked until very early morning, developing ten rolls of film. Not many for two jobs, he usually took at least four or five times the amount on any given project. Finally feeling weary enough to sleep, he would turn the negatives into something exciting the following day. One image in particular demanded exacting clarity; and he would ensure its preciseness for someone imminently important to view and consider. Approximately 3:00 a.m., he opened the door and entered the main living area, turning off lights and making his way to his beckoning bed. He noticed the overhead light remained on in the guest quarters, and he peeked inside the slightly open door. The kid lay motionless under the covers, sleeping deeply. Switching off the light and closing the heavy wooden closure, he smiled happily, unable to get Mr. Thornton-Jones out of his head. This particular day he would not forget; the change he looked for may lay close by.

A deep breath, a stretch of his firm body, confirmed he had lost little weight this trip, and felt the need for a workout in the morning. His hard living fifty-five years had not diminished his body structure of solid steel, well-defined muscles, and rippled scrub-board abdomen; even his chin had not drooped enough to warrant plastic surgery. Suddenly shivering, he saw the beautiful face before him, shaking a head of tussled pastel layers, and those bewitching eyes penetrating his soul. The man said the most peculiar thing: he had no face to take a picture of, and a plastic surgeon reconstructed a new one, one too beautiful for a man. The vision faded, and Trevor vowed to forego someone touching his own handsome features, particularly with a knife that could cut away more than skin. He did not wish to awaken with a new face, terrified at what could happen, possibly changing who he was. Liking himself was a monumental task in his youth. His mixed heritage, his large size, and his alternate sexuality had been difficult to understand without a mentor to speak with, but now he reveled in his uniqueness and an exciting lifestyle that offered change without notification. Phoenix would be a constant reminder of becoming a different person; and he wondered about the boy. What had he looked like at seventeen? Had he shown the same enthusiastic, yet bashful character? Who had this young man been; someone he would have liked? On such ragtag thoughts, he turned off his light and settled in.

On a shriek, a thud, another scream, a skittering of footsteps, something crashing into pieces on the floor, followed by another shriek and a thud, Sloane leapt out of bed and dashed for the guest room while trying to climb into his denims. More wailing and thunderous drumming against the wall, Phoenix found the doorknob, pulling at it frantically to get out, while Trevor attempted to turn the twenty-four carat gold knob from the other side. The muscle man won out, forcing the release of the smaller hands and quickly opening the door. As Sloane turned on the overheads, a white-haired sprite, in a gray flannel sweat suit, dashed passed him in one direction and a harried silver-colored cat in the other.

"Phoenix, stop, you're bleeding! What happened?"

"The... the..." Thornton-Jones pointed at the fleeing feline still a fluster over the sudden burst of yelling.

"Bogart? That's my cat! Come here, Bogie."

"No! Please, no more! Don't let him! No!" The shrill shrieking could stir the dead.

"Afraid of cats too. Shit." Trevor mumbled, as he gingerly approached the man still in the throes of a nightmare. "Wake up, Phoenix. Steady now, you're okay. Talk to me. Whatever you're thinking; just keep talking."

"The cat jumped on me... and the room... it was dark! I couldn't find the door! I was trapped with a cat! Stop! Please, no more! No more!" The small man fought wildly for an escape. The feline had been a Russian Blue, not the Tabby with nails as long and curled as the woman's dragon talons. He felt his arms tighten against restraints; the feline eyes glowered at him from below. One scratch had him screaming; a second nearly had him blacking out; the third accomplished the task.

Sloane tapped him lightly on the cheek, calming the hysteria minimally. Drenched in sweat, shivering in shock, and widening his terror-filled violet eyes, Phoenix's fear rejected the attempt by the larger man to touch him, immediately scurrying away and slipping down into a corner, out of reach of the grabbing, hurting hands that he believed them to be.

Rattled at the abrupt awakening and the strange position he found himself, the photographer looked about the room sizing up the dilemma. The exit of Bogart came first, lifted out of his safe nest on top of the refrigerator and locked within the master suite. Sloane then returned to the small, shaking bundle of humanity, contemplating three new problems: fear of cats, fear of the dark, and possibly, fear of being touched. Unfortunately, his huge frame created a dark silhouette against the light, causing more panic in the man now too afraid to yell. Trevor's unidentifiable shadow loomed black against the harsh glare, blocking any escape for a phobic driven kid.

"Phoenix, do you know where you are?" With no answer, the

large shadow bent down on one knee, wishing for some kind of response. "Do you know who I am?" Still no reply, Trevor wavered in a precarious position, deciding his next move. He left Thornton-Jones cowering and picked up the wireless telephone no one had used since the call to Colorado. Pressing the redial button, it rang several times before a low, weary voice, as sweet as southern honeysuckle, answered.

"Yes, hello. I'm sorry to call at this late hour, but I must speak with Mr. Jones or Mr. Thornton."

"Twister Jones here."

"This is Trevor Sloane; and I need..."

"...something's wrong with Phoenix. God Almighty, Caly, wake up; our boy's in trouble! What happened, Mr. Sloane?"

"I'm in somewhat of a quandary. Phoenix neglected to identify his phobias, and I believe two of them hit him at once. A cat jumped on him in the dark." Keeping an eye on the unmoving creature in the corner, he raked his fingers through his silver tipped dark hair and left his hand on his head.

"Damn! He's found himself a corner to hide in, unless I'm mistaken. Why was he sleeping with the light off?"

"My fault, as was the cat. I wasn't told. He's trying hard, sir, but I have to know about these things before we leave, or I can't take him with me; something I am loathed to tell him."

"Failure would kill him, Mr. Sloane, and call me Twister; Caly's listening on an extension. Phoenix will stay still as a mouse for as long as it takes to come out of the attack. Fill a bath of fairly hot water, add something scented to soothe his psyche, and allow him to soak until he can make sense. Once he tells you he's better, you can believe him, and then send him back to bed. One more thing, he's also afraid of anyone seeing him undressed. He won't realize it when you set him in the bath; so I suggest, if you have bubble bath, fill the tub high with foam. After drying and dressing in private, he'll come out on his own, but a little disoriented for a few minutes." The alarm, in the most melodic male voice he had ever heard, forced Sloane to think quickly.

"Scented bubbles I have, plus a Jacuzzi to keep them frothy. My grandmother swore by chamomile tea as a mild sedative. I think I have some stashed away."

"That would be helpful. Sage is good too, if you have any, plus a great deal of honey. His blood sugar level will be down, and he'll need a little power boost." A new voice responded; this one was higher, more excitable, and definitely worried.

"No problem, I have both."

"I'm sorry, Mr. Sloane, truly sorry. We had hoped he would tell you these things. He has a number of phobias; some have been conquered, but others remain. During our telephone conversation this evening, he said you were an understanding man. Please be gentle with him, give him the chance he so desperately requires, and I can promise you, he'll try his damnedest to do anything asked of him. He told us of the coffee you made for him; and we're proud he succeeded in drinking a little. You have no idea what you accomplished, or the courage it took on his part to even try." The stronger accented voice returned, any quiver dissipating after calming the initial fear over his son: a son two lonely cowboys happened upon in some strange way and loved as their own. Phoenix was the heir they could never produce between them.

"He's a good sport, and after your call, drank another cup without hesitation. Once accomplished, he trusted me enough to walk away and return to it. I'll give him the chance, if he tells me everything."

"He won't do that, Mr. Sloane."

"Trevor."

"He's never spoken to anyone about what happened to him, Trevor, and neither can we: a promise to be kept. Although fragile mentally, he is clever, bounces back quickly, and is extremely strong for his size. Let his determination help you both overcome his idiosyncrasies. You have already started, and we thank you. Take care of him, and if his behavior becomes uncontrollably erratic, we'll travel any distance to pick him up." Twister finished and wished upon the stars shining over Colorado that it would not come to such an end for his son.

"We'll struggle along."

"Give him our love. Better yet, don't remind him of the incident, unless he brings it up. We never spoke." Caly chimed in, hearing his partner's voice drop in sadness.

"Agreed. I'll get him fixed up, but you're sure he's okay to leave alone?"

"Leave the light on, the door ajar, and he'll be fine. Thanks, Trevor. This will be a long night for you." Again, the higher southern voice gave the directions, and Trevor understood the love being sent to their greatest treasure.

"Been there before, and if you don't hear from me, you'll know everything went smoothly. Good night." Sloane hung up and headed straight for the guest bathroom, twisting taps, filling the monster tub with fragrant bubbles (mango had to do), and then turning up the lights. Finding clean sweats that the young man appeared to favor as sleep wear, Trevor left them on the vanity, along with bandages and an antibiotic cream for the minor lacerations, and then quickly left to boil water for a tea concoction of wild herbs and plenty of honey. Phoenix proved Twister correct, remaining curled in the corner motionless, except for the uncontrollable quivering. With everything prepared and in arms reach, the photographer's biggest difficulty hid in shock within a tight corner, bleeding from the foot, and clinging to his knees with his head tucked between them. "Up you get, kiddo. We have a hot bubbling Jacuzzi for you to relax in; and if you scream at that--trust me--I'll drop you in. At least you're small, which will help me lift you over high locked gates." He chuckled, hoping a little humor would bring the man back.

Undressing the white statue, the keen-eyed photographer tried to ignore the prominent scars; some remained ghastly reminders of hurried mending, while others appeared painstakingly corrected by an immensely talented cosmetic surgeon. A few of the latter looked recent, with fine lines of pink, while others had been done earlier, disappearing as grid lines of white on the creamy alabaster skin. Phoenix compared to a very small replica of 'David' under the brutal scarring that covered his body, at least from Trevor's one discreet glimpse. By the easy lift, however, he knew the frame of the man, strong as titanium, tight as stretched wire, although diminutive in size, and light as a handful of feathers; the white-haired anomaly appeared perfectly proportioned, made for the endurance, speed, and agility of an aerialist.

Without a sound, a moan, or a whimper, the small man's slight but toned body slipped into the suds. Phoenix offered no help and slid through the foam like an eel, disappearing into the waters pulsating on full power. Quickly grabbing the strangely colored hair, Trevor hoisted him up with only a slight splutter from the drowning man to catch his breath. Nary a look, the purple eyes fixated unblinkingly on the finely painted tiles of a life-size dolphin swimming low over the ocean floor and around the tub enclosure. Although Trevor loathed large bodies of water, the sea mammals fascinated him, believing their presence, on the immense mural surround, honored the intelligent creatures, while giving joy to his overnight guests who did not share his bed. He looked skyward and hoped the water-dancing mammals would ease the fright of his new friend.

Keeping one arm in the water, to support the neck, allowed him the use of his other to squeeze the soaked, beige terry toweling and wipe the delicate face. The small figure did not stir to his manipulations, and the bath continued. First, the shoulders were washed, and then the arms, down the back, and over the small chest, although Trevor cringed upon touching the hideous marks inscribing the history of the man. Even the nipples had seam lines of pink, an unusual injury from an accident. Swallowing hard and growing excited by cleansing between the legs, up and down, in and out, Sloane played nursemaid and not the seducer, sponging Phoenix clean of sticky perspiration that only came off with soap and a light hand.

A gentle, innocent rub of the hidden cock made his head spin, and he immediately stopped. He felt no resistance from pubic hair, but only the smooth silk purse holding secret gems and an unseen penis as soft and innocent as a baby. Lifting and cleansing the hairless yet manly genitals, hidden under fragrant bubbles, gave Sloane a rush he would dream about later. For now, he had to remain attentive to his task; one he had never pursued innocently, but only as a prelude to sex. Unworthy and disrespectful of the catatonic man, he dropped the washcloth in the water and silently cursed his thoughts. The kid felt nothing, but the photographer's passion increased. Wicked imaginings were dispelled with a few profanities and a shake of his head. Sloane vowed to pleasure the misbegotten tragedy of a man when the time was right, if only to touch, to taste, to love every part of the abused body, inside and out, and to care enough to melt all fears with a kiss. A shaking hand picked up the cup of warm, sweet tea, and gently placed the vessel against the lips; again, those perfect lips enchanted the older man who teased them with the china cup and tempted the petit nose with an unusual honeyed scent. On cue, Phoenix blinked and sipped the brew.

"Hey, kiddo, you with me, son?"

"Yeah... No... I think so. How did... Oh God! The dark! The cat!"

"Bogie is secure in my room, and Master Chui will care for him while you're here. I'm sorry about turning off your lights. I thought you had forgotten them, considering your weariness."

"How did I get in this tub?" The tea took time to work, unable to stop Phoenix's harsh-sounding question, although the man seemed to settle in the comforting waters.

"You felt chilled, so I ran the bath, gave you a few bubbles to play in, and left you to undress and get in. I then made this tea, thinking it might help. It's my grandmother's best remedy for ailurophobes." Trevor lied with all the willpower he could muster, unaccustomed to storytelling. Seeing a look of relief on the disquietingly beautiful face, Sloane's nonchalant reasoning quelled the man's fright over the bubble-covered scars.

"Thanks, the tea tastes good. Sorry about your pet. I knew I should have gone to a hotel." Phoenix accepted the cup to hold on his own, while submerged to his chin in fluffy froth. Sloane remained at ease, or the best pretense of such, leaning leisurely against the vanity and gazing in wonderment at what had fallen from the sky this day. He shook his head in disbelief; a broken angel had dropped into his life when least expected, an innocent creature needing care and all his attention.

"I found a fresh sweat suit for you to don after your soak. Stay as long as you wish, or until the water cools. I'll take Bogart down to his sleeping quarters near Chui's doorway. Too bad you don't like him; he seems to like you. Never seen him take to a stranger in his entire life, wanting to share a bed."

"Lucky me. Even the barn cats want to get close, and they were slowly breaking down my barrier. But to be jumped on! Man, he scared me shitless. Sorry, Sloane."

"Hope he didn't push your progress back too far. My cat's a loveable character that won't bother you again. I'll see you when you emerge, after I clean up the vase that one of you wildcats terminated. You're cut, so check your hands and feet. There's a first aid kit on the vanity. Yell if you need help." Trevor shut the door behind him and leaned against it, breathing hard. Pulling himself together, he found Bogart sleeping unflustered in the middle of his emperor-sized bed. Picking up the large male cat, he stared into the mellow green eyes and sleek face of silver gray. "Sorry, Bogie, but it's back to your babysitters until I decide what to do about Thornton-Jones. He is puzzling, my friend; in just one day I don't want him to leave, wishing to hold him tightly, smothering him with more affection than I probably have to offer. After all these years, numerous relationships, I have found someone flawless, and yet paradoxically imperfect. Time to follow my heart, which I swear will be kinder than the head currently raging between my legs. I will behave and wait. Even with his many problems, I'm attracted to him like no other. I wonder who will be more frightened in the jungle darkness: our nyctophobic Phoenix, the wild beasts ready to eat us, or me, the one ready to pounce on our guest this very second. It's all about love, hey Bogie, all about love; and I think I've truly fallen. May God help us all, whichever one is listening."

Chapter V

Sloane exited the guestroom, leaving Phoenix shaken, but dressed head to toe in clean navy fleece and a bandaged foot, sipping a second cup of tea, while sitting on the bed refitted with fresh sheets, and stewing over what had transpired during his dementia. Again, the photographer bid his guest good night, reassuring him that the cat had no entry into the apartment. Bogart remained safe and comfortable within Chui's warm doorway, his favorite place while Sloane was traveling. The feline would content himself chasing mice and whatever else night creatures pursued in the darkness.

The cat's owner, on the other hand, felt unglued, unable to close his eyes, ready to spring out of bed at another tirade of screams. He lay prone, wondering about many things, including a long, grueling trip, although the kid seemed capable of coping with the physical challenges. Phoenix's mental gymnastics, however, plagued the more experienced man with the eternal question of *the accident*. A severe trauma at seventeen had left the kid sexless and afraid of his shadow, and yet pleading to follow the photographer to the ends of the planet to capture a story. With a guttural groan of confusion, he flipped onto his back, studying the ceiling fan that remained inactive this cold night. A loner--a drifter of sorts--he felt comfortable wherever he came to rest. With work his only responsibility, he had little else to fuss over, until a badly damaged angel flew in from Colorado to spin him around.

A gay bachelor's life, now an accurate term with same sex marriages abounding, took hold early in his development. Passing the occasional night with another man came easily for the handsome he-man who attracted attention and appreciation wherever he ventured; his blatant advances never suspect or refused. Safe sex had taken away the fun, especially for a man just off the fringe of the sixties generation; but at fifty-five, he had learned from the young gay crowd that experimenting with new toys returned the pleasure he remembered. The wild Joey Calloway had also introduced him to enjoyments beyond ramming into a flaccid asshole. Contemplating the sexual act in this day of latex, he discovered how much carnal intimacy meant to him, and now turned each encounter into a meaningful moment, one in which he recalled every touch, every scent, every sight, for one night may be his last. This midnight episode he would remember as a single touch, the smell of mangos, and violet eyes staring vacantly. He immediately drew in a deep breath and turned on his side, preventing his non-thinking head from rising.

Sex and breathing for Sloane was one and the same, even as he aged, often satisfying his lustful nature by unleashing his engorged beast upon someone inconsequential; Mr. Thornton-Jones would never be placed in such an insidious category. Performing many pleasurable acts in his life, his first time was a threesome with the quarterback of his college team and a visiting linebacker. He continued from there with little reverence: the bars, the bathhouses, the beaches in Greece, and Boogie Street in Singapore, where the boys looked like girls and played as such. Not to his taste, often mischievously fooled, he found discreet ways of finding quality male whores, with some regulars in various cities. With the current gay community forming tighter bonds and taking vows, a deep loneliness had taken hold within; he wished to fill the missing piece. Perhaps the lack of a partner (for those intimate conversations and gestures) arose and snarled at him, particularly thinking of his friends, as well as these new acquaintances, a devoted couple with a mature gay son.

Two men had made a serious lifestyle adjustment, accepting responsibility of a troubled and injured teenager, and tending to his every need for a decade. Eagle spirit filled them both, and Trevor knew he had forgotten many of his grandmother's teachings. He felt her presence whenever he looked through a lens, capturing a beautiful, sensitive moment of someone or something. Her spirit ran through him, like the sparkling river they had gazed upon, calling for the spirits to heal and help, changing them into that which could not be, but happened nonetheless. With an indigenous upbringing of sorts, he had made the transformations and quests required, but he missed something of her lessons, too young at the time to comprehend those important spoken and unspoken words. Seeing details had been only part of her equation; he had not listened, and listening was the other half. Without hearing the sounds around him, he had missed years of wonder, such as Phoenix's silly giggles slowly changing into quiet sobs. On a sudden impulse, which he refrained from acting upon, Trevor wished to awaken the kid immediately, to hear him sing and play just for him, and to remember the words--his missing piece was Phoenix Thornton-Jones--the writer of those words.

Sloane finally closed his eyes, intently listening for anything that may stir in his hidden domain. Silence filled his ears; he had reinforced and soundproofed the old building to such an extent, he could not hear a passing fire truck with alarms drowning out the city's life: real life. Melancholy and regret overwhelmed him, while he considered checking on his more than slightly off-centered houseguest. There seemed little need, as Phoenix appeared emotionally exhausted after his run-in with Bogart. Listening would start on the morrow.

The man clad in warm fleece, hearing no sound from his famous host, limped out of his room to place an ear against the door left ajar to the master bedroom. Sensitive to sound, he heard the breathing of a man deep in slumber; he closed the door gently and returned to the sofa to stare at the last of the smoldering embers. Dejected and haunted by another nightmare, he sat with his arms wrapped around his legs, his chin resting on his knees, praying for an idea to redeem himself as a man worthy of the challenge presented. An hour, and then another, 5:00 a.m. he flipped up his laptop and went to work. His flying fingers clicked the buttons on his keyboard, taking his mind off the mistakes he had made the previous day and concentrating only on his work. His social ineptness clouded his insight and disabled him from understanding one important form of communication--body language--the language displayed by the photographer who had him intrigued; leaving him unaware that Sloane was equally bedazzled. With both men at an impasse, the younger of the two could not let go of his past; he could not allow anyone to come close. His hope laid with the job at hand, one of intellectual thought, creativity, and with luck, a few thrills he could cope with and relish.

A new sun, sparkling like the finest diamonds against Sloane's bedroom window, lightened the clear winter morning. Wishing to get on with his day, the photographer shaved, showered, and dressed, desperate for life sustaining coffee. On opening his door, he spotted him instantly. Still outfitted in his dark blue nightwear, the kid appeared in a trance, scanning the screen as his fingers danced to a tap rhythm. Trevor flexed a few muscles, deciding to forego the workout, until finishing the task of developing his images, and perhaps, enticing Phoenix to partake in breakfast at the java café a block down the road. "Morning, kiddo. Have you been up since I dropped off?"

"Good morning. I couldn't sleep, so I tried to grant your wish after you retired. Sorry, Sloane, your plan isn't feasible. First, the tickets: too many airlines, too many possible destinations, and too far off the path of any vapor trail. Second, I looked up the number of potential wilderness areas of concern. Their various governments and international organizations protect many; and since they are only in their beginning stages of conservation, I say we give them a chance to rectify their problems. The forests of the Northwestern States and Western Canada, where strong logging regulations exist, have suffered severe droughts, followed by heavy downpours and dangerous lightning storms, creating major fires up the west central and the coastal areas, a harbinger of global warming. They have the knowledge, the skilled and volunteer work force, plus the money to fight the devastating results, but everything takes time. Fire damage will always exist in both countries, a natural occurrence that can be rectified with replanting immediately after clean up. Without forests, the earth can no longer hold water, and new seeding becomes more difficult. No woodlands, no clean air, we will all suffer the consequences if Brazil and other rainforest domains refuse to act responsibly. Off the direct subject of rainforests, but exacerbating the problem, were you aware that the State of Washington has the highest carbon-gas emission rate in the world and is singularly blamed for the disappearing Arctic lakes? The Inuit of Canada are filing a lawsuit against the state! Awesome, someone is reacting, but we can hardly go after unaware nations if our own government doesn't curtail such pollution, particularly when the current administration publicly denounces the threatening issue of climate change. I'm surprised we're part of the innocuous G8 nations, if we're that negligent regarding our own controls and dismissing global warming as an environmentalist's joke."

"Ah, but we have God in charge."

"Oh, yeah--God and Country--indistinguishable and inseparable. Here's another news flash for you, one that scares the hell out of me. The various military academies, in our nation, heavily favor an evangelical belief, which means we're training officers to fight under a fanatical religious banner rather than for democracy. No wonder we're so fucked up." Phoenix pulled away from his computer, only for a second, to see the surprise registered on his partner's face.

"We're in worse trouble than I thought. This is going to make our task immensely more difficult. No wonder people are at a loss as to what to do. I think we need your real God down here and quickly, kiddo."

"Pray that some Holy Spirit shows up soon, since his stand-in doesn't know shit about global warming, planning to forego the G8 discussion on climate control, while leading his people down the righteous path of intolerance." Phoenix looked dismayed as he spoke. Their task seemed a pointless experiment to change political thinking.

"Our country is out of control, growing more isolationist and conservative, merging state and religion. Scares the hell out of me as well. I had heard that the President was backing off on the environmental issue, but believed it only a rumor. Where did you read it as fact?"

"Every newspaper from *The London Times* to *The Toronto Star*. His stance has been ongoing for sometime; but another news bulletin, from a domestic paper, spurns the new American policy of leaving the environment to the heavenly host, while our country forges a pathway of tyranny, Christianity, and filthy air, decimating those who stand up for freedom of speech, religion, abortion, gay rights, etc. etc. etc. Be prepared to be trampled, Sloane. We all voted, but who gained the power--our first dictator--good God."

"Which one are you speaking of?" Trevor smiled and winked at his already discouraged partner.

"Very funny, now back to our original problem. Our job is to influence those people, who voted for God, and those countries, which harbor the last forests and jungles, to jump on the preservation bandwagon, by proving they'll be hurting themselves if they don't. Unfortunately, some countries dismiss the urgency of the matter, unlike the more enlightened nations who at least acknowledge the oncoming threat with some form of recycling and environmental impact control, although said nations are still polluting their own lands, as well as the exotic paradises where their citizens choose to invest, retire, and holiday. Man, could I tell you some horror stories happening right now, instigated by the righteous few who should know better. We, as an international group, spout technological and environmental advancements, but remain, in theory and ideology, as lesser world powers, acting as the worst contributors to global warming and weather shifts, even with proof rammed down our throats. Our objective is hopeless, Sloane. I can't see how we can make a judgment call." Phoenix returned to scan the monitor, as more data flashed in front of him with another couple of finger taps to his mouse.

"Slow down, you're giving me a headache. So what are you suggesting?" Rubbing his temples, a sure sign of an onset of another chronic migraine, Sloane listened for an answer while fumbling for the coffee.

"The whole world is fucked; and it depends on the day and the current leaders as to which country is the bigger pain in the behind. The Group of Eight nations are a contrived, powerless, and elitist group. Who thought of the idea in the first place? Moreover, when it comes to militant action, the United Nations is sorely lacking in guts. Why would anyone want to follow the advice of the United States, God forgive me, considering what we've just discussed. Russia is laughable, considering the ethnic civil unrest and the terrorist tactics used by all those in the foray. No one learns, man. Then there's France, which, by their veto power, has caused dissention and chaos in Europe. They join a cause, back away, and then return, until you're dizzy from their *volte-face*. What I'm saying, Trev, is that our job and Graham's vision is stupid, and if the greatest nations can't abide by the rules of common sense, why should anyone else. Let's quit while we're losing and losing badly." The white head fell against the keyboard of the computer and banged against it several times to clarify the absurdity of politics, religion, and day-to-day strife.

"We must take baby steps first, kiddo. Before contemplating more disasters in the making, what have you found out specifically on our main subject?" Trevor agreed with his enraged partner and had been quietly troubling over the scenario handed them the day before. The new magazine could be shut down and all copies confiscated as a libelous attack against their own government, even treasonous if God had his way, or cause said government to topple as Warren Graham gleefully predicted. The many wars, in which America participated, would always stand as the primary issue, due to the horrendous number of lives lost and the billions of dollars spent; but the sudden insurgence of the most insidious type of terrorism, the creation of a subservient society under a tyrannical and religion-based government, was growing malignantly and very quietly. The thought was beyond frightening for the free world and for the country he loved and called home. Only the upcoming election could dethrone the villain and return common sense to government, although that also could be deemed as just a dream.

"Okay then, I'm over my fury." Phoenix inhaled and restarted his thought process. "Drought, fires ignited by lightning, and never-ending rain are out of our hands, so we must narrow it down to man-made shit. We may be looking at the status of a country in its world ranking, heaven forbid, considering what I just said. If freedom from poverty is a nation's priority, which it is in most, environmental issues show way down their list of concerns. An extraordinary dilemma, considering they could be paying the unemployed, giving them hope, teaching them a trade, making them aware of what happens outside their home situated on top of mountains of garbage, as the poor live in Mexico City, Rio de Janeiro, Sao Paulo, and many other sprawling metropolises without controls, facilities, and money. I'd suggest that the people who successfully clean up and rebuild an area remain there, caring for the land they saved, making it economically viable, and setting up fine new communities that are environmentally aware. It's all in your pictures, Trev."

"I know the image you're referring to, and I immediately thought of Kimmie. It broke my heart seeing such a tiny girl, in her ruffled, hand-me-down, special-day dress, climbing a slope of tin cans and rotting boxes hundreds of feet high and miles long to reach her home. Using her hands as well as her feet, she was trying so hard not to get her white dress dirty. Even in the slums of Mexico, families celebrate third birthdays extravagantly, as the child has passed the infant mortality rate to face an uncertain future. Too bad I didn't take that picture."

The younger man nodded and continued. He had made more progress than Sloane thought possible. One family-owned forest in the Eastern United States seemed a good starting point, with a proven method of removing specific trees with care, rather than obliterating an entire area that would normally take decades to recover. A strange anomaly in Mexico took both men by surprise, and they added it to their list as a potential site to investigate. Two woodlands leveled by deforestation in Guanajuato created differences on a corrective measure. The western section of the state had burned to the ground, but due to its mountainous terrain, the continuing rain, and the consequential mudslides, stabilization deemed impossible; but the eastern slopes, with the same conditions, intervened quickly to save their forest with terracing and new planting. This important but little known catastrophe needed reviewing, finding the reason behind the rapid action on one side, and the delay and consequent devastation on the other. The same scenario could lay in wait on their final stop--the big one--Brazil.

Something, which re-ignited Phoenix's wrath, was a plan devised and proposed by five South American countries: to dredge, deepen, and straighten the large Paraguay and Paraná Rivers, building a seaway for two landlocked countries and opening up economic development for Brazil, Argentina, and Uruguay, while ignoring the existing inhabitants and a fragile ecosystem. The Hidrovia Canal Project was a blatant circling of sharks ready to devour another natural habitat, the last of its kind, a microclimate that curbed flooding and seasonal drought in all nations involved. Allowing access, for ocean-going vessels, would upset the balance of delicate resources already in use for livestock and farm crops, and cause a swift change in a natural environment, from rich grasslands and cattle ranches to deserts and empty haciendas, not to mention risking international outrage at what many would view as blatant stupidity. The plan made no sense to anyone but the greedy and ignorant.

The concerns of the ranchers and farmers, dwelling and working along the two rivers in question, were ongoing; and the journalist felt the controversy was something only known by a few outside the countries in question. The warnings of cattlemen and a handful of ecologists may have stalled the billion-dollar project, as well as South America's fear of further international wiggling of fingers. Even the G8 nations remained unresponsive, considering how they obtained their wealth in the first place. The world had seen many cataclysmic results of dam and river projects improperly studied for environmental impact, including those controlling the Mississippi, the Nile, and the Saint Lawrence, all of which destroyed nature's original plan. Thousands of hectares of important wetlands in South America--the Pantanal--would be gone next, and global warming would advance further.

The kid shook his head in disgust and turned away from his computer to accept the hot coffee offered by the photographer. Both men agreed that nature did its best to lay the planet to waste and did not need help from humankind. Between slow sips, the scenario developed further. The encroachment of the Sahara into the African jungles would give them a different slant, a natural condition serious enough to consider a major threat over decades. In India, Phoenix found another conundrum of a different sort. People problems in their northern tropical forests were descending on the lands occupied by a declining tiger population; and in the south, herds of once domesticated elephants marched through whatever they pleased. India's citizens grew tense, as a battle raged between humans, animals, forests, and farmland, all fragile and all for want of the bulging populations of the major cities. Their government did embrace outside advice however, proving their willingness to come up with solutions, bit-by-bit, state-by-state. The process would take time, but the wealth and awareness of India, even with its poor and the climatic forces against it, would help them succeed.

Europe maintained a progressive stance, although, like North America, it also suffered from the effects of changing climatic patterns: too much rain and long periods of scorching temperatures. The weather had already altered dramatically over twenty years, proving something on the planet had metamorphosed, and whether it be one country's fault or the world's, the question stood before them. One hope lay in China--a very small hope--the carefully monitored, but very tiny bamboo forest had survived the encroachment of farmers. The Chinese Government, their zoologists, botanists, and environmentalists had succeeded in protecting the small woodland, before the famous roly-poly Giant Panda became extinct, only to be found in pictures and a few zoos. Recognizing the problem, the large nation responded quickly to outside fears, and now attempted a study to solve the animal's delicate dilemma with propagation. A definitive success story, one country accepted and reacted to save their symbol, shutting out the angry demands of farmers who had no concept of what they were doing, or had done. If Brazil allowed deforestation to continue, reducing the jungle's size to that of this small portion of China, not only would it devastate the country, but detrimentally affect the entire planet.

"Good suggestions, Phoenix, although you've crushed my dreams. Of course, my way would take years, and our boss would have his baldhead rubbed shiny by the time we returned. So, the plan: investigate the various areas through my contacts, the scientific community through your fingertips, and government officials via Daddy Warren. I'll call Sting, if I can find him, and see what he knows administratively about his charitable organization and what information his people share. He must have a few names to give us. We might want to add Costa Rica as another spot. They're doing wonders in the small country--their tropical vegetation and wildlife increasing rapidly--an inspiration to others. As the photographer, I'd like to give the world a little hope, as well as slam-dunking a few governments and would-be saviors who know nothing. Your research and current conclusions will singe a few nerve endings raw; so, we had better know all the facts before condemning anyone. By the way, I happen to know one of those Brazilian ranchers who would invite us to visit, considering his continuing battle over the rivers in question."

Trevor's friend had a long time feud with his government and what they planned with others; his life lived in peril by unseen forces-- greedy industrialists, overly eager government officials, shoddy environmentalists, foolish academics, and blood-sucking entrepreneurs clinging to important coat tails--the rancher had many enemies. The big man's thoughts turned to the one in front of him who looked drawn and tired. "Great job, and as you said, we'll play Phileas Fogg this trip. Perhaps you should go to bed, kiddo. You haven't slept an hour in the last twenty-four."

"Plenty of time for rest when we're finished. Plan on dressing and continue working, now that I've started and feel sufficiently agitated. Did you sleep? I'm truly sorry about last night." A little pink in the face from shame and his violet eyes ringed with red, Phoenix could not meet the sympathetic brown ones.

"Cats won't be too much of a problem, but nyctophobia, man, that's huge. There will be times and conditions preventing the use of campfires, lanterns, car lights, and flashlights. How will you cope?" Trevor felt paternal for the first time in his life, and he rather enjoyed it.

"Just like drinking your coffee, I'll do the same with the dark." After another sip of proof, the white-haired wonder finally looked into the softening eyes and handsome face to illustrate his resolve.

"If you wish, but I insist you remain here. You may need help; and a hotel does not supply the necessary service when called upon. Starting tonight, no overheads, only a bedside lamp, and tomorrow, I'll purchase stair lights to plug in, giving you a little more than moonlight through your window. Now, how about breakfast? I'm starving. Get dressed, and we'll eat out."

"I... Trevor, I hate people staring at me. They don't recognize if I'm male or female, and this hair... I'm a freak!" Phoenix threw his hands up in despair, and then grabbed the strange but intriguing mop, tugging at it for emphasis, as if it needed more.

"Jesus, you're in New York. No one will give you a second look, except a few double-takes at how perfectly gorgeous you are, and no one would mistake you for anything but a man in your tight jeans. Don't be afraid of your looks, which you must be used to after ten years. I personally would like to photograph you and put your picture on the biggest billboard in the city. You'd have cars running off the road and people clicking off their cells just to gape." Another strange phenomenon puzzled Sloane. In front of him stood an extraordinarily beautiful man who did not disguise the fact, but enhanced his looks with the soft highlights of the oddest pastels in a trendy haircut, one to be copied if on a magazine cover. Phoenix was the epitome of a walking, talking, sexy rock star or pin-up boy; the world would be eager to eat out of his small hands on seeing him, and yet the man seemed too shy to leave any sanctuary he found.

"No, not ten years, maybe three at the most. Like I said... the last surgery wasn't that long ago, and the white hair... well, it grew back this way. On a whim of my younger female nurses, and their wacky hairdresser, they did a radical cut and color job. Trying to brighten my life, they always came up with something weird to make me laugh."

"I should have realized from what you've told me. I can't imagine waking up one day with a new face, not to stare into this lined, sagging one. At least I can accept the gray slowly overtaking the black."

"You say I'm good looking, but all I see is some pretty, androgynous character, the color of my eyes the only thing I recognize. You're naturally a very handsome man, Sloane. Tall, very tall, well built without being heavy, an infectious smile full of humor and secrets, and eyes that change color from melting amber to smoldering black. With so much dark hair with silver sprinkles, you'll never go bald. I like it. How many men are in your little black book anyway? They probably crawl after you on their hands and knees, begging for your attention and affection, not to mention salivating in their sexual craving." Phoenix stopped his comments abruptly, having forgotten to inhale with a pause.

"Thanks, kiddo. Salivating sexual craving, hunh? Best keep my boots polished. We're a mutual admiration society; so, let's admit we're a terrific and unique looking pair wherever we go. Shall we start today with breakfast at the café around the corner?" Sloane pressed, but received an unconvinced shake of the head.

"If you don't mind, I'd rather try a different test. Can you cook?" A fluttering of pale butterfly lashes baited the bigger man, but the twinkling of dew-drenched violets stole his heart. Phoenix settled his own anxiety, although his new appearance continued to unnerve him. An unnaturally beautiful face bestowed upon him, he had to accept the dramatic change. Nothing less than perfect, corrective surgery made him a 'Barbie' instead of a 'Ken' doll.

"Sure, I can throw something together, but tonight we eat out.

You want to try a friend's cooking first, like the wine bottle thing, right?"

"I'm trying, Trevor, I am; but I also have a practical reason. There's this little matter of putting my boot over this bandaged foot."

"You're right. How bad is it? Do you need stitches?"

"No, the wounds only amount to a few gouges that will heal if left for a few days. Besides, we have other things to do. I need to pull up more data, and you must finish whatever you're conjuring up in your formidable darkroom." The younger man finally smiled, raising his hands in pretense of fearing the dreaded works in the off-limits area, particularly when the bright red light lit the door a scarlet hue, quite out of character with the rest of the décor.

Sloane chuckled at his young workmate who gestured eerily with his fingers and arms splayed like Frankenstein. He twisted Phoenix around and shoved him playfully toward the guest quarters to change, while he ventured downstairs for breakfast supplies, knowing that the tiny cereal boxes presented only an appetizer for his larger appetite. Taking only minutes to find the items in Chiu's shop, he smiled at the wizened old man who raised his eyebrows over things his landlord never purchased. The photographer only shook his head and shrugged, while watching his tab slowly climb.

Chapter VI

Dinner out came many exhaustive days later, since both men had immersed themselves in their work. Once Sloane had finished his prints and sent the best shots via courier, he turned his attention toward Phoenix, a man growing weary of gazing at the subtle light vibration of the monitor and writing copious amounts of notes. As suggested, their trip would flow with the importance of each place. Having enough data to make them appear somewhat informed, the journey would start after Christmas in the Northern Hemisphere and would reach the southern half of the world approximately three months later, just as the wet season slowed to a few torrential downpours a week.

Observing Phoenix over several days, Trevor found him a quiet, respectful man, working hard, disguising his fear of ordered-in food, and in the evenings, happy to play his guitar, allowing both men to relax a few hours in the darkness of winter's cold nights. Lust turned to friendship for the photographer; trust replaced fear for the journalist. With a glass of wine dangling from a former Tight End's long fingers and one very sturdy leg thrown over the arm of his chair, Sloane made his decision to invite Phoenix to a special gathering of friends. All in professions related to investigative reporting, from scandalous innuendo to cutting-edge political cartoons, the seven men came together once or twice a year to vent their feelings and rid themselves of the perversely unexplainable events they had to hide from the public. The entire stories, and what truly had to be said, ended in a shredder, as the group of friends danced on a tightrope politically, socially, and religiously: a strain on them all.

Phoenix accepted, his mind whirling with thoughts of Joey and what Sloane fancied in a male partner. In his mind, the two men still slept and cavorted with each other sexually; and having been on assignments for many months, they would both likely be suffering from a scoreless stretch. A suggestion to Trevor that he participate only a short time that evening, and then spend the night in a hotel, was adamantly discouraged. The bashful offer stirred the older man to hoist his petit partner up like a doll, stand him on his feet, and order him to dress for a casual dinner out. End of further conversation, they would depart in ten minutes.

Darkness fell early in winter, but New York City lit up the night sky, along with the famous Rockefeller Center Christmas Tree. Phoenix had seen nothing of the metropolis but through the giant windows of the apartment, and this evening offered him fresh air and a sense of freedom. After a week of studying copious amounts of data, stepping onto the sidewalk of Mott Street startled his quiet reverie with raucous noise and confusion. The exhaust fumes suffocated him and his ears rang the entire way, until he entered an Italian restaurant four blocks down and around the corner. The clamor continued inside with the bustle of a busy night, but after shedding their winter gear and Trevor taking his arm, they were escorted immediately to a select table. Apparently, nothing prevented the famous photographer from bypassing those in line; and both men received stares of wonderment while walking through the throng.

A delicious dinner and caring company, surrounded by new acquaintances of the friendly variety, put Phoenix into a peaceful zone. After scanning for possible faces seen ten years prior, he relaxed, knowing that nothing sinister could happen to him within such a crowd, particularly with his giant protector always in sight, who asked the waiter to bring an uncorked, expensive wine to the table. Insisting he would open the bottle and pour the liquid himself, the photographer also ordered a sealed bottle of water and requested the liquid already served over ice be discarded. Having carefully executed a simple plan for handling Phoenix's problems, the older man looked up to see a happier face and those purple eyes glittering with thanks, perhaps even a little joy for the first time in years.

The two talked about the trip and what the fledgling journalist had discovered, redefining their sojourn. With more research to do and contacts for Sloane to make, the problems fell away; this night ignited a little laughter in the younger man, and certainly stoked the flame higher in his friend's adoring eyes. The subtle seduction went unnoticed by Phoenix who flirted naturally, not knowing he did. The dancing violets, the flutter of white eyelashes, and a rush of pink to his cheeks over something of embarrassment to him, captured the attention of all in the restaurant, including the chef and maitre d' whom he met. Long standing friends of Trevor's, they promised to grant any wish asked by the young man, including cold, sealed, bottled water, and food directly off the heat.

Out the door and on their way home, their laughter and joking continued, particularly over their size difference. Trevor demanded proof that the smaller man could hold his weight if the photographer found himself hanging from a rope, although a rather absurd scenario that was unlikely to occur. Streetlights lit their way as they strolled along the slippery sidewalk, taking in the wondrous display of fresh snow falling, sparkling, and then twinkling to ground. The large white flakes gently kissed their faces on this calm, cold night, which was no matter since the distance was short and both men were happy to hike back. Looking through the low lying cloud, Phoenix tried to find a recognizable star to wish upon, when a large arm unexpectedly knocked the wind out of him, stopping him abruptly. Trevor's voice came out in a harsh whisper, only for Thornton-Jones' ears. "We may be in trouble. Whatever I say, follow my lead."

Bewildered, the journalist squinted over the arm, seeing five men carrying baseball bats. In the moment immediately, he responded appropriately to Sloane who wrapped around him protectively, bent down to stare worriedly into his face, fussed paternally over his coat collar, and then caringly touched his forehead with one bare hand. The kid leaned into the army-green Arctic parka, as the gloved hand pulled his head into the cold feel of waterproof canvas.

The largest of the five men stepped forward in time to two beating hearts and bludgeoned them with verbal insults of the gay variety. Trevor did not hesitate to look directly at the boss man, while standing his full six-foot five-inches. Growling back, the sounds and words--father, son, sick, hospital, may be his last day to breathe fresh air--created more laughter. Phoenix, nonetheless, came through, collapsing against Sloane. "Dad, I need to sit down."

The sniping attacks grew more vicious between the photographer and the hulky leader, particularly the remarks of being an old trick to escape a beating of two fags. The younger man again supplied proof, pitching forward, leaving the meal he had enjoyed on the curb. The instant memory of another group of hostile men created the actuality; Phoenix was sick over the number of men ready to assault him. Only five assailants encircled them, where were the others and the redheaded woman with the cat? His mind twisted around, attempting to secure some footing in the real world. Snowing and cold, the same conditions prevailed, but someone held him together, not down on his back. The smell was different, a scent he craved; he regained his senses and remembered his famous friend who again attempted to seat his son on the closest stoop. Both huddling within earshot, Phoenix deciphered the whispered instructions and readied himself. His comrade turned to snarl angrily at the approaching thugs, throwing more fuel on their ire. "Look, you son-of-a-bitch, my son is dying. He knows it, and this was our last special day we may ever have. If you had any compassion, or a soul, you'd wave down a cab and help me get him back to the hospital."

"Yeah, right. Seems you like fuckin' boys. Maybe we'll just beat on your sorry ass, you old queen. He sure ain't your kid. Look at his eyes and the size of him." The sound of beating bats against leather gloves drew ever closer, as two men ticked off the time in their heads. Sloane firmly clasped the smaller hand, which returned the signal with equal pressure; and the two athletes flung themselves straight into the oncoming mêlée. Their clenched hands downed the leader hard, with a controlled double-fisted jab to his testicles. The victims split apart; Trevor ducked one swing, catching the bat on the return. Holding fast his position, the man on the other end of the weapon struggled to regain control, attempting to release it from the mighty grip of a vice. While struggling with one thug and a deadly weapon, Sloane caught another attacker with a high karate kick to the chin, felling the man like a pine tree, straight backward onto the concrete and out cold. Now with two hands on the fat end of the bat, he easily swung the third man through the air, landing the thug hard against the one still in a crouch. Both gay bashers lay flat on the ground moaning, thanks to the former football player's strength developed over years of expert training. Hissing through his teeth, Trevor steamed at the three barely conscious men, "Who are the fools now, suckers? Go back to school and look up genes, recessive and dominant. Better run home to your mommies, little girls."

Trevor suddenly twisted his head around, remembering Phoenix, praying he still stood. Surprisingly, his young friend's agility came into play lightning quick, diving under two swinging bats, rolling to stand up, and inflicting precisely aimed punches into vulnerable body parts: the throat and a nose. Seeing the journalist move with such speed and force, Sloane stood amazed, while his one foot held the two struggling to get up. He watched his new partner burn the last two assailants; however, one look at the beautiful face forced him to intervene, to hold Phoenix back from picking up a weapon and beating both fallen men. The perpetrators of the assault, or attempted murder, received their comeuppance; and Sloane pulled the kid away, yelling for him to run. Both men dashed away, led by Phoenix who had no idea where he was going. Once Trevor caught up to the deer, fleeing from unseen street wolves, the small man froze at the touch of a hand that pulled him around.

"Easy, kiddo. Slow down. We're safe. Breathe deeply." Trevor held him steady against the cold brick wall of the deserted alley they found themselves, while he whipped out his cellular telephone with the other hand. Placing a call to the police, he notified them of the incident, where to find the injured attackers, along with the address of his apartment if they needed their statements. The photographer had no reason to suspect anything further than signing his name on a complaint document. The snowy night grew bitterly cold, and two men, struggling with the horrible surprise and their expeditious retaliation, walked quickly and silently down Mott Street. Climbing the inside stairs and entering their safe haven behind the black and gold door, both collapsed into chairs, sitting quietly, waiting for the inevitable ring of the doorbell. It sounded.

A gong disrupted the silence of the apartment where two men breathed heavily, recovering from their ordeal. Unfortunately, one heart jumped at the unexpected clang, and Phoenix flung his arms around the bigger man, nearly knocking him backward onto the floor. "Please, Trev, they can't know my name. Give them this number to call. Tell them anything, but who I am or where I'm from. Please, Trevor." The young man dangled from his position, arms about the strong neck, pleading with those violet eyes as soft as velvet, and yet scared to his grave.

"Why?" The older man clung to the body he desired; the scent and feel saturated his being so intimately, the astute, easy-going photographer was rocked to his curling toes. Love at first sight and now the chemical attraction of scent, Sloane held his breath, waiting for an answer and wishing the unexpected embrace would continue.

"I can't tell you. Just give the police a card I must carry with me." Slowly set on shaking legs, Phoenix reached for his wallet, pulled out an official looking plastic-coated card, and ran for his room.

Releasing the locked door at the bottom of the stairs, Sloane opened the lacquered black one, unperturbed at the presence of two plain-clothed detectives. He welcomed them in, introduced himself, and settled in to discuss the events of the evening. Reiterating every word said during the incident and the slow march toward them, his eloquence and diplomacy won the skeptical detectives over. However, their assailants were pressing charges, considering the carnage two average citizens had created in their frenzied defense: a broken nose, a damaged larynx, a severe concussion, a dislocated shoulder, and one who continued to speak in a high-pitched voice. The damage inflicted did not look good for the photographer with nary a bruise.

"Sorry, detectives, but our only weapon was surprise; and it worked. They were the ones with the bats and attitude." Trevor maintained their self-defense scenario; truth always won over a series of lies.

"This is an unusual case, the victims seizing the opportunity to divert their attackers' attention and grasp the moment. Is your companion the same size? I imagine two men of your stature very capable of defending themselves." The head detective continued his questions, seldom diverting his eyes from the big man sitting opposite him. His partner, however, noticed every nuance the room provided of an alternate lifestyle; and Trevor watched the disgust rising in the silent one.

"He won't speak with you for some reason; and please, do not assume anything about him, considering this is my home and he is my guest. Having only just met, our full focus has been on our assignment, nothing more. This card, which he asked me to show you, means something. By the looks of the government stamps and seals, you can use this telephone number; but the big bold letters state you cannot confiscate this particular piece of plastic. Never seen the likes of it; and by the way, he's smaller than average." Sloane reached over to the receiving calloused hand, thinking the detective had a very different hobby other than asking questions.

"Is he hurt?" The detective inquired while reading the card. He immediately arose and went to the telephone, jabbing the numbers as if prodding a dead body to awaken.

"Shit, I never thought to ask him."

"He's staying with you then; and I'm not reading anything into that, Mr. Sloane. Perhaps you should find out if he's injured, while I make this call."

Trevor immediately went in search of his guest, feeling ashamed of himself for not inquiring after the man's physical and emotional needs, while gathering their wits and fortitude. He found Phoenix in the bathroom, leaning over the toilet, the last of his dinner gone. "You need something to stop you from gagging. I'll be right back. Did they hurt you, before you tried to kill them both?" Sloane bent down and wiped the sweating brow.

"Not bad, but I'll have bruises. Did they ring the number? I won't show them any injuries those thugs inflicted."

"Yes you will, Mr. Thornton-Jones, if it comes to pressing charges against us. Where were you hit?"

"My shoulder, a couple of whacks to my right side and lower back."

"Sit quietly against the wall; here's a cool cloth; and I'll get you something for your stomach. Some night, hey kiddo, welcome to New York. You handled yourself extremely well. I need a partner who isn't afraid to engage in a scrap." Sloane gave him a comforting smile, although it turned downward at the response.

"I've learned to protect myself from everything and anyone. I will kill whomever messes with me. Never again, Sloane, never again." The voice lowered, growling vengeance. Ten years of trauma came through loudly; and Trevor now knew the *accident* involved others the kid had no control over.

Sloane heard the click of the phone; a signal the two detectives waited for him. Excusing himself temporarily from their next set of questions, he found the pink fluid, which usually made one sicker, and returned to place several teaspoons between those amazing, quivering, perfect lips. "Hold on until I see what they want from you." Exiting the guest quarters, the man returned to face two men puzzling over something "Sorry, Gentlemen, but it seems fright causes an instant purging in my writer. What did you find out?"

"This card is extremely important, Mr. Sloane. They should have tattooed the number across his forehead in case he loses it. We do need to ask him a few questions however, only about tonight; and we can discount his name thanks to this card. Did you determine if he sustained any injuries? It would help dismiss the charges against you, if we had a visual to attach to your statements." The head detective looked far too concerned; while his partner appeared as puzzled as did the photographer.

"He caught a few hits from the bats, which will probably be black and blue by morning. His sheepskin coat provided some protection. Please note he's extremely shy about shedding his apparel, so be gentle. I'd like to see him stop vomiting first. Oh, one more thing to ignore besides his name; he's acutely embarrassed about his looks. I warn you now; they are unusual." Trevor quickly sought out Phoenix, edging him toward the waiting police who retained their stoic appearance, although unable to stop their mouths from dropping slightly at the perfection drawing nearer.

"Sit down, son, and tell us what happened, so we can collaborate your story with Mr. Sloane's version. I hope you didn't discuss the situation with your colleague before our arrival."

"Oh no, sir. We saw it from two different angles, considering we were fighting off different men."

"Good, then you concur that your actions were in self-defense."

"Yes, sir."

"We can't use your name, understanding your FBI connections, but they are concerned about you. They divulged nothing, only asking us to handle you with care and to inform you to call Agent Donahue, using this same number, when we're finished. Start from the beginning, after you left the restaurant. Just a few words of confirmation from you, I'm sure we can put this incident to rest immediately." The primary detective returned the card to its distressed owner, but continued to stare in astonishment at the young man.

Phoenix described every detail, just as a trained journalist would have observed. Leaving nothing out, he did balk at the possibility of an examination. With a little convincing, he pulled up the right side of his gray and yellow striped ski sweater, along with the same yellow-colored turtleneck underneath, giving them a quick glimpse of his right side and a close up Polaroid taken by Sloane. The red marks had started to turn color, but did not disguise one ghastly scar requiring cosmetic work by a skilled surgeon.

Satisfied, the two detectives left with a farewell and a wish for a safe journey for Sloane and the strange young man who wielded a card of power. They promised to purchase the first copy of the *PlanetTerra Journals* and put the costly magazine on their expense account as evidence. Laughing politely and shaking hands, the fiasco was over, until Trevor turned to face Phoenix. "The FBI?"

Chapter VII

Forgetting his injuries, Phoenix whipped around, causing an involuntary emission of the quietest groan. He had to say something about a number only used once and for the strangest of reasons. "Can't talk about it, but you're secure."

"I sincerely hope so! You grow more intriguing, kiddo. That card must be worth a Sultan's ransom. You should have this--I guess this number here--branded on your butt. I won't ask, although I wish I could. What's the matter? Still feeling unwell?" Sloane questioned the face full of pain, anger, and secrets with the uplift of a brow, while mentally registering that he had gone too far with his statements.

"I've concluded that unexpected bodily attacks make me puke, considering potential assaults and retaliatory actions are not a normal activity for me." The reach for the back of the couch threw the big man into action. Lending a hand, Sloane felt the small body straighten and tense.

"I won't hurt you. Come and sit with me. I think it may be a good idea to talk about what occurred."

"You sound like Twister; but there's nothing to say. We both know what would have happened without your quick plan. Can't believe we whacked them and weren't charged." The younger man relaxed enough to sit back into the softness of the sofa, thigh-to-thigh against one four times the size of his own. The appendage felt tight and powerful, as did the arm hanging over his shoulder. His breathing shortened at the touch of the photographer, while the strong squeeze of his shoulders ignited flames doused years earlier. Wishing time to stop, he needed to catch his breath to prevent another agitation that was growing within his confining jeans.

"Hell of a night. Sorry about the Polaroids, but they will show some bodily contact. I think we managed to delete any extraneous exposure, except the bruising. How do you feel?" Trevor had no expectations of his light touch, but the inexperienced, awestruck journalist felt the hot breath and soft voice vibrate next to his ear, creating a detectable tremor to shake his stiffening body.

"Sore and a little frazzled." Phoenix swallowed a tortured scream, hiding every confusing thought exploding in his brain.

"Frazzled? I haven't heard that word for some time. Hey,

you're still shaking. I'll start the fire; considering the adrenaline rush, which we're both suffering from, always results in the shivers. Are you able to handle Agent Donahue?"

"Yeah. I best get it over with." With a reprieve, the shaken youth inhaled deeply, his life and feelings on hold for the length of a telephone call.

"Want privacy?"

"No, just need to tell him why I handed the card to a police detective whom I thought particularly considerate. I can tell you this much, Trevor, and then we can drop the subject. I did a few favors for the Bureau and receive a few in return." With his swelling bruises throbbing, he reached awkwardly for the wireless telephone, made the quick call at several paces distant, and turned to watch Sloane stuff kindling under the larger logs. The troubled man hesitated on hanging up, undecided as to the appropriate place to sit.

"Everything okay?" Sloane continued his task, now believing his partner under some bizarre witness protection program. What could a youngster, from Colorado, supply the FBI to warrant the drastic measures? He kept quiet, puzzling over the strange dilemma of the man, while coaxing the twigs to spark before returning to his former position on the sofa.

"They're just concerned; since this is the first time they've heard from me. They're cool with my explanation. Smells good in here, Trev." The dry logs caught the flame, quickly filling the room with the aroma of hickory and cedar, as the heat slowly fogged the windows that once glittered with diamonds. Susceptible to scents, Phoenix loved the smell of home; even the thought of Christmas crossed his mind and erased the doubts of what had occurred this strange night. Solemnly, he sank back into the engulfing furniture and against the warm thigh. His first outing in New York ended in a near disaster, a possible arrest for their actions, and his identity close to uncovered. He desperately desired to take the first jet back to safety and loving family, but the sensation within had not subsided. Unable to understand why his dead manhood stirred to create more agony, his only reason lay in the presence of the man sitting beside him. Squirming slightly to rest the demon forces, he controlled the physical anomaly, forcing it into submission. Severe damage, from a decade ago, wreaked more mental scars on the fragile mind, and no one could convince him otherwise. Coming out of a long lost world, he gazed up into brown liquid pools clouded with sympathy. His soft heart broke;

his holy tears fell. He had not cried in years, but fear, frustration, and a famous man, who could and would break his heart, drew closer. The photographer looked worried, and yet mellow and kind, as he offered him a haven within strong outstretched arms. Drowning in sorrow over many things, Phoenix released his soul to a special person; he could not receive enough of the tender embrace.

"It's okay, kiddo. You kicked arse tonight, defeating a few fears. Your anger rather upset me, nothing wrong with that considering the circumstances; but your spirit burns with rage. Can I help? Anything you need to make you feel better?" Stroking the sweet-smelling hair gently, a large hand encircled the entire pastel head, while rocking the younger man who quieted quickly. Trevor understood the humiliation that came after an emotional outburst and the acceptance of a paternal gesture.

"Just scared shitless, and honest to God, I would have bashed their heads into mush if you hadn't stopped me. I'm okay, thanks, just another rare moment for me." Phoenix pushed away, but on this night that grew more peculiar, his new protector refused to release him from the strong hold. His body stiffened, waiting for something.

"The incident frightened me as well, and I thanked every star in the sky you comprehended my few cryptic instructions. Surprise was on our side, not to mention we're both fit for a brawl."

"Nothing brave about defending yourself, fighting off a deadly menace. Pure survival, man. Try voluntarily jumping off a small ledge, sailing through the air on skis, and doing triple twists head down. Every new trick puts your guts in your mouth, but the thrill is beyond imagining. I think our adventure could almost top it." Phoenix settled, cautiously easing into the comfort of the offered warmth, while lapsing into dreams of Twister and Caly's fatherly hugs, and feeling the rush of freedom his former pastime instilled.

"That's right, you told me about your university days in Denver. So... you were one of those suicidal, out-of-their-mind aerialists. Man, did you pick a tenacious and dangerous sport. I should have recognized the body type and training method." New respect grew for the kid, understanding where Phoenix's swiftness, agility, and courage originated.

"I'm a body type, hunh? Guess every sport has one that aids performance. I started long before anyone thought of hanging ten with snow skis. My first competition was at age eight; no one, not even my family, had heard of the sport. It's come a long way since then, with

moves I can only dream about trying. I was good enough and did well
in competition, but the love of it kept me going. We lived between
Denver and the closest ski resort heading west. Every Saturday and
Sunday morning, I'd walk down the road to the security guard who
would open the locked gates of the estate and wave down the bus
heading for Breckenridge. I'd ski all day, never resting, until I
returned on the last bus. My only obstruction was the church, but with
some major whining, the family agreed to attend night services. I must
have thanked God a million times for the reprieve."

Back to leaning against the soft cushioning, the two men
warmed up from the cold walk home and the chill induced by shock.
Coffee, with a shot of flaming Sambuca, finished them off, but they
remained close, with some body part resting on the other. After
several minutes of mutual warmth and comfort, Sloane turned to the
young man, put his arms about the small torso, and brought the
beautiful face around to stare longingly into the violet eyes. "Phoenix,
don't flip out on me, but I want to kiss you, right now, right here."

A look of horrific surprise shot from the journalist's eyes, while
the beautiful head shook back and forth frenetically, creating gulping
sounds in the raspy throat. "No, Trevor, no! Don't touch me! Let me
go!" Squirming like a wild man caught in a trap too small, he fought
ferociously against Sloane who refused to release him, causing a near
catatonic attack in the former daredevil.

"Easy and gently. Just a tiny lip-to-lip touch, nothing more, and
you'll calm my racing heart. Please, Phoenix, settle down. I won't
force you, nor would I ever hurt you to play out my own desires, but I
am besotted by you. If that one feeling scares the hell out of you--trust
me--it has me shaking in my shoes."

Blinking at the gentle brown orbs flecked with gold, the smaller
man had no response. Fear stood in his way, but the strengthening
hold and the feeling of safety overcame the terror. A passionate hug
seemed the moon away without a reliable friend to try such an intimate
gesture, but he found himself releasing his anxiety enough to submit to
the kindness expressed in an older handsome face. Studying every line
around the loving eyes full of fun, now softening to amber and
twinkling like topaz gemstones, he veered his gaze to the
mischievously grinning mouth. Each aging wrinkle deepened with
affection. Every line seen was a result of worry, harsh working
conditions, and a life unknown; the young man wished the chance to
discover every detail of the Herculean. Phoenix smiled shyly back

when a thumb stroked his cheek lightly; serene bliss fell upon him with the innocent action.   He drifted unknowingly toward the full lips saying something, leaning into the hand that now held and raised his chin slightly upward.   Shivering with the sublime touch, he instinctively breathed in the ecstasy of a man filled with passion and smelling of wild animal musk mixed with licorice from the Sambuca. In ten years, he had not shared an intimate moment, except for family caresses. He watched his captor's movement forward; his lips softened with the touch of a large finger gently manipulating his malleable mouth to open a sliver. A slight brush of his lips, a tingling sensation of another's warm breath, Phoenix released his inhibitions with an anxious moan.

As promised, Sloane took it no further, attempting to pull back, but two small hands reached up and laced themselves in the graying hair, enticing the photographer to linger against the perfect lips. Phoenix quivered as a wet tongue slipped over and into the small opening, and he whimpered softly, struggling with his need to satisfy the giddy feeling deep in his crotch, but refusing to give into a rush of lust. Another plaintive groan, he lost himself in the sweet sensation of the larger man who gently, but forcibly, removed the fisting fingers from his graying hair, kissed the fluttering white eyelashes, and captured the anxious tears before they fell.

"That was an amazing kiss, Phoenix. I knew you'd taste divine and smell like heaven." Trevor put his hand on the small beating chest while keeping his other arm around the man's shoulders. Surprised by the response of someone unwilling to participate in sexual activity, he wondered if the simple caress created other stirrings and glanced at the pouch hidden under very tight jeans. No normal movement showed itself, and Sloane suppressed his own growing concern, calming the devilish serpent with years of experience.

The receiver of the gift said nothing, not comprehending what had happened, only placing his fingers to his lips. A release of the caring arms did receive an unexpected reaction. "Don't let go!"

"I won't. You're quite the sprite, kiddo. Did I tell you how much I care about you?" Sloane understood the kiss meant more than simple affection to the confused man, although sexually impervious to his seduction. He held on firmer, attempting to quell the sudden quivering of another phobic attack, possibly due to their intimate position. "Thank you for granting this old man's request. Now, come closer, move your feet nearer the fire, and we'll just sit, enjoying silent company. If I scared you, please forgive me." With only Phoenix's wide-eyed expression as an answer, the bigger man adjusted their sitting arrangement. He desired the disquieting kid; unfortunately, he realized how easily someone could force attention upon a weaker victim. Silently cursing himself for his premature actions, again he pledged to wait until Phoenix asked, just as he did to be held. Having secretly called a psychiatrist, of his acquaintance, to learn the definition of sexual inertness, he also ran into a terminology problem, as the tags *sexual aversion* and *asexual* encompassed many mental afflictions applicable to the condition. In the photographer's mind, Thornton-Jones' psychosis lay deeper than a word, more akin to a pretense hiding something grimmer. He could not believe the flirtatious purple-eyed flower felt nothing, even upon initiating a delightful response. Disturbing for a man whose sexual appetite had never diminished, the thought of one so young incapable of receiving the core rush of maleness saddened him. He held on tighter, his petit partner accepting the giant hug like a child to his father. Sloane wanted more.

"I'm sorry I can't express my feelings any further than I have, but we better stop now. I don't wish to lead you into something I can't finish." Phoenix's hot breath whispered against the larger hand holding his own. Wishing to lay his head against the warm, broad, pounding chest that sighed heavily, he dared not try and left the wanton desire as an unrequited dream.

"If that's what you want, my friend, but I find you irresistibly attractive, and not only physically. Give me time, and I can grow accustomed to the position we're in now--your security blanket--and happily so." Sloane released his hand, freeing it to tussle the crazy hair and bringing the head to rest against his chest; he swore he felt the vibration of a satisfied purr.

The stroking of the pastel tresses continued, the fire warming both men, and together they fell asleep, one curled snugly within the other's arms. Several hours passed, the room grew colder as the fire slowly died. A few mumbling words from Phoenix woke the man who rousted at the sound of a feather duster swiping a table. Painful little grunts and moans, breathlessly murmured, startled Sloane who listened for an intelligible word; he heard nothing clearly. Gently speaking to the troubled sleeper, another man who woke at a running start, the photographer suggested they retire. Thornton-Jones sheepishly agreed, wished Trevor good night, and disappeared into his own room. As promised, he turned on the bedside lamp, before returning to switch off the overhead.

Through the small crack of the guestroom door, Trevor watched closely, content to see Phoenix quickly climb into bed and fall asleep. More enlightening thoughts had surfaced, certainly the journalist's willingness to conquer fears that could be hushed over time. Sloane undressed to his usual night garb of sky-clad tanned skin, and without further thought of the night's antics, he also started to drift off, prepared for a wet dream during slumber. Sensing movement in the dark, he spotted a small figure, with moonlight turning the white hair glowing silver, wandering into the master suite. Saying nothing and keeping still, Trevor looked on in astonishment as Phoenix slipped into his room, appearing unconcerned of where he was. Walking easily in the dark, avoiding any troublesome obstacles, considering he had not set foot in this particular room, the young man stepped toward the bed and climbed in. Without a word, the kid closed his eyes and slept normally.

"I'll be damned, you're a sleepwalker! That's just great. I can imagine having to chain you in the center of a stilt hut in the jungle, or I'll be hearing the scream as you plummet headfirst out the open sleeping area. Sleep tight, kiddo; we'll make it somehow." Trevor thanked the stars, dancing in the uppermost windows, for his purchase of a bed big enough to accommodate two athletes of substantial size. His new friend cuddled deep under the thick duvet, barely taking up five square feet.

On guard the rest of the night, Sloane finally arose at the first sign of dawn, quietly dressing and tiptoeing from his room, not to awaken the spirit who had slept motionless the rest of the night. He declined to embarrass his young guest further; considering the two fear-filled crying sprees had unnerved him enough. Understanding the truth when he felt it in his heart and head, he believed the younger man did not cry readily, considering the painful therapy endured. Something about staying with the photographer created Phoenix's macabre behavior; the listening promise came to mind. "Okay, Sloane, keep your mouth shut and pay attention to all sounds and occurrences surrounding the kid. He's out of his environment and feeling the loneliness; that's all it is." On that affirmation, he collected the paper, made coffee, and stretched out comfortably to catch up on world news. Nothing of interest caught his eye; political bantering avoided at the expense of unsubstantiated knowledge, and worse yet, the entertainment section full of non-essential news about the goings-on of irrelevant people. Only a friend's comic strip made him laugh, and of course, catching up on a variety of sports he enjoyed. The football season was slowly closing on winners and losers, and he delighted in reading who led the league the past year. A squeak of a door alerted him, but he continued to read, glasses perched on the tip of his nose; he waited.

"Morning, Trev, how did I end up in your bed? I didn't flip out or anything did I?" The voice sounded casual, although weak and very scratchy from their lengthy conversation of the night before, plus a smoke filled restaurant.

"You walked in, slipped between the sheets, unaware of your actions. Kind of cute actually, like a puppy finding something warm to snuggle against." Sloane turned and grinned at him, wondering if the man could tolerate a little teasing.

"Oh brother, you're psychic; and I'm back to sleepwalking. It started when very young, and as soon as I could walk again, I often ended up with Caly and Twister. They never said if I interrupted them at an inappropriate moment, but I assume I did on occasion. I seem to wake in the oddest places, but as you said, always close to something warm. I thought we rectified the problem when they gave me two loveable pups trained to sleep with me. They stopped my midnight wanderings immediately." Phoenix laughed hoarsely, coughing to ease the strain, while downplaying his strange behavior that would have mortified most men, but one he shook off as an everyday inconvenience. Underneath his façade, however, he felt his heart shatter, but he would never forget that a show of bravado always lightened a sensitive problem.

"Too bad you don't like Bogie. He loves curling around my feet under the covers; and he likes you. He would certainly keep you warm."

"Along with scaring me senseless. Good God, the thought has me shaking." Phoenix could not hide the involuntary quiver, flashing back to angry eyes squinting at him, the claws extended, the blood, and the stinging sensation each scratch inflicted. The memory rattled him within; he wavered.

Trevor leapt to his feet to stop the fall. "Steady, Phoenix, I won't mention Bogie again. Come; join me for coffee. Sounds like your throat is sore and you should be sucking on a lozenge."

"Definitely would help. My vocal cords aren't exactly strong.

Do you have something? I'm sure Master Chui stocks a medicinal cure in his apothecary section of weird herbs and spices. I'll run down and get something."

"I have what you need, and you shouldn't be racing around in the cold until your throat problem's corrected. Back in a flash. Here's your coffee. Warmth helps dry sore throats. Maybe a little rum and butter should be added, in case you're coming down with a cold."

"Thanks, but no thanks. I have work to do, and my throat is scratchy from talking too much. This foot bandage needs changing as well. The damn thing's bleeding again from our mad dash. I should have looked at it last night." Sitting at the table, the sleep-ruffled man sipped the stimulating brew carefully while contemplating his life. Thornton-Jones had regained his composure, although truly demoralized by another anxiety attack over something he believed foolish. How many times, over the years, had he discussed cats with doctors, nurses, psychiatrists, Granny, Caly, and Twister? Taking years to numb the implications of the dreaded feline, he found himself, once again, fighting the word--cat, cat, cat--it would never end. With a red bitter candy handed to him, he popped it into his mouth to ease the rawness, while Sloane checked the lacerated foot and re-bandaged it. "Thanks, Trev, but with everything that has happened since my arrival in New York, this latest episode takes the proverbial cake. You really don't want me on this journey, do you? Look how I reacted to a stupid three-letter word. Why I have cried in front of you--twice--is beyond me. I get mad; I don't cry. Then letting you kiss me, and my response; man, this is so ridiculous. I'll never make it." Phoenix leaned back and sighed, but did not take his eyes off the man now sitting across from him.

"Let's forget all that has transpired since your arrival and start again. We made a plan that we're sticking to. Not only are you a talented writer, you're extremely clever, positively brilliant in your quick but methodical research. Having created the scenario of our adventure primarily on your own, there's no way I'm letting you off the hook. Besides, if I'm never allowed to kiss you again, I still enjoy your unorthodox company; you're the perfect companion for a long grueling trip. Enough said." Trevor believed himself out of his mind with his decision, but this was one trip, one trial run, nothing more. Having telephoned earlier, to find Warren continuing his workaholic schedule, the two old friends planned to meet that afternoon. Friday was not the best day in New York for publishers, particularly during

the Christmas holidays, as they were kept busy selling book and
magazine ideas to backers, while running from one cocktail party to
another somewhere in The Hamptons; one glorious circus he loved to
miss. Nonetheless, he needed to confide his doubts to someone and to
support his decision regarding the monumental puzzle ripping strips
off his heart.

"Unorthodox? A good description, I think."

"Earns you points for not being average. I have errands to run
in Manhattan today. I'll be back before eight. Will you be all right by
yourself?" A squint expressed some concern, but the kid jumped back
to life rapidly.

"Sure. Tonight your guests are coming. Do you want me to do
anything, or should I keep working?"

"Take time to rest, strum your guitar, keep your weight off your
foot, and absolutely no singing. Please, Phoenix, try to quiet that
racing heart you're concealing. I'm sure you need rest after the hard
hits you received last night."

"Don't think I'll remember all that, but a day to myself sounds
good, not that your company bothers me." Phoenix swiftly apologized
for the wording with an instant retraction of his ill-perceived callous
statement. Unnecessary, his next words erased a worried frown. "Oh,
I should call the family and tell them we're coming on the 23rd. The
work is almost complete, with a week to spare. Let me find the exact
location of that tree farm. We could leave tomorrow or the next day,
and then continue on to Denver."

"A perfect plan. You did a great job, but please, relax enough to
enjoy yourself when my friends arrive. Now listen up, kiddo. If any
of them start discussing a subject you'd rather not participate in,
simply excuse yourself, and return when you're ready. This group
meets to vent the problems associated with our god-awful job
assignments, which we can't rid ourselves of in any other way. I have
one of my own I need advice about, a little mental therapy to share.
You cool with that?" Sloane peered into the violet orbs, hoping to use
the lens of an eye instead of a camera, while listening for the slightest
hint of hesitation. With the usual *'no problem'* response, he settled
back. The day would be long, particularly if the young man fled the
apartment, a likely possibility if blindsided by something unbeknownst
to the photographer. Perhaps his meeting with Warren was too hasty,
or conversely too late. The problems Phoenix experienced now
bubbled too close to the surface after being long guarded; his

outrageous friends could hit a button he had not yet pushed.

"Who are these friends of yours? If delayed, I had better know whom I'm letting in the door. Please, Trev, don't be late." The crossed fingers expressed it all.

"Not to worry, I'll be here. Joey usually arrives first and can take over if something extraordinary happens. You already know he'll have a load on his shoulders. Wolfe is an old friend from my football days, a giant of a man with plaited Rastafarian-styled hair and attitude that will catch you by surprise. He's written several sport related novels, currently working on a third, uncovering drug use amongst a myriad of athletes, ready to punt kick a few people out of their cleated booties. His cub is a sweet guy who creates satirical four-frame comics. This is one of his." Trevor pointed at the comic, after switching the paper around for Phoenix's viewing. The crazy little characters merited much giggling behind a clenched fist, and the younger man immediately expressed a desire to read the preceding frames of the continuing saga. Promising to find one of the paperback books, which were rapidly becoming classics, brought a happy smile on the lips Trevor could still taste.

"Wolfe and Cub; what strange names."

"Sorry, Phoenix, I used Wolfe's correct moniker, but neglected Sebastian's. *Cub* refers to his role in their daddy/boy relationship. I guess Seb would be about your age, whereas Wolfe has a few years on me."

"I understand. Who else?"

"Gregory and Denis, an interesting couple of look-alikes, the same generation as me and Joey. Gregory investigates cold case murders, very highly respected and in great demand, as is Denis, our notable forensic scientist. You'll enjoy and learn some interesting facts from the pair, and they assuredly do not resort to grisly details."

"Thank God. Does Joey have a partner coming?" The violets opened to the sun filtering through the windows, and then returned to focus on the steam rising from his mug, creating tiny rivulets of perspiration on the perfect face. A fluttering of white eyelashes, however, was noted with curiosity.

"No, he's currently on his own from what I gather, as is Will. Speaking of our old lecherous queen, he'll love you to death in his silly way, wanting to squeeze you into porridge. He covers the seedy side of gay life for several tabloids, digging into the scummy part we try to ignore. The attack perpetrated on us last night should interest him."

"I'd rather not talk about it. He won't try hitting on me, will he?"

"Most assuredly, and in the most effeminate manner, which drives me uncharacteristically crazy. He's been a friend for years, and as such, we put up with him. If he makes advances toward you, just stick your tongue out and snarl at him. He'll back away, being a harmless oaf."

"What fun; I haven't committed the effrontery since I was six." Another bright smile appeared, believing Sloane would not allow any of these men to touch him after the sweet kiss of the night before. He also felt some relief; happy in the knowing he may have a potential friend in the youngest member Sebastian. With confirmation of who was who, he now looked forward to meeting the eclectic group of individuals.

Trevor nodded farewell, pulled on his boots, struggled into his parka, and headed out the door. Braving the transparent elevator, he walked passed Gina with a Merry Christmas wish on his lips and opened both heavy wooden doors in a grandiose gesture of repressed anger. Sitting behind his desk, Graham startled at the abrupt entry, immediately laying down his pen and standing up. "What's up, Sloane? Are you two packed and ready to go?"

"Tell me everything you know about Thornton-Jones. Everything." The big man thumped down hard in an oversized chair, placed his arms on that of the comfortable piece of furniture, and settled into his thinking position.

"You read his resume: degrees in Journalism and Foreign Languages, minors in English Literature and Communication."

"A minor in Communication! Probably in another one of his languages besides English. What else?"

"Graduate of the University of Southern Colorado, lives on the family ranch about an hour out of Pueblo, seems extraordinarily polite with the usual nervousness under the scrutiny of an interview. He's a talented writer and a sweet kid. Hell, you're the one living with him, or he with you. What's your problem?" Warren's frown could not deepen further with his concern.

"I don't know details, only a feeling. Hell, I don't know anything. He is talented: quick, methodical, creative, inventive, practical, yet wildly imaginative, but..."

"...but what? Don't you like him?"

"Damn it, Warren, I've fallen for a man who terrifies me."

"Slow down, Sloane, you're starting to hyperventilate, and even together, Gina and I couldn't lift you off my floor. Why does he scare you, because you've finally fallen in love?" Graham came around and leaned back against the desk, to peer down at a very disturbed photographer.

"He's doing so well, trying so hard, but I don't think he can handle the trip mentally. Something happened to him, something grotesque from what I've pieced together. I've lost count of his phobias, but I'm telling you, Warren, he's still hurting after years of physical therapy and counseling. The variables of him falling apart are astronomical, but I don't want him to leave. He's pulling at my heart, wanting to care for him, not putting his brain in mind-melt with some oddity that I know nothing about. Just leaving him on his own today has me in a sweat. Twister and Caly must be going through hell." Trevor leaned forward and put his face in his hands, rubbing the fear away. He felt so at odds with Phoenix, his verbalization skills could not phrase the absurdities experienced over a week with too many days.

"Who?"

"His parents."

"Look, Sloane, you said he tries, and tries hard. How is he to work with?"

"Fantastic, and I can't believe I said that. An amazing researcher, he can sift through mega amounts of data in seconds, retaining every detail in his beautiful head."

"How is he to live with?"

"Odd, just odd. He's tidy, quiet (most of the time), gentle in his mannerisms, plays the guitar beautifully, cooks like my mother, as well as being capable of beating the shit out of a couple of punks we ran into. You couldn't ask for a better houseguest." Leaning back, he caught the slight smile of the older man who remained mystified as to what possible problem there could be.

"Do these oddities and phobias interfere with his work? What about traveling?"

"Remains to be seen. He's tiptoeing along a slick ribbon, but I'll be there when he slips off." Sighing heavily, once again Trevor succumbed to the luxury of the chair.

"Sounds like an adventure for you both. I saw no indication of any mental problems, as he had me hypnotized by those astounding purple eyes that begged for the job when I first met him. Just try,

Sloane; you can always send him home." Graham returned to his chair, crossing his arms in a dare for the photographer to take another risk.

"I know, but I'd never send him packing. Okay, I'm off, and Phoenix will send you our fly-by-our-butts itinerary. We leave before Christmas, but will be spending a few days with his parents who are both gay. Ain't that a kick?" Sloane slowly rose, zipped and buttoned his parka, and turned to go.

"Does he love you back?"

The remark caught the former football player by surprise. He turned back to look quizzically at his old friend. "No. No, I don't think so. Of course not. He can't."

"Why not? You're not a bad catch in your social circle."

"Thanks, but you ask too many questions, Warren. We'll see you sometime this summer, considering the long, hard trip we have planned, investigating rainforests and deforestation around the globe." A smirk finally shone at the startled face.

"Oh no you won't. How many stops have you pinpointed?"

"At least eight."

"No deal. In the small amount of time you have, I would suggest only Amazonia as your focus of investigation. I want Thornton-Jones' take on that colossal nightmare."

"You said no censorship or editing." Trevor lashed back, annoyed at the curtailing of their six-month journey, which would have given him time to seduce his young partner.

"In words and pictures, Sloane. You have only three months, so rethink your plans."

"Should have given us a deadline from the start." Another sniper attack did not faze the publisher.

"The first edition, with your story headlining it, rolls off the presses in six months. You have much to do before jumping into scandalous notoriety on July 1st. Get it done and submitted by the end of March. You know the drill and the timing."

"Consider our dreams derailed, but you're right. Just pray Mr. Thornton-Jones doesn't fall out of a hut." Trevor laughed aloud and opened the doors. He at least had a timeline to work with.

"What?"

"Private joke. Have a happy holiday, Mr. Graham."

"You too, Sloane. A hut? What in hell does that mean? Gina!"

Chapter VIII

Trevor rushed around Bloomingdales, searching out items he thought appropriate. Using buyer's guides, for suggestions and to lead him around, helped him tremendously, and he exited carrying a large number of parcels. The door attendant easily waved down a *yellow*, receiving a surprised look from the former athlete standing on the curb. With a laugh and a wink, the man in uniform opened the door, and Sloane climbed in, protecting his treasures and wondering what he had been doing wrong his entire life in New York. By 7:45 p.m., he urged the driver to travel at speed, but to stay mindful of the icy streets and bumper teasing traffic. Decorative lights colored their route; little gems of glitter reminded him of his holiday promise to Phoenix. Stepping out of the taxi and gathering his packages, he knew he was late when he saw his elderly tenant beckoning him inside with a flurry of hand gestures. A few quick words, Sloane took the stairs three at a time.

"Phoenix! Phoenix!" The call came out in alarm, but settled on hearing a familiar voice.

"Hey, you handsome hunk of male virtues, you took your bloody time. Put down the bags and plant a bruising kiss on these neglected lips. God, I've missed you and your equipment." Joey stood with a drink in hand, looking like a poster boy selling Glenfiddich Scotch thirty years later. His blatant attempt at seducing Sloane failed however, without a mention of Phoenix.

"Good to see you too, slut. Let me rid myself of boxes and parcels, take off my coat, and then I can look forward to warming my freezing hands on the hottest part of your body." Sloane chuckled, while frantically hiding his concern over his missing houseguest.

"No thanks. A kiss will do until your hands warm. I wouldn't want my rising excitement to extinguish."

"You're insatiable. Where's Phoenix? Was he here to let you in? Chui said he had some trouble."

"You mean TJ? He's in the guest room, busy with something. Seemed fine when he let me in, although a rather bashful, nervous piece of candy. He's knock-down-dead gorgeous and such a tiny little sprite. You are a lucky man, Trevor. Where did you find him, and have I been replaced?" Joey grew a little flamboyant with his wanton posturing, something Trevor found distasteful, certainly bad enough to give his long-time friend a warning squint while struggling through the entry to his private quarters. Tidied up, packages stowed, he emerged in a rush, quickly kissing Joey to fulfill one promise and playfully squeezing his genitals hard enough to score a squeal and a silly wincing motion. The gong threw them both into action, Joey opening the door for Gregory and Denis, and Sloane tapping on Phoenix's door. It opened a crack to expose one violet-colored eye.

"Hey, kiddo, what happened? Are you okay?" Trevor entered and closed the door behind him.

"Yeah, just settling a surprise. Better get used to putting this jigsaw puzzle back together. You didn't tell me to expect a food and liquor delivery. I wasn't sure what to do, since I didn't recognize them immediately. Rang Master Chui and asked him if he knew who struck the gong. I'm sorry, I should have known your friends from the restaurant would cater this affair; and they were two of the waiters I met. I felt like an idiot, particularly when that poor old man climbed your long flight of stairs to ensure they stowed everything in the correct place, or to see if he had to pick me up off the floor. How humiliating is that?"

"You can slow down now. You did fine."

"Was I supposed to pay them? They didn't ask, but a tip would have been appropriate. Master Chui stayed a short time, hovering about, while this fool stood as still as one of the marble statues in the foyer, except with clothes. Anyway, he put things in order, I think. God, I'm sorry, I must have sounded nuts when Joey arrived. Can't remember what I even said to him." Phoenix rambled on, perspiration beading on his forehead, which Sloane dabbed away with one of the monogrammed handkerchiefs always neatly folded in the young man's pocket.

"Calloway thinks you're cute, so he didn't notice anything peculiar. Besides, you are Mr. Nuts. Now, deep breath... another one... much better. I apologize for my oversight of the delivery and being late." A few more wipes of the face, Phoenix slowed the reggae beat of his heart. Obviously no longer looking forward to a rendezvous of strangers, Sloane had to liberate him from his anxiety. "Okay, we're all set. Gregory and Denis are on their way up. Ready?"

"I guess, although I still feel like a fool. Socializing is not my forte, but lead on, Mr. Bolts. I'm ready to puke, but I am ready."

"Good man. By the way, you introduced yourself as TJ. Is that the name you prefer?"

"Amongst friends and acquaintances. Only family calls me Phoenix."

The two men exited the guest quarters, the bigger one smiling upon hearing the implication that he was family. Sloane greeted his guests with hugs and kisses, while his new sidekick settled for shy but firm handshakes, maintaining a distinct space between him and the others. With cheerful seasonal welcomes upon Will's arrival, Thornton-Jones deviously ducked behind the closest tall man who happened to be Joey. The overweight, ogling lecher spotted the diminutive creature immediately, but instinctively retreated with a dangerous glint from the two pair of darkening eyes of his friends. Sloane and his former lover saved their latest member from a slobbering kiss and rubber handshake; the flustered journalist whispered his gratitude to the tall man guarding him. Calloway stretched six-foot six-inches, and when asked, the old friend was once a known basketball player who attended the same university as Sloane and Wolfe. All alumni, Will also came from the same group, a wrestler of some distinction, now a replica of a standing Buddha. The man created instant mirth in the journalist, but he held his giggle in check upon finding that the circle did not end there.

Caught by surprise at Wolfe's formidable presence, the kindest, softest voice murmured a seductive 'hello', and Thornton-Jones timidly shook a hand bigger than Sloane's. So impressive, the man not only was tall, but built like a Kenworth truck--a tandem--and just as powerful. Finally able to close his mouth, another enormous smile appeared from behind the giant, one that created a shy grin of his own. Sebastian pushed passed his lover who was renowned for the plaited graying hair reaching to the middle of his back. The wily cub was also astounding to look at, with a child's face and an athletic body. He greeted Phoenix with an extended hand while introducing himself and his bear. Looking at the group as they all cheered the holiday, Phoenix felt like a Lilliputian in the land of mighty men. Even Will, although shorter than the rest, formed a formidable barrier to pass readily. Six strangers, one acquaintance, and a cat lurking somewhere close by, his heart nearly stopped. Why now? How could he stop remembering the minute details of the *accident?* Only one person missing, he turned toward the door, praying a redheaded nightmare would not barge in with thigh-high stiletto-heeled boots and a bustier with points so sharp, they pierced the skin a quarter of an inch. A large, dark-skinned hand on his shoulder turned him around, startling Phoenix who inhaled sharply at the sudden touch.

"Are you all right, son?" Wolfe's voice could entrance a cobra with the soft hush of a whisper from such an extraordinarily imposing man. This one person could have annihilated the five assailants on his own without breaking a sweat; the idea caused the diminutive one to waver between liking the man and being intimidated by him.

"He's a little shy, Wolfe. I'm gathering drink orders. What would you two fancy?" Trevor came to the rescue, leaving Phoenix tongue-tied, and two older men understanding they had done so.

"Scotch... two fingers for now."

Sloane grinned mischievously. "Dirty beggar. Keep it for Sebastian. What about you, kiddo: beer, wine, or water?" With Phoenix's shaky gesture toward the water bottle held by Will, the host received the message and disappeared.

"Are we rather overwhelming for a kid from Colorado? Never mind, for we all started somewhere and shall return one day. Joey, Trevor, Will, Denis, and I once called Montana home, although we all now live in different states with bases in New York. Let's see; whom have I missed? Gregory hails from Kentucky originally, and my partner, who just left with our host, is too Californian for his own good. I dare hope you and Sebie will get along, both being similar in age, at least younger than the rest of us old dreamers. Once he helps Sloane prepare whatever they're doing, you and he may enjoy sharing a conversation more suited to your generation." The man continued to tower over him; but with newly acquired practice, Phoenix controlled his heart rate and uttered a few words he hoped made sense.

"Thank you, Mr. Wolfe, I'd like that. I read his comic strip this morning and wish to read more. He has a great sense of humor."

"Just Wolfe, white angel child, and Sebastian is usually your equal in shyness, until he gets to know you. When that time comes-- beware--he suddenly explodes into his riotous, hyperactive alter ego you see in his comic strip. Sebie also requires a tender hand, but a firm grip. Now, come along, and let us join the group." The friendly arm encompassed Phoenix's entire upper torso, giving him little choice but to move forward and listen to the others laughing over something you needed the full story to appreciate. The evening would be a nightmare, but then Trevor handed him a sealed water bottle, took his hand gently, and insisted he sit next to him. Phoenix took a breath of hope that he could survive another party of strangers.

Feeling very small and inconsequential, the journalist sat quietly next to the photographer, as the men gathered around a lavish spread of Italian delicacies to savor, and too many wine bottles, beer mugs, and other assorted glass liquor containers to drink from. Sticking to water, Phoenix felt safe and attentively listened to the others who grew more intense with their discussion. Denis and Gregory seemed a very solid couple, thinking alike, as well as looking alike. They could pass readily for brothers, and probably did when needed. Both had been basketball players, meeting when their opposing teams took to the court. A tight group as a whole, they had known each other their entire adult lives, a good reason to share their morbid occupations and ghastly discoveries.

From across the table, Sebastian winked knowingly at Phoenix, both understanding they were outsiders of this particular circle. The younger men, however, enjoyed the blond-haired couple and the telling of their latest hair-raising discoveries. Amusing but never degrading the victims, the playful duo did laugh heartily over the follies of the perpetrators of minor crimes, pulling the rest of the party into their merriment. Phoenix relaxed for those moments with an embarrassed chuckle, but just as suddenly would stiffen to fight the need to run away, thinking of another group of men, an acquaintance, a redhead, and a cat. Getting up to find another bottle of water and to calm his edginess, he heard Trevor's baritone voice asking for assistance. He remembered a vague mention of a problem on first meeting, causing him to prick up his ears and return to the table.

"I seldom have much to vent, except for poverty, environmental devastation, and crumbling ancient cities. Tonight, however, I need your personal views on whether to go public with these pictures."

"You old dog, Sloane, you've been peeking through keyholes." Will laughed, receiving a few smirks from the others who knew better.

"That's you, Wilbur. Don't mess with me; this is serious shit. Look at these, and it goes no further than this room." Trevor handed out a half-dozen different 8 X 10 glossies to circulate around the table. He was disturbed about the significance of these images and unsure as to who should see them. Taken in his favorite out-of-the-way eatery in Bangkok, the photographs captured two men who should not be dining together, let alone speaking and laughing in such close proximity. Snapping shots at political gatherings and state affairs were boring but profitable jobs. Now, he held pictures that could throw the struggling balance in the Middle East into a Hurricane 5.

"Who are they, Trevor?" Sebastian asked respectfully, shooting a glance at Wolfe to ensure he had not crossed a line. With a nod from his bear, he returned his big brown eyes, outlined with thick ebony fringes, back toward Sloane and an answer.

"Leaving it simple, the one on the right is a minister of a Middle Eastern country, which is attempting to remain neutral; however, the other is an al-Qaeda terrorist who disappeared off the radar years ago and is linked with mass slayings in both Europe and the Arabic nations. They were enjoying their tête-à-tête while my camera sat hidden under a blanket of lilies. Thank the stars new shutters make little noise, or I could have been shot right there. Even the knowledge of their existence makes me a target." Trevor looked at Phoenix to see his mouth drop and the purple eyes open in shock. "Easy, kiddo, no one knows."

The small man said nothing, but contemplated the situation as the others went through all the possibilities: the White House, the CIA, the Department of Defense, the *New York Times*, and the list went on. Hearing nothing that would not end in Sloane's assassination, along with the major political and social outrage, Phoenix quietly interjected with a single word, stopping the conversation abruptly, "Interpol."

"Why do you say that? They could spread the news like a brushfire around the globe just as easily. Besides, no one ever hears about them; or if they actually do anything."

"That's unfair, Trevor. You don't know anything about them because you're not supposed to. They lead the war on international crime, and you had better open your eyes to the bigger picture. You all sound like a bunch of paranoid isolationists. First, you have the most recent picture of this al-Qaeda creep on record. Interpol has probably been searching for him on a continual basis since he was first suspected of planning the various attacks. This is about taking out the terrorist as expeditiously as possible. With these photos, the time, and the location, they can concentrate their agents on what could be his hiding place in minutes, somewhere in the Far East, not in Afghanistan, Syria, wherever. Once they have him, if they are able after such a long delay, there will be no leaks from Interpol that they have a new lead. Let the proper authorities deal with this state leader later, however they see fit; and I guarantee you, both deeds will be done with tremendous discretion. This is Interpol's job, and not one for high-flying, fucking, don't-obey-order, bad-boy heroes to screw it up. We Americans portray the anti-hero as the main character in movies, expecting we're all stupid enough to live up to such an insidious make-believe reputation. If I see one more film with Tom Cruise playing another arrogant, no-rules, son-of-a-bitch who wins the day and the girl, I'll puke. Personally, I would like to see that shit stopped and trust those who know what they're doing, without the major flag waving and applause. We're all part of a huge global village, with allies better trained and disciplined. I say we start acting sanely and co-operatively." Expounding his anti-American opinions had Phoenix unraveled. He stood for communal righteous behavior in an isolationist's world.

"He's right." Denis confirmed.

"He's right." Gregory also acknowledged the idea.

"Sounds like your easiest solution, Sloane. No glamour, no high profile, just get this one man, no matter how." Will leaned back, wiping his forehead; now knowing they all knew too much.

"Make two sets of prints without your trademark seal and perfection, Trev. Getting them into the right hands is crucial. Who has a connection with Interpol?" Phoenix felt in his heart that he protected Sloane's life, while ridding the world of a proven psychopath hiding behind religious fanaticism.

"I suppose that would be me, TJ. I can get a package into the right hands." Calloway rubbed his face hard; believing those sitting high on Interpol's ladder would not ask him questions when presented with such invaluable information. He could leave on the next flight for Lyon, although certainly enough time had passed for the man to vanish again. Nevertheless, he could tell them the name of the restaurant, while the real crime fighters quietly took care of business.

"You need two, Joey, to cover the possibility of one department deciding the problem is not theirs and feeding the proof to a shredder. Mistakes can be made by anyone." Phoenix had thought the plan through; Trevor's former lover volunteered to dare the dangerous mission; and Sloane's name would be kept out of the scandal.

"No problem. I always use one disguise and set of documents for Interpol, so they can't connect me to Joey Calloway, or this group. Now you know why I suffer from burned fingertips and wear gloves. Too late to travel tonight, I'll try wing walking on some carrier tomorrow. This is the correct route, TJ, a very good suggestion that should have been my first thought." Getting up, the tall dark-haired man picked up the telephone and organized a trip to Lyon, France,

under another name. The group had never understood Calloway's
need for his many aliases, although they respected his silence and
privacy, believing he balanced tenuously on a swinging tightrope
whatever the skirmish. Whether or not the international authorities
knew about his numerous identities, he had never been caught--an
indication of his cleverness or of someone manipulating him--a very
frightful thought.

"I should have asked you when I recognized your research
skills, kiddo. The simplest, most efficient plan, you came up with it
faster than those X-Men cartoons you watch. You are a wonder, and I
promise not to take you to a Tom Cruise movie." Trevor laughed,
beaming proudly at the young man who bowed his head to watch his
hands shake.

"Common   sense,   Sloane.   Everyone   makes   things   so
complicated; I've never understood it. This is international crime, at
least the terrorist falls under that category, and who better to inform
than the organization that handles it. As for the other guy, they'll
expose him to the proper authorities, such as the United Nations, which
now appears superseded by the G8 Nations.   What a fucking
debauchery that is. At any rate, the cards will be on the table, and
whether the sticky situation is dealt with secretly, or in a public forum,
will be anyone's guess." Phoenix fumbled to get up, leaving the table
on wobbly legs. His first major decision had him quaking on the lip of
an avalanche; and he stared through the crystal-clad windows into the
exotic lights flashing about Chinatown, wishing on every artificial star
that his suggestion was correct. Conversation returned to other things
of little interest to the younger man, still unsure of the appropriateness
of his opinions stated to a group of more experienced and worldly men.

Sebastian sidled up to him with an invitation to sit and talk of
other matters. A welcome respite, for the one transfixed on neon
lights, the cub handed him a small paperback. "Someone told me you
liked my comic strip. Here's an early Christmas present for you."

"Thanks, man. I think this morning was my first real laugh in a
long time, and your quips fit my own opinions about the ridiculous
side of society. I appreciate your gift, and one autographed by the
cartoonist! Awesome!" Phoenix shook the black hand and looked up
into the cutest male face he had ever seen: perfect white teeth, full
laughing lips, the shiniest curly hair plaited tightly and tied back, and
huge round eyes of milk chocolate with an added frosting of glitter.

"Is you hair naturally white, and who thought of the rad highlights? Very cool, very cool indeed." The cub reached forward to touch the unique hair of the smaller man.

"Whiter than white, and the colors were added for fun. Is yours naturally shiny, and I've always wanted to ask, how do you create all those tiny tight braids?"

"Shine from a bottle and the plaits take hours. Damn, you are one fine looking dude. Never seen nobody with such delicate features. Shit, you're the size of a twig." Sebastian may be well educated, but street grammar unhinged him occasionally. The smaller man fascinated him, wanting to touch a face too delicate; and Phoenix felt equally spellbound by the extraordinary face of the African-American.

"I could say the same of you, except for size. My features resemble a girl's, but yours... well, you're cute... incredibly cute. Oh man, that was a stupid thing to say, but if you were my size, people would mistake you for twelve, as they sometimes do with me. This group's an example of how I'm often spoken to. Very weird, but together, we'd stand out like a couple of circus clowns." Phoenix smiled at the surprised face, which broke into a huge beguiling smile and a chuckle.

"Clowns, no; handsome, devilish rogues, yes. We'll stand next to each other, at the first party we're invited to, and watch the double-takes." Sebastian leaned down to whisper and received a snicker back, although answered with concern.

"I'll hide behind you and pop up from under your arm on occasion."

"Coward."

"Definitely, but not afraid to ask something really stupid. Consider me curious and uninformed, but your relationship with Wolfe... does he ever hurt you?" The question came out of no man's land, and the answer surprised him.

"Jesus, TJ, he couldn't squash a bug. He's my bear all right; and he keeps me in line. I need that, as much as his unending support and adoration." The voice did not falter; the answer was the truth.

"Can I ask a delicate question, Seb?"

"Thought your last one was. Never mind. Shoot."

"If bears discipline their cubs, is spanking part of it?"

"Man, are you blunt, and yes, in our particular relationship and only when necessary. Since the sex afterward is absolutely dynamite, I often instigate the rough handling, but don't you dare tell Wolfe. For a rare time in my life, since I met him, I have a father who cares, along with a lover who is gentle, warm, and extremely affectionate. He's my bear, and I love every inch of him. There's certainly enough to squeeze and bury myself in. Hell, I bet you could do chin-ups using one of his arms, and there are few men who we can say that about." Sebastian glanced sideways, catching Wolfe's eye and smiling at him with great tenderness.

"Sorry, I'm just not sure what..." Phoenix hesitated, lowering his head in embarrassment.

"...I think you've read too much on different relationships without hearing the entire story, believing a daddy/boy affair only includes whips and chains. It may be in some cases, but physique and age are the main considerations. Whatever happens between two men is a private matter. I personally like large, burly, much older men with lots of padding, while Wolfe prefers younger, smaller men who he can baby and who like to be treated in such a way. He no longer keeps in shape, like Trevor and Joey, although extremely strong under those rolls around his waist that turn me on. I assume your main squeeze seems somewhat patronizing toward you; but he is twice your age."

"My main squeeze?"

"Whatever, but protecting you is a natural response for him; natural for anyone who is older. Don't let that consume you with fear of pairing with him. I wouldn't put him in the bear category; he's too fit and clean-shaven. What say we get together, when you return from your trip, have some fun, go shopping, whatever, and I'll tell you about the birds and the bears."

"I know about the birds and bees, but bears and shopping? How about a hockey game instead?"

"Perfect. I wasn't sure if you were into sports."

"Freestyle skiing. An aerialist."

"No shit! I played varsity football, until my behavior proved too daunting a task for academia to handle discreetly. They tossed me out on my arse, even with a good grade point average and the highest yardage in our division. I think they noticed too many hugs and bottom love pats, as did my teammates, although some didn't mind. Rather funny actually."

"Man, they sure couldn't get away with discarding you now, without a major march on the university campus. Glad you're here, Seb."

"Glad I accepted the invitation. I usually don't come."

"I thought you did, or so Trevor implied."

"No way. These guys have been meeting like this for twenty-odd years. I've known them for maybe four. Always an open invitation, I've only been to one of these get-togethers, although Wolfe and I visit Trevor's ranch regularly. I'm happy to meet you as well, TJ; very glad there's someone here I can relate to. Our photographer friend insisted I come this time, just to meet you. I think he's always understood my reasons for not coming; they would apply to you as well."

"What's that?"

"Age and the generation gap. Cool dude, your Trevor Sloane."

"My Trevor Sloane! Why do you keeping inferring..."

"...shit, you know: the way he looks at you, touches you, hovers over you. It's hard not to acknowledge the love in his eyes."

"Now, you're shitting me."

"No way, bro. He wanted us to meet, showing you off to his friends."

"No, that's impossible. He couldn't. He wouldn't!"

"Maybe not, but you have him captivated. Let's go, before he sends out a search party looking for us." Sebastian clasped Phoenix's hand, towing him back to the group where Joey began iterating his latest findings. The group's white angel pulled away immediately. 'Sadist' and 'masochist' hit his heart hard, obliterating his thoughts of Trevor and flashing back to the meaning of the words. He felt it, the snap, a crack, another broken bone impossible to break, and then another. Unable to scream through the pain, he had passed out with cruel laughter ringing in his ears.

Sloane looked up, immediately seeing the white-knuckled clench on the back of a chair. Excusing himself and asking Calloway to wait a moment, he locked his arm around his failing comrade and rushed him into the bathroom. Phoenix retained the contents of his stomach and thankfully felt himself eased onto his bed. "A trigger word for you, hunh? Was it from Sebastian or Joey?"

"I'm okay, just tired. I like your friends, Sloane, really; but I think I've had enough. I'm not used to the profanity and blatant sexual innuendoes, although I spouted a few radical statements when I had the floor. Hope I made sense through my opinionated diatribe." Phoenix gazed at the man sitting beside him on the bed. The photographer was a remarkable individual; his easy-going manner, his instincts, his sensitivity, and his quick reflexes had once again come to aid a distressed friend, although Sebastian's words had rattled him further.

"Colorado and the Christian College didn't prepare you for Will and Joey's crudity. Gay society is a mix, as is the heterosexual variety. As for your opinions, they're always a good start, but keep your mind open. Investigative reporting is just that--investigating first--followed by an informed opinion. Your suggestion of Interpol was very sound; an idea I'll accept willingly. Thanks, kiddo, and I won't tell Cruise what you said."

"Shit, you know him too!"

"We've met. Now, considering something shook you up, maybe a sleeping pill would help get your mind off what was said and implied." Trevor did not wish to leave his friend who was telling more lies, but other guests had been left on hold.

"Thanks, but I've taken so many painkillers, muscle relaxants, and tranquilizers, they don't work anymore. Perhaps I'll go to bed and meditate on the rainbow. It usually works."

A half-hearted grin helped Sloane let go of his need to stay. He quickly opened the door to leave, puzzled by his youngest guest who now sat cross-legged on the bed. "I didn't know you meditated."

"You don't know much about me at all; and it's time you told me more about your Cherokee grandmother and her healing ways."

"During a quiet moment, kiddo, alone and in private. Should I leave the door open?"

"Please. I'll put my earphones on until I fall asleep, and as promised, one child's nightlight. Couldn't you find something other than a set of the Seven Dwarfs?"

"No, or I would have picked up Wolverine for you. I don't know what you see in those cartoons."

"Mutants, maybe I can relate."

"No more degrading yourself, for you're the marvelous creation of a talented plastic surgeon. Twenty years ago, they may not have been able to rebuild you. By the way, do you have any sensation in your face?"

"For the most part. A few places still have a fuzzy feeling, like around my hair line, where they cut the skin to pull it back in order to set the bones properly."

"Is that why you have no facial scars?"

"I sure didn't have a face transplant, thank God. They left me with broken bones without facial lacerations. Luck played a huge part, as far as my face was concerned."

"Okay then. Get some rest and we'll see you in the morning.

Sweet dreams, kiddo."

"Why did you want to know? I did feel the kiss, if that's what you're thinking." Unintentionally blurting out his feelings, he suppressed further emotions created by the caress.

"Good, because I felt it down to my curling toes and wanted to make sure you felt it as well."

"Oh brother. Night, Trev." With the shutting of the door, although a small sliver remained, Phoenix changed into his warm sweat suit and plugged in the frivolous nightlight of Dopey. If nothing else, Sloane had a dry sense of humor. Putting on his earphones, he settled against the soft pillow, attempting to relax by silently chanting a Sanskrit mantra, which usually sent him into a fantasy world of his own making. The attempt failed; Sebastian's words leapt to the frontal lobe of his brain. Trevor had said the words directly to him, but he did not believe the man then, nor could he believe a new friend now. Many thoughts whirled through his muddled head: some happy, some wistful, and others so terrifying they superseded the first two emotions. He wondered about the meaning behind the kiss from a man who proved his protector this night. A strange bond had formed between them, blinding Phoenix from anything further, except for a green feeling running head to toe. Sloane knew Joey very well: the teasing playfulness, the private jokes, and the intimate gestures. Feeling like an outsider, he had retired from the oncoming stories that grew increasingly difficult to deal with mentally, as did the effects of too much wine on Mr. Calloway, bringing out his flighty side. Phoenix thought it odd, that a man, as steady and solid as Sloane, would find the posturing to his liking.

The hours dragged, counting the steps while pulling an old-fashioned plow behind him. He listened to his third CD; he could not sleep for the memories. Why had they returned so vividly? His nightmares were also intolerable; they were resurfacing in demon force. Thankful for the soundproofing of Trevor's home, the barrier prevented his host from hearing his abrupt awakenings accompanied by a shriek and a great amount of heavy panting. Throwing off the covers, he would pace off the panic attack; exercise often helped. He passed by the tiny opening of the door, believing everyone had left, leaving only a flickering of flames to illuminate the fireplace. On his second pass, his hands gripped his hips, and he limped the twenty-five feet from one end of the room to the other, mindful of the cut he had re-bandaged. He pushed everything else aside to regain the control he had fought so long to achieve. Crumbling with every moment spent in Sloane's company, he had turned into a whimpering idiot. He would not tolerate the return of vanquished anxieties because of one man.

On his third pass, a groan caught his ear. Stealthily peeking through the small opening, he immediately put his hand over his mouth in surprise and interest. Two silhouettes moved rhythmically against the backdrop of the fire. A tall slender man arched his back dramatically, his arse in the air, his head buried in a cushion, while a bigger built man hunched over him, whispering and grunting profane words, while penetrating the other man who attempted not to squeal in pleasure. Phoenix watched in wonder, the controlling force of one man over another. Having never witnessed Twister and Caly making love, he imagined their attentions gentler and more fun. He would never know, nor did he wish to find out.

Turning away, he wiped the perspiration off his forehead and leaned against the wall breathing heavily. Overtaken by an excruciating need inside, another rare moment forebode a dangerous plight for Phoenix, one he did not want, unequivocally scared out of his mind at the thought. The pulling, the tearing, the plummeting of his penis, the insidious memories returned as clear as the expensive crystal on the table. Never again! Never again! He would never allow his cock to harden again! The cruelty had nearly killed him, and then coming to with a bucket of icy water thrown over his head, only to splutter and look down at red--red blood spurting from his organ--the agony had given way to unconsciousness.

With his fist pressed hard against his tightening lips, he scurried to the little light plugged into the wall and crouched in the corner. The memories would go away, as would his hardening manhood. Breathe deep, calm down, maybe a shower, but then they would know he had seen them. Pulling his knees tight to his chest, an embryonic position in the hidden corner made him feel safe; ready to deal with a problem of such painful magnitude, he had only allowed it to happen once. Too soon, he never touched himself again; the feelings of torment too great for anyone to tolerate, no matter the delicacy. Unable to lay one finger on the living beast between his legs prevented him from relieving himself in public urinals, for he had to use a pencil to lift the rebuilt, dysfunctional tool, and a sponge to buffer the feel of his fingers against the wrinkled, scarred skin when washing. Four surgeries made him a man who mentally could not cope. He continued to hide in a ball when a voice called out. Who is it? How long had he been watched? Only knowing the sensation had not subsided, he had spent at least ten minutes fully extended and ready to rupture, only to be exposed to someone who was never to know.

"Phoenix? Where are you?"

Trevor's voice, but Thornton-Jones refused to answer. Believing himself safe from sight, the younger man forgot that the treacherous Dopey lit his face a blue-gray against the blackened wall. He could not let Sloane see him. A lie seemed the only answer; he had to think quickly.

"Good God, Phoenix, what are you doing?" Trevor hurried around the bed and knelt down beside the flannel-clad figure. "Did you fall, or are you hiding from something?" Sloane remembered Twister's first thought.

"Shit, you startled me. Don't you knock?"

"Sorry, but I wanted to check on you before retiring. Why are you huddled in the corner?" The concern sounded paternal; Phoenix had heard the fear in too many voices.

"I feel comfortable sleeping while sitting up. I was just nodding off, but man, you gave me a fright." Phoenix lied, stilling the quiver of his voice, pretending his position normal. "Sometimes I start meditating lying down, and then try a lotus position, which usually turns into this. I couldn't concentrate or relax, so here I am, quite comfortable actually." Phoenix gazed into the worried frown, attempting to coax a smile from the man. The gesture was difficult enough to accomplish on his own accord.

"Are you planning to spend the night sitting in the corner?"

"For a while."

"You drive me absolutely nuts. I'll get your pillow and comforter. At least I won't find you rigid and blue in the morning; and perhaps their warmth will prevent your midnight wanderings. Maybe I should buy you a large stuffed toy to take with us." Trevor quickly snatched the items, returning to find the odd character had loosened his grip enough to allow a glimpse of the bulge under the sweatpants. He bit his lip hard, wondering if he should offer to help. A ridiculous notion, the man should not be in this condition, being averse to any sexual activity. "Hey, I didn't think you could do that!"

"Mind your own business. Leave me alone and stop teasing me; I'm not a child. Man, this hasn't happened in years, but I can will it to go away." The younger man grew angry, jabbing at the pillow on which he placed his head and snuggled deeper into the corner.

"How often have you stopped yourself? Tell me the truth." Sloane intended to keep this going, as repressing sexual climax deemed exceedingly dangerous for both the male and female of the human species. Over time, irreversible medical problems could arise, causing toxins to build in the body, resulting in the lack of any kind of sexual response.

"A few times. Hardly ever. It shouldn't matter to you anyway."

Draping the comforter and securing it around the shivering body, the photographer could not believe what he heard or saw. He may have a chance with this young man and help him overcome the fear. Kindness, gentleness, and no pressure seemed appropriate, his natural behavior with the inexperienced. Love--it was all about love-- and for this love, he would be patient. "This feather duvet is warm and soft, so you should be somewhat comfortable sleeping in corners. You handled yourself well tonight, and everyone adores you. Good night, Phoenix; thanks again for expressing your opinions. You are the amazing white angel the others have nicknamed you."

"I'm no angel. You can tell them that. Good night." Left with his sorrow and the memory of what his unleashed cock once wreaked upon him, Phoenix clenched his eyes tightly, refusing to let natural fluids flow. Trevor had made love to Joey, creating uncontrollable envy and sadness, an emotion not felt in years. A hard-on, he could not touch, had him breathing deeply; his hands stretched to try just once; but his fingers splayed above his rock hard crotch, unable to do anything to satisfy the tension rising. Mortified and issuing small groans, he succeeded in subduing the evil organ; his strength of will finally sent him into an emotional, exhausted slumber, nestled in a corner cradle within a luxurious duvet, a feather pillow, and an unhappy Dopey face lighting his perfect features.

Chapter IX

Waking up with a headache, which beat a calypso tune in his skull, Sloane vowed to stop drinking; and now, overloaded with too much worrisome information from his friends and concerned about the kid he barely knew, he felt sick. Rolling over, he almost crushed Joey, although impossible considering the former basketball player's physical stature. A groan and an unconscious push in sleep from Calloway, Trevor arose, tiptoed from his room, across the main living area, and into the guest quarters. All appeared quiet with the new sun brightening the earth-toned Cherokee wall hangings, ones that blended with the Asian influence throughout the rest of the room. A little of his ancestry lived here, and he raised his eyes to the dreamcatcher his grandmother had made, knowing she protected the exotic bird rising from the flames once more.

The bed remained as he had left it, pulled apart with the removal of one pillow and the duvet that now buried the small body in a crumpled heap. Still sleeping, still in the same position, Phoenix appeared capable of resting in any tight spot; his flexibility would come in handy on planes, trains, and other forms of compact quarters, such as a two-man tent. The thought of the delicate bundle, who curled beside him a few nights previous, squeezing next to him under a canvas cover, created a mischievous grin; the twinkle did not leave Sloane's eyes as he left to shower, shave, and take a half-bottle of headache remedy.

Respecting Phoenix's presence in the apartment, he ignored the normal ritual of showering with Calloway, not desirous of the affection and sexual advances of the man, although exceedingly satisfying after a long dry spell. Guilt filled his heart. Could the young man's trigger be Joey and his gestures toward him? Unable to think further of the two very different men and their feelings, he readied himself for a busy day and to break the news of their shortened trip to the younger one. Their first itinerary being virtually impossible to carry out, Warren had rightfully grounded them. Brazil would be their destination: their kick in the arse for the world, or their destruction professionally.

Busy cooking breakfast, he gave Joey a shout to get up, and then quietly tapped on Phoenix's door, requesting him to hurry. He heard only a muffled groan and the rustling of the crisp cotton that covered the down comforter. With clean dishes placed on the counter (the only area he found clear), three stools pulled up and arranged methodically, plus small cartons of orange juice for each man beside the plates, he left the sausages and scrambled eggs in the oven to stay warm. He stood back and surveyed the aftermath of the previous night's gathering. The tall, thin man emerged first, holding his head with one hand and the other reaching out in a plea for the rest of the vial of tablets. Trevor understood his need and laughed at someone else's self-inflicted pain, and he tossed the small bottle for an easy catch. Gratitude came with a full body press, a seductive rub between genitalia, and a kiss that could erase any memory of the young man who unexpectedly appeared.

"Don't you two ever quit?" A vicious snarl came out of the man clad in faded, tattered, too tight jeans still in style for the young cowboy, a purple turtleneck that enhanced his eyes brilliantly, and a possible favorite worn-out ski sweater with the appropriate matching colored striping down the sleeves and across the chest. Trevor pulled away from the embrace on the pretense of putting breakfast on the counter, while shoving Joey toward the oven to handle the task. Cringing at the underlying implication, he realized Phoenix had seen their performance in front of the fire. He had hurt the younger man, the man who could love and potentially make love, if the photographer could remain patient. His heart shattered; the arousal meant something drastic. The young man suffered from a sexual aversion all right, but a condition more dire and damaging: fear of sex!

"Morning, kiddo. How about some breakfast? I have news from Warren, which is good and bad."

"Probably cut back the trip and the time involved, if he has any sense." The mood became more hostile; happy news was vital.

"Correct. We're in for a hell of a trip, considering it's the worst two months of the wet season in the jungle, but we can start by spending a few more days with your family. What do you think?" Sloane glanced at the man who turned away after picking up a juice.

"The latter sounds good, but the former... do we take hiking boots or rubber galoshes?" The snipe at least illustrated some humor, although reminding Trevor his partner had the wrong equipment and clothing for their venture. They would take care of the discrepancy that afternoon, and then pack for an early flight to Denver on the morrow. A quick alert from Phoenix would give the Colorado crowd advance warning of their son's earlier arrival.

"Come on, kiddo, take a seat and eat."

"Not hungry. Juice is adequate. I'll start on the mess from last night."

"Join us, TJ, and partake in Trevor's cooking. Personally, I've never had the pleasure and am somewhat dubious about his culinary talents. So, a family style breakfast, very cool." Joey immediately felt the underlying tension and quickly decided to forego the meal to allow the two men to sort out whatever their dilemma. He iterated a good reason for retreating, as an emergency trip to Geneva with a connecting flight to Lyon lay before him. As soon as Trevor had the two envelopes sealed, he would be off. Anything for a friend, he never failed.

"You didn't eat last night. Sit down and munch on something, as we have a busy day ahead." Sloane did not get far with his gentle command to the youngest in the room.

"Stop treating me like a child! I'm not your cub, boy, baby, or kiddo! Whatever you think of me sexually is unimportant, as is my false face and body. I'm Phoenix Tyler Thornton-Jones, a man fast enough to kick the living shit out of both of you." An outpouring of screaming rage, after a sleepless night and Joey's reference to family, caught the two much larger men with their mouths open. Staring down a trapped, snarling snow fox was not to their liking at the early hour, and both men stepped back from the force of just the look. "And I'm nobody's white angel. If you'd shut up and listen, instead of misinterpreting everything I do or say, you'd find me out of reach of heaven, burning in hell every moment of every day. Can you understand that? You know nothing, despite all your pictures and undercover investigations, of how a fire feels within, scorching flames that singe every DNA molecule in your body, leaving only the necessity to kill, just to..."

"...hold it right there, Phoenix. The various nicknames we've affectionately bestowed upon you are only words to describe a gentle human, one who could very possibly kick the shit out of us all. I've seen you in action and have no doubt about your feelings of frenzied panic and abilities to hurt someone. I don't know why, but I have seen it. We're not your enemies, Phoenix, and would never hurt you knowingly." Sloane raised his hands to his shoulders, his palms facing outward to ward off the anger spewing from the growling fox.

"I would've killed those thugs the other night; I would have! The trip's off. I quit. You know too much about me from my regrettable behavior and stupid admittances. I should have never allowed you in. Merry Christmas, Joey, good luck in France. I'll gather my things and be on my way as well." Phoenix whipped around, physically illustrating his ire. He would leave without a backward glance. The slamming of his door had both Sloane and Calloway staring at each other in disbelief.

"You have a wildcat by the tail, Trevor."

"Don't I know it. I have the two envelopes for you and can't thank you enough for moving so fast on this. My fault for not thinking this through myself and neglecting to ask the man with the best answer. I only hope Interpol finds the son-of-a-bitch quickly and terminates him quietly." Sloane stood looking at the guest room door, while handing the envelopes to Calloway. Leaving breakfast untouched, a quick kiss of farewell, and a hasty retreat, Joey bounced down the stairs at full speed.

Sloane gathered his shaken wits, waiting for Phoenix to open the door, not believing he would desert him and the job. While he anxiously abided the journalist's reappearance, he tossed the food in the garbage disposal unit, tidied the apartment, and returned to gaze out the window, a coffee in one hand, and the fingers of his other rubbing his temple. Not yet recovered from the hangover, the first slamming of the door had nearly derailed him; the squeak of the same portal made him flinch. He had some explaining to do, although silence would be preferable. Trevor slowly turned to watch his tense young friend set the familiar backpack and computer case by the front door, and then hustle over to place the magical instrument, of many delightful evenings, in its case.

"I'll miss the sound of your voice, Phoenix, and your guitar. The days we spent together meant a great deal to me and were more enjoyable than I can explain. I doubt my sentiments mean anything of consequence to you, but they do to me. Tickets for Denver, which had us leaving tomorrow, are in the left-hand bottom drawer. Take yours and exchange it for today's flight home. Have a happy holiday, Phoenix. I'll miss meeting your family. Where will I ever find another writer and friend such as you?" He turned back toward the frosted window to fight off the oncoming tears, unable to remember the last time he cried. Everything ghastly about the world and life had been filtered, making them beautiful with his camera. His mind could cope seeing suffering through a lens, but this disaster stood undisguised beside the exit.

"You don't need a writer, Sloane; your pictures tell the story. No one will take my words seriously anyway. I called Granny to let her know I'll be arriving early. I'll stay with her in Denver tonight. Remain well, Trevor. It was a pleasure meeting you." Donning his sheepskin jacket, he buttoned it up to his chin and pulled on his warm gloves. He stood ready, his backpack over his shoulder, along with his guitar and laptop. Juggling his load, he quietly opened the door and left. For only one sorrowful moment, he stopped outside the black lacquer door, giving up his dreams, his ambitions, his life, his heart, discarding them along with the man he loved in his special way. After years of work and hope, he had failed miserably. His only chance of a real life lay in a famous man's hands; and he had incredulously slapped them away without a handshake of farewell.

Struggling with all his paraphernalia, Phoenix descended the long stairwell, caring little of life or death. He walked into the middle of the street in a trance, unaware of the cold and icy conditions. One of New York's famous yellow taxis, which glided slowly over the shimmering morning's glaze, ably stopped before hitting the runaway. Without saying a word, but on hearing a destination, the cabbie drove away, taking special care of the white-haired, porcelain-faced kid with the swollen red eyes. The driver was cognizant of the sorrow spreading through his hometown this time of joyful greetings, sparkling decorations, and crystal-glazed windows.

Looking down from a very large pane of glass, a tall silhouette stood, wandering why and how to correct an error he did not understand. After pacing and fidgeting for an hour, to calm a headache that would not go away, Trevor found the ranch telephone number. Punching in the numbers, he hoped for a relieved answer. Phoenix would have called his fathers, leaving them frantic over their son's angry decision. Upon the fourth ring, he almost hung up, but a voice responded, sounding so upset that the man, on the other end of the line in Colorado, seemed to vibrate through cyberspace.

"Hello, this is Trevor Sloane."

"Trevor! This is Caly. I'm so glad you called! What happened? Why aren't you coming? This is terrible; the last catastrophic blow to Phoenix's ego!" The one-time bull rider, who wore his heart on his sleeve, began to unravel while sputtering into the telephone.

"Hand me the phone and settle down, buckaroo. Listen quietly on the extension. Trevor, this is Twister. We're glad to hear from you so quickly, after hearing the heart-wrenching news of our boy fleeing New York. He's no quitter; I assure you. Can you tell us anything?" A calmer personality than his partner, Jones exhibited more restraint.

"I have no idea what set him off this morning. Perhaps not my place to speak for him; but a few nights ago I kissed him very gently, and miraculously he responded favorably. I didn't think of it again until last night, when I found him curled in a corner. We had guests over, and perhaps he heard something he couldn't handle. I went to check on him and found him attempting to mentally subdue an aroused, twitching organ. He is suffering from a sexual aversion; inert as he calls it, but Twister, his condition... your son's afraid of sex! The kiss meant something, as he went ballistic on witnessing me and my friend kissing in the kitchen."

"Good God, you're the first person who has seen through his secret. The doctors have been unable to diagnosis the mental disorder due to an implied falsehood created by our son. I can't believe Phoenix would do such a thing! Can you still come, Trevor? I think he needs you as much as he needs us, if I have interpreted this correctly."

"Don't know how much help I can be, or whether I can exchange this ticket at such a late date. Did Phoenix manage to catch a flight?"

"Yes, from Kennedy to Denver, where he'll stay with his grandmother."

"I'll try to arrange something. If I'm lucky, and the Christmas sprites are with me, I could arrive before he reaches you tomorrow. I'll call as soon as I have the particulars. Will that be a problem?" Sloane breathed in some relief. With the slamming of the door, the white angel had disappeared into the falling snow; a famous name would open a window to allow him to fly again.

The photographer had learned over years to pack quickly, this time for the cold climate of Colorado. With his heart full of hope that the journalist would reconsider his desertion, Trevor would purchase the required gear and apparel for he and his partner on a stopover in Miami, as a direct route to Sao Paulo from Denver would be impossible. Calling on Master Chui, he gave the storekeeper instructions regarding the apartment, not giving a return date or a reason for his hasty departure. After a quick snuggle with Bogart, a gift handed to the old man for Kimmie, he was off. He had managed to arrange a stand-by seat from La Guardia, with only one flight change before reaching Denver. Christmas was not the time for expedient travel, but once on board his second carrier, he stroked his aching temples, satisfied the route would connect with a commuter to Pueblo. As he felt the pull of the small aircraft climb through winter clouds, his head ached with the vibration until the plane leveled off. He had much to contemplate; he needed Twister and Caly's advice on how to handle his presence at the ranch. Barely able to think, he gave into a short nap, which stopped the pain aided by a pillow shock absorber.

Touching down safely at his final destination, he easily walked the short distance to Baggage Claim, where he spotted two men, in dark felt cowboy hats and sheepskin jackets, nervously waiting for him. Neither man could hide their apprehension over their runaway son, although they greeted his working partner enthusiastically. They had much to ask about Phoenix who had allowed someone to kiss him and had an erection on witnessing a sexual act between men. The two cowboys were very aware of the inherent dangers of their son subduing natural bulging blood vessels, thus making his manhood an instrument of torture. They sympathized over his problem, but could not reveal the circumstances behind the phobia. With this first new clue, they asked the photographer if they had time to speak with his psychiatrist. Sloane shrugged his shoulders with no decisive answer, believing talk and time may help. Whatever created the insurmountable fear of an erection seemed irreversible behavior; and no one was talking.

While at the airport and during the hour drive to the ranch, Trevor studied the two men and their ways. They sat in the front of the luxury British-built Land Rover, driving carefully with the legendary passenger in the backseat. Twister sat behind the wheel, asking further questions in a honeysuckle drawl and frequently touching his partner's hand that gripped his thigh nervously. Unconscious transference of tranquility steadied the much smaller man. Barely five-foot six-inches tall, perfectly proportioned, extremely intense, and inordinately powerful, Caly fit the epitome of a bull rider in size, strength, and exuberance. An odd thing, Sloane thought, such small men daring the ride of a dangerous beast that outweighed them by two-thousand pounds, not to mention sporting horns. Twister, on the other hand, had the rangy look befitting a saddle-bronc rider, with equally wiry muscles stretched taut over his long, thin body. Both devilishly handsome, one man was calm and easy-going, while the other appeared excitable and high-strung. They balanced each other.

Throwing a disturbed young man into the mix drew them closer, giving them something of immense importance: a son's love. Sloane liked them immediately.

Arriving at the ranch in darkness, he did notice the large wrought iron gate with the TJ brand at the center. As the extravagant entrance opened automatically, a long country road led down an avenue lined with evenly spaced naked aspen, their branches stretching between columnar cypresses. The trees stood pristinely in the glare of the headlights against a backdrop of ghostly white. Opening his window, the cold crisp air hit the New York nostrils, and he inhaled the fragrance of winter in Colorado. An entrance into a different world, even his ranch in New Mexico did not have this particular drama. Two cowboys had created a magical setting for the extensive ranch-style house; a grand wrought-iron porch chandelier welcomed them home. Before entering the heated four car garage, he noticed the road passed the main house, to disappear behind a knoll that was lit like a bedside lamp, indicating a possible snug oasis for the stables, the bunkhouses, the treasured horses and bulls, until extending into the darkness of pastureland dotted with cattle. Trevor's best guess was an accurate one. The image lingered in his head, an acknowledgement of the power such a vista held for his reclusive runaway. This was home and always would be Phoenix's safe haven.

Once inside, additional lights flickered on, and the three men entered more wonderland. Large stone fireplaces dominated all the rooms, along with a rock wall partitioning the front entry from the grand sala where a roaring fire invited their pleasure, along with a hotpot of chili steaming on the coffee table. Beside it, neatly set, were three bowls, spoons, mugs, and the best smelling coffee and fresh baked bread the photographer could remember. These men lived graciously in a western themed house, full of trophies and pictures taken with famous rodeo stars, not to mention many other well-known personae of the arts, business, and politics. A couple of recent ones displayed Phoenix's likeness, the understanding of so few hit Sloane hard. Only two years since his perfect face had healed, no remnants of scars, changes, or surgeries need remind the young man of his former life. Several distinctive trophies did catch his eye, not of horses and bulls, but two tall statuettes, resembling aerialists frozen in layback triple flips, stood prominently amongst the silver buckles and World Championship saddles. Sloane could only stand staring, thinking of his much smaller case, holding his fancy crystal awards, all looking the same. Invited to sit, relax, and eat, he had no hesitation in devouring the delicious offering, comfortably sitting alongside his cordial hosts who had put in as hard a day as himself. It was a nice welcome. Sloane, however, did not miss an eye flutter, wondering what really happened to Phoenix, yet knowing not to ask.

"A fear of sex! Why didn't they know, Twister? They should have known. Hell, we should have guessed! He's hurting himself because of those sons-of-bitches and idiot doctors."

"Be kind, Caly; those doctors saved his life. Now, we have to get him back on track with Trevor first, since our new friend seems the only person our boy has connected with, other than family. What do you think, Sloane? Do you still want to take him, or is he a lost cause to you?" Twister dealt all the black cards to the man in question; three men exchanged worried glances.

"That's why I'm here. He's a talented man, a gifted troubleshooter, and a fighter, the perfect combination for what we have to do. I'll try to convince him, but he might need some tough love from his fathers to get him excited again, or feel guilty enough to come with me. I like Phoenix, boys, but I may frighten him with all his problems. Like you, I can be patient in showering my affection upon him, until he trusts me; but you both have helped him for ten years, while I've only known him a dozen days. My feelings for him do go deeper than paternal, however, making our relationship an entirely different ballgame."

"You've fallen for him and your hands are tied. Good God, Twister, we never thought he'd ever drop his guard to allow someone in. More than the job itself, this could change his life, if he can return the adoration. I hate this. We're always in control, but now our son's world is collapsing because of something we wanted for him. What do we do?" The small man leapt to his feet, ending up on his partner's lap, his face in Jones' neck, and his arms strangling the man.

"We'll work it out with Trevor, Caly. Don't jump to conclusions about Phoenix's feelings. Right now, we know three things: our son is afraid of sex, his new friend loves and desires him (a sorry situation), and to top it off, they must work closely together. A loving relationship may prove too difficult for both men." Twister looked up with a pained expression, imploring Sloane to help him out with his devastated partner.

"The unfortunate truth, plus a few other snags in the plan. I know he enjoys my company, and his erections appear triggered by something I've done. If I am the catalyst, I could destroy everything he's conquered, or enrich his life with untold dreams. I do love Phoenix--a word I have trouble saying--but he's twenty-some years my junior. Hearts could be broken, while I wait and he tries. A coupling could blow up in our faces, and who would suffer the most: your son. Let's leave it to him to decide before I cancel the deal. If he agrees to continue, whatever happens during our sojourn, I'll handle. I think it best not to tell him of his condition. A smart man, he's probably figured it out; but being young and virile when this so-called *accident* occurred, he probably can't deal with the mortifying label. In close proximity for several months, we may develop a bond strong enough for me to assist his desperate need to touch himself, a rather personal task to take on." Sloane rubbed his face, leaned forward, and sat in his thinking position.

"Okay, we wait until his arrival tomorrow and follow his lead for the next few days. In the meantime, we'll make this holiday particularly special."

"You know it, buckaroo. Now, let's get Trevor to his quarters and comfortable. As for you, I'm shoving a sleeping pill down your throat, so I can sleep." The taller man laughed heartily, picking up his pint-sized partner who wrapped his legs around Twister's waist. Both wore a smile whenever they looked at each other, brightening the night with hope. Their son may find his sexual identity with a famous stranger, one who had compassionate feelings for him. Much lay on Trevor Sloane's shoulders.

Colorado residents did rise early; and although Sloane lay sleeping at the end of a long corridor of rooms, he awoke on hearing his hosts crunching through the deep snow, likely heading for the barn. The day of reckoning dawned through the bedroom window; the day in which a future may take root or unravel. Before going to bed, however, they agreed to keep Phoenix's phobia a secret, one possible to rectify slowly with gentle gestures and innocent words. Unfortunately, the only man capable of aiding the mentally scarred was dragging himself out of bed half-past dead, until his feet hit the cold floor, alerting him to quickly dress in his warmest attire. Although centrally heated, the house appeared too large for the two full-sized furnaces raging, and only scatter rugs covered a small portion of the highly polished wooden floors. A knock on his door caught him by surprise, and a spirited young cowboy greeted him with firewood. Both laughed at the bad timing; nonetheless, the staff member, dressed neck to ankle in denim, promised to light the fire earlier the next day without awakening him, as he did with the family. Since the important guest was already up and stirring, the lad left the wood piled next to the fireplace for the upcoming evening's warming blaze.

Discretely exploring the house, Sloane heard the clank of a cast iron pan against a gas burner, and he poked his nose into the kitchen to catch the best smell of frying bacon. The cook happily acknowledged his presence, particularly after a thank you for the late night fireside feast. Continuing his unauthorized tour, he strode onward, peering at every detail with a photographer's keen eye. A longer walk through the rambling house found him in another long corridor leading to the private family rooms where another young man made beds.

"Good morning, Mr. Sloane. You look lost." A toothy grin was acknowledged with a nod from Trevor. "This is Mr. Thornton and Mr. Jones' quarters. Master TJ resides in the suite next to theirs. I better get to work on that one quickly. Sure will be good to see him. We're riding mates, since neither of us is truly affixed to the saddle yet. A hand comes with us to baby-sit; in case one of us sees blue sky through our boot tips." Another genuine laugh erupted at something not quite accurate, as both men, over a few years, had become competent equestrians.

"There are certainly enough of you to take care of the place." Sloane chuckled with the sprite, while dodging another flying figure coursing down the hallway with towels and sheets in his arms.

"Twenty men work the ranch, and six of us tend to the big house as well as the bungalows. We're mostly partnered here; and if your mate isn't a ranch hand, then you're on the domestic roster. Works just fine for us all."

"The entire ranch is gay? Now that would be an interesting court case of job discrimination, considering society wants to burn us all at the stake, unless we sing, dance, act, or look gorgeous on a billboard."

"It would go down in the history books, although their other holdings employ many women. We do have the occasional female visitor, since we all have women in our lives, like my sisters. Phoenix's grandmother comes often, along with his many doctors and nurses who are on call."

"How many doctors care for him?"

"Lost count years ago, sir, but we're seeing them less often.

Well, must keep moving. Looks like Mr. Thornton is on his way from
the barn and in a very big hurry. He's so excited; he probably can't
tend his horses properly. They'll sense his overly stimulated heart
beating and become as nervous."

"I'll head back toward the kitchen to meet him. He's probably
craving hot coffee. Talk to you again..."

"...Jazz, just call me Jazz."

"Jazz. I'll remember." Sloane departed the family area to cross
paths with the pink-faced, diminutive, attractive man who wore a
broad, hopeful smile, barely containing his excitement, and yet
dreading a final ending. The hat came off first, tossed at the
appropriate peg where it caught and hung. Gloves came next, and then
the heavy barn coat, covered with new snow, was dropped on the floor,
along with the discarded coveralls, boots, and vest, all picked up by
another lanky denim wearer who quickly hung them up and
disappeared. Caly smacked his hands together and ran into the large
living area to warm his derriere, fingers, and toes by the fire.

Sometime during the night, a tree had appeared center stage in
the sala, waiting to drop its frozen pine needled limbs in the warmth
before decoration commenced. The scene brought Christmas back to
Sloane, the pagan rituals from his Irish connection, as well as those of
the Cherokee. This was the time for the tree to take over the house,
bringing the outdoors in with its scent and wildly imperfect beauty.

"Awesome, as Phoenix would say. We've been waiting for a
special holiday for this magnificent tree, which should keep us in
firewood when it dries out. Unfortunately, we use far too much, even
though we close off your end of the house unless Granny shows. Man,
it's cold out there. Until yesterday, the weather's been very pleasant,
just soft snow at night and sunshine during the day. Shoot, where are
they? Come on, old girl, pedal to the metal, but be careful with my
son." Caly once again proved the excitable one, while Sloane stood
laughing at the mixture of joy and worry in the former bull rider's face.

"It's only 8:00 a.m. They won't be here for hours. Where's
your partner?" Trevor continued to smile at a man ready to explode.

"You don't know Granny. She taught her grandson to rally
drive when he turned sixteen. Knowing those two, and how much
they're alike, I bet they left before dawn. As for Twister, he's
checking our prize mare. Foal's due any day. Hope it comes soon to
brighten Phoenix's homecoming; he loves animals. Oh, shit, his dogs.
Damn. Jazz! Jazz!" Shouting the name in alarm, the man, rubbing his

backside by the fire, refused to search out anyone in the catacombs of the large house. "Where's Snow and Sky? Are they clean and brushed?"

A yell from down the hall confirmed the two dogs were happily bouncing in the new snow, sensing the excitement of the day, and perhaps, instinctively knowing of their master's return, particularly with a change in the room they shared, smelling of fresh sheets, mulberry scented potpourri, and a cedar fire crackling. Phoenix's suite took on the air of Christmas, welcoming him home with his favorite things.

"Those two never forget him no matter how long he's hospitalized. They wait at the front window, right there, watching for him. A wrestling match will occur, as both dogs will take him down before his feet touch ground."

"Something fun to look forward to. He misses his dogs."

"Come on, let's eat. Twister will be here any minute. He's all gnarled inside, believing we've laid too much on you, Sloane, and worried that Phoenix has taken on something impossible for him to handle."

"Only the work for now, nothing but the job at hand and the journey ahead. I won't touch him until he asks, but the wait could kill an old guy like me."

"Lord love us, don't say that. Both Twister and I are your age, and we haven't stopped the giddy feeling of our toes curling up at the sight of each other." Chuckling merrily, the two men accepted the coffee handed to them as they came through the batwing doors and into the massive kitchen. "We have the entire staff at this monster table for festive occasions, including Christmas Eve dinner, and then we're left to ourselves. All thoroughly screened, our employees have been with us for many years, except for the younger lads who are fitting in nicely. We've known most before our son came into our lives. He trusts them all, and we couldn't be more grateful to the bunch. By the way, the family enjoys a traditional sleigh ride around the ranch on Christmas afternoon, weather permitting, although we all ride once a day. We would enjoy your company, if you're willing to risk the cold."

"I'd be honored, but I think a family ritual should not be broken. Granny and I'll find something to do, or tend to the new baby coming soon."

"Nonsense, since Granny always comes with us. She wouldn't

miss the outing for the world. We may call her Granny, but she's not much older than us."

"All right then. Sounds like fun. Even if I speak from a non-Christian philosophy, the season is special for whatever reason. Do you think the mare can hold out and deliver her Christmas bundle on the day of peace and joy?"

"Oh, I do hope so. Here comes Twister; better grab some breakfast before he chows down."

Sloane delighted in sharing the morning meal with the cowboys, while the house-staff ran the distance to their own warm dwellings to prepare a similar breakfast for their mates and comrades. A good place for Phoenix to be surrounded by men who cared about him, and quite a group they were: some young enough to be friendly company, like Jazz, while the rest happily acted as brothers, uncles, and grandfathers, certainly giving him a large, happy family. The ambiance felt tranquil but busy, inspiring a sense of home in the frontier tradition. With the décor fitting the former rodeo competitors, their inheritance money, plus the influence of wealthy upbringings, showed in the fine leather furniture and priceless paintings of famous western artists. Two men lived and worked in their own Nirvana, training and raising horses and bucking bulls, plus nurturing a few hundred head of cattle; their main herds cared for on other properties. Each of them had inherited ranches, Caly's in Oklahoma and Twister's in West Texas; both estates equally grand from the pictures shown to him and in the paintings displayed on the walls.

Using the twelve passenger family jet, they flew to one state or the other to acquaint Phoenix with staff members and the difference in running three distinct properties, as well as the business side of the Thornton and Jones fortunes. All would be his one day, along with his grandmother's titles and industries, although she hastened to sell everything, unwilling to leave more responsibility on Phoenix's dysfunctional head. The load seemed too heavy for one so mentally fragile; and it dawned on Sloane how devastated his young friend would be upon the death of any family member; they were his only connection to the real world. The loss of the fathers and the grandmother would leave Phoenix alone with the colossal burden of vast wealth. The boy would never starve, but he would be bait for any gold-digger who toyed with his sorry psyche, taking his love, his money, and leaving him more reclusive and isolated.

Enough to break a heart, Trevor's hit the polished floor, but the sudden honk of a horn had two men out of their chairs and hustling to put on boots and jackets, while their guest remained inside, wishing to blend into the landscape, until the excitement died down and the dogs stopped their crazed barking.   Watching unseen through one of the many windows, he saw Caly had been correct; Phoenix fell heavily into the snow with two white Samoyeds wrestling him to the ground for a good face washing, until both started pulling him by his boots toward the house.   Yelling for mercy, the trio of friends played, as snow flew in the mayhem.

The grand dame, of this alternative family, disembarked with Twister's assistance from her own distinctive Land Rover, receiving generous hugs from both cowboys and some secret information whispered into her ear. A discreet turn toward the window, she spotted the photographer; simply giving him a smile and a nod of recognition, an indication she was glad he had arrived.   A diminutive creature, strikingly good-looking for her age, she had a distinct resemblance to her grandson's new face and was a dead-ringer for Francesca Annis. Perhaps, the plastic surgeon had used Granny as a model for him, making her fine features a touch more masculine for Phoenix, or he may have always looked like her. For a wealthy woman, she dressed appropriately for the trip and the country setting she appeared to love, as seen in her sublime expression over the beauty that lay at her feet and over the horizon.   Trevor instinctively felt her presence in Phoenix's spirit.

The rescue of their snow-covered son seemed a scramble of the fittest, but Caly managed to yank him onto his feet and into an embrace so tight, both men let loose their tears. Twister's turn, he swung his heir off the ground and once in a circle, ending with a flurry of paternal kisses. Two large hands clasped the youngest face, wiping away salty liquid with calloused thumbs.   A family homecoming, Sloane whispered a Comanche prayer that Phoenix would accept his presence. Serious challenges faced the photographer, ones he never thought possible in today's world of safe but easy-going sex, and a journey that would extend thousands of miles into the darkest, rain-soaked jungle. He had to be out of his mind; until he remembered--'*listen, boy, listen and watch, always with love in your heart*'--he raised his eyes and thanked his own grandmother's spirit.

Chapter X

Voices at the front door trilled with four different accents: Coloradoan, Oklahoman, Texan, and Granny's unique speech, the long ago Easterner who sounded like Katherine Hepburn. A wonderful commotion of sounds echoed through the house, with dogs slipping across the polished floor (their nails too long and their paws too encrusted with snow) amidst the excited human chatter. Sloane heard jackets and boots come off, while the family members stuffed their cold feet into house slippers that sat ready in the foyer. Smiling behind the rock wall, concealing him from the family, the photographer listened closely, happy to be a bystander sneaking a view of the chaos.

The tone suddenly grew serious; the happy gathering finally ignited the demons afire in Phoenix's soul. "Before you all start razzing me, I quit; that's it, the end. I failed; I messed up; I ruined everything. I'm sorry for disappointing you, but I don't know what to do or say. I can't even come up with a valid reason. A freak, even in New York, I don't belong anywhere but here. Then again, I've screwed up an incredible opportunity so badly that you probably want to see me gone as well. All I've given you is worry and a financial burden I can't ever repay. My one chance, folks, and I fucked up royally."

"Phoenix, stop. We can't give you an opinion on your decision until we know the facts. Did you talk to Granny last night?" Sloane heard Twister attempting unsuccessfully to calm the blithering tornado.

"No, Dad, because I've made up my mind. How could I believe, in my insanity that I could pull this off? How?"

"Come in and get warm by the fire, Diablo. The discussion's closed for the day. You seem out of balance and need some quiet time." Twister, now also known as Dad, tried maintaining control of the runaway, but lit the fuse of a second stick of dynamite.

"You're damn right I need a whole lot of quiet time. I'm going to my room, count to a thousand several times over, kick my arse around the room a few circuits, and drown myself in a Jacuzzi bubbling out ice cubes. Just leave me be and leave my bags alone. I handled my gear to New York and back; I think I can carry them the long stretch to my room."

The sarcasm spewed out, as did the defeat, creating a little wrath from Phoenix's spitfire grandmother. "Phoenix Thornton-Jones, you are being cruel. I am ashamed of you for talking in such a manner. No grandson of mine is going to get away with such bad behavior toward his parents. Enough! Go to your suite and return in ten minutes speaking civilly and with an apology. You did this to me last night, but today, you had better compose yourself like the man I'm proud to call my grandson. Another outburst will not happen again."

"Yes ma'am."

Sloane heard the shuffling of feet and two dogs heading in one direction; a tiny pair of feet went in another, along with a member of the house-staff to assist the still striking looking woman; while the two distressed fathers entered the grand sala with their arms about the other.

"He hates us again, Twister. We'll never convince him."

"Sorry about that, Trevor, but he'll be out soon. He said it all, Caly; he's not mad at anyone but himself. His words were directed at his own decision, making me believe he may recant. For now, he feels defeated, and we know how that affects him. Let's all settle down, and if he's not out in ten minutes, I'll go and throw him over my shoulder as he yells profanities at me. Please, buckaroo, let go of my arm and relax. You are such a baby under that tough rawhide." With the tenderest of embraces, the fathers could not let go of each other in their disappointment. A long ten years for these two men, they had hoped a writing career, their son's first love, would enfold him softly into the real world. A setback, however, could drive him into a solitary corner, writing the memoirs of his short life, a potential disaster for the only one who could tell the full story.

Within five minutes, Granny walked in, striding forth in her casual gear to shake hands with the famous photographer whom she prayed would save her grandson. While Twister and Caly commiserated elsewhere, Sloane had the opportunity to meet the tiniest but most powerful person in the unusual family.

"I thought this little escapade might happen and hoped you were hidden, for he would have broken down completely. Phoenix, even as a child, walked a fractured line, using a make-believe pole to maintain his balance. For years we have handled his frustrations, as has he, and as a family, we will deal with the continuing battle. I must be blunt, for we have little time before someone walks in. What are your feelings toward my grandson?" The purple eyes caught Sloane off guard, proof that Phoenix's genes came naturally.

"As I told the boys last night, I care a great deal for him. In all honesty, I wanted this trip to bring us closer together, despite his sexual problems. I'm old enough to require Viagra before engaging in a liaison with a wild sexual dynamo half my age. I only wish to hold him when he needs me." Sloane slid over the truth, not wishing to make his serious pronouncement if a harried young man interrupted him a second time.

"The only thing he divulged last night was his fondness for you. It makes little sense for him to run from a friend, considering sexually he would feel nothing. Very odd, Mr. Sloane, unless you know something different." She looked at him with those remarkable eyes, searching for a truthful answer, one he could not supply.

"I have some suspicions; but for now, I pray he changes his mind." The large athlete offered the woman a chair before sitting down to stretch out his long frame. With his surprise postponed, and failure, rejection, and regret racing through his young friend's mind, Trevor felt he should leave the job to those who knew him best.

"Pops! Dad! Where are you? I'm sorry; the last thing I wanted was this." From the distant door of his quarters, Phoenix's shouts echoed through the vast house, causing one man to fly out of another doorway. Caly responded quickly on hearing the yelling and hastened to catch his running son in search of one of his fathers, either father.

"It's okay, Phoenix. It's okay. We just need to understand your reasoning for quitting a project so exciting; something you've dreamed about for years. You love adventure and risk. What happened? Come here, Sugarhead." Caly waited in full view of the sala, as Phoenix ran toward him with his arms outstretched and a face full of remorse. The warmth between the two was undeniable; a slightly smaller, older man comforted his grown son who had done nothing wrong.

Twister rushed out and embraced them both, finally attempting to separate the family clench; but each of Phoenix's hands held fast to his fathers' shirts. "Please, Dad, I wanted this so much, but things grew so confusing. I need you both, but I want more; a close friend maybe, one I can trust, one who will just hold me. Can you understand that? I want to be normal, but I'm not. It doesn't stop me from desiring a partner, another man to love me without the sex. Oh Jesus, this is the worst pain of all. Who would want someone who can't return affection physically?" Phoenix unraveled, blithering his sorrow into two chests, not knowing whom to hold tighter, or that two others were listening.

"You just never know, poco Diablo, and we understand your need. We love you, as caring fathers should, and would hope someone special comes into your life. You trust and like Trevor Sloane, feeling comfortable enough to stay with him. You have an opportunity, right this very minute, to develop a solid friendship with a man who seems willing to give you another chance. Turn around and look." Jones twisted his son gently around to face forward, while clasping the small hands and embracing the heaving chest from behind. "Sloane didn't give up on you, Phoenix. Rethink your decision."

The white eyelashes fluttered at everyone in the room; the violet eyes finally rested on the big man with deep furrows in his brow. Phoenix's knees gave way, but Twister's supportive arms prevented him from crashing to the floor. "Trevor! What are you doing here?"

"Told you I needed a writer and a friend. Now, get your butt over here, apologize for giving your grandmother grief, and let's talk about the plans we laid out. I want to know how you wish to handle the trip, the things you want to see, what you wish to avoid, all the places and sights to help you with our task, and more importantly, those that may give you joy. I'm determined to take you with me, kiddo, or Warren Graham will be very disappointed. We wouldn't want to ruffle a major mogul's feathers. Besides, I believe, in that brilliant but opinionated head of yours, you already have come up with some conclusions." Sloane stood with his arms crossed, wearing his most reassuring smile, attempting to make light of a serious matter, while watching the young man grasping his dad's hand until he had walked too far and had to let go of his only security.

"I may have a possible solution and wish to investigate its merit, but I need to cogitate further on the job and its consequences."

The bashful young man returned; and Sloane had to believe he could win the match. Phoenix's utterance showed some interest, yet he remained unwilling to commit or proceed too quickly. The likelihood of the young man being embarrassed for running away, as well as someone discovering his sexual malady, could be reason enough to shy away from accompanying the older man on a long journey. Trevor would gladly attempt to rectify the misconception, assured that the kid could be helped, even at the expense of his own heart shattering in the trying.

"Of course, but on this beautiful day, we have a tree to trim, a baby to wait for, and I haven't seen the ranch in daylight. What do you say, Gentlemen, my Lady, of partaking in the hot brunch currently being prepared for us, and then ambling down toward the stables? Who's up for a stroll in the cold?" Trevor immediately lightened the load pressing down on too many shoulders.

Granny eagerly clapped her hands at his suggestion. "That is a marvelous idea, Mr. Sloane, and I am appreciative of you inviting this old woman to accompany her favorite men. Phoenix, will you truly think about the offer over the next few days and join us for some invigorating air? Snow and Sky look excited at the prospect of a romp. Come along, pooches, we're going walkies with him or without him." The elderly matron flashed the same eyelashes, ones coated with dark mascara to enhance her bodacious eyes further.

"Yes, ma'am, and I'm up for a walk. I need to smell hay, fresh air, leather, and horses. I forgot Dancing Doll and her baby. It hasn't arrived yet; I haven't missed the birth?" Phoenix looked hopefully at Caly; his purple eyes sparkled back to life when the answer came back negative.

"Okay, something hot to eat and we're off. We'll leave the tree for something special tonight. The lights are up, and as per tradition, this Colorado Spruce will be set a twinkling when the staff gathers for Christmas Eve dinner; and then, my wild son and equally crazed partner, the grand spectacular will flare." Twister laughed heartily, grasping his son around the waist, twirling him around, and tickling him until he collapsed in uncontrollable giggles. With a shaking of hands between two lost souls, Phoenix agreed to weigh the pros and cons of tackling a long journey and a tough job. Trevor agreed not to push him, and the uncertain deal waited on the runaway.

The days before Christmas were enjoyed to the fullest, although someone often caught Phoenix drifting off, muddling his decision in the labyrinth of his head. Once aware of being watched, his perfect pale peach lips would part to flash a set of bright white teeth. The weather turned warm enough for the four men to ride the fences of the ranch, checking for breaks, runaways, and something not understood by Sloane. The barbed wire and posts unnerved the other three, particularly tensing the riding position of the youngest. Subdued chitchat and the slow pace continued, seeming a transparent disguise to hide something of significance.

The mood changed once in open space and softer snow, which made walking easier for the horses. Caly and Phoenix would set out on a wild chase, urging their animals forward to break a trail of frothy white. In a full gallop, they hollered to the wind, inviting the element to join them in a mysterious game the two men played. Sloane and Twister followed at a gentler lope, laughing at the pair who rode as fast and hard as their sparring; each man attempted to unseat the other and to dump him into the softness of a breakaway cloud.

All smiles, they would turn toward the ranch, always from the same direction, to pass the bungalows and greet all those working the domestic shift: shoveling new fallen snow, enjoying the vista always before them, and catching up on pre-Yule jobs, while their mates tended cattle and horses. Two cabins seemed of importance; always the first stop, Phoenix would dismount to accept a hug from an elderly Arapaho tribal member who took the role of wise grandfather to an unsteady heir of a vast fortune. The man spoke in puzzling phrases much like Sloane's grandmother, evoking fond memories in the photographer. Always a whispered conversation between Phoenix and the old man, a distinguished character with long silver-streaked hair, the two seemed in tune with one another. Jack Eagleclaws and the snow fox could speak without a word said, only a look, one remembered by Sloane from his Cherokee heritage.

While the others rode on, Phoenix would walk his mount until he reached the fifth dwelling, where he would speak with a ranch hand who always threw on a coat before emerging with a smile to talk to the young man. A horse trainer by occupation, the lean, thirty-something wrangler seemed a sensitive person, with a contagious grin and an extended hand of welcome. On medical leave, he rested from a solid kick to the stomach by an unhappy horse, causing no harm but severe bruising. Not privy to the quiet conversations, Sloane puzzled over the intimacy and intensity of the talks, which he witnessed from a distance. Kindly smiles cloaked more secrets.

Twister finally explained one day, while waiting for his son and the ranch hand named Grant. "Eagleclaws has been with us since we started the TJ Ranch, which seems a million years ago. His lover, of twenty years, died several months ago of heart failure, and he continues to grieve. Being a healer, he also tends to many indigenous people in the area. Unfortunately, he takes the blame for his partner's demise, although impossible to detect such a condition, considering the man looked healthy and strong. As he soothed a temperamental cutting horse, he suddenly fell over--dead--a massive coronary killed him instantly. Yesterday, our Arapaho elder informed us of his desire to move in with our best wrangler, another sad and lonelier story. Phoenix's friend tested HIV positive after a wild affair with a young, promiscuous partner; a man our son never met. Grant handles his job, shows little signs of weakening, although symptoms could show anytime. He's been healthy since the diagnosis, which thankfully hasn't developed into full-blown AIDS; and we will never abandon him. With Jack's idea, we think the companionship will help both, taking away much of the loneliness. Everyone here knows of our wrangler's health problem, and we went to great lengths to make it understood, to all our employees, just how to deal with his malady and keep a harmonious flow throughout. It worked. All of us, living at the ranch, admire him and are willing to work at his side. He has much to teach, although his job may seem too high a risk for such an illness."

"So, how does this involve Phoenix? He seems to have an affinity for both men, an affectionate one, wanting to be with them."

"That he does, Trevor. Caly and I did something we'll regret forever, forgetting important lessons taught to us about HIV and AIDS, its victims, and how the dreaded disease spreads. When we first brought our son home, he was far from well, covered in bandages from surgery after surgery, and still unable to move on his own. A whisper from Jazz, our sprightly cub, informed us that Phoenix had met everyone on the ranch except for Grant. Our best hand felt neglected because of our own inner struggle and stupidity. We almost lost him, throwing him into greater despair. It will not happen again. The two decided on their own rules: open sores on either man require bandages, and if lacerations develop in time, they will avoid contact with the other. These rules were of particular importance in case of a work related gash on Grant, or Phoenix's healing surgical wounds re-opened. All staff agreed to the rules, and our small infirmary is always stocked with bandages and antibiotics for the many cuts and blisters we're susceptible to in a physically intense business. Sneezing and coughing from colds remains a danger to Grant, due to the pneumonia it could create. We worried about this rule for both when our son lay in such a fragile state. They have such a good time together; we hate to see either man have a bad day. Both are currently in good shape; Grant will certainly be sitting at the Christmas Eve dinner table. With approval from their many doctors, they remain good friends and affectionate ones, as long as no one sneezes. Everyone takes this seriously, staying in bed with colds or influenza, Caly and me included, which ironically keeps us all healthier. To maintain in contact, during these times, we purchased individual computers and cell phones for everyone. Cute and sad, we watch two men who love each other, but are unable to express the affection physically, except for the holding of hands. Does their relationship bother you, Sloane?" Twister sped through the conversation quickly, but understandably concerned over two men he cared about.

"No problem with me. You've handled their plights delicately, and I'm including Jack. A handful of acquaintances have died holding my hand. Grant looks sturdy and strong enough, standing in the cold, although taking short breaths and holding his gut from the kick. Phoenix has been healthy, since staying with me, and easily stands up to the cold, happily chatting to his friend who puts on a brave face, considering the dire consequences of a reckless renegade partner who may have been one of those vindictive types: *'if I have AIDS, so will everyone else'*. Taking the hand of your elder will be of tremendous help from what I have experienced with the afflicted, a rather bad term when they are healthy, yet knowing the end will come. The quiet ways of your healer will provide easy company for Grant, although their different heritages could prove perplexing. My grandmother confused the hell out of me on occasion, but her words return in dreams, reminding me of who I am." Sloane drove his horse forward alongside Jones, while Caly waited for Phoenix. He liked all these men: true of heart, strong as titanium, and sweet as Twister's honeysuckle drawl.

Darkness came quickly this time of year, and the entire ranch bustled around for the grand Christmas Eve event. Already decorated by the family a few nights before, the tree waited upon this special time, when it would burst into its full shining glory. After a few pinecones and intricately handmade baubles were hung by the staff and hot toddies passed around to warm festive spirits, the first switch was flicked; the sala shone in splendor with candles, tinsel, and tiny lace lights. The smell of juniper and mulberry filled the room; fragrances awakened Sloane's memory, that he happily welcomed, including the savory scent of a massive dinner of several turkeys, hams, goose, and assorted side dishes. Phoenix and Grant decorated the table elegantly, with cut crystal, fine china, red roses, and white poinsettias. Caly, Twister, and Granny served dinner, filling large bowls to pass around for the sharing. Time came for everyone to sit, ring out toasts, eat heartily, laugh loudly, and clink glasses together. The huge family celebrated freedom, all devotedly caring about each member. The bright countenance of Phoenix, during this shining season, gave Trevor hope, recognizing the seventeen-year-old boy in the heart of a troubled man.

Before dessert, Twister slowly arose; everyone hushed. Time for the spectacle, another tradition before Christmas pudding lay in wait for the uninitiated. A rare, uninhibited moment for Phoenix, his demeanor changed to that of the teenager lurking within. Clasping Sloane's arm with his two hands, he hustled the larger man into his winter outer gear and dragged him outside toward the only light visible. A single lantern sat on the remains of an old tree trunk rooted fifty yards from the house, strategically left on a rise to guide the spectators to view the show from exactly the right location. The staff gathered in the darkness, and Phoenix held on tightly to both Trevor and his grandmother. His eyes grew wide and sparkling; they belonged in the heavens that clear night.

Caly stood in front of Twister, wrapped safely in long arms. The taller cowboy asked if the excitable one was ready, and with a quick nod of his forever partner's head, he clicked a series of timed buttons on a remote control, making one section of the ranch glow, and then another, and another. A magical realm of colored lights, fireworks, and strangely devised animated figures lit up the night sky, unlike anything Sloane had seen at Christmas. He laughed with delight and wonder, along with a clapping Phoenix with each new timed event. The long road to the gate glittered with every naked tree dressed with hoar frost and twinkling white lights, reminiscent of a Disney fairytale. Turning toward the bungalows, Twister had magically placed a tree in each log cabin and decorated them in different colors like gingerbread houses. Even the horses had sweet smelling wreaths hanging on their doors, with lace lights adorning their stalls inside and out. Nothing, however, could compare to the main house that shone the brightest and in the most elegant of style, at least for the first five minutes and strictly for Caly's taste.

Sighs of enchantment turned to laughter, as faces looked to the roof where cartoon characters flashed into view. Phoenix giggled so hard; Trevor had to hold him up. However and whoever created the scene had done a masterful job. The X-Men flew through the air, shooting red laser beams at unseen foes. Gambit threw decks of flashing playing cards; Wolverine scratched lines of light into the black sky; and a blizzard whirled around the character called Storm. Created only for Phoenix, he stopped laughing to stand bewitched, his mouth open, his eyes bigger than Sloane had seen them; and they were full of joy. Another round of fireworks, far out in the back paddock behind the house, were cheered with a chorus of bravos from open smiles so broad, they were a show unto themselves.

"Twister, you've outdone yourself! You continue to amaze me with your imagination. No wonder I shacked up with you. Just look at the road and cabins; they're magnificent. Thank you for the grandest finale ever: it's truly wondrous. I think you've hypnotized your son, however, with the action on the roof and using the original characters he favors. You are one hell of a cowboy." Caly turned away from the display to give his companion a smoldering kiss, turning every man on who gaped at the torrid embrace. It did not take long for the others to show their equally intense feelings toward their partners. Even Jazz hung from the biggest, burliest bear on the ranch.

"Dad, this is so rad! The X-Men! Awesome! You even have Jubilee throwing off sparklers to ignite the fireworks! Man, this is the best! Isn't it amazing, Poppy? It's so fantastic; I don't know what to say. Can we turn them on and off at will?"

"You bet, mi poco Diablo, except for the fireworks. Now, with the excitement over, and everyone has approved, hot Christmas pudding is bubbling on the stove. I need a volunteer to check on Dancing Doll, in case the fireworks scared her into a quick delivery. She seemed okay when I was doing a little testing for loud noises." Twister's face glowed with enthusiasm, always loving the secret extravaganza he planned together with a special-effects company who put his ideas into motion. Even the ranch hands were kept in the dark, except for a few of the wiliest.

"I'll go, sir. She quiets with me."

"Thanks, Grant, but as soon as she's settled, return to the house for a hot toddy and dessert. I'm still worried about your injury." Twister shook his hand, expecting him to walk slowly to the stables.

"Don't worry about me, Mr. Jones; I put blankets outside her stall in some fresh straw. I'll join you, but it would be my pleasure to watch her tonight. This is new life; and I need to see it awaken."

"Of course, but make sure you stay under the lamps as well. Although the barn is heated, it certainly isn't as warm as your bungalow. I'll send someone down with a few sheepskin rugs to make you more comfortable. Bang on the door if anything stirs." Understanding smiles between both men were exchanged, and the usually slow moving wrangler ran the distance to the stables, worried about the mare, believing the fireworks inappropriate and too close to the million dollar baby.

With Christmas Eve over, the staff strolled back to their

bungalows hand-in-hand, but for a few. Time came for the Thornton-Jones-Granny family to settle by the fire, sing carols, and listen to Phoenix's original melodies played on a finely tuned instrument. Packages were placed under the tree, and a family fell away one-by-one to their rooms for an early morning rising, and a very early call it was. Four in the morning, the household heard heavy banging, and no one needed to ask the circumstances of the abrupt awakening. Running as they dressed, the entire family dashed toward the barn, following Jack's rapid pace and quietly entering the dimly lit stable. Everyone intently watched Twister slip into the birthing stall where Grant gently soothed the struggling mare. After some initial difficulties, the dapple Arabian mother gave birth to a bundle sheathed in white protective packaging. Gently exposing the nostrils, Twister stepped back, listening for its first breath, and it came. The mare struggled to her feet, wet with sweat, to commence her maternal job of licking off the substance and nosing her pure white baby onto its feet.

"A filly, Caly! That priceless stud gave us a beautiful little girl!" Twister exited the stall, turning on extra warming lights to keep mother and daughter safe. The gender seemed particularly important to him, but in reality, the cowboys were happy that the foal looked healthy and strong enough to live a long life.

"She's beautiful, pure white like her sire. I doubt she'll turn dapple after losing her baby fluff. This is fantastic, cowboy, a possible outstanding brood mare no other will match. We need to cross our fingers that she throws foals as beautiful as her mother's offspring, together with the appearance and conformation of her sire. What do you think, Phoenix?"

"Awesome! She's magical and what a moment to arrive: a full moon, sparkling stars, and soft snowflakes glittering as they fall. She's worth every penny."

"You keep referring to this little darling as prize material worth a great deal. I know horses are expensive with specialty jobs, but this filly..."

"...this filly will introduce a million dollar business, Mr. Sloane, for breeding purposes. The sire belongs to a Sheik in Saudi Arabia, whose horses' lineage date back several thousand years. The stud is pure white and pure fire; the boys will show you videos of one of the most famous Arabian stallions in the world; a horse seldom seen and heavily guarded. Caly and two top men in the field of insemination made the journey to ensure the semen came from the correct animal, and immediately packed and handled the precious fluid to arrive safely. Dancing Doll was impregnated successfully and has been secretly guarded twenty-four hours a day, as is the sire. This filly is a million dollar baby, Mr. Sloane, many millions of dollars, with a pedigree longer than any horse alive, except for a handful of foals sired by the same father, our baby's half siblings. All parties involved are praying that she will stand atop the breeding pedestal, to continue the lineage of her ancient ancestors." Granny told the story, her eyes never leaving the little thing, which acted like the royalty she was, only willing to stand when ready after her first awkward attempt ended in a thump. They would wait until the new life contentedly suckled on its mother. The two had a very long night.

"Would you like to name her, Phoenix? Snow and Sky came readily to you, but remember her name has to incorporate both dame and sire, and be eighteen letters or less." Caly put his arm around him; both small men smiled at something of wonder.

"Snowbunny's name represents her silly, flirtatious sense of self. Skyflyer is a risk taker, which suits me just fine. However, this little one is from the desert, which may fit, considering the similarity of white sand and snow when hit by the sun. The father's name in English translates to Sheik's Diamond. I have a name that has meaning to me and fits both sire and dame."

"I'm sure it will be perfect."

"Well, Pops, since Snow and Sky were named after skiing terms, perhaps our newest family member should be as well, considering she's a Colorado citizen of winter's color. When skiing under brilliant sunshine, and like tonight, with the moon sparkling on the snow, it looks like a field of diamonds, as does white sand. The conditions bring to mind a Paul Simon song that Rory and I would sing as we skied. '*Diamonds on the Souls of Her Shoes*' was how we felt when experiencing the natural wonder. I'd like to call her Dancing on Diamonds. She's white all over, her black hooves will glisten lacquer black when shined, and her beautiful brown eyes already dance with mischief."

"Our first Christmas present. We dub thee Dancing on Diamonds, but DD for training purposes and familiarity. Agreed?" Twister hugged everyone, including Grant, Jack, and even Sloane, with the excitement of a successful, expensive enterprise.

"I'll remain here the rest of the morning, Mr. Jones, just to keep an eye on them."

"I'll stay with them as well, Twister." Eagleclaws stepped over to stand next to Grant, exhibiting his caring nature toward the man who treasured every waking moment, considering the death threat looming over his head.

"Thanks to you both, but please join us for breakfast in two hours." Twister again took charge of a touching moment filled with sadness mixed with joy, as the Arapaho healer put a tender arm around the more fragile wrangler. They needed each other.

"We would be honored to accept your gracious invitation. When the sun reaches its zenith, however, we must bring the filly outside into the sunshine to be blessed."

"Thank you, Jack. Your power will add to her father's fire." Caly smiled up at the old man, while sadly eying his son's slow movement toward the stable door.

Phoenix had turned his face to the open portal upon feeling the faint hint of light touch his face. Dawn approached, and in his habitual manner, known to all but Sloane, he walked out to greet the new sun, in what his comrade thought a trance. Following the young man outside, Trevor wondered what the strong drawing power was to this particular moment of the day. "Every morning, since arriving at the ranch, I've watched you stand on the porch gazing east. What fascinates you about the sunrise?"

"You never know if you'll see another." The plaintive but factual reply came innocently from Phoenix who continued to squint into the oncoming brightness.

"The rising sun seems to send you to another place and time, one that puts the serenest smile on your face. The look is so ethereal, you break my heart."

"I remember one so special in color and texture that it brought me a few moments of happiness. Now, everyone I see confirms I'm still on this planet to face another day."

"I'm sorry my apartment doesn't allow for sunsets and sunrises."

"It's okay, Trev. I know the sun still comes out. Thanks for sharing this one with me."

"You're welcome, kiddo. Sun is now officially up, and you're feeling chilly by the sound of your chattering teeth." Sloane noticed the shiver when he put his hand around the smaller shoulders to walk his wistful partner back to the house. With his hands stuffed into his pockets and his cowboy hat hiding much of his white hair, Phoenix accepted the friendly gesture and returned contentedly, strolling leisurely beside the bigger man toward home. Two natural wonders gave him joy, relieving the burning fire searing his soul.

Life settled, as the family warmed under hot showers and bubbling baths, dressed for Freedom for Rights Day, while looking forward to the surprises under the tree. With each one opened, a happy laugh erupted, particularly over the gifts from New York. All appropriate, all approved of, Phoenix finally arose, staring at his feet and cuddling his chest with his arms. "Trevor, I neglected to buy you a gift, unaware you would actually follow me. Nonetheless, I hope to compensate for my negligence, and the lack of a new sweater or socks, by accompanying you to all points south, if you still wish my company." A fluttering of absorbent lashes stopped the sentimentality; two dew-filled violet eyes waited for a single word.

"Your company was the only thing I wanted for Christmas. I humbly accept, very thankful of your gift. Again, I bear no socks or sweaters for you, but maybe this will help you on good days and bad." From behind his back, Trevor gleefully pulled out a stuffed white dog, looking very much like Snowbunny with her pink nose, and tossed the fuzzy object like a football into outstretched arms. "Nice catch, but you're too small for a receiver."

"Now you've embarrassed me. I can't take a stuffed toy with me, Mr. Bolts. You're nuts." Phoenix may have sounded displeased, disliking any childish treatment that he had coped with for years. His comment, however, came from the private joke shared with the photographer, and they both chuckled, confusing the rest of the family.

"It's wrapping paper, Mr. Nuts. Stick your hand into its belly. It won't bite." Sloane received the reaction he wanted. Carefully watching the younger man, he finally saw the paper pulled out of the pocket where pajamas were meant to be stored.

"What's this? It's a gift certificate to... I'm sorry, but I don't recognize the store. This is too much money, Trev. The entire family agreed, including you, nothing over a $100."

"Too bad, but the store is in Miami, a three-day stopover to get you outfitted. You don't have a damn thing for torrential rains or hot, humid days, so no more complaining. You need clothes, as do I, since I'm running low, plus equipment that must fit into larger, lighter backpacks than we now carry. I was in somewhat of a rush to pack for a week of winter." Sloane again cracked up at the look on the surprised face of a grown man who clung unconsciously to a fluffy toy.

However, he did catch the sad dimming of the purple sparklers. "I realize it's not as personal as your gift, but in true meaning, I wanted you with me badly enough to prepare for the possible eventuality. It's all about trust and friendship this trip. Besides, I thought the dog was very personal, considering Jazz drove me all over Pueblo to find a white pooch with a snow nose."

The latter statement brought smiles and laughter to start them on their journey. Time had come, and after many quiet tears shed into white fur, two men shook dozens of hands, hugged a good number of people, and said farewell to the entire ranch family. With Granny at the wheel revving the engine, a last minute hug came from Jack, and a tighter one from Grant who whispered he would be waiting for his young friend's return. After kisses and lasting embraces from Dad and Pops, they were on their way.

Twister held Caly for a long time, watching the Land Rover head east, then finally swinging north and out of sight. Their son came through with barely a tear shed, but with the last wave of farewell, two men fell apart in each other's arms, holding a stuffed white dog between them. Snow and Sky sat dutifully beside the two cowboys, the famous Samoyed smile straightening into alert mode, instinctively understanding their friend had left for more than a couple of weeks stay in a hospital. Phoenix and Trevor would hold the image close to their hearts for a lifetime.

Chapter XI

Forty-eight hours in Miami gave two men the opportunity to apologize and get on with their work. Leaving the laptop behind had become an intense dual several hours before departure from the ranch. No amount of explanation from Sloane could convince a man who insisted that all his wireless electrical devices would work anywhere and could tap into an electrical power source to charge the battery. The older partner's many guffaws irritated Phoenix, certainly enough to make the journalist tap his toe against the polished wooden floor, while he crossed his arms in defiance over the precious information source that he held firmly against his chest.

With firsthand knowledge to the contrary, knowing you had to take a straight razor and not a battery charged one, if traveling off road, Sloane insisted the various commercials, selling communication devices, fell under fraudulent advertising. He swiftly yanked the small but heavy piece of equipment from the tight grip, tossing it over the white head for Twister to catch, causing a sharp inhalation of air by the youngest man. Giving his annoyed partner a little shake, he tried another approach, pontificating on specific advertisements: the man on the cellular in the jungle was an illusion, as was the monk happily working on his laptop in Lhasa, for both places had no regular telephone lines, no cable hook-ups, no transmitting towers, few satellite dishes, and sometimes no electrical power. After another valiant effort by Phoenix to bring a useless item, the photographer challenged him with a test. Before leaving for Miami, they would travel fifty miles into the Mexican desert, where Trevor would drop the stubborn man off for four hours and wait for him to contact anyone via his remote access computer or cellular telephone. With that much ranting and intensity, Thornton-Jones relented. It would take time to print the papers he needed, and he had better start. Grumbling over the situation, the small man accepted the return of his computer, to plug into the printer and begin the task. His specialized equipment was supposed to work everywhere!

A shopping spree for Phoenix, with an expert in the field of jungle attire and equipment, went quickly and methodically. One exception had eyes rolling, much chortling, and a constant shaking of the pastel-hued head over a very important selection out of dozens: the choice of underwear. Keeping the different styles coming, with the help of a store assistant, the photographer maintained a reddish blush on his young friend's face, one attempting to frown while snickering. The questions appeared straightforward behind closed doors, but in a busy store, just after Christmas, their overt interest in the unmentionables department brought puzzled stares. Did he want to stay cool, or wear something to absorb the sweat created by the hottest part of his body? Which seemed preferable, long legs to avoid chafing, or no legs, again to remain cooler? Was it to be light cotton or stretch latex, Brazilian jungle green or Colorado snow white, thong or boxer, or something in-between, perhaps a butt-lifting jock strap?   The choices were endless and each held a good reason for their purchase. The final decision was longer legged (no chafing), slightly stretchy (prevention of insect intrusion and riding up), cotton (sweat absorption), and skin-toned (looked clean longer and virtually invisible under light canvas cargo pants).

Giggling long after their excursion, the two continued the merriment in their double bedroom suite at the hotel. With the final garments washed and starch free, they stuffed the new packs appropriately, tied on their rain-slickers, checked each preferred piece of photographic equipment in the smallest camera case for Trevor, and took stock of notebooks, pencils, researched documents and licenses, along with tickets, passports, and visas, all organized in an over-the-shoulder bag for Phoenix. They were ready and would purchase, if necessary, essential camping gear in Belém, the city 90 miles up the Amazon River. Thornton-Jones soon forgot his laptop.

Their journey started with an eight-hour night flight from Miami to Sao Paulo, to arrive at their destination early the next morning, and allowing enough time to catch a domestic rollercoaster flight to Guaira where they would meet Sloane's friend, Rojerio Vianna. During the first leg of the trip, Trevor remained vigilant in case Phoenix drifted off, a highly unlikely possibility. Without his computer, the young man drafted scenarios, created lists, drew pictures, anything to keep his hands and mind busy. The photographer understood the blatant working façade acted as a preventative drug for sleeping. An overnight flight seemed a perfect plan for resting before a full day of travel into the pasturelands of Paraná, the state south of Sao Paulo, but the photographer immediately understood his mistake upon settling into first class. The table in front of his partner flipped down before takeoff, assuredly annoying the flight attendant along with Sloane.

On their bedraggled arrival in Guaira, Rojerio Vianna easily recognized his large, muscular friend, towering over the throng of travelers, and came forward with greetings and help with their luggage. The drive seemed endless and treacherous; the new luxury truck endured the mud-filled potholes interspersed with hidden rocks below the surface. The jostling created lurid thoughts for the older man, as his lightweight friend bounced into him constantly; near misses were part of his fun, as were the reddened cheeks of his companion. The well-traveled trail passed dozens of impressive gates of wood and wrought iron, as they grew nearer the ranch, one of which opened thanks to a gatekeeper waiting for guests. Moving the heavily carved doors with effort, a gaucho swung them from hinges embedded in a rock wall. Once the entry was closed and locked, the Brazilian cowboy mounted his horse and rode away into the hills, not to be seen again. Like the rest of the hacienda employees, he had much work to do during the wet season. The road continued further west; and the passengers were informed that several ranches lay beyond before reaching the border of Paraguay. Small bridges crossed the many minor waterways of the ranch and along the main road, creating easy pathways for strays. Exchanges were customary and cordial, even when involving bordering countries.

Arriving at the hacienda early evening and having been welcomed with a large dinner by Señora Vianna, the two men could finally rest on their first night in Brazil. Phoenix looked glassy-eyed upon retiring to the guesthouse, which he would share with Trevor who remained cognizant of the sleepless hours and how they may affect an excited phobic man. The seasoned traveler eliminated one worry upon checking the large two-bed suite for animal life of the feline variety. Vianna had offered them the luxury of private bedrooms in the main house, but midnight discussions between workingmen convinced their host that the guesthouse was more appropriate. Exhaustion prevailed, and Phoenix slept soundly in the next bed. Another body close by seemed to settle the man; the photographer could finally sleep.

Because of their shortened investigation, they had only one week to discuss the proposed Hidrovia Canal Project with as many parties as they could interest. Starting with the livestock community of Paraná and the bordering Paraguayans, their first session raised issues of more flooding, longer dry seasons, changed courses of the feeding tributaries, and of most importance, the annihilation of their natural system of water storage to the north: the fragile ecosystem of the Pantanal.   Covering thousands of hectares, the wetlands were a naturalist's playground of rare species, an environmentalist's nightmare if tampered with, and the pastureland's stabilizing force for flooding and drought.   Decimation of the area, which the planned dredging project would accomplish, could only be called flora and fauna genocide. A disaster ill conceived by greed for two landlocked countries and for three wishing to expand economically, the project lingered for more than a dozen years. A shovel had not yet dug deep; the world had a window to act.

A good beginning, in Phoenix's mind, the opportunity provided a feel for the sophistication of the governments involved in the multi-faceted quarrel, as well as the awareness of Brazil's science and environmental communities, considering they always stood on the international firing line.   Questions would prove the metal of the ranchers and farmers, determining their knowledge from an irrational reaction to change. Trevor also believed a crucial start necessary. His naïve partner needed to meet Brazilians in a less dramatic setting than the controversial battle over the rainforest, and in comfortable surroundings, before being unleashed to iterate his suggestions, to formulate a method of presenting the problem, and to write a plausible solution, by an average man, to correct a world travesty in an upscale glossy magazine. The sophisticated readers, of a $40 publication that came out only twice a year, would immediately recognize a false statement or hasty opinion.

After a day of rest and exchanging pleasantries with the Vianna family, they met the following day with ranchers from Argentina, Paraguay, and Brazil, listening in finite detail to all their problems and concerns.   Unfortunately, without their respective government officials, all of whom neglected to respond to a polite invitation, not all ideas were heard. The decision had been ongoing for years, and perhaps the project drifted while waiting for the ruckus over the rainforest to calm in international forums, a major calamity for the largest country to rectify, particularly while squabbling with all ten nations butting its border. Case closed for now.

They spent their third day traveling with Rojerio and his ranch manager, Carlos Silva. Up at dawn, they headed toward one river in question, with Vianna pointing out various important features that would be destroyed if the plan went through. Flooding had started early this particular rainy season, and they spotted a number of dead animals in pools that were slowly receding after a week of sunshine, a reprieve allowing the gauchos to regroup before the next torrential downpour. Knowing the climatic disaster would strike the ranch every year, Vianna and his men believed that dredging, deepening, and straightening the two main rivers, as well as building a canal large enough for oceangoing vessels, would result in the erosion of farming and ranching lands through worse flooding and longer droughts. The influx of hundreds of thousands of workers, builders of the canal and the new port cities along its route, had the current inhabitants in an uproar. Historically, such an invasion meant a harbinger of millions of poor, the usual byproduct upon completion of a major construction project, and the consequent squalor created by those who had no place to go or to work; their existence sustained on the waste material left behind; a condition that the smaller states could not handle financially or environmentally.

According to Carlos, who drove the modified vintage Jeep, and Rojerio, who adamantly agreed with him, one eventuality of the proposed disruption would be the change in the flow of the tributaries, where large trees and thus shade prevailed. By building a seaway, using the large Paraguay and Paraná Rivers, nature would start again, redirecting tributaries to sculpt new routes through potentially dangerous locations, causing a different form of flooding in the future. Since waterways evolved over years from their original source, a watchful eye on their progress seemed of utmost importance, uncertain as to their direction, and the possibility of forming new, more treacherous rivers.

The ranching community struggled with the quandary, fighting continually to leave things be, but on the other hand, requesting some type of flood control. A change in both rivers would certainly increase economic growth for some, and both sides of the argument were valid. Phoenix, however, only saw an important ecosystem sitting on the brink of oblivion, albeit the project sat in limbo, with rumors spreading as rapidly as the white churning waters. The human conundrum of economic development always won over the environment; the thought angered the journalist to the point of falling ill and taking to his bed in despair. No consoling helped this night.

The fourth day grew busy, and Phoenix's distress eased with an invitation to participate as a gaucho, helping Carlos save a yearling stuck in a mud-hole, a simple task as the animal grew weary and did not fight the rope. Once out and still caked with mud, the animal shook himself, caught his breath, and slowly made his way to the grazing herd to find drinkable water and the new grass poking through some of the damper areas. Nearing the major tributary, which crossed the Vianna rancho, they heard the roar of the swollen river and the unstable banks giving way to the force. Having subsided substantially in a week, nonetheless, the speed of the water remained perilous. Three men stood in the back of the Jeep, attempting to get a better view of a possible new river, if not allowed to drain into its natural reservoir. With a single glimpse--just a glimpse--Phoenix yelled for the driver to stop, immediately climbing on top of the cab roof, swearing under his breath, and just as quickly jumping down.

"What's up, kiddo?" Trevor questioned his young friend who frantically checked the number of lariats stashed in the back of the truck.

Without answering, Phoenix issued orders, "Vamos rapido, Carlos! Cut that cow off! Someone has to rope her and hang on. Her new calf is drowning! Rapido, Carlos, rapido!"

Silva spun the truck around at speed, understanding the situation through Phoenix's excited Portuguese. Trevor and Rojerio hung onto the roll bar with Vianna shouting, "Carlos is our best roper, muchacho. He will get the calf, but the rest of us must detain the mother. I can see her now; she is big and in a very dangerous state. Hurry, she readies herself to jump."

"I'll rope the mother, Señor Vianna, if Carlos tries for the calf. Mas rapido, por favor!"

The driver complied, stopping 200 feet in front of the mother, and as close to the water as safety permitted, but able to block the cow's route momentarily if Phoenix missed. The violet-eyed muchacho vaulted out of the vehicle first, landing on solid ground along with Carlos; the former ran at maximum speed toward the oncoming cow, while the latter scrambled to the river's edge. "I see it! It's coming this way with its head above water, but the calf grows tired and starts to sink!"

With no time for another idea, the Colorado cowboy snagged the mother with his first toss, yelling at Trevor to hold him and the rope as she rushed passed. A riata and a small man would not be enough to deter her. As she swept by, still unaware of the noose around her neck, she maintained her frightened gaze at the rushing river and her baby. Phoenix yelled, and the two Americans pulled her around sharply, consequently being dragged thirty-odd feet, until the anxious beast reached another obstacle: the truck. Once in partial control, yet fighting every second to maintain it, the younger man glanced at Carlos; the gaucho had missed his first throw. A small bobbing head was a daunting target for anyone to lasso, but the second attempt miraculously caught its mark. Vianna joined Silva, running along the slippery bank, not wishing to strangle their catch or break its neck, as they pulled the small animal closer to the steep bank. They scrambled to keep pace with the racing water, while attempting the impossible. Seeing their predicament and the two men having trouble maintaining their footing so close to the raging waters, Phoenix wished Trevor luck and let go, scrambling quickly toward the two Brazilians who finally had the calf out of the water, but with little chance of getting the awkward body up the bank.

The calf fell exhausted at the bottom of the slippery rive, unable to help itself. With the tenacity of a pit bull, Phoenix lay on his stomach, demanding the men hang onto his boots while he slid down along the rope to bring the drowning baby to safety. Not liking the idea of this white-haired American taking the risk, they relented, as he was the smallest, and yet, still strong enough to handle an exhausted week old calf. Wrapping his arms under and around the mid-section, Phoenix yelled to pull. In minutes, a very muddy cowboy rested on solid ground, wiping the small animal's nose, mouth, and eyes to see if it had survived the ordeal; he could not feel a sigh of a breath.

"No, come on! Don't die! Please, don't die! I'm here, little one. Blink your eyes for me. Look at me; you're not alone." Phoenix's yells turned to whispered pleas, unable to do anything but rock the creature. A sudden rush of expert hands pulled him aside for Carlos to perform the save. With some effort and unorthodox tactics on the gaucho's part, the calf blinked several times and snorted the dirty liquid out through its nose. Taking little time, the baby stood gasping for air and coughing out more fluid, while shaking from fear and a cold-water bath.

Another heart-stopping yell from Trevor had the three men leaping aside, as he no longer could restrain the mother that rushed passed them to protect her calf. All in a day's work during the wet season, four men stood drenched in red mud, but smiling. Saving one out of hundreds felt overwhelmingly good, all pleased they had come this day and at this moment.

"Excellent work, muchachos!" Rojerio Vianna slapped the backs of his comrades, steering two toward the truck while leaving

Carlos to remove the ropes and to ensure the bovine family moved away from the river. It took little prodding to convince the animals to walk on, although the calf had difficulties regaining its leg strength. A gentle nose push and an all over sniffing by the cow, the week-old little darling finally stumbled away, following close to its mother, until they stopped on firmer ground for sustenance from the swollen pink udder.

"How did you know?" Trevor asked, once sitting beside his partner in the back of the truck.

"Just lucky to see the mother in post-natal condition. Cattle are generally rather stupid, so the only reason she would panic, watching the rapids so intently, is if something important to her had fallen in. The only thing important to a cow is her calf. I had to take the risk, Trevor; I had to." Phoenix drew very close, refusing to start babbling in front of the two men in the closed cab of the modified vehicle.

"I know, kiddo. You did an impressive job; and I quite enjoyed wrestling with the mother. Very exciting." Responding quietly with an upbeat tone, Sloane felt the quiver; the young man's actions meant more.

"Wasn't fun holding a calf that had stopped breathing." Phoenix controlled his shaking to open the back window of the cab. "Señor Silva, would you show me what you did?"

"Carlos would be delighted to demonstrate a gaucho technique, Señor TJ. First, we shall return to the hacienda for dry clothes and dinner. Perhaps tomorrow would be a good time for an exhibition." For Vianna and Silva, this day would not stand out as anything special, but the ranch owner heard urgency in the white-haired journalist and thought it best to return home immediately.

"Something to take back to Twister and Caly?" Sloane heard himself only asking questions, unable to converse normally with a man badly shaken by the unexpected experience. Perhaps he had been listening, fitting the pieces of Phoenix Thornton-Jones together. He reached over the white head and put his arm around the wet, shivering body. Even though the sun shone brilliantly above, dark shadows threatened on the horizon. As the temperature escalated along with the humidity, the ominous storm clouds moved quickly to envelop the ground with a suffocating blanket of heavy, damp air.

"No, for me. They probably already know, but haven't had reason to use the procedure. My God, Trevor, that newborn almost died today. I would have held it until it took its last breath, even if the mother had trampled me. No one, no creature, should die alone."

Tears sprung from the violet eyes without a whimper or a sob.

"Let's be happy you didn't have to. Quick thinking on your part; and Carlos is equally fast. Good work, Gentlemen."

"Gracias, Señor Sloane. The animals, which fall into the raging waters this time of year, usually have little hope of survival. Without Señor TJ, we may not have seen the situation, or tried the difficult rescue."

"Thanks, Carlos, it's in my nature to save everything and everybody. Now that the crisis is over, I feel sick." Phoenix flopped down on Sloane's wet thighs, encircling his arms around his chest for comfort.

"We'll be home soon, but it sounds like you're speaking from experience." Trevor closed the window and leaned forward, bending his back to get closer to the mud spattered head. "You were dying alone until Twister and Caly found you. The sunrise was the last thing you saw before they arrived. Is that correct?" The sad ending to the long tale of *the accident* concluded with many parts missing. The photographer could only surmise his partner had been trapped in a vehicle for some time, but that did not fit the strange phobias. He certainly showed no fear of cars, trucks, or other means of transportation.

"Yeah, I thought I'd die alone. It scared the hell out of me, Trev, but the sunrise stayed with me until I fell peacefully into oblivion. I knew my trial was over, relieved to accept the ending." The skilled rubbing of his back, by a large hand, eased the troubled spirit who finally opened a portal to the mystery he kept secret.

"Not to worry. You're alive, calf and cow are busy feeding, and you did a remarkable job of roping that feisty critter. Man, she was strong. I didn't know you could do that."

"Physiotherapy for my shoulders and arms. Something Grant came up with."

"Sounds like an idea hatched by a thoughtful man." Continuing to rub the small back, Trevor attempted to roust the exhausted creature slumped across his thighs. He wished to hug the white-haired youth, kiss him with the passion he deserved, and ignite his dying heart. A revelation struck him hard: Phoenix lived for those who saved him, not for the torment of years in a hospital. His young friend risked his life for a calf, believing every minute he existed was borrowed time, snatched from the arms of the grim reaper. Sloane felt sick at the thought and leaned further forward to handle the job that needed doing immediately. Lifting Phoenix into a sitting position, he held the small body tight against his chest; two men embraced in fear, need, and confusion.

Hearing fragments of the conversation through the closed window, the men in the cab kept their eyes on the trail home. Nothing needed saying of an older friend aiding a distressed new one at least twenty years his junior. On reaching the settlement of buildings that comprised the large hacienda, the four men watched the sky darken with a mist of oncoming rain and the formidable black clouds growing ever closer with sharp thunderclaps to jolt them back to the reality of the wet season. Thornton-Jones immediately scrambled out of the truck and sprinted for the guesthouse. A few words from Sloane, and a shrug of his shoulders, sent the photographer rushing after the runaway. "Phoenix, are you okay?"

"Yeah, just tired of being covered in mud, and my insides doing a fine impression of a washing machine on maximum. Sorry for the clench." The yell came from the bathroom, as did some soft grunting and moaning.

Trevor chuckled to himself, realizing there was more to his friend's dash than saturated, caked-on clothing; the man's actions were understandable, considering new food and different water could upset the digestive system of the uninitiated. "The clench? Always a pleasure to hold you, Phoenix. Would you care for something that will help your present condition?"

"Anything. I've been holding this since the rescue. Man, I hope it stops soon. I feel like I'm generating a highly polluted Niagara Falls into their sewage system."

"Feeling sick as well?"

"A little, but it will pass along with everything else." Chirpier, Phoenix went about his business in the bathroom, also showering and thanking Trevor for the clean, dry clothes the older man handed him at the bathroom door. He came out with a sheepish grin and wet hair.

"Throw me a towel, and I'll dry your mop. Glad you weren't running from stress or frustration about the calf's condition. Did you see enough today?"

"I'm not upset, just in a hurry. Nearly didn't make it. I'll apologize to Señor Vianna at dinner. As to your question, I'd like a closer look at their flood control plans and a longer study of the Hidrovia Canal Project itself. After today, I feel something must be done, although changing the landscape would not be my choice. The idea of building an enormous seaway would certainly open up economic development for all five countries, but how does one calculate the cost to nature? Another sacrifice of a few for the good of the whole; unfortunately, it's not just a few. For the Pantanal, it means genocide of hundreds, maybe thousands, of species of living beings: both plants and animals." He threw a dry towel at Trevor who gladly patted out the pastel hair, before leaving Phoenix to tussle the humidity created waves into a wild frenzy of twists.

"We'll look at the plans again tomorrow. Seems we'll be rained out anyway. An indoor job will allow us one last stab at the problem."

"Wish we had some government assistance to stand in their defense. This isn't as easy as I first thought; and I've had to discard and rethink many of my original opinions."

"Our task does seem more daunting now, not to mention obscure, considering the length of time five governments have hovered over a single matter, and one of such importance to so many. We need their insight, as you suggest, before making sound conclusions on a project that wavers. It was their choice to refuse an interview, possibly because of who we are: crazed American journalists. We're not particularly well respected outside our borders. Now, how are you feeling?"

"Better, but you mentioned having a cure. I hope it's not that god-awful pink shit."

"You're suffering from a different malady than charred nerves, Mr. Thornton-Jones. I'll dig out our ever-ready first aid kit."

"Thanks. Thinking further on the canal, both the Paraná and Paraguay River Systems are sprawling disasters naturally, considering the original ranches were built and remain on a flood plain where the larger waterways and their rivulets meander. Drought and then heavy rain happen, and have been happening for hundreds of years. Don't quite know what to make of Señor Vianna's ancestors who first built in this particular area; they had to have known of the problem. Of little consequence now, they're here and need a solution. By the way, I enjoy your reassuring hugs as well. You have great insight, Sloane. Fighting for a life scares me. Can't imagine what Twister and Caly went through. I smelled and sensed their presence somehow; their caring can never be repaid."

"You've been hinting at your injuries, and to tell you the truth, finding a body, in the condition you've alluded to, would unglue the staunchest of men, not to mention watching others put you back together over years. Your fathers are strong, stoic men. Enough of the past, which usually puts you into a downward spiral; now, *'open your mouth, close your eyes, and I'll give you something to make you wise'.*" Trevor laughed off the foreboding picture of a broken body with no face, as he put a couple of tablets into his partner's mouth, making sure he let them melt under his tongue before swallowing the mint-flavored remedy.

"Just where do you and Twister get these weird sayings to administer medicines and food? I think I've heard every nonsensical rhyme on the planet."

"Not of your generation, or of mine, but my mother used them. They always worked, because if you didn't swallow, she'd come up with something more childish. All you could do was accept the ghastly tasting inevitable. Today's tablets are candy coated, making them at least palatable. Think you can eat something?"

"I'm quite hungry, after two days of fresh air and activity, although I may be running back here. Oh, man! After my actions today, Vianna will think me a blithering idiot with no manners for racing to the casita without a thank you." Phoenix lazily walked over to the mirror to ensure his lengthening hair remained twisted to his satisfaction, while he formulated a polite apology for his host.

As Trevor started for the shower, he turned back with a wicked grin. "Just smile and tell him the truth; the bathroom has become your friend for the rest of the night." Ten minutes later, the muscular man emerged from his shower wearing only a towel. He glimpsed at Phoenix who quickly diverted his eyes from the temptation of the bigger man's naked body. Trevor had no inhibitions about his own looks and was slightly disappointment that he could not catch the eye of his young bunkmate. Musing to himself, upon seeing the quick eye-flutter as Phoenix turned away, he whipped off the colorful terry toweling, and in one fluid motion, cracked it at the rear end of the tight fitting jeans, probably purchased in the boys' department of a Western wear store. They certainly had problems finding the small size when looking for appropriate attire in Miami.

"Ouch! That hurt!"

"Don't be a baby. I'll be dressed in ten."

Sparring as only good friends could, they soon joined Rojerio and his family, along with the Silva family, to plan their next outing and to dine in lavish comfort. A full day was set aside to review topographical maps and the Hidrovia Canal projections; the cost in money and ethics still upset Phoenix. The method for saving animals with too much water in their lungs, however, proved extremely interesting. His search for the Vianna computer the following evening, to send the information to Twister and Caly, brought great laughs from all. Finally looking around, the innocent traveler came to realize just how correct Sloane had been.

The knowledgeable photographer opened his mouth, but immediately stopped his dissertation when the worldly Brazilian arose. Rojerio put his arm around the small but strong shoulders, walked him through the massive dining room (the only room he had seen), and into an even larger sala full of antique furniture. Trying not to gape at the extravagant pieces, Phoenix did calculate their value as a six-figure sum if auctioned at Christie's.

"Sit, my friend, and I shall explain to you what life is like in remote areas of any country. You believe we have electrical power due to the number of lights in the dining room and your own accommodations. Have you seen any wires leading to the hacienda to suggest we can easily flip a switch?"

"No, sir, but I never really looked."

"One takes electricity and communication devices for granted when raised with the luxuries, but we are far from a major city and must use generated power--gasoline generators converted for ethanol consumption--just a minor inconvenience. The lights are subdued in the casa grande and even in your casita to conserve gasoline, as delivery comes only every two months. The new solar panels and wind powered energy towers have been ordered and requested, which should allow us to have uninterrupted electrical service. A new computer is the first thing we'll buy, as the one we own has become worthless with constant energy surges."

"Considering the Itaipú Dam is just downriver, the largest hydro-electrical power plant in South America, I assumed power lines crisscrossed the state of Paraná in all directions and much further beyond." Phoenix continued his journey of investigation.

"Yes, the Iguaçú Falls and the Itaipú Dam generate 20% of the power in the South and East Coastal Region, and supplies 80% of Paraguay's electricity. Power poles extend east and west, bypassing we inlanders."

"But you do have power--ethanol power--just like your car manufacturing industry."

"Quite correct. Brazil is the leading manufacturer of ethanol-powered vehicles, and our gas, made from sugar cane, receives high accolades worldwide for an inventive solution to shortages of natural gas and coal, which are both heavy contributors to air pollution. As for computers and surfing the web, we cannot use the unique service, as a generator's fluctuating power will cause undue damage to such sensitive equipment over time. A satellite link will be a possibility one day, but few Brazilians have access to the technology, considering who owns the satellites and where these satellites are situated in the sky. The price tag is astronomically high and can only be reached by large industries and the scientific community. It will come, as did satellite television, but again the equipment requires consistent power; the picture is often distorted and finally disappears, indicating signal loss. Technicians are few and do not come this way when needed. We must also wait for telephone service; our telephone company rations out lines and numbers in the interior, and even in the very small towns along the coast. Due to the close proximity to several mountainous areas, cellular telephones are out of range for most outlying ranches; you must be very close to a tower. We hear promises, but currently we have new radiophones, thanks to military technology. You will need one when you journey deep into the jungle, just as your armed forces used them in Korea, Viet Nam, Kuwait, Afghanistan, Iraq, wherever the war zone. Indispensable for communication in a good part of the world, a radio signal can receive and transmit in the remotest of places. So, there you have it. I am sure the same problem exists in the northern part of Canada or a single cabin in your mountains. Electricity and telephone companies cannot spend the money for one isolated family." Rojerio finished, smiling sympathetically at a confused young man.

"That's what Trevor said, but the communication industry leads you to believe your computer and cell phone can be used anywhere."

"The information continues to be falsely conveyed, considering the reality outside your borders. Maybe in another ten or twenty years, the entire planet will have access to inexpensive electric power, clean gas fuels, and satellite communication systems, including telephones. I'm afraid, muchacho, our world is not yet there. Supplying what you consider the necessities of life means economic bankruptcy for most governments, resulting in rising costs that are out of reach for their clients in the major cities, even in a blessed country like Brazil. We may have the largest, grandest hydro-electrical plant in South America, but it means little to those who are few in number and live far from a large population. The old adage comes to mind: '*sacrifice a few for the good of the whole*'."

"Is that why Trevor threatened to drop me off twenty miles into Mexico?"

"I would venture to say yes, as I have been there. Although the cities have power, telephones, cable, and satellites, the outlining villages and smaller towns have limits and far less money. For instance, a village of 5,000 people may be allotted only 40 telephone lines, if and only if they are close to a road with wires running along its route. The number remains stagnant for years, with telephone numbers being past down to kin, or sold for a very high price. The facts do not coincide with American advertising, not even within your own country."

"Thanks, Señor Vianna, I hope I didn't embarrass you."

"No, muchacho, for how can one be embarrassed about a fact based situation. We make do and have done so for many years. As I said, we're blessed to own several powerful generators, ethanol delivery, and a first class radiophone system. We lack for very little. Now, are you feeling better?" Rojerio arose, as did Phoenix whose eyes sought out Sloane to apologize.

"Yes, sir, although I think it best if I retire early and stay close to the much needed plumbing facilities."

"We can provide contemporary luxury in that regard. Ah, here comes Trevor."

"Hey, Rojerio, did you straighten him out?"

"Our young journalist friend would have discovered our power source given the chance to investigate the telltale signs on his own." Vianna laughed and escorted them to the guesthouse, via the pathway lit by ethanol lanterns.

Chapter XII

Mr. Sleepwalker returned the last night of their stay at the rancho, but again appeared unperturbed over his position, tightly sleeping against Sloane. The big man said nothing, for they had a long day of travel in front of them, leaving before sun up. First, the harrowing country road to Guaira, a small city with an airport where they boarded a direct flight to Sao Paulo, a spectacularly beautiful city sparkling in the night. Trevor made his way to the penthouse suite of the luxury hotel, while Phoenix found the business office and an Internet station. The younger man oozed with glee at the touch of a keyboard--his only friend for too many years--his partner would never understand the connection.

He answered his email from Twister, Caly, and Granny, next a supportive note from Grant, and an unexpected, comical greeting from Sebastian. Their words put a lump in his throat. The next task, given to him by Trevor, left his heart intact, simply searching for addresses and telephone numbers. Having jotted down the important website URLs before leaving Colorado, he quickly found the needed information and tentatively closed the window to the world. In search of a detailed map of the central core and specific directions to various locations, he found what was required at the front desk. With everything plotted and the site of the hotel marked, nothing prevented them from walking or taking a quick taxi ride to the different possibilities. This may be their chance to find someone knowledgeable regarding the canal project and the latest news on the rainforest.

Feeling hungry, Phoenix pushed the elevator button and waited for an empty car to deliver him to the top floor. After three openings and closings, he skittered into the fourth, quickly pushed the appropriate button, and even faster, hit the close door switch before encountering unwanted company. He breathed heavily, wishing all elevators were built of three-ply acrylic, like the one leading to Warren Graham's office. Emerging into the brightly lit hallway, he found the door to their suite and opened it quietly, to find Sloane sitting forward in one of the chairs, rubbing his temples. "Hey, Trev, you okay?"

"A headache. How did you make out?" The baritone voice sounded uncharacteristically tired and withdrawn.

"Fine. Everyone sends their regards. I found the necessary

addresses, plus directions to each destination and a map with a strategically plotted course for an early start. The city's vast, but this hotel is centrally located, relatively close to federal governmental offices and a few environmental authorities."

"Amazing what you, in particular, can do with a computer."

"Me and the concierge. What's wrong? You don't sound happy this evening. Maybe some food will help your migraine." Phoenix warily sidled over to the man, unsure of the appropriate action to a new situation. His partner appeared distressed, and the young man had no experience in dealing with such an emotion in an older man. Although his fathers worried and obsessed over him, they were his parents, seeking out each other during confusing times. As the only other person in the room this night, he felt compelled to offer as much assistance as he could dream up, which seemed very little.

"Worth a try. The room service menu is on the table. It's getting late; they'll be closing soon." Sloane still did not meet the worried violet eyes.

"Okay, what do you feel like? I understand red meat, wine, and cheese are not good for your type of headache. How about a seafood salad and a juice, or maybe water?"

"Sounds good, but perhaps something simpler, like chicken broth and a cheese sandwich, which might settle my stomach."

"Feeling ill as well, hunh?"

"A little. You also should order something your stomach can tolerate before retiring." Trevor finally took his hands away from his head and leaned back slowly against the back of the soft chair provided by the largest suite in the hotel. There seemed no reason to skimp on a few nights of pampering when he had so much on his mind. Flooded with doubt, the photographer tensed, making his pounding head feel worse. He heard the telephone conversation through a fog, only to open his eyes to see a nervous and confused white angel emerge through the thickening clouds to stand before him.

"I guess there's no remedy for headaches such as yours, except rest. What about a cold compress and I'll handle the rubbing part?"

"Thanks, kiddo. Do you give good massages?"

"You tell me, since this will be my first attempt. I've had enough of them to know what they're supposed to feel like, at least for me. If I make things worse, tell me." Phoenix found the bar-fridge, gathered sufficient ice, which he folded within a damp towel, and placed the makeshift compress on the brow with the deep furrows.

Tentatively he started, receiving a slight smile for his trouble.

Trevor did not respond with words to the featherlike manipulation of his temples. Such a light touch would have seduced the photographer given any other time. His migraines felt exactly like ice headaches, the instant pain of drinking very cold liquid too quickly, but lasting hours longer. The small gentle hands did very little but comfort him, considering the subject he needed to approach.

"Does that help?"

"You're doing fine. Can you keep it up until dinner arrives?"

"No problem. One thing I have is physical stamina." Phoenix continued, still unsure of the method or the amount of pressure required to ease the pain he felt within the tense man. "What about your neck and shoulders? I know mine always cramp with muscle spasms when I'm not feeling well; or maybe it's the other way around. Caly rubs my neck, and if the tension remains, we know I'm coming down with a cold or something." Trying his best, the younger man could only ramble off his concerns, cluttered with useless information. Overtaken by serious nervousness, he wished upon the lights beyond their window that dinner would arrive soon.

"Feels good and the ice helps as well. Thanks." Trevor did not move, nor did he open his eyes, leaving Phoenix to finish in silence. Dinner arrived; the bellhop set the table and vanished. The smaller man aided the larger one to the table, every step taken slowly. Both men picked at their food; both men felt ill; and both men wondered about the other.

"Something is terribly wrong, Trevor; I can feel it. What's causing your migraine? Is it my fault?" Phoenix laid his fork on the plate before him and clamped down hard on his trembling lower lip. Beyond worried, he had no recourse but to ask.

"Of course not. I'm simply concerned about our job. Come on; let's go to bed. Sometimes lying supine helps. We can then talk without me gagging." Sloane rose to his feet and headed for the largest bedroom that accommodated an emperor-sized bed with ease. Using the small man for support, he felt able to walk the distance, but standing increased his dizziness; the food made him sicker.

"Maybe we should talk in the morning. You look pale, Sloane, and there's no way..."

"...I know, you can't pick me up off the floor either. No wonder my close friends are larger than average. They're my security blanket." Trevor tried to laugh as he slowly sat on the bed, not willing to jar his head.

"Let me help you undress. I must be good for something." Dejection ruled the younger mind, feeling discarded as even a potential friend because of his physique. Not only small, he had sustained irreversible damage to his body that only plastic surgeons could improve over time. Sloane broke his heart.

"You're good for much more, Phoenix, like putting me to bed without further advances, considering how deathly ill I've suddenly become. Besides, who revealed his feelings toward you and even followed you to your fathers' ranch? I've never done such a thing, always leaving people to their own devices and concerns." Trevor helped the small hands remove his shirt and pants, reassuring his diminutive friend he intended on wearing underpants to bed for decencies sake.

"What can I put beside the bed in case you need something during the night?" The younger man perked up immediately with the supportive words and pulled back the covers. Extra blankets would be necessary due to the overtly air-conditioned suite, for which he could not find the controls.

"Just you. Get undressed, climb into your flannels, which are very much needed tonight, and snuggle next to me." Trevor lay with his eyes closed; his one arm lay on his brow to still his head against the pillow.

"What?" Phoenix startled at the invitation, although the bed seemed large enough, and they had shared a room for over a week.

"I refuse to let you loose in this suite. We know where you'll end up, considering the temperature in here. Come on. I'm just as warm as your dogs and equally as safe. Your pack is next to mine."

"I should shower and ensure my scribbled notes are readable." The smaller man hesitated, wishing to disappear from an awkward and frightening proposition.

"It's late; we've been traveling all day. Tired, ill, and smelling ripe is part of the job. Now, strip down and come to bed, before I drift off without knowing where you are." The large hands returned to the graying temples, his head spinning about the room like the lights reflected off a mirrored disco ball. A bad migraine he could tolerate, but this one roared at him, making him sink deeper into cloaked doubts and worries. "Hurry up, before I'm really sick."

"Okay, okay, let me get my things. Can I use your bathroom?" Phoenix lifted his hands, palms outward to thwart any misinterpretation of the man's request.

"What do you need the bathroom for? Just undress here. Jesus, I won't look if that's what you're afraid of, although we may share a tent if we camp. Oh, but you'll find a place to hide. Man, you are hellishly shy."

"That's unfair. I usually take a leak before sleeping, if that's okay with you. What's wrong with you besides a headache?" Phoenix stormed back, hearing words that hurt. He understood Trevor had no inkling of his leftover horror, but there seemed little excuse for cruelty.

"For one thing, I haven't set up my equipment for one decent shot. The calf thing would have been a given; unfortunately, I was wrestling a frantic beast that only Caly considers an every day job." Sloane immediately knew his words came out wrong, and he squeezed his eyelids tighter at his stupidity, waiting for a sharp and deserved retort. Unable to look at the young man, he needed a chance to explain his concerns before they encrusted his soul. A wistful response, from the ethereal creature, caused the dark eyes to flicker open, only to close against the harsh overhead lighting.

"I'm sorry, Trevor. Your work is so important to you, and I selfishly ignored the fact I may impede your creative drive." Phoenix turned away to find his flannel sweat suit, his heart bursting with regret.

"No, the problem's me, kiddo, only me. I'm not used to company while working. Not your fault, I'm the selfish one. I honestly don't see what we're doing. Our objective renders pointless if we can't get answers, and I sincerely doubt we ever will. You're already confused over the canal conundrum, as the problem may only exist for the ranchers. Hell, I don't know, but me thinks, Master Thornton-Jones, we've conjured up an unsolvable horror story. I just don't see any plausible answers: my enthusiasm snuffed out by bureaucracy, too many variables, and lack of imagination on my part. What do you honestly think? Do we continue, or call time-out with Graham?" Remaining in the same position, Sloane vented his concerns, believing the time had come to retire, hang up his camera, and lose himself in obscurity. At odds with the request from the publisher, he understood boundaries, working under strict rules of protocol, deadlines, and ethics, not to mention social consciousness. The younger man's opinions, although valid with the little they knew, disrupted his usual conservative approach toward any subject; a conventionality he hated admitting to. He had much to rethink and possibly discard, including his new working partner, his hope of a loving relationship, and his sudden lack of confidence to accomplish their mission.

Phoenix said nothing, contemplating the defeated words, also in a quandary of indecision. Perhaps the bigger man was right, for they had little evidence to prove any theoretical proposal had merit. Many experts worked feverishly on Brazil's on-going struggles, whether the country wanted their help or not. Considering the seriousness of the nation's continuing disputes, which the government also engaged in problems with its many neighbors, not to mention their international forays over the rainforest, he truly wondered if the beautiful but harsh land could justifiably be referred to as a world power, or would ever be. Brazil had everything to become a leader in many circles, already established in numerous industries, but remained unstable and defensive politically and economically. Power and money lay in the hands of 5% of the population, while 90% were considered below the poverty line in other developed nations. The numbers seemed ludicrous, considering the splendor surrounding them at the rancho. Rojerio Vianna mentioned he and his family were part of the few 5% listed as middle class. Bogged down with thoughts and ideas, Phoenix could not comprehend a country, so poor and yet so rich, that barely recognized the money accumulating in the World Bank specifically for them and for a single purpose. Billions of dollars, from many concerned lands, awaited the Brazilians, certainly enough to rectify the potential global disaster they seemed bent on escalating through deforestation of the world's largest rainforest, just to satisfy the greed of a handful by exploiting 90% of the population. Nevertheless, it was their country, to do with as they pleased, and heaven help the rest of the world waiting on the brink, waiting for a sane, knowledgeable decision, but receiving only retaliatory accusations of interference. The fifth largest nation in area and population adamantly tapped a national toe, and justifiably so, on the ill-conceived notion of turning the rainforest into a sanctuary; an idea that had no bearing, considering the uselessness of a plan instigated by a handful of fanatical ecological groups. The political and environmental arenas wished to see the South American continent stabilize and prosper, without destroying the climatic conditions of the Northern Hemisphere. There had to be a way for all.

"Come on, kiddo. Hurry into your flannels and come to bed. I've upset you and myself."

With his sweats in hand, Phoenix turned to ponder the man who finally gazed up with haunted eyes burrowed in the deep sockets. "Since tagging after me and running with my thoughts inhibits your creative juices, I have an idea. What say I follow you, keeping silent as you scout for subject matter and set up your compositions? Whatever you photograph, I'll sit and watch, write and contemplate, viewing the image and how you perceive it. Pretend I'm not around, only Passepartout to your Phileas Fogg. The only thing I need to study intently is Brazil's boating industry, a few major and minor tributaries yet unaffected, those that have been, plus the current road system and future development. I think we could salvage something of our working partnership."

Trevor looked at the hopeful face and smiled. "Why not. I'll do my thing in the normal fashion, but it won't prevent us from conversing. I can hardly deny the existence of one who makes me smile with a look. Just let me get my feelers back, and we'll be on our way. Their boat industry, hunh? Something new?"

"Just a thought. Rest and I'll be right with you. I'm tired too and have always been dubious about the scope of the article. Scares the hell out of me, Trev." Phoenix scurried into the bathroom, quickly returning to the bedside. Still unnerved and distraught, he lingered, staring at his designated side of the enormous bed.

"Get in. What's the difference between sleepwalking and scrambling in on your own accord?" Sloane pulled the covers back, inviting the paling man to share a warm, comfortable place to rest his white head.

"Simple. Sleepwalking is a bodily reflex action, which I can use as an excuse." Phoenix finally crawled in and sank into the softness.

"You don't need an excuse, kiddo. Good night, sleep tight."

"There's another one! What the heck does that mean?"

"Have no idea." Trevor chuckled lightly.

"Thought as much." The smaller man turned on his side and fell asleep with his partner's quiet merriment singing a lullaby in his head.

Chapter XIII

Sloane woke first after a short troubling sleep, his migraine not easing, and his stomach churning until very early the next morning. Without disturbing the small figure, curled in a tight ball next to him, he managed to run for the bathroom, purge himself of demons, and return to bed in a sweat several times during the night. On one of his jaunts, he remained awake for an hour, placing a call to the concierge to request a technician turn off the air-conditioning system in their suite. While waiting, he messed the second bed into a frenzy of rumbled sheets and head-dented pillows. No need to antagonize the hotel that could legally confront them over the blatant disregard of church law, although Brazilians left the homosexual population to cavort on the beaches and discreetly in other public areas, if not disturbing the largest Catholic social structure in the world per population. A contradiction in acceptance of same sex familiarity and church doctrine, the double standard kept foreigners straddling an undefined line.

Feeling better, and with the sun reflecting off the glass and mirrors of the crystal city, he nudged Phoenix to awaken. The two quickly showered, dressed, ate breakfast in the main dining area on the mezzanine floor, and hit the streets with loaded questions in hand. Agency after agency, organization after organization, they ran in circles, always ending up with little information from people who did not know. A frustrating situation, only the second day brought them in contact with a group of researchers blessed with funding from the billions of dollars available. The Pilot Program to Conserve the Rain Forest willingly explained their multi-layered study in accordance with relief guidelines, the location of various protected areas under their scrutinizing eyes, as well as showing the travelers a current video of the laboratories and explaining their specific tasks. Appearing pristine and orderly, not to mention diplomatic and friendly, the scientists and administrative staff had impressed the investigators, until the pair walked out and realized they had learned nothing. One could only shrug and laugh.

Next stop--Rio de Janeiro--Sloane wanted the younger man to touch down in one of the most famous cities in the world, to experience its wealth and its poverty. Phoenix alone reveled in finding the city's equivalent to the Chamber of Commerce, which gave him a list of names and website addresses of various shipyards and boat builders in Brazil. Traditionally a sea-faring people, the descendents of the original Portuguese settlers, the Brazilians proudly displayed their various models, plus the latest in boating technology, from houseboats to trawlers, jet boats to yachts. Mainly a domestic business for the transportation industry and the handful of rich, the visit did give Phoenix a direction in which to expand his plan. He nodded with a smile and would later inform Trevor that the vessels were beautifully constructed, but not what he looked for. Keeping his idea a mystery, from a curious Sloane, had the small man chortling in delight.

On one unsettling day for Phoenix, the two men ventured into territory not on Rio's tourist map. Traipsing gingerly through giant hills of garbage, passing tin shelters and wide-eyed women, children, and those looking very elderly but probably only in their thirties, they saw and smelled the journalist's first encounter with extreme poverty. The favela reeked of sewage, rotting food, and no hygiene, bad enough to make heads reel and stomachs reach for the throat. A thriving community this was not, but a decaying cesspit of humanity and all the vices it created. Mainstream society ignored those regarded as lesser beings than the flies invading the three-sided shelters. Phoenix held fast, while the photographer snapped pictures of only a handful of the millions who lived in the dramatic and dire conditions existing in every major city in Brazil. Shaken to his boots, the young man begged to leave the city of beautiful beaches, stunning architecture, and steamy nightclubs, to which the world's rich and famous flocked while praising the city for its sophistication. It was an outrage.

Arriving in Brasilia, with the hopes of a new city freshly unwrapped, they encountered more slums fringing the limits of the capital, with an expanding population of unemployed who originally built the capital, confirming the fears expressed by Señor Vianna. Dismissing a trip to the outer areas, to protect Phoenix's unstable mental state, the pair again ran the gamut of offices, finally finding their way to the Pilot Program's headquarters. Cordial and gracious, as were their people in Sao Paulo, the coordinators left them still guessing as to exact locations of various research groups living within the forest. An offer was extended, however, to join a party of foreign diplomats for a field trip in three weeks. Trevor thanked them, but turned down the proposition, aware the guides he arranged would know precisely where scientists trod, if they actually did. Telling his young friend he had doubts, Sloane received a solid objection from the shaking white head. Phoenix remained resolute, adamantly believing the World Bank had a stake in the program as holder of the funds, along with the backing of the Group of Eight nations that furnished those funds. If they said a study group existed, then it existed. With much more faith than Sloane, the journalist prayed the Brazilians had made a start. This new organization had much to prove to the international community, while dodging political aspirations, environmental attacks, and entrepreneurial contamination.

After two more exasperating days passed with little success, the photographer and his Passepartout flew to Belém, an important starting point and port on the Amazon River, where Trevor rented an all-terrain vehicle and headed toward the Atlantic. Traversing ninety miles of paved highway through the jungle, they arrived at the mouth of the great river, unable to see anything but brown water flowing miles into the ocean, interspersed with a few delta-made islands. The size and wonder kept his passenger bubbling with excitement, and Sloane relented to the constant badgering, stopping long enough to allow an impatient Phoenix to jump out of the Jeep and scramble to the river's edge, just to dip his hands in the famous waterway. Here they would meet with friends of the photographer, in a place hidden from view by the mighty ships picking up cargo and passengers to take upriver or out to sea. After a five-day voyage to the next large city of Manaus, then passing many tourist lodges, villages, and established plantations, they would eventually head for the Peruvian border; their final plans depended on the advice of their guides and what lay between.

With much merriment and high spirits, Trevor introduced Phoenix to two botanists: British expatriates who regarded Brazil as home the last twenty years. Doing their own freelance reconnaissance of the jungle, and its thousands of miles of tributaries, they lived on the river in a comfortable vessel they called home, anchored nightly in the vast Amazon water system to prevent trouble due to their politics, their environmental activities, as well as their blatant sexual orientation. Warned previously that he may have to dodge bullets, Phoenix remembered and immediately switched to alert mode.

Nigel Foster and Kenneth Baldwin stood astounded; their jaws hit the decking when the white-haired angel reached a small hand upward for assistance with his backpack. Quickly recovering, Nigel, the blond-haired half of the duo, hoisted him onto the firm deck, shook his hand, welcomed him aboard, and toured him about the boat. From the description provided, Phoenix understood that the Greenpeace Organization had approved the craft's usage as unobtrusive, a rare stamp of acknowledgement by a group known for its outrageous tactics, sometimes warranted, but often times not. A little radical for even someone of his generation, the journalist accepted the organization's high praise for a brilliantly designed water vessel. Clean, quiet, with no underwater blades to harm what lay beneath, the boat instilled a powerful message in the young man; his idea had potential, using similar but contemporary designs for a variety of purposes.

While Thornton-Jones chatted with Foster, Kenneth interrogated Sloane over his relationship with the astonishingly beautiful one. The well-built American accepted an imported lager and sat down to contemplate his next words, remembering to use the correct name of his partner. "The relationship is ongoing platonic for TJ, although he must share my bed for reasons I can't explain. I certainly wish more, Kenny, but the kid has a host of ghosts chasing him, disqualifying me from seducing the man at my normal speed. My patience may wear thin before an honest relationship can grow. By the way, if you hear screams, sudden outbursts of rage, or run into him in the middle of the night, ignore the circumstance and find me." Trevor swallowed the ice-cold liquid, happy to have friends who prepared for larger than average-sized guests of a different culture and taste. The two Englishmen had successfully escorted the photographer to many an isolated region to capture elusive shots. They knew his routine and obliged his every creative whim.

Their first night onboard, hidden in the third or fourth tributary, the fledgling traveler became quite turned around after leaving Belém, lost in the jungle's maze of waterways. Remembering Trevor's inability to focus on the job, Phoenix pondered the rowdy trio who grew increasingly inebriated as darkness fell. An unasked question arose in the younger man's mind. Could Sloane work amidst the cacophonous drone, albeit extremely witty and exceedingly charming? The uninitiated would wait and nervously crawled into the largest bunk provided, with the photographer as his bed-buddy in the posh but cramped stateroom.

Very early morning, the rustle of activity and a wristwatch alarm alerted them to rise. The first day out, Phoenix slipped through the hatch, feeling the sunshine that tickled the water to sparkle and cascaded prisms through the formidable trees. The rainforest welcomed him with the drama of sound. He never worried about Trevor's tolerance again, as everyone grew silent. On their only day of waking after sunrise, the journalist came to understand that Sloane required much more time. The photographer wished to arise in darkness, after anchoring anytime of the day, wherever he felt a shot might be important, or possibly indicating a venture into the terrain. Sloane had a method that worked. No one understood his actions or what he saw, but the man had style and foresight, an instinctive knowledge for light and color, along with how a composition would look under different conditions. He held magic in his mind and hands, insightfully finding the right time of day for each shot taken, and the emotion he desired to express. Fogg's Passepartout learned quickly.

The journey by boat would take several months, faster if they missed the traffic of oceangoing cruise ships and industrial transporters. Having read too many books and hearing too many stories, the young man discarded his preconceived notions of the landscape of Brazil, coming to respect the country's varied terrain and its immensity. From the many aero-flights taken to get this far, he saw the deserts of the northeastern region infiltrate the scrub moving south, ending in the flood plain pastureland investigated in Paraná. The east coast was separated from the inland by a long stretch of mountains, but supported the majority of Brazil's population in extremely large cities, sprawling endlessly along white beaches. Ranchers and crop-farmers inhabited the countryside inland, on high plateaus between mountains, attempting to increase their holdings by spreading into the jungle. Amazonia covered the rest, with thick jungles, extensive waterways, and thousands of birds and animals. The staggering size of the rainforest hit home, for it covered two-thirds of Brazil, starting at the Amazon River's mouth on the Atlantic, reaching into Peru, Columbia, Bolivia, Ecuador, and Venezuela, as well as the smaller countries to the north. Hundreds of tributaries flowed from the north, south, and west; the source river only a stream originating in the land of the Inca, proving to the journalist that the problem of the rainforest extended beyond Brazil's borders politically and economically. Many countries wished to reap the benefits of the jungle, while others cared little about entering the dangerous terrain.

Baldwin cooked a full breakfast, as they would eat twice a day and snack in-between. While he managed the kitchen, his blond partner navigated the boat into the Amazon, close to the north bank. Nothing of interest for Sloane, he remained quietly vigilant, but took the time to inform Phoenix of what he proposed to do and would confirm with their guides. A single nod, from the white head wearing a tan hat, assured him the younger man paid some attention, although the purple eyes remained intently fixated on the ribbon of green on the starboard side. Innocent to the wonders of the Amazon, the journalist stood on the edge of a lifetime's adventure, refusing to miss one instance of changing landscape or a hint of wildlife. The small hands worked non-stop, writing copious notes without looking at the paper. A writing exercise from his university days came in handy, observing while explaining his feelings in words for those who could only wish they stood by his side. By early evening, a drizzle replaced sunshine; Phoenix scanned their damp, hidden anchorage, mesmerized by the rising steam and ignoring the rain ricocheting off his hat. Called to take cover, he finally accepted a plate of dinner and sat quietly next to Trevor who laughed at the wild violet eyes, ones that grew larger as the day ended.

"Hey, kiddo, how are you doing?"

"You tell me, Phileas."

"You're doing fine. Quite a trick you have going with your writing. I've never seen such a beautiful pair of eyes go unblinking for so long."

"Afraid of missing something. Besides, how would you know, considering these rad shades you bought me? Very cool, Sloane, but they probably won't be needed deeper inland, and certainly a put away item in the rain."

"Glad you like them, and you're absolutely correct; seldom will we see the sun hit the lower floor this time of year. The humidity and heat will increase dramatically, and there's no stopping the rain. Our luck won't hold for long."

"What do you call this?" Phoenix held his hand out the opening to catch a few drops.

"Jungle mist that adds drama. Look through the fog hovering over the river. Between the rising steam clouds, you can see the forest, and the deeper we penetrate, the hotter the day, the better the pictures will be at dawn and dusk. We pray for clear days and rainy nights."

"You paint a great picture, Sloane. This is more than I had hoped. Glad you arranged this river excursion, as I wasn't looking forward to investigating the road system inland."

"We'll check how far the roads lead after this venture. With Kenny and Nigel, however, we'll find deforested areas easier and travel into far denser woodlands. As per your research, the Brazilians are trying to populate the jungle to make use of its natural resources. Small settlements lay along the Amazon itself and some along the waterways feeding it. Once we pass Manaus, traffic will become lighter, but humankind extends upriver on any habitable land. Our friends plan on taking us to places I haven't seen, particularly burned tracts of the man-made variety. We'll see how devastating a fire can be over the long term. During our flight to Belém, you saw grazing land and areas of leveled jungle that indicate farm encroachment. You've read about the problems between jaguars and cattle south of the rainforest; the ranchers bordering the treed area are creating a like situation if they don't stop felling trees, much like the problems in China and India. The latter two countries pushed hard to stop the intrusion into natural habitats for the giant panda and the tiger, but both animals remain in danger of extinction. India has instituted harsh punishment for poachers and is relocating thousands of people who reside within the tigers' many designated reserve areas." Trevor seemed full of information regarding Brazil and other areas they had touched upon when they had first met. He had Phoenix fascinated with whatever information he could provide.

"Yes, I read about India's actions as well. Very good news. A similar confrontation between man and beast exists in the Northern Hemisphere, that of cattle and misplaced wolves due to logging and forest fires. Zoologists had a difficult time convincing ranchers to stop killing wolves when they were reintroduced from Canada. The ratio of calves taken per population is very small. Mountain lions, per number of animals, kill as many. Jaguars, however, are a more dangerous threat to man, simply because of their size and power." The smaller man also understood the wildlife conversation efforts, and the trying problem of correcting them.

"They are ferocious and have no hesitation in killing anything that moves. I tried my hand at wildlife photography years ago, a very dangerous job, although fascinating. Both the big cats go for the neck; the leopard attacks from the rear, while the jaguar is strong enough to snap your head off from any direction, giving you no chance."

"Who's going to be watching whose back then?" Phoenix snickered, although serious about the existing threat, having been told that the photographer liked to hike into dense jungle looking for rare finds. He eyed the ever-ready digital compass the man held in his hands since boarding; the experienced trekker knew exactly where he was at all times. Sloane's skill in the wilds brought a sense of comfort to the smaller man.

"Creatures of the night, unless they've had poor hunting; the big cats won't be a real problem for us. You can take bravery too far but we will be armed." Trevor waited for the shaking to start, which surprisingly did not develop.

"You're a comfort. At least I know how to shoot, but killing... man... I just don't know." Phoenix shook his head, dreading the possibility of murdering anything, even in self-defense.

"Glad to hear it. I don't like the idea of dodging your bullets at an inappropriate moment. Nonetheless, if one crosses our path, fire a shot over its head, or kick up debris into the face with several shots to the ground near its front paws."

"Just as you do with aggressive cougars, bears, etc. etc. etc. So, are we talking about leopards as well as jaguars in Brazil, not to mention panthers?"

"Man, you have a long memory, so I best not lie to you. This is jaguar country, not the leopard. As for ebony cats, the coloration is found in many feline species. Their differences show in head shape, body size, the way they hunt, and their coat. For instance, the leopard panther is slightly smaller with slicker, shinier fur, while the jaguar has a tufted coat, showing its natural spots through texture."

"Have any panther jags been killed by ranchers?"

"I don't recall any. We'll have to get the statistics on the subject, before we hear about the killing of one."

"Let's hope the situation rights itself with the tagging of a particular cat, following the movements of said cat, to see if it repeats the act. Like any predatory animal, easy prey is exactly that, once they start. A tagged jaguar, however, could innocently amble too close to a herd and be eager to return to its own habitat. Seems a good reason to stop on-sight killings." Phoenix sat quietly in the dark, listening to night sounds he had never heard in reality, while contemplating large jungle mammals. He could only count one at that moment.

"Do you realize what you've done tonight, without freezing into a statue, or going nuts on me?" Trevor's smile shone white under the few small lanterns that lit their way to the bowels of the boat and warned passing night visitors of their presence. His dissertation on the jaguar had worked.

"No. What did I do?"

"You've been talking about cats, in the dark, for the last twenty minutes."

"I have, haven't I?" After years of therapy, Phoenix wondered why now. He finally had said the word without thinking, or a bad memory surfacing. Although talking of large jungle cats, the word remained the same and should have triggered a response, not to mention his normal reaction just contemplating the subject. Having succeeded in conquering the dark, at least a full ninety percent thanks to Sloane and the Seven Dwarfs, he said nothing about blinking at an ethanol lantern throughout the conversation.

"Maybe you've vanquished a few phobias since leaving New York."

"I don't know, Trev. How could something so unexplainable just happen? If I ran into Bogart, or came face-to-face with a jaguar, would I still panic?"

"Got me, kiddo. Let's go to bed, and you stop thinking about it. I don't relish a sudden awakening by another type of wildcat pouncing on me." The big man laughed and reached out his hand to assist his partner off the covered prow. Once in their quarters and dried off, a new suggestion came from beyond to startle the journalist. "This bed is too small, Phoenix. Damn, I should be calling you TJ, but I forget. No matter, life would be easier with me on my back and you on your side, your head resting on my shoulder. We'd have more room, and I'm used to the position. I stay very quiet with a sleep-over."

"Oh! Well! Okay. Which side, my back against you, or my..."

"...whatever feels comfortable; and please, discard your flannel, since it was hotter than sin in here last night and will become worse. Remember we're on the equator, experiencing a Brazilian summer: meaning hot, stifling, wet, and did I mention sticky? I don't know how you bear these temperatures."

"Turn off the light then. The heat doesn't bother me, and as you know, I seek it out. Can I leave my underwear on?" Phoenix grew anxious. No one had seen his body except Twister, Caly, and a handful of doctors and nurses.

"Of course. I'm down to mine, as you can see. Now get undressed, with the light on, while I settle in. You don't have anything I haven't admired before."

"Oh yes I do." Phoenix insisted, praying the large man would back off. Revealing his scars would sicken the staunchest of men, not to mention a gay perfectionist.

"I know you have ghastly marks, if that's what you're worried about. We included one in the Polaroid for the police. A brute of a reminder I will admit, but you must be riddled with them, considering the injuries you've subliminally mentioned. Why do you go to such great lengths to hide them from me?" Sloane quickly covered his tracks, forever concealing the knowledge learned of the small body while lifting the man into the bath. A shock then, he could prepare himself for the horrific damage on one too young.

"Because they're revolting and I'm shy."

"Fine, but you're still stripping. Hurry up; I'm way ahead of you. You also need to coat yourself with more insect repellent." Trevor climbed into the bed bolted to the floor, readjusted the coverings down to a single sheet and the mosquito netting. He glanced at the man who turned his back, believing in the old adage: *'if I can't see you, you can't see me'.* The second viewing still upset the intrepid photographer, seeing the gouged markings running red up the legs. Whatever caused the mess, money luckily existed to ease him of the psychological problems by eliminating the physical.

"I'm feeling very awkward, Trevor. I don't know about this." Phoenix quickly turned around, attempting to ascertain the discomfort level of the photographer's facial expression. No disgust registered; he breathed a little easier.

Sloane, conversely, wondered if he hid his horror. The knees, the elbows, the shoulders, every joint detailed massive injuries, some corrected to a degree by plastic surgery. Each scar proved Thornton-Jones endured years of therapy to walk on his own; compound fractures had wreaked havoc on the fragile frame. "So... nice undies. What do you think of your choice?"

"Very comfortable, as are these singlets. I would have thought layering inappropriate for insufferably hot, sticky weather." Phoenix stopped his racing heart, slathered on the disgustingly odorous lotion to fend off unwanted bugs, and crawled in next to the bigger man who smelled the same. Settling his body (facing Sloane seemed best), he bent his knees to prevent intimate contact, although his head fit perfectly in the indentation between the man's clavicle and a hard pectoral muscle.

"Loose clothing feels cooler, while layers absorb sweat, keeping you drier without showing through your outer layer. We would have dressed in fine layers of cotton if in the Sahara, but conditions in the rainforest brutalize the skin, especially insect stings and bites, not to mention the various plants that scratch and gouge. Both flora and fauna can be deadly. Now, are you comfy?"

"Yeah, how about you?"

"Perfect, if I can rest my hand on your shoulder."

"Okay." Phoenix waited, holding his breath. The touch could awaken the dreaded beast, but tenacious determination rendered the menace quiet.

"Good night, kiddo. You can breathe now." Trevor chuckled, as he reached for the overhead light, finally feeling the tense body relax.

"Night, Trev. Sleep tight, whatever it means. Sounds physically impossible."

"You are a trip, Mr. Thornton-Jones."

"Another one. Good grief."

"From the sixties generation and the dying fringe of it."

"You were a hippy!"

"A little too young, but wanted to be one."

"Cool."

"Very cool. Say good night, Phoenix."

"Good night... Phoenix."

"Stop."

"Stopping."

"Don't get me started. Close your eyes and shut up." Sloane put his hand over the perfect lips, starting a bout of uncontrollable giggling in the smaller man. With nerves stilled by silly chatter and a few laughs, he smiled knowingly in the blackness. Nothing wrong with a proven remedy for the giggles, he fell asleep with the white angel cradled next to him. Phoenix had not noticed his changing mental condition since arriving in Brazil: ailurophobia and nyctophobia conquered, haptephobia subsiding.

Chapter XIV

"Good morning, Kenny."

"Good morning, luv. Are you ready to speed to our first destination?"

"You bet. Trevor told me the plan, but I wasn't really listening. So, where're we going?" Phoenix scanned the dark forest through the fine drizzle, hoping for signs of nightlife before the dawn. Nothing stirred, not even a bird.

"I suggest you step out of the rain for a bit. I'll play Mom and pour the coffee. First, we continue up the main river, adhering close to the north shore. By nightfall, we'll safely anchor inside the entrance of our newest discovery; a unique waterway where Trevor will find untouched jungle. While you and our photographer friend spend a week or longer shooting, Nigel and I will scavenge for flora specimens on the lower floor. A good location for picture taking, Trevor should delight in this part of the forest, particularly near its source. Although small of size, a dramatic waterfall spurts from an unusual split in the rocks, spewing a great deal of water into the air and falling into a small pool before starting its journey. When assured that your work is complete, we'll hasten to another north side rivulet, situated close to the Peruvian border, where we've asked Trevor to hike inland, although there's considerable risk involved. Unauthorized emerald miners have found a load; but remember *caution rules*; you must go unseen, as the law does not reach all places." Baldwin poured the young man a coffee and quickly returned to stir something smelling delicious but possibly burning. With Nigel emerging from one direction and Sloane from the other, passengers and crew met in the galley.

"Morning, TJ, Trevor. Everyone happy and well rested this morning. We have a long day ahead, and I'm sorry to say, a rather boring one until we locate our turnoff."

"Very well rested, Nigel. Thanks, Kenny." The photographer accepted the hot Brazilian brew handed to him, one of the country's finest exports. "I understand we'll meet little traffic our first week of exploration. Why haven't we seen it before?"

"We've discovered a great deal since we last saw you. This waterway is narrow and quite shallow for most boats. If you make the distance, the river suddenly widens halfway up, breaking into three small rivulets that flow into the Amazon. Two of these waterways can accommodate only narrow dugouts. With their mouths hidden from most that pass and their routes covered by a forest umbrella, they merge quietly into the main body of water, virtually unnoticeable to rapidly moving vessels. Quite extraordinary, little is known of the waterway. Difficult to even pinpoint on aerials, although it is situated between the busy cities of Belém and Manaus, the lovely little sanctuary is only known to a few."

"Sounds exciting. I guess it has been years since I've seen you two. Always a pleasure I might add."

"Kenny was explaining our route, Trev, since I wasn't exactly paying attention to what you said." Phoenix lowered his damp head and bit his lip in a gesture of remorse.

"I didn't think you were, kiddo. You should be wearing your hat. Don't want you saturated the entire day. So, what has Mr. Baldwin been telling you?" Sloane reached through the hatch to the coat rack and pulled out the tan hat, comically pulling down hard on the brim to make the lengthening white hair stick out wildly from underneath.

"First, two north side tributaries, and then I assume two southern ones." Small hands reached up and readjusted the hat appropriately, accompanied by an annoyed roll of the violet eyes.

"Right you are. Our other areas of interest include those of deforestation by fire damage, both lightning and man-made, as well as authorized lumbering. They don't particularly like our presence, although they cut trees to specified guidelines that are inconsequential, meaning no replanting and indiscriminant chopping, leaving healthy, noncommercial trees as waste."

"For the fire part, has anyone suggested cut-lines to stop their spread?"

"Yes, TJ, but the forest is too tall to make the idea viable. Even large highways are inadequate to stop the highest canopies from igniting the other side." Sloane explained further, remembering the important name, which Foster or Baldwin seldom used, preferring their own nicknames for the young man.

"The Brazilian stretch of the Amazon River is wide enough to act as a cut-line, stopping fires from spreading across to the other side. As you've noticed, traveling along its northern-most bank, we saw oceangoing vessels and cruise ships capable of sailing the length. The river narrows once in Peru. Good photographic opportunities do not readily show themselves along such a large river's shores until crossing the border. Between our turnoffs, on the southern side of the river, lies one of the Pilot Program's laboratories and research centers, where you can see for yourself whether they're doing a proper job." The blond captain smiled back at the happy face of the youngest.

"Huh! See, Sloane, they at least try." Phoenix smirked at the larger man; relieved the Brazilians had organized something out of the chaos.

"Glad I was wrong. So, what's cooking, Kenny?"

"Spiced sausages, hash browns, fried stuffed tomatoes filled with tropical vegetables and herbs, plus fresh fruit, and several more cups of coffee."

"Good God, I'm going to weigh a ton if we don't start walking it off." The four men laughed, three understanding one's appetite waned and food consumption diminished the hotter and stickier conditions became.

They ate in dryness, happily chatting in the screened and planked covered area used for food preparation, dining, and gathering. As dawn brightened the sky to overcast, the vessel once again slipped quietly into the Amazon. Traveling at speed, Phoenix sat and watched the passing landscape of blurred green, unable to see its likeness on the other side. He had not realized the great width of the river, growing more aware that the pictures he admired, of the largest water system in the world, were shot either up the tributaries or closer to the source in Peru. The day disappeared as two friends sat close together, both contemplating the number of miles to travel and the quantity of work required. Turning into the first designated tributary had the Americans stirring; Trevor climbed the ladder to the uppermost seat with Phoenix at his heels. Something new in an ancient habitat for the former, an eye-opening spectacle for the latter, both men settled in for a drastically slower pace. A hint of a beautiful, entrancing photograph played out; what the old world once was and the new world hoped to see and save--a primeval forest--the last on the planet of such magnitude and grandeur. The jungle cast four men and a boat as pinpricks on a canvas of deep green.

Connecting with the widest part of the tributary, from where many rivulets ended their journey and some only started, the vessel stopped several times for Sloane to set up equipment, finally to rest in the damp, graying twilight. Their anchorage location gave Trevor an instant hit of possibilities, and he fired off a roll of film over an hour's time. Before night descended, he captured the distant green covered mountains, tall trees overhanging both sides of the river, and the water sparkling under a short moment of sunshine, which highlighted the wet upper canopy, the sharp rocks, primordial ferns, and the natural watering hole. Rain started to fall softly and the mist slowly rose, but Trevor continued to shoot several exposures offered by the eerie silence of a jungle in transition. Birds and monkeys grew silent; other nocturnal creatures came out to play, including several alligators awakened by the camouflaged vessel that came to a final stop in a safe position. A good start, Sloane climbed down with his camera case, to lean with the others against the railing, a time for reverence of the majestic forest.

"Can't deny the awesome beauty of the place, Trev, but why here? What do you see? What makes this place different from any other part of the forest?" Phoenix assumed the role of journalist, waiting for the insightful wisdom of his partner and what the man perceived in a finished photograph.

"Something untouched; something of magic. Look at the floor before it becomes too dark. You'll discover plants from an ancient time, perhaps before the evolution of man and other forms of life. Very few places in the world have such ancient woodland growth. Even in South America, such foliage can't regenerate after fires, logging, mining; even the spreading tourist eco-destinations kill these rare species unknowingly, decimating many entirely. This rainforest can grow back over time, but never with these species of ferns, or the trees that may be indigenous to only this small area."

"A delicate dilemma."

"Too delicate, kiddo, and thus the need for protection."

"Same for rare species of insects and birds. What wildlife exists in there?" Phoenix pointed toward the forest floor, while listening to the bewitching baritone voice that seduced him to his knees. His friend had regained his feelers and wallowed in the sanctity of life and death, danger and beauty, silence filled with life.

"Thousands of different insects, multitudes of birds, monkeys, and snakes, plus our friend the jaguar: all live here, kiddo, including the alligator checking out the boat."

"Really! Where?"

"Directly below us. One of the reasons I'm not a big fan of water." Trevor laughed, pulling the young man away from the railing and wiggling a pointed finger at the petit nose. "Remember, no feet in the water, no hands in the water, no walking along the edge of the water without undue caution and deliberation. Let Nigel, Kenny, or I help you find a safe path before venturing on your own, something I hope you won't try. We know the dangers lurking beneath and along the shore. One of us will tell you when it's safe, until you get an idea of jungle survival. If we have to wade in, the proper equipment will be used; those remaining onboard will watch the person's every step." Trevor looked down into the beautiful eyes, wanting to kiss the perfect lips a second time. Refusing to draw away, he continued his gentle gaze at the diminutive figure who looked exceedingly adorable in the paling light.

"Whatever you say, Trev. Why are you looking at me like that? What did I say?" Phoenix tensed, not understanding the slight smile and the flash of fire in the dark eyes.

"Just wondering how we made it this far, Passepartout. After the problems we've hurdled, you're still with me, doing a fine job. Even though we're hot, wet, and uncomfortable, I can't wait to hold you close. Don't misinterpret what I said as a come-on line; just go with the flow of our platonic relationship." Trevor blinked away the stare and turned at the call of their names. Dinner was ready.

"I feel safe with you, Trev, although wary about your intentions sometimes, like right now."

"No intentions but to hang onto my first and favorite partner. Come on. Let's get out of the drizzle and eat one of Baldwin's massive dinners. Now that we're skipping lunch, I'm up for a large meal."

Two friends slept unperturbed under one sheet, swathed in a cocoon of mosquito netting. They ignored the heat, the smell of insect repellent, and the tiny rivulets of perspiration coursing down their faces and chests. Trevor's musky scent enveloped Phoenix, as if sleeping with his fathers, and yet the intimacy stirred other emotions, all hidden discreetly after years of practice.

Allotted only a week of intensive photography in this enclave of magic, the journalist became increasingly aware of Sloane's insightful abilities, experiencing the magic on his own. Enraptured by the awe-inspiring visuals during the day, he spent the wet dreary nights writing his impressions to jungle sounds; even the roar of a large cat snapped him to attention, searching immediately for words to describe the lone hunter's powerful snarl and what it meant to him.

Their last few days near the source, Sloane gathered enough equipment for an overnight stay at a higher elevation, to look down at the gushing falls during various lighting conditions. With sufficient resources for several days, they tackled the climb, stopping halfway up the slope in a clearing, which offered a magnificent view of dripping foliage, misting mountains, flittering birds, vibrating colors, and the splashing source of the falls that spilled into a dazzling pool. The sound of the cascade would lull them to sleep this night, both men at peace after a sultry, hot ascent, with clear sky overhead that promised a break from the light rain. They set up camp early: Phoenix busily secured tent awnings, ensured their lighting system worked, and read instructions on the dried food packages before darkness fell.

Sloane planted his camera and small tripod in an appropriate position and began the task of waiting. With the first shots rifled off before the sun dropped below the trees, a second set captured the rising sequined veil of the falls, mingling with the obscure moving shadows of the spray. The minimal differences of the play of light and dark were difficult to catch on film, but the artist snapped image after image anyway. His last set for the night, the fastidious photographer returned the important equipment to its case and stowed everything in the tent. Checking and securing the camp once more, he could rise safely at the first hint of light.

From his strategic perch, to witness the sunset behind the upper canopy of the jungle, Phoenix watched every move Trevor made, until the tall, handsome man turned a tranquil smile toward his awe-struck partner and the scene that framed him in the background. Also diverting his attention afar, beyond the range of distinguishable shapes, the younger man attempted to view the vista with an artistic eye. The wild land held him spellbound, while he sat on a precipice overlooking the spectacular. No words could interpret the feelings tingling every molecule of his body, or the joyful tears washing his face. Majestic, inspirational, spiritual, a natural wonder filled his head with dreams to keep the forest safe. Trevor's presence jolted him into thinking of words; nothing came to mind.

"What's up, kiddo?"

"Not a thing, and that's a problem. You're lucky, Trev, able to capture a moment, never to see the same view twice, like those snowflakes you mentioned. How can I catch the essence in the limited art form of words?" Phoenix shook his head and placed his forehead on his knees, securing his bent legs with his arms.

"You'll find them for those who can't visualize the magic in the photos." Trevor put his hand on the back of the pastel head and laced his fingers through the thick, but finely textured hair, which grew wavier in the high humidity. "Sun's almost gone; we have just enough light to eat and ready ourselves for bed. We'll get another early start tomorrow. Stay in the circle of solar lamps, which will remain on throughout the night and well into morning. They'll continue to glow forever with a touch of sunlight each day. How many more trail packs of food do we have?"

"Plenty, although, if left alone for long, one could certainly grow tired of nuts, grains, and dried fruit. Water is sufficient, as is our juice supply. Kenny believes long hikes require a sugar fix. Could use one now, considering the effort climbing takes out of you in damp heat. I felt like I was slogging through mud with an equal weight on my back."

"The high humidity has finally affected my inland partner, has it?"

"No shit."

"Better leave the juice for extraordinary circumstances, but drink lots of water. Even though the atmosphere may be humid, a person still sweats profusely. You'll sleep tonight, preventing a header off our perch." Trevor tightened his grip on the pastel locks and affectionately pulled the head up from its resting place on bony knees.

"Yeah, I'm really tired, although enchanted by this land. Would be nice to jump into the pool created by the falls. Any chance of that happening tomorrow?" Phoenix batted his flirtatious eyelashes, obviously forgetting his phobic desire to remain dressed. The action could drive the photographer to leap in himself, if he could not net the white, fluttering butterflies with his fingertips, or kiss them gently before they flew away from the dewy violets.

"After morning shots from this vantage point, we'll head down to the pool for a few more and have a look. The water at the base of any falls is usually safe from predators that hate the pelting of a heavy deluge. How will you manage a skinny dip without freaking out on me, because if you go in, so am I?"

"Oh! Actually the idea of being naked never occurred to me." Phoenix pulled away, considering his ongoing struggle over his mutilated body, although Sloane had seen parts of it. "I'll stay in my shorts and singlet."

"And walk back to the boat wet and uncomfortable. I don't

think so."

"Man, I'm already drenched from the humidity. What difference would it make?"

"Come on, Phoenix, I've seen most of you, and I know you're comfortable with me by this time, certainly enough to shed your last remnants of apparel. Time to start loving yourself, kiddo. There's no sin or ugliness in unavoidable scars. Look at them as a source of intrigue and mystery, making up a great story to explain them, while protecting whatever you're hiding."

"Who said I was hiding anything?"

A rolling of eyes and a deadly squint from under the dark lashes, there seemed little else to say; the photographer was laughing at him. To turn the frown into a smile, Trevor switched gears immediately. "You've never explained your *accident*, Phoenix. I can't imagine what occurred, but I did promise never to ask. I don't intend to." He ruffled the hair playfully, wishing he had left the subject until ready to leap into the refreshing pool.

"Something I can't disclose as yet; I'm sorry, Trev. One day maybe, if I can spit it out." A frightening memory stiffened the small body, unable to shake off the lawyers who had forced him to relive the terror, blinking answers to awkward, accusing questions. Every conscious second of a never-ending nightmare had been exposed to ridicule. Caly and Twister always stood by, holding his immobilized fingers and calming his severed nerves; he thought himself better off dead than another round of torturous reminders that hurt so badly.

"Phoenix? Where are you, baby? You wandered off again. Time to turn on the lamps to ward off preying animals and go to bed. Nervous?" Having felt the small body tighten, Trevor changed the subject, nullifying the usual shiver that ran from the man's nose to his toes when questioned further.

"Not really. Spent many a night under the stars when young. The wilds of Colorado have plenty of ferocious animals wandering about, trying to find your stash of camping goodies. My body's weary after the slippery climb; a cot, to stretch out, sounds almost lavish out here." Phoenix rose and extended a hand to his larger partner, a useless gesture, but a welcome one. The two lay comfortably with a solar generated lamp overhead, lighting the mesh and canvas lodging. Awnings would protect them from a sudden downpour, while elevated cots would deter those creatures that had entered in a moment of fluttering flaps before zipping the closure shut. Sleep prevailed, although both men were vigilant of the slightest paw or footfall.

Phoenix startled from his slumber at an unknown noise. Keeping very still and holding his breath, he whispered, "Did you hear that?"

The older man responded with a disgruntled groan, as one large hand reached for the solar light and turned it on, accidentally blinding his young friend. "This noise?" Sloane continued after the rude interruption, rather dismayed being caught doing the unthinkable.

"Yeah. What is it?"

"Just me."

"Are you okay? Not a headache I hope." Phoenix uncovered his eyes and moved to a supine position, turning his head and blinking at the distinguished profile of the man lying a foot away from him.

"I'm fine. Wait a second and let me finish."

"Finish what?"

"Shit... Unh... I'm jerking off. Do you mind?" Trevor had woken to one of his wet dreams, certainly early enough to capture his essence in his hand. Every dream gave him pleasure, and more so on waking halfway through, to receive the satisfaction his own hands lovingly bestowed.

"You're kidding!"

"No, and... Oh, man... Yeah... Much better." The older man immediately relaxed, chuckling lightly with the eventuality finally actuated. Keeping tight control of his needs, since Phoenix started lying next to him, time came to reveal his sexual side to a naïve phobic friend.

"You're kidding!"

"You said that. Leave my wet dreams and their pleasurable results to me, Phoenix. I enjoy them." Sloane planned to continue the dialogue in some manner, wishing to obtain a few answers.

His partner, however, could only glare at him, aghast at the wanton actions, and then, to add fuel to the fire, turn away in disgust. "This is way too personal, man."

"Nonsense. You and your straight college room-mate probably had jerk-off contests while waiting for an early morning exam."

"I attended a Christian college remember."

"I forgot; Christian's go blind if they masturbate. You've never played how far, how many times?"

"No! Never! You're grossing me out! Can I look now? Have you secured the beast in your shorts?"

"Divert your eyes if you feel uncomfortable, because I'm not quite finished. I happened to like playing with myself. Look at it. What amazing hardware we men are blessed with. Like a living creature, separate from its host but yet attached, your cock reacts to a multitude of emotions you can't face yourself. We carry with us a soft serpent looking for a warm place to harden, nestle, and spill its seed."

"Give me a break!"

"Why so defensive, Phoenix? You have one, which you won't let out to play."

"Unfair, Sloane. You know what I am, and there's little you or I can do about it."

Trevor turned his head to stare at a tasty earlobe, one to nibble on during a long rainy afternoon. "How much is riding on such a bet?"

"Go away."

"Good response, considering where we are. Pull that pecker out and let's play."

"Did you arrange this little side trip to molest me? I'll kill you first." The low growl threatened with the vengeance Sloane recalled from one night in a dark New York street.

"You actually would, wouldn't you? Why, Phoenix? What's your real problem? I know your juicy rod grows hard on its own, and you control the impulse until you're writhing in pain, not ecstasy." Sloane sat up, adjusted his own relieved snake, and swung his legs over the side of the ten-inch high cot. Feeling he was in a comfortable squat, he leaned forward into his thinking position.

Terror hit Phoenix first: another night alone with someone bigger and stronger. Unable to cope, fear continued to rise, as did the hated monstrosity under discussion. A single sob started an onslaught of pleas, as a large hand touched his arm and turned the emotion of oncoming tears into a yelp of frightened surprise.

"Easy, kiddo, I won't touch you. Nonetheless, we should talk about his particular phobia. You're not *sexually inert*, although you do have an aversion toward anything sexual. Give me the truth. My gut tells me you've thoroughly studied the matter, wishing for an easy cure. Unfortunately, discovering your symptoms gave you a name for the real condition, causing you more strife. The term is as terrifying as the problem, isn't it?" The tender touch brushed the quivering face, but Phoenix pulled away, preparing for an attack.

"Stop, Trevor. I can't deal with this. You're scaring me." The potential downpour of salty droplets stopped abruptly. Phoenix tried to subdue his racing heart and a hard-on that fear created.

"Why? Why are you so afraid? If your woody frightens you, then you're probably terrified of sex. Listen, kiddo, the condition only manifests more fear. I'd like to help in some way, even just talking with you." Sloane continued to brush his own lips with his fingertips, knowing he had gone too far, but unable to stop. He needed information from the sole person who kept the most important part of his life secret.

Phoenix lay still, controlling every emotion felt. "Why are you doing this to me? I thought we were friends."

"We are; that's why I'm concerned. At your age, you should be having wet dreams and jerking off regularly."

"Wet dreams--eons ago--and long forgotten. Tell me this, Sloane, since you're bent on ruining this expedition, what causes your wet dreams, like the one tonight?" A change in subject may be an escape; the smaller man gathered his fortitude to retaliate gently, forcing his inquisitor to answer rather than ask.

"A recurring one, always pleasurable and always sinful. I see three young men, with firm little butts, dancing and cavorting naked down Broadway. They giggle, they're adorable, and they make me horny as hell." Trevor stopped his compulsion to stroke his lips, leaving his hands to dangle between his bent knees.

"Young, like me?" Phoenix could keep this up until his interrogator grew weary of the game.

"Yes, if I could get you to giggle more. What were yours about so very long ago?" Returning quickly to questioning mode seemed a likely way back to the intense conversation originally started.

Phoenix gulped and blurted out the unexpected. He did remember and in detail. "I'd be flying, turning, spinning, hair blowing in the wind, my ski tips in the foreground. One last flip and Rory would be under me, his..." The tears finally started with a fond memory. After years of stowing away his secret desires, a handsome man challenged him. He lost the will to fight.

"Please continue. Don't be shy."

"You know, and I can't say it."

"Yes you can. His what--pecker, arse, ski poles--what?" Trevor refused to give up. Freeing Phoenix from his cocoon was more important than sleeping through the night partially satisfied.

"His... his... I'd fall to ground, impaling... No, I can't do this. Please, Trevor, stop." More gully washers coursed down the perfect face, the violets drowning in grief.

"Okay, slow down. Steady, man. You certainly can't talk about sex, let alone masturbate. Will you do something for me?" Sloane touched the heaving chest, calming the heart rate with a gentle rub. "Deep breath. Good man... and another."

The downpour eased, breathing grew deeper, and Phoenix had a few seconds respite to answer. "That's a hell of a question after our discussion."

"Yeah, but hey, we're in the middle of the rainforest, with little else to do but share experiences and secrets. Come on; look at me."

The shaken kid wiped his face with his hands and raked his fingers through the avant-garde colors. Once settled slightly, he turned to look at Sloane who smiled and shook his head. "You're one enormous conundrum, kiddo."

"Sounds painful."

"Very funny." Sloane smiled wistfully, continuing to apply warmth and a little pressure to the quieting chest. "The last time I saw you with a woody, you seemed unable to deal with it. I want you to touch yourself, just once, to let me know the extent of your fear."

"Don't be absurd. You're so wrong. I'm a non-sexual entity; and what you perceive as normal, I'm a long way removed." An attempt at a chuckle failed; Phoenix was devastated.

"I've never seen you scratch yourself or use a urinal. Now, just put your hands over your crotch. Nothing drastic or harmful, just a hand on your genitals." Trevor pulled his own hand away to meet the frightened eyes. "I'm sure you can prove me wrong."

"I... No, I... Please, Trevor!"

"Try." Sloane watched a resolute young man attempt to conquer a fear just for him. The small hands splayed, reaching down and hovering over the designated goal. Fingers stretched to their limit; hands shook violently. With a reflex action, a larger hand forced the smaller pair down, and the photographer jumped on hearing a banshee's scream coming from the body suddenly flailing about.

Phoenix twisted in the small cot like a trapped wildcat. His organ stiffened against his will; his own touch suffocated him in terror. Someone pinned him down, but his own hands pressed against his genitalia for the first time in ten years. He roared at the man holding him. "No! No! Don't. God, please don't!"

"Easy, my friend. I'm just holding your hands. Relax and breathe deeply. The hard part is over. It's time, kiddo, time to feel something good, something nice. You've held back so long, you've forgotten how wonderful your wet dreams of Rory felt."

"No!   No!"   The negative response came out in little whimpering pleas, but the large hand prevented escape. Phoenix clamped down hard on his lip, waiting to be hurt, waiting to be used by too many.

"Hush now. I'll take my hand away while you leave yours where they are. Slowly, baby, slowly. No one's going to hurt you. Leave your hands right there and hold yourself. You're doing fine." Trevor pulled away again, but left his hand an inch from the two vibrating against an organ that required no further stimulation; an arousal induced by unspeakable, unbearable fear.

Sloane had taken his experiment too far, and Phoenix's brain spun back to the last attempt made and the resulting agony. Pressure mounted within his body, reaching a point even an experienced man could not avoid. He cried in alarm, unable to come, but also incapable of holding back. "Trevor, I can't. Help me! Help me stop it!"

"Too late, kiddo. Settle a bit and relax if you can. Take your hands away." Concerned out of his mind, the big man had little difficulty with his last request; Thornton-Jones pulled away as if scalded. Settling onto his knees at the foot of the cot, Trevor issued soft commands to lay still. With his partner hysterical and out of control, he slipped the tan underwear down, without much more ado than already exhibited, and exposed the strangely lined stick of dynamite. Wetting his lips, he leaned forward, engulfing the explosive in his mouth, instantly receiving a reaction. The white angel came, and came again. Years of anguish spewed sporadically into the talented orifice, while a tongue unintentionally teased a terror-stricken man to his grave. One long scream and satisfied groan, Phoenix laid wasted, panting heavily and sobbing like a hurt child. "Hush now. Hush." Easing the young man into a sitting position, the demons of ten years saturated Sloane's singlet.

"Trevor..." The whimper could break the most stalwart heart.

"I know, baby. Take your time." Holding the shaking body firmly against his chest, calming the fright, soothing the mental pain, the older man licked his lips, savoring the salty ambrosia on his tongue and swallowing the remarkable taste of an unearthly creature. "Did I hurt you?"

"No." Timidity and wonder oozed from the sigh exhaled by a man who misunderstood the moment of his first loving time.

"Do you feel better?"

"Yes."

The two men sat together through a long night enveloped in a quivering, fragile embrace. A soft kiss on top of the white head seemed the only recourse to quell the thumping heart. Trevor had overstepped the relationship, but succeeded in easing a man's anxiety, if only for a moment. Phoenix clung to him, coming to grips with the occurrence and stifling a burst of rapture.

Chapter XV

Rain bombarded the canvas dwelling as one man clutched the other, both awake, both frightened. Still in the dark, but for their solar lamps, including the one in the tent, they waited in silence until the surprise torrential downpour eased enough for them to break camp. Concluding that morning photographs from their precipice were impossible, the photographer plotted a course downward to the pool's edge. Slippery going, they stopped several times to adjust bags, apparel, and footing, forever unspeaking, always waiting.

At one rest stop, they sat overlooking the bubbling pool, hypnotized with the close-up view of nature's fountain. Remarkable, even in a black storm, Trevor pulled out his camera, snapping picture after picture, attempting to show heavy rain in a still photograph, while stewing over his unprecedented behavior the night before, regretting every moment. His blatant molestation of a man obscured every thought; something he would never contemplate, let alone consider doing. The savageness of the jungle played out his torment on an innocent so frightened, Sloane reeled at his intent. Nothing justified the action: nothing.

Phoenix remained transfixed, watching the water gush through the tight rocks, comparing the dance to creamy fluid sporadically oozing into a sensuous orifice. Overcoming his shock, he drew in his breath, strangely feeling better for the assault he craved, yet unable to take the next leap. A forced gesture created a new man; Trevor Sloane supplied the impetus. The naïve journalist loved the tall, attractive man on first meeting; he now grew intensely besotted over the legend. Wanting more, but unable to ask, he continued to stare straight ahead waiting.

An unexpected treat, the rain subsided to allow a sprinkling of sunlight to shine through the dark clouds, enough to create a rainbow that ended in the pool. The spray from the falls glittered with color, dispersing the prism as it touched the fractured golden mirror. Treasure lay before them in natural wonder; the soft clicking of a camera the only sound made by the intruders. Turning frowns into wistful smiles, they sat and watched, forgetting what went before, keeping still in this land of magic, and expecting an elusive unicorn to emerge from the dark forest to drink from the mystical fairyland waters.

Gone as quickly as it appeared, the sun hid behind a gray thundercloud, enclosing them once more; the resulting deluge broke their enchantment. In silence, two men slipped and grappled their way back to the vessel; a wielded machete cleared the way with little damage done to awaken ancient spirits. Phoenix reached for Foster's hand and received a merry greeting, which he did not return. With no eye contact or a hint of gratitude from their youngest passenger, the Englishman turned to the next man climbing aboard. Trevor shook his head, a subtle warning not to disturb either man's countenance. While changing into something dry, two men wrestled over something to say; two men could not open their mouths to speak.

Sloane emerged first for a needed nerve settling coffee, finding the British couple fingering their teacups, as if contemplating the drinkability of a potion steeped too long. Again, the photographer shook his head and poured himself a mug of hot, strong java. Unable to handle the troublesome situation, Nigel arose, placing a reassuring hand on his partner's shoulder. Gathering his will, he poured a second cup while Sloane took a seat across from the brunet with the deep frown. Without looking at the tall American, the equally concerned skipper stepped through the hatch, descended the stairs, to find Phoenix drumming an empty page in his notebook.

"Brought you a cuppa, pet. A sweet treat you're probably ready for after two days without hot food and beverages." He set the steaming coffee beside the agitated fingers, receiving only a soft thank you for his kindness. The perplexed blond botanist withdrew and climbed up to the galley, the natural gathering place in any home. This particular evening life grew increasingly tense.

"Did you get some good shots, Trevor?"

"Possibly a few outstanding ones, Kenny; if they develop into what we saw. May take my entire technical prowess to achieve the effect I'm after."

"Did TJ enjoy the outing?" Trying not to pry, normal questions seemed appropriate. While Baldwin continued, his partner watched for reactions.

"For the most part."

"Seems rather withdrawn this evening."

"I need to speak with him, but have no idea what to say, Kenny. I'm sick... sick in more ways than one." Sloane rubbed his temples, his headache mushrooming into a severe migraine.

"Are you still getting those headaches, Trevor? Have you seen a doctor?" Baldwin reached over to touch the large man's forehead, an automatic reaction for one who could heal.

"Went to several, but there's no cure. We've tried changes of diet, sleep patterns, light therapy, nothing works but relaxation. Unfortunately, they seem to be growing worse." Sloane leaned back with mug in hand, sipping slowly. Caffeine was a substance that did not help either.

"Stress induced, old boy, and I'd say the young man below might be the cause. Anything you'd like to share?" Foster took over. Distress in both men was obvious, and for friends and co-workers on a long journey, they needed to find a solution to their undefined problem. "What can we do to help, mate?"

"Feed me to the alligators and put TJ on a flight home to Pueblo."

"Sounds serious. I'd suggest you speak with the lad first. Depending on your crime, we may just throw you in ourselves." Nigel quietly sat next to Sloane on hearing footsteps from below and continuing up the steep, narrow stairwell, while Kenneth eyed the forlorn creature stepping out of the hatch to top up his beverage.

The small figure turned toward the others, having gathered his wits and walking the few paces to sit next to Baldwin. "Hi, guys, did Trevor say anything of our overnight adventure?" The voice sounded subdued, depressed, while the eyes remained downcast.

"We hear you may have captured some brilliant shots. Anything particularly special you can tell us about." Reaching for a towel to finish drying the damp white hair, the brunet quizzically eyed the two across from him, only receiving shrugs, and a strange, quiet utterance from the journalist.

"Yeah. There's a pool of gold at the end of the rainbow."

"How wonderful! You've discovered the Leprechauns' secret." The surprised Englishman again glanced at Trevor who only nodded before they all withdrew into their own thoughts. Knowing the youngest needed time with his partner, the long attached couple uttered excuses to leave, one to plan dinner, the other to finish labeling their findings.

"Phoenix..."

"Trevor..."

"Allow me to go first, kiddo. I don't have your words to describe how badly I feel. Well aware of your concerns over your body image, and now realizing the extent of your fear of sex, I can't imagine what made me believe I could help. Overcome by madness is my only excuse. I am sorry, Phoenix, so terribly sorry. I'm deeply ashamed over my behavior toward you, inflicting another horrendous act upon you physically, and one you couldn't cope with. Please forgive me." Trevor rubbed his face, attempting to regain circulation in his throbbing head, concentrating on one particular area to ease the worsening pain. Never willingly would he prey upon the weak; he had done so with the man he adored.

Phoenix could not lift his eyes to meet the gaze so full of regret. Scared to stone at living in the real world, the journalist sat quietly across from a man who had opened a door. Satisfied, after a ten-year battle with fear, the deranged snake between his legs had brought him pleasure, but Trevor Sloane rued his actions. Shattered in mind, mortified to his inner core, the young man stifled his sorrow, but needed to say something without revealing his unfathomable feelings. His heart was broken, not for the doing, but for the man's unfavorable response to the events of the previous night.

"Please say something, Phoenix. You're ready to cry; and I'm certainly about to."

"No, Trevor. God, don't cry over what happened; but I need to know why you're mad at me. Did performing oral sex on me disgust you? Was I too unattractive, too repugnant, too horrible to see more scars? Was the act too repulsive? Oh Jesus, I taste ghastly! No wonder you hate me." Salty droplets bubbled under the white lashes, the tiny nose ran, and further troublesome words were sniffed back, causing Phoenix to choke. He immediately stopped his compulsion to leap into Sloane's arms; he could do nothing but sit and shake.

"Oh, baby, no! You're perfect--sight, smell, taste--what have I said to make you believe such a thing? I'm bewitched by you and have been since I saw you in Graham's reception room." Sloane reached for the vibrating hands, taking one in each of his. "Come here, kiddo. Come." Twisting his body lengthwise along the secured bench, he maneuvered the young man to his feet, finally to straddle his lap with little fuss. Releasing the small hands, he reached to touch, to appease, to capture the delicate white angel in heart, spirit, and soul.

Phoenix flung himself around the strong neck, not knowing what to say, except sob for eternity into a broad chest. Having misinterpreted the man's silence as anger and disgust, he had ignored the love. Now lost, he wished, but did not want: an unexplainable paradox. With his limit fulfilled, he had nothing to give. He had no idea how.

"Hush now. I could never hate you. Lift your head and look at me." Trevor gingerly pushed the smaller shoulders back to place his hand under the quivering chin. "Making love to you is a future hope when you're ready, and only if you desire the extreme affection. I pushed too hard, too fast, too suddenly; now you suffer from the consequences. What have I done? Tell me, baby; say you forgive me?" Wiping the perfect face with his trembling hand as he spoke, Trevor heard the clattering of red shards hit the deck. A heart broke as he predicted, but two, he never thought it possible.

"Yes." A warm stuttered whisper, exhaled through lips wet with sorrow, signaled a beginning.

"Thanks, Phoenix. I do love you."

"But, Trevor, I don't know. I don't know anything. Why is this so difficult?" Phoenix landed a light, frustrated fist against a chest too hard to make a resonate thud.

"What, expressing your feelings?"

"Yeah."

"I'm not the one to ask, considering what I said and how you interpreted the words. Just spit it out any way you wish, and we'll sort out the misunderstandings as they come." Trevor continued to stroke the face, preventing any precious liquid from escaping.

"I don't know anything about love, or making love. How do I return the gift you gave me? Perhaps only a one-time occurrence, what if you're not around if it happens again? I couldn't come on my own, Trevor. I couldn't." The devastation of the young man was complete. After one satisfying moment in his adult life, failure loomed before him.

"Time, Phoenix, you need time to get over years of doubt and fear. As for learning the techniques of a great lover, maybe I should listen to Wolfe, and you speak with Sebastian. We both would learn something." Sloane chuckled, dismissing what he read in Phoenix's words.

Unfortunately, the smaller man grew increasingly agitated, unable to connect the dots of reasoning. "I don't understand, man. How could I not know? How could I be so stupid? If I conquered the first bodily function, withstanding the agony, why not the second? Why? Why couldn't I put it all together?" Breaking away from one fatherly gesture, Phoenix again buried his head into a warm neck, wishing to suffocate in the scent of musk and to drown in the nervous perspiration dampening a clean khaki shirt.

"When in intense pain, a person may be unable to distinguish between a normal reaction and an excruciating memory. I have no understanding of your injuries, but your last ejaculation must have been a horrendous experience. Perhaps not fully healed when a subconscious act happened, like a wet dream, you immediately catalogued the pain in your mind as unbearable, closing the door, never willing to try again. What I did last night, did you find it hurtful?" Holding his breath and his diminutive friend in trouble, Trevor recognized the fine grid lines for what they were, a reminder of a number of operations. Whatever the cause, to necessitate surgery on a sensitive organ, one difficult to damage unless the testes were involved, was beyond the photographer's comprehension to calculate even a guess.

Phoenix continued to cry, now a need to release his stupidity, humiliation, and frightful anger in the easiest manner. His fathers wept in frustration; he learned from them that a man's sobs came from justifiable torment. Nonetheless, he had staid his emotions for years, hiding from the world until meeting the legendary photographer. Through all the surgeries, he remained resolute, refusing to give in to the pain. Time came to shed every tear held in abeyance by conflicting thoughts; each salty droplet saved in the shirt worn by a man who had aroused his consciousness with long forgotten sensations.

Sloane held tightly, one arm around the small man's waist, the other holding the heaving shoulders. Placing his chin on the white head, he felt the increasing desire of his partner for affection. He allowed Phoenix to nestle deep into his arms, while rocking him gently to ease the sorrow. The journalist struggled to get closer, while Trevor grew increasingly tense, feeling his manhood pushed against by an open crotch and thighs tightening around his waist. Fists loosened and pulled away from his chest; the small fingers reached up and entangled themselves in his hair, forcing the older man to look down at the closed crying eyes and the perfect lips whimpering unfathomable words. Those lips searched for a caress. Startled into full arousal, the photographer held the pastel head and kissed the softening moist mouth. He tasted the salty fluid dispensed from overflowing eyes, from a runny nose, and from the sweet coffee-flavored mouth. He moaned between the quivering perfect lips, as he swiped them clean with his tongue.

The damaged angel left reality to those who understood the concept, strangely letting loose his arousal, to grow hard against another engorged shaft. Hard and rough against his clothing, he commenced a rubbing motion aided by strong hands clasping his arse to cause greater friction. The harsh movement had his head swimming and his hips in constant agitation. Up and down and in against Sloane, he fell into the pleasure, whispering little pants and purring sounds into the mouth ravishing his lips. Struggling to maintain a rhythm, he let go of all fears, suddenly wetting canvas trousers and skin-colored briefs. A tremor quaked through his body, and he held the graying head tighter against his mouth.

The older man pulled away to breathe, stricken with shock at the momentous achievement and the intensity of his small friend. An unexplainable reaction, he would wait for the resulting relief or regret. A tongue tickling his ear brought him back into the action, to kiss the wet cheek, to untangle the savage fingers, and to subdue the hysterical caresses lavished upon his face and neck. He had never felt the likes of the seductive attack on his person. "Hey, kiddo, slow down." Trevor could barely speak; his own arousal ready to inflict more telltale stains on his clothes. "Come on, baby, loosen up. I won't let you go."

The small body relaxed slowly; the urgency to rub himself against another man climaxed. He blinked his violet eyes to focus on a slight frown, deepening the squint of the worried brown eyes. Feeling sticky and uncomfortable, feverishly hot and tired, his actions came straight at him, fast and hard. Confused, he released his hands, stared wildly about, and collapsed into the powerful arms that held his head and backside tightly against a larger body sweating and smelling of sex. Wanting to gag, Phoenix was mortified.

At a sudden clearing of a throat, Sloane looked up to see Baldwin speculatively arch his eyebrows, a signal whether to leave or invade the private moment. The stunned photographer nodded his approval, but continued to cradle an insecure young friend. With nothing settled, one man left his heart on the table, while the other muddled through the shame building in his head.

"Tea time, mates. Shepherd's pie tonight. A little comfort food for the misbegotten."

"Thanks, Kenny. We'll just sit a while and watch you work." Trevor held his position, lovingly caring for a fragile psyche. The cargo on his knee felt feather light, but the journalist's guilt weighed too heavy on the broader shoulders. Hearing nothing in his state of anxiety, the younger man hid his heartache in a warm recess. "Time to move, kiddo. Hurry now. We best go downstairs and clean up." Trevor pried the trembling body off him, standing him up, and handing him his wet tan hat to cover the results of his humiliation.

"God, I'm sorry; look what I've done!"

Sloane immediately stood and hurriedly helped Thornton-Jones through the hatch and down the stairs without a word to Kenneth. He had a mess of a man to sort out, and he had no idea where to begin. Regaining his composure and his voice, he started, "Everything's fine, Phoenix. You managed to come on your own, and the wonder and pleasure of the fact should excite you to your curling toes. Never regret this time, for I enjoyed your love making immensely, and hope you'll do it again."

"No! Never! I made a fool of myself, and it landed all over you! I thought you hated me, and what do I do: jump on you and hump you like a goddamn dog. What's wrong with me?" Phoenix struggled to shut the world out by reaching the stateroom first. A large hand prevented the slamming of the door. For a few minutes, two men stood silently, unable to look at the other. Another moment of quiet, Sloane dug out clean clothes for them both, while Phoenix stood looking down, covering his wet pants with his scrunched up hat.

"Nothing, nothing at all. Let's change and join the boys upstairs. Perhaps next time, we'll find a quieter, more private spot to lavish our attention on each other. For now, neither of us will mention the incident again, until it becomes clear in our minds as to what we felt and what we wish to do about it. Hurry or we'll miss dinner."

"I'm so embarrassed; I don't know what I did to you?"

"You aroused me unlike anything I've ever felt; that's what you did, behaving like the sexually aware male you've always been. I'll handle my arousal in the bathroom. Give me a minute, and I'll bring warm water so you can freshen up before changing."

Neither man was hungry, albeit the occurrence temporarily laid to rest. They both washed and donned fresh clothing, one in the stateroom, the other in the head. Trevor knew the stained clothing would go unnoticed by Baldwin; all three older men understood unexpected events. Tired and overly emotional, two men emerged through the hatch to take up sitting positions beside each other.

"You two ready for dinner?" Easy to see the strain on both men, Kenneth changed the seriousness of their predicament with trivial chitchat. He called for his partner to join them and to help him out of an awkward moment.

"Although we had a bitch of a hike today in the rain, I feel too wasted to eat much, Kenny." Trevor's baritone voice apologized, truly too exhausted after the exertion placed on his body, although he might have found a cure for his headaches. He hid the smile, not wishing Phoenix to misinterpret another expression or nuance.

"How about you, luv?"

"Your shepherd's pie smells good, but maybe just a small portion to settle my stomach." Phoenix also suffered from his uncharacteristic behavior, while hiding his own wondrous discovery.

Foster overheard the conversation, remembering the condition of the two men before he and Baldwin had departed to allow their friends a private moment. He did not like the idea of illness in either man. Climbing around from the side and ducking under the covering, he puzzled over his subdued passengers and squinted at his partner for some clue. He only received a shrug and a blinking of the eyes; the cryptic movements gave him a hint. "How's your headache, Trevor?"

"Gone for now, Nigel. Thanks."

"Good. Sip on this drink made from a wild herb we've been cultivating for its medicinal qualities. The tea seems to alleviate many an ailment. Now you, pet, let's stand you up and take care of those red eyes." The skipper first handed Sloane a cup of bitter tea, before forcing him to release the small man from their mutual clutch. With a tender touch, Phoenix did the man's bidding, standing precariously on wobbly legs. Hearing several sniffs, Nigel plucked out his clean handkerchief, handed it to one who testified to their use, and insisted the young man blow his nose. Like an obedient child, or a man whose fathers had administered aid when he was unable, Thornton-Jones complied and stood quietly, as the captain of their vessel wiped his face with a warm wet cloth and held the white head back to drop soothing lotion into the red encircled orbs.

After a thank you and now composed, the young man suddenly startled. "Trevor! Why didn't you tell me your head hurt? Are you feeling as sick as you did in Sao Paulo?"

"I'm much better after our chat, TJ. This tea has a rather sedating effect as well. Try it."

Phoenix took several sips from the cup offered, and immediately mellowed, able to eat dinner with a shy smile and enjoy the evening's conversation, while sticking close to the photographer's side. Weary physically and emotionally, two men retired early, both falling into a troubled sleep, deathly worried about the other. The photographer spooned himself around the tinier body and held fast.

Chapter XVI

After many inconsequential days of high-speed travel, bypassing the large inland port of Manaus and moving ever closer to the Peruvian border, the vessel finally slowed, quietly moving over the water of another feeder river. They slowly passed two deserted Yanomami villages, both of which would be forever remembered as unique historical documentation of the river people and on display in a Trevor Sloane coffee table book. Sightings, of the various tribes of indigenous people living in the rainforest, grew increasingly rare, the Brazilian Yanomami the most frequently seen and abused, whether exploited, diseased, or alcoholically repressed. Numbers diminished and certain tribes had succumbed to genocide by militant loggers and miners who trampled and ravished the land and its native people. In time, without government intervention, by all countries of Amazonia, most would perish; their culture, rituals, and ancient beliefs gone in the jungle mist, with only photographs of empty villages as their legacy. South America had much to answer for.

Keeping the significance of his images to himself, Trevor put away his camera. They drew closer to the drop off point, and once in the shadow of the northern mountains, overwhelming silence tensed nerves. All eyes alerted to anything human. Another branch of the tributary seemed easily accessible by boat, but the two Englishmen warily sought shelter for the craft elsewhere. With compass directions to the mine and their backpacks restocked, Trevor and Phoenix headed into thick forest for another overnight trip, a quick one, but a difficult traverse on a dangerous mission. Both men holstered handguns across their chests; both toted rifles at the ready. They entered the wild frontier of Brazil to capture the bad guys on film. Unauthorized mining and lumbering created a lawless society; the government turning a blind-eye if they saw profit in the venture. Two American journalists, along with two Englishman who discovered the travesty, would obtain proof of the rumored atrocities for the international community and wave the evidence in the faces of those who failed. Man-made misfortune awaited the careless, but Sloane was not a reckless man; his every move weighed heavily on the safety of a violet-eyed angel, one who had become withdrawn and tentative.

The co-ordinates led them to their first sign of humanity; a wheel-rutted road carved a straight line from the minor waterway to the mine entrance. With great caution, Trevor watched Phoenix scamper across the trail, ducking safely into the trees on the other side. On a hand signal, the photographer ran the distance, as a keen pair of eyes attentively scanned for armed lookouts. Warned of the possibility, no chances would be taken.

Quickly disappearing into dense ferns, they remained at the base of the mountain, taking the same route inland as the road, but a half-mile out of viewing range. They took turns cutting a narrow track. Sloane wielded the sharp blade, while Phoenix trekked vigilantly behind, securing their back and sides. Too soon, the sweep of the knife stopped, and the smaller man felt a hand cover his mouth, preventing an utterance and deterring further progress. In whispers, the two hikers exchanged instructions, remaining very quiet as Trevor pointed to an unusual sight. Agreeing over the importance of the shot, Phoenix nodded; both men dropped to a kneeling position in the underbrush of the jungle floor. Straining with the stillness, the youngest jumped when a webbed vine caressed his cheek; the same hand, which reined him in, stilled his racing heart.

With a finger to his lips for reassurance, Trevor found all they needed in a few shots, so close yet so very far away. The large zoom lens came out of the case, and with speed and dexterity, he mounted the invasive weapon onto the camera, finally screwing the equipment onto an equally heavy tripod. Their hazardous position justified the carrying of the ponderous objects and proved the insightful sixth sense of the photographer. While Sloane adjusted the focus, his Passepartout continued to watch for life forms: two-legged and four. The forest quieted closer to the mine entrance; few birds sang and the monkey population had nearly disappeared with the human drone and mechanical whine. Whispers were the key; a silent shutter a necessity.

With a handful of shots fired, the two men had little time to retreat to the other side of the road. Silently and swiftly, they moved far enough to stop and catch their excited breaths. A smile from the photographer eased the tension. They succeeded in capturing not only the camp, but also a large beer-bellied blond man, wearing steel-toed boots, a hard hat, and the latest in mining gear, staring down at a pint-sized nude Yanomami tribesman, with ornamental feathers in his black hair and shelled husks of tropical fruit to protect his male hardware. The second picture had caught the naked backside of the native running barefoot into the mine, while his blond-haired oppressor laughed.   A human-rights activist's dream photograph, the shot illustrated tyrannical force, and a wrongful act perpetrated on a primitive people.   Of anthropological and sociological significance, this image alone warranted the long trek and potential dangers.

A sudden yell in a Germanic language startled the pair; they listened.   Phoenix understood the term *jaguar* and gestured the information to Sloane.   Still unseen by mining personnel, the investigative team had another dire problem--a prowling, dangerous wild cat--they stood in its oncoming path.   Trevor quickly scanned the area all around, up and down. Pointing upward and tugging at a thick vine, he found their escape. "Can you hand-over-hand climb?"

"You bet."

"Take off your pack and climb to that large, flat leaf about 20 feet up. Hurry."

"I'm hurrying.   The third one up looks broad enough to stand on." Phoenix removed his pack and laid it down.   Pulling at nature's ladder, he felt like Tarzan, but the thought of the ferocious animal, which may be stalking them, stopped his flight of fantasy.

"Take your climbing gear. When you've found a solid location, stop, and throw down the rope. We'll repeat the effort for each pack. Nothing indicating our presence can remain. I'll be directly behind the last bag, scrambling up the vine to get the hell off the floor. The cat could sense our trail and come hunting for us. Remember, they're tree climbers. Quickly now."

The smaller man climbed expeditiously, feeling secure in his ability to overhand the vine while bracing himself with his feet against the trunk of the ancient tree.   Many hours scaling the false cliff face, specifically built for him at the ranch, had honed his skill and strengthened his arms. Without letting go of the vine, he tested the immensely wide limb of an unrecognizable tree. Feeling very small, he glanced upward, seeing green foliage rising more than one hundred feet above his head. No time to contemplate the majesty, he dropped the knotted end of his rope, hoping he had climbed high enough. Catching on branches, the yellow nylon was lowered numerous times, but vines, leaves, and a variety of natural protrusions hindered every attempt.

Trevor nervously watched, unable to hasten the delivery of the needed rope. Prepared to take flight if he had to, the thin thread of escape finally hit his head. Two sharp jerks, he received a signal indicating Phoenix held the other end firm. Tying several secure knots, he fastened the first pack loaded with heavy camera equipment that would break a path for the next bag. Another tug indicated that his partner had received his message, and the pack moved upward, while Sloane prayed the small man could withstand the strain on his breakable arms.

Thornton-Jones managed the task with great effort and secured the first pack. Eying Trevor's gear, he snatched a second nylon cord, tied a knot in the end, and lowered it, not taking precious minutes to untangle his own climbing gear. This time he had a maneuverable space to weave the strong but light rope through the branches, finally to feel the two tugs and to hoist the second pack. Again, he pulled an awkward bundle through palm fronds and assorted jungle foliage, while the natural ladder, which he had originally used, moved and straightened: Sloane had started his ascent. Ten minutes of fierce struggle later, the pair found a perch, safe from jaguars but not from men. A sharp crack of a rifle had them in a huddle; a second crack they waited for confirmation of a death. "Trevor! They're calling the men to fan the jungle. They'll be right under us!"

"Damn. Means the cat's still in the area, and if wounded... hell, he'll be fighting mad. We had better ensure our position goes unseen. Cut a few branches of overhead leaves to camouflage the packs. Be careful and quiet."

Phoenix busily hacked off a few leafy-covered limbs from a neighboring invasive tree. Sufficient to hide their bags, and taking only minutes to accomplish, they now needed cover for themselves and a few more branches were cut. The journalist finished the task expeditiously; and Trevor motioned the white-haired man to lie prone, to stretch his arms to the side fully extended, and to grip firmly to the edges of the wide, flat, but exceedingly thick leaf they rested upon. While the smaller man adjusted his position, the photographer heard the voices grow louder. He had little time, but carefully used his tall frame to hide his partner, distributing their weight evenly and covering them both with the cut foliage. Barely breathing, the two nervously waited, their precarious location only visible when Sloane forced the uncovered head to lie flat, using his chest to hide a color conspicuous amongst the forest green.

A third unnerving crack, from a different gun, brought excited chatter from below. Phoenix grasped the meaning of the important words and noticeably drew in a relieved breath. The larger man, protecting him, felt the tension ease as his young friend relaxed, a significant all clear that the lone cat could be scratched from their list of potential dangers.   A sad fact, but an appropriate necessity, a territorial, solitary animal, growing used to the scent of man, created too great a threat.

Once the miners returned to camp, Trevor slowly pushed himself into a kneeling position, looked carefully about, and then aided his young companion.   They remained quiet, only speaking with hushed voices.   The hot, sunny day darkened; evening descended.   Ill prepared to spend a night in a tree, they were stuck.   The fully charged solar lamps remained tied to the packs, their usefulness negated as the hidden perch, Trevor and Phoenix sat upon, swayed dangerously close to the camp.   Making the best of their precarious position, the two men remained alert through the long, humid night, one man leaning against a stronger one.   Awkwardness diminished, shyness subsided, two friends silently reflected on the exciting events of the day, plus the physical exertion of a long trek and a harder climb.   The rising vapors of the deadly jungle enveloped them.

Alerted by the dawn, tired eyes searched the surrounding area for signs of trouble.   The forest fell silent, not a whisper of air, only a muggy cloud of heavy humidity had the two men sweating.   Cramped by their unmoving position, Phoenix stretched first, strong hands holding his thighs to keep him from falling.   Assured his legs functioned normally, he changed places with Sloane to allow the bigger man room to maneuver.   With the snap of a spine, a relieved groan, the photographer straightened to full height, ready to tackle the descent.

Fastening their packs firmly, both men agreed to carry their unstable burdens, making the downward trip quicker, quieter, but much riskier.   Although the heavy foliage afforded some soundproofing, they waited until the miners were stirring, creating enough noise to deafen the repetitive chopping of a machete.   Trevor tried first; fully aware his trained strength gave him an edge over the smaller man.   Remembering a promise once made, he would be ready for a fall, softening the hard blow.   Once on floor level, he whistled to alert Phoenix, knowing sound traveled upward.   Disturbing nary an insect, he quietly waited for his young companion.

Far above the photographer's head, Thornton-Jones readjusted his pack, finally confident with the extra poundage.   Unafraid of heights, he was also a cautious man, testing everything before leaving the safe, naturally strong platform.   Grasping and stroking the vine, the texture felt strong enough--rough enough--to give him a decent grip. He started slowly. Halfway down he heard a groan and a thud; the sudden slack of nature's ladder indicated his partner had released the end. A breathless whisper for help had him sliding down the vine, now too rough, burning his hands. "Trevor! Holy shit!"

His best friend lay on the ground wrestling frantically with an anaconda! The twenty-foot snake formed a second ring to encircle an expanded chest and a full pack, while the first coil squeezed the lower rib cage.

"Quick, the machete." The lungs, once full of air, began collapsing with each word uttered; but Sloane understood they still required quiet. It was a matter of death or death.

Frantic, the small man took the cue, unsheathing the cutting device, now a weapon to strike a blow to kill a living creature. He stood clueless, unable to release his sight from the mesmerizing eyes staring him down.

"The head... Unh... lop off the head."

Weaving back and forth in motion with the large open mouth, Phoenix swung, as Sloane released his hands from the serpent's thinner neck. The head flew into the ferns, but the body continued to tighten, the tail flipping sporadically from the cut nerves to the brain.

"The tail... is coiling... Slice the damn thing off... close to me..."

Once again, the breathless instructions gave the inexperienced a direction to follow, and without hesitation he came down hard, cutting through powerful muscles, but not with sufficient power to severe the last ten feet of living, struggling contractions. A second try embedded the machete into the ground, the tail end wrapping around the blade.

"Jesus, let go! Let go! Step away... It's squeezing harder... Grab mine."

The death rattle sounding in the strong lungs had Phoenix leaping away from the twisting tail, finding their second machete, but again freezing at the sight.

"Hard... come down hard... lengthwise... Cut the sucker off me... Kill it!"

Two swift movements, the blade cut through the shimmering body, splitting the anaconda up the middle in two places. The pressure it exerted decreased, although the photographer continued to stutter directions in a whisper. "Place the knife... flat side down... between me and the snake... Turn the sharp edge up..."

Without further explanation, a man running on adrenaline

released his partner from the last remnants of the anaconda and hoisted Trevor into a standing position with extreme difficulty and tremendous willpower. "Shit, you're bleeding, bleeding badly! I cut you!" Phoenix put his arm around the big man's waist and used his other to grip the wrist hanging over his shoulder. He moved Sloane and their heavy loads away from the still twitching muscles of the dying snake.

"Better bleeding than dead... Let's get the hell... away from here." Sloane could barely breathe, his ribs broken, his fortitude waning with the pain of deep machete lacerations.

Phoenix supported too much weight, as he walked the larger man a fifty-yard distance. Sitting the photographer down, he removed the man's backpack, unbuttoned the shredded shirt, and carefully slipped it off, along with the equally bloody and cut singlet. Two deep wounds across the chest and abdomen caused the scarlet flow down the man's front. The youngest reeled, hanging onto an overhead vine for support while gulping for air.

"Easy, kiddo... Check my bag... Is everything intact?"

"Forget your bag. What about you? What do I do? Water, you need water!" Phoenix grappled for his canteen, handing the half-full container to a man unable to raise his arms.

"Yeah. Water's good." Trevor opened his mouth, making his frantic savior understand he required help. With fresh liquid trickling down his throat, he regained his voice, and his head cleared for the meantime. "My ribs are broken... Need to wash off the blood... Scent could attract... unwanted visitors. Hurry, kiddo, if we hope to make..."

"...rest, Trev, while I find the first aid kit. There should be something in there to clean your wounds. I'm sorry, man; I didn't mean to cut you." Phoenix dropped his pack to fumble for the Red Cross symbol and extricated the box from its secured position. Rummaging through the small containers, he had little experience with the various items marked.

"There... the brown bottle... Pour the liquid directly onto the cuts." Trevor felt himself failing, an unusual occurrence for the man. His ribs hurt and the cuts went deep, but neither should affect him to such a degree. Hurriedly done, the application forced him to gasp with the instant pain; he nearly passed out. Again, he shook his head to clear his mind. They were in trouble; their lives depended on the frightened white-haired angel. "We have decisions to make... It's up to you..." The brown eyes rolled skyward, making his upper body waver like a tree about to topple.

"Stay with me, man. I'll get us back. Where's your compass?"

"Pant pocket. The coordinates are set... just follow the heading." While the injured man gasped for words, Phoenix rummaged through both packs, taking out items essential for survival, which in the photographer's case meant his camera equipment. Rearranging his own pack, adding articles and removing others, the smaller man hoisted one heavy load onto his back and tightened it securely. The handguns and two half-full canteens hung from his neck to balance his load, as did the rifles strapped to the overly weighted bag. Now in a frenzied but organized race for time, he jostled the weight, regaining his equilibrium, and then awkwardly wrapped gauze around the large chest and the fat pad he had made with two shirts. Both men were down to dry singlets and canvas dungarees, enough clothing for a sweltering day. Once done, Phoenix stood ready, the compass now meaningless to him. The offshoot tributary seemed his best chance of finding transportation, a necessity for a man too big to carry and too weak to traverse the six-hour hike in one day. With only one idea, Phoenix assisted Sloane to stand, while willing his overstrained muscles, once again, to support the larger man with one arm secured at the waist and his free hand gripping the forearm that dangled over his shoulder.

"Ready, Trev? Hang onto me; we're going for a walk. Just put one foot in front of the other. Come on; help as much as you can." Struggling with too much weight and responsibility, the smaller figure guided his partner through stinging brush, heading directly for the road. Taking an hour to cover too short a distance, he made up his mind to attempt reaching a recognizable point first. He had to use the man-made trail, the only clearing in the dense forest, enabling him to see and hear anything that may follow. The walk to the road was unmerciful and daunting without a path to follow, unaware of what lay hidden in the thick foliage; but he kept his eye on his marker and continued in a straight line, seeing his objective as a line of light through the trees. Finally reaching the road, he stopped, sipped a small portion of water, and rested a few moments without the strain on his back and around his neck. A little water for his rapidly fading friend, he staggered to his feet, expending too much energy to lift the large man a third or was it his fourth time, and to secure him on his left side. His arms ached; his legs burned; and his back was ready to snap, but they stepped onto the wheel-rutted road.

Inhaling deeply, Phoenix began to count, resolutely coaxing

Sloane to pick up his feet and attempt to walk. Fiercely battling to maintain a straight line, he took two steps, but his load pulled him backward three. Another two steps, he veered right and fell with a 230-pound Tight End pinning him. Scrambling out from under the entanglement of bags and a motionless body, he looked around, and started again. He dared not look at his watch, but the sun hung overhead without a cloud to hide behind, reminding him of the hours spent traversing such a short distance. Again, he tripped, recovered, and stumbled once more; his mind played out cruel imaginings, while he concentrated on the number of steps taken and the hours of time passed. There had to be a boat.

A branch cracked like a rifle shot, and the men fell to ground, startling the hallucinating man-child. He shoved his friend into the ditch and leapt off the road himself, scanning for the shadow that lurked behind. Nothing; he saw nothing. A thought scared him witless; jaguars attacked from any direction; he would never see the creature coming. Back on the road, he felt eyes piercing through him; he continued his march. Losing his fight to roust Sloane, he received only mumbled replies. Looking up for help, the sun had moved further west, but burned deep into his face and naked arms. He wanted to stop, to sleep, to die, but the responsibility he toted weighed as heavy as his backpack.

Another sound alerted him; the face of the blond-haired miner flashed before the violet eyes. The man laughed at him, not accepting any of the explanations he had made up for their presence. Ideas came and went, but the man still laughed. Phoenix was the man who ran naked into the mine, attempting to escape the clutches of the pompous blond pig chasing him. He had to keep moving; he had little time. They would ensnare him again in a dark hellhole. Step after step, pace by staggering pace, he continued his struggle, seeing another line of light on the horizon. The river lay not much further; there had to be a boat.

Smelling water like an injured, dehydrated animal, he forged ahead, finally reaching the sparkling green waterway. Off the road, he settled Sloane and the pack out of sight, while he checked the river for miners and a gift of a vessel. He found nothing; his heart sank; he had failed. Dropping exhausted at the river's edge, he slowly reached for a taste, but a rustling of leaves stopped him. He had left his partner alone with alligators! Unable to get to his feet, he pulled out a handgun and started to crawl.

"Trevor! I'm coming..." He collapsed, but attempted to raise his head, although knowing, if he opened his eyes, he would see an open mouth full of jagged, sharp teeth. Death drew nearer, and he had not a sunrise to console him.

Chapter XVII

Opening his eyes to ochre light, Phoenix quickly shut them again. Lost in mind and time, he thought the spirit world would glow bright white and would allow him at least one chance to reach heaven. The orange fire, behind the daunting black obelisks, meant only one thing: he waited in the southern end of purgatory, close to the gates of hell. His eyes already burned; his skin seared in painful red; unknown hands turned him over; he could not face the monsters convicted on his words. They had promised he would never see them again; the District Attorney had lied.

A cooling substance eased the burning sensation of his face, as gentle fingers applied a mixture smelling of ferns and earth. The scent wafted over him, and he opened his tortured eyes. A Yanomami tribesman smiled brightly, while finishing the mudpack on his raw nose. Too late to fear the indigenous people of Brazil's rainforest, he caved in on the man who hoisted him into a sitting position, to rest his head on a strong bony shoulder. A strange language and a pointing finger directed him to look at a sparkling green strip. The river: he had made it. The day's long trek ached through him; he had to find Sloane. Struggling to sit forward, he felt too heavy, unable to move a finger. A flashback returned him to a forgotten reality; plaster and plastics held him forever fast; but he inhaled deeply on seeing his partner awkwardly emerge from the trees, supported by two other tribal members.

"Phoenix..."

"Trevor..."

"They're friends... with a boat."

The younger man returned his gaze toward the water. Missed on his first glance, a long, unstable dugout lay disguised against the wooden pier used by the miners. He closed his eyes as a salty tear stung his face, but a comforting finger touched his lips, forcing them to open for a quenching drink. Needing as much as he could swallow, Phoenix moved his mouth to indicate his thirst; the naked man understood and poured the life-saving liquid down his throat, bringing some clarity to the journalist's world. He blinked away the dryness of his swollen eyes to focus on the primitive rescue craft. Two backpacks occupied the front; someone had followed him.

Although able to sit on his own after the reviving beverage, Phoenix still required assistance to stand and to stabilize his weight on shaky legs. Every muscle flamed with fire, every joint tightened in defiance, but he walked with assistance to the vessel. Settled near the back, by the gentle people of the river, he watched the Yanomami help his partner. The half-naked men had tremendous difficulty keeping the tall, muscular frame walking in a straight line, even after nursing him with the exotic cure-all. They finally had Sloane lying in the dugout, his head resting on Phoenix's thighs. Never had the young man been so grateful to look down into half-closed brown eyes and a muddy face. He touched his own, understanding how his new friend cooled his skin.

"You with me, Trev?"

"Phoen..."

"I'm here. Rest now. We're on our way." The smaller man laced his fingers through the graying hair, watching the glazed eyes close. His partner seemed very ill, shifting from lucidity to hallucinatory, consciousness to oblivion. Phoenix could only speak softly with consoling words that he hoped Sloane heard.

The long day stretched into early evening, when they stopped to pick up an older man who replaced one of their three saviors in the dugout. Laden with medicine bags, the healer immediately pushed Trevor's singlet up, removed the blood soaked makeshift bandage, and applied arrow-shaped leaves over a green paste on the open wounds, while the younger Yanomami pushed away from the bank, paddling a course downriver. Phoenix's attentiveness weakened; his eyes no longer able to focus. He ached to be home on Nigel and Kenneth's vessel, able to stretch out at will. Remaining in the same position as the rowers, he felt trapped, sick, and unbearably dizzy. He closed his eyes to the passing landscape, missing the alligators that swam too close, the boar that drank along the water's edge, and the birds that alerted to their quiet presence. Thoughts of Sloane prevented him from blacking out and falling into the dangerous, murky-green water.

The medicine man stared at the face too young for white hair and eyes of a color seen only in the feathers of a hummingbird. Fascinated by the paling creature behind the red face, blistered lips, and bleeding hands, he reached out several times to touch, to help the stranger, but withdrew the moment an eyelash fluttered. A few words, although not understood, seemed to console the silent man who appeared as ill as his supine comrade.

The journalist felt the naked man's intense study of him; but rather than freeze in fear, he breathed in a lungful of humid air, relieved the healer helped Sloane and, with luck, would return two lost souls to their friends. After more long agonizing hours under a blistering western sun, he opened his eyes with a sudden lurch forward caused by a heavy bump against a hard object. Blinking at the camouflaged hull of a much larger boat, he heard vaguely familiar voices breaking through the twilight. They were home.

Foster secured the two ends of the wooden dugout, giving some stability to the potentially dangerous vessel, one that may tip if the uninitiated moved incorrectly. With much chatter in a new language, Phoenix understood part of the intent through his confusion and waited for a signal to move. First, the bags were hoisted aboard the larger boat to make room for more difficult tasks. Through his hallucinations, he heard a voice calling his name. With much coaxing, he realized his turn came next, while the healer held fast to the comatose Sloane to prevent a fall into the dangerous water. Aided by the rower in the rear, the young American tried to clear his head, as he was lifted under the arms and balanced until steady. Strong calloused hands ensured his grip on the ladder and one booted foot found the first rung; but a larger hand reached for him and tightly grabbed his wrist when his weak grip failed. He looked up to focus; his blurred vision and fogged state only saw blond hair. The last blow, he faltered and fell back against the rower, causing the unstable dugout to rock.

"Easy, TJ. I have you, pet. Now, move one hand up, grasp the next rung. Come on, lad; you can do it."

The voice sounded reassuring and spoke in his native language. He reacted to the kindness, the softness, and he fought his way into some clarity. "Nigel?" With a hoarse croak uttered in a whisper from a parched throat, he received immediate confirmation.

"Yes, it's me, pet; I'm here waiting for you. Take one step up at a time." With one arm firmly held, the young man forced his clutching fingers to release and stretch for the next hold. His leg moved with the aid of the rower, to bend and raise his knee, and with intense coaching from above, found the second rung with his toe. The short ascent took time, but those who waited, in anxious frustration, would allow the ailing man the many minutes needed. On reaching the deck, his stiffening, burning legs buckled, saved from a fall by the captain's bear hug. "Good lad. Slowly. You're safe. Kenny will take you below, where you can lie down, out of the way of a more difficult task."

"No."

"Yes, luv. Come with me; we'll get you lying down before you fall. Nigel and I will take care of everything, but we need you to tell us what happened if you're able." Baldwin immediately had his arms around him, ushering him toward the hatch, an unlikely scenario for one whose legs operated independently from his brain.

"An... anaconda."

"Bloody hell! That explains his condition."

"What?"

"We'll explain later. Right at the moment, I need you lying on the closest bunk."

"Wait! I'm..." Phoenix had no time. He pitched forward and vomited; his empty stomach churned out of control; his head spun in circles of shadowed trees and early evening stars. Kenneth stopped immediately, tightening his grip around the small waist and allowing the man to purge green bile; the result of the medicinal herb the journalist had swallowed eagerly. The cure kept him upright on the journey downriver; the malady remained long after.

"When did you last eat?"

"Can't remember. Maybe yesterday."

"And water?"

"This morning... I think."

"Okay, luv, I must help Nigel with Trevor. Can you lie on this bench without falling off?"

"Yeah. Go. Go help. I'll be fine."

"Steady now. Here's a cold towel for your face. Don't move or you'll be trampled. One of us will be back shortly to ease your suffering." The worried botanist touched the sweating forehead, hesitating over the responsibility he had to leave. Nonetheless, his partner needed the information about the snake; it would change the treatment of their friend on the gurney currently being hoisted aboard.

Taking time, the men had Sloane lying on the biggest bunk below, stripped naked and hurriedly shot with a cocktail of antibiotics and an antihistamine. Baldwin cleansed the wounds, relieved that the medicine man had used recognizable herbs; a remedy he would have tried himself under similar circumstances.

After checking the photographer and ensuring his partner had everything he needed to mend the ghastly injuries, the captain crawled wearily out of the hatch to bid the Yanomami farewell and to thank them profusely for assisting strangers in grave distress. He heard the story before the men returned to their dugout, now laden with the extra supplies that the larger vessel stowed for emergencies. Under a veil of Sloane's jungle mist, the natives disappeared into the night, when Nigel turned to spot Phoenix sitting up, although his head rested on the table. "Well, TJ, sounds like you've had a hell of a day. The Yanomami would have helped sooner, but tend not to interfere with strangers, unless they sense it appropriate. They did remain close, however, watching you and Trevor climb the tree, coming to understand you were separate beings from the miners."

"They were there at the end, the only thing that matters." Phoenix sat up, coming to terms with the world out of its natural orbit.

"Yes they were. Let's get you cleaned up, your stomach filled with something you can tolerate, and your bumps and scrapes seen to. I hear you fell as much as you walked. You should be sleeping comfortably before night fully darkens, considering the exhaustive trip you lads trod. You're probably extremely pale under your crimson skin."

"Felt like I walked forever, and falling--I've never eaten so much dirt--and the weight. Hell, I should've only been thinking of Trev, leaving everything else behind."

"Not to worry, pet, you did just fine. Now, how sick are you?"

"A little better, Nigel, but I should be helping Trevor."

"Not after the trauma you've been through. Our large friend's wounds have been disinfected, temporarily stitched, and bound. We gave him a local anesthetic to numb the pain before we started. Kenny is now giving him a sponge bath to lower his temperature, as well as awakening him from his shock. Whether you like it or not, I'm taking care of you. First, a cool shower to alleviate your heatstroke and ease your sunburn."

"Heatstroke?"

"Yes and a bad case of it. You traveled a great distance in an open area, under a very hot sun and with little water. We've been straddling the equator since our voyage began: a treacherous place to walk without sufficient fluid, a hat, or sunglasses. You're also suffering from sunstroke, a dangerous combination that will make you very sick for a few days. Trevor is not the only one hurting, is he?"

"With more water to drink and cleaned up, I'll be fine. Really. I didn't think I'd make it, Nigel, believing the road shorter and easier than a jungle trek. Man, was I wrong."

"No, you were quite correct. Walking the road takes a fraction of the time, but you burdened yourself with three to four times your body weight. You're not an ant, TJ, but you did a fantastic job in spite of the load. Here's some cool water to get you hydrated. Drink slowly, only small amounts at a time. You don't need a stomach-ache along with everything else." The man in authority came around to sit by the ailing creature, carefully holding the white head attached to an aching neck no longer sufficient for support. With more care, he tilted the young man backward to trickle lifesaving liquid down the parched throat.

"Thanks. I prayed, to every god known to man, for a boat, believing the miners kept an emergency vessel in sight. There may have been one, but by the time we looked over the water, I couldn't think. I couldn't feel..."

"...shock and exhaustion, pet. You're barely able to function now. Have another sip." The captain again helped the young man take several small gulps from the glass, and then gently dabbed the blistered, swollen lips that cracked when they moved. "Come on with you, for we have a layer of mud and sweat to wash off, a lovely ointment for your tender skin, and fresh soft clothes. Kenny washed the apparel you left on board."

"Nigel, what's wrong with Trevor? The cuts are bad, I know that; and broken ribs are excruciating, but why's he delirious? He lost a lot of blood and couldn't breathe after the attack, but he wasn't hurt badly enough to slip in and out of consciousness as we walked. I thought he'd be strong enough to help me."

The blond graying man rubbed his chin, formulating a theory on a subject he could only guess at and hoped sounded plausible. "Do you know anything about phobias and shock?"

"Yes." Phoenix adjusted his position, unnerved at how much he knew of both conditions.

"Our friend's in shock over the snake. He's in a very bad way, more than likely succumbing to the incident in his head. Dehydrated and physically exhausted, from the struggle and long walk, hasn't helped, but he'll recover. We'll watch him while motoring across river to the next location. Not to worry, he'll be up and about before we reach our next target." Foster eyed the ailing man intently, noticing a flicker of puzzlement in the red-rimmed violet eyes.

"I can't believe he's afraid of snakes. Ophidiophobia would make him freeze or panic, but Trev remained calm, giving me instructions while the serpent continued to coil." Phoenix looked up, needing further explanation for his own concerns.

"I'd say he held his fear in check because he had to. Facing the Furies is a difficult task, but when one's life is in peril, you're forced into the appropriate behavior to survive. Trevor had a good reason to curb his panic, his life and your safety in jeopardy. He did it for you, pet; he had to fight the anaconda to get you home safely."

"But, Nigel, you can't stay a phobic attack. You lose control of rational thought. Snakes, cats, redheads, they surround you, breathing down your neck. You can't escape from the terror."

"I may overstep boundaries here, but Trevor loves you, and that one emotion conquers all others. My opinion only, but I'm confident our friend would face hell to protect you from harm."

The smaller man fumbled with the thought. Twister and Caly had set aside their private lives with a declaration of fatherly love toward him. He understood family adoration, for he loved his fathers and grandmother who had no reservations in expressing their mutual joy toward each other. Sloane, however, ensnared him in another emotion; one night of frightful pleasure in the jungle, one evening of unguarded sexual craving, he dared not submit to further temptation. Another phobia reared up and growled at him. He saw no recourse in correcting his own fears with a similar confrontation. The idea nearly stopped his heart.

"You're fading, pet."

"Just thinking. I'm okay; but can you tell me why he's afraid of snakes? Doesn't his Cherokee ancestry deify them?"

"I'm unaware of Cherokee philosophy, but Trevor's phobia lies in an incident that could have ended his life, along with that of his mentor."

"I suppose he keeps it secret."

"No, for many of us saw his rescue attempt."

"Did you?"

"Yes. We all seemed so young and invincible then, never fearing what life may throw at us. His first trip to Brazil coincided with Kenny's and mine. We plunged into unknown jungle with a handful of fellow adventurers. Trevor and Ben Willoughby, his photographic mentor, were on an assignment for *National Geographic*. Traipsing into the trees, scouring for plant life and great images, Willoughby suddenly screamed and your friend shouted for help. Several of us came running to find Trevor lying prone over a pit filled with snakes, like in *Indiana Jones*; but unlike the intrepid archaeologist, our friend unsuccessfully tried to save his comrade who had fallen in. The man had broken both legs, unable to grasp the hands reaching for him. With too many lethal serpents and vipers, the most experienced of our group succumbed to poison and strangulation. Trevor went berserk, trying the impossible while fending off multiple attacks. Bitten twice before we could rescue him, he then had to watch us pull out the remains of the grossly contorted dead body of his friend. Sloane fought the poison for three days before opening his eyes. The battle affected us all, but our legendary photographer holds the incident close to his heart. He survived, but carries the mental scars of the death of his friend and mentor."

"I can sympathize with his plight. A close encounter with death does that to any man."

"It certainly does. Now, come; we'll get you set up for the night."

"Thanks, Nigel, but I can take care of myself."

"Given any other time, you are very capable, but not this evening. No arguing, as I help you descend into the living compartments." The captain stood and offered a hand of assistance to one very likely of falling over without aid. Phoenix was ill; and the concerned blond intended to make his life a little easier. Without a thought of the ghosts Sloane had mentioned, he turned on the shower, adjusted the temperature to cool, and returned his attention to the small figure who remained dressed, looking distressed and confused. "Hurry; before we lose too much water. Don't be shy."

"No! I can't! I won't!" Fear overwhelmed the journalist, again facing exposure of his damaged body; a drama heightened by his other phobias while talking of one belonging to another.

Foster turned back toward the shower, shut off the water, and peered from under a furrowed forehead to study the wavering creature. "What's wrong? I can't leave you alone; you're far from well."

"Just leave me be. I said I could handle it." Phoenix snarled at the man doing his best to help. Unfortunately, he ignited a spark not counted on.

"Enough, TJ. I have two ailing men to tend; one is you. Whatever your problem, I don't much care; however, I am concerned about your present condition. I don't need another injury to deal with if you fall and hurt yourself. Now, strip!"

The unexpected attack jolted the frightened man into a response seldom uttered, "You can't see me! You can't!"

"Don't be absurd. What do you have that the rest of us don't? Right then, if you won't, I will."

"No! No! I'll make you sick!"

Nigel stopped his forward progress, as well as his plans to rip off the man's sweaty, blood-splattered clothing. "I've seen much in my life; any oddity or abnormality will go unnoticed."

"I'm scarred, damn it! I'm ugly, disgusting, riddled with revolting marks. Hell, I've lived with Trevor for two months, and he's only seen a few!" Phoenix caught the sob in his throat, waiting for a fist to his face from another acquaintance. How many times had they punched him for screaming? He nearly blacked out, remembering what his reactionary yelling once rendered upon his battered body.

"Listen, pet; we all carry physical reminders of one kind or another. Trevor will add two more to his chest; Kenny has some nasty reminders of a boar attack; and I have them from a car crash. Yours can't be more outrageous than ours, except mentally, and the rest of us eliminated those years ago; you best as well. Now, hurry, or I will carry out my threat."

Phoenix heard the word and held back his scream. Torture waited, forcing him into an act of indecency. His coping skills shut down; he closed his eyes to stop the flood. Visibly shaking over a torturous untruth, he undid his pants and dropped them to the floor, forgetting his boots remained tightly fastened to his feet. "Help me."

The whimpered plea snapped his antagonist to attention, and the blond man quickly came to his aid, sitting him down slowly and finishing the task. Kneeling in front of a wild-eyed youth ready to bolt, Nigel scanned the legs without any notice taken by the frightened young man. "Okay, boots are off, pants away, and the scars on your thighs are reminiscent of my partner's. Nothing wrong with these, but we need to clean up the gouges on your knees and shins. You took some nasty falls today, and we don't want to add more scar tissue if we can help it."

"How can you touch them?"

"I can't deny their severity, but your arms and shoulders gave me a hint of what you hide. You forgot you're down to a singlet. Let's have a look. It appears some are only fine lines, intentionally placed and stitched by a skilled plastic surgeon. Another few years, they won't be noticeable. Now, off with the rest of your gear." Nigel waited as a hesitant man removed his top, but stood stone still unable to finish the task. The Englishman remained wary of the smaller man's stance, ready to catch the faltering figure. He knew more than he let on, waiting for proof of his theory.

"Please, this is extremely awkward for me."

"Thank goodness I'm not so inclined; and we can get something accomplished. Hurry, for Trevor may be alert and calling for you." The older man turned the embarrassment switch off. Phoenix removed his shorts and staggered toward the shower stall, leaving Nigel to contemplate the rest of the scars. The small man had surgical reminders on his penis, but other vicious markings etched deep into his hips and lower back, between his thighs, and spreading out from the hidden anus. With no doubt in his mind, the worldly blond wondered if Trevor had uncovered the travesty.

Phoenix showered and emerged brighter red, to step into the embrace of a large, soft, white towel waiting outside the door. Setting him down, the captain patted out the wet hair, produced a fresh singlet and clean briefs, and insisted the young man would be abed soon and need not dress fully on such a hot night.

Reluctantly agreeing, Phoenix only wished to see Sloane, having had no word about his partner. Some rectification of his worry came via the brunet who exited the largest stateroom. "How are you feeling, TJ, still dizzy? You look better."

"Feel better, thanks, although still a little wobbly on my pins."

"The condition will last a few days. How's Trevor, Kenny?"

"Lucid. We talked awhile, but his ribs prevent him from breathing normally, spending a great deal of energy saying one word. He's resting while I fill his dinner order."

"Hunger shows improvement. What about you, TJ?"

"I should be, but can't think of anything that won't make me gag."

"Your partner feels as nauseous, but has requested soft boiled eggs with toast to dip. Swears by it to settle his stomach and ease his headache. Doesn't sound bad the way he described the dish."

"A lovely light dinner on a hot night; I'm game. What say you, lad?"

"I guess. Can I see him now?"

"Let's leave him to his nap, while we nourish ourselves. He drank a great deal of water, something very necessary for you both. Have you seen to TJ's needs, Nigel?"

"We've taken some time to clean up; and he's been steadily sipping water. Let me help you stand, pet, and we'll get you drinking

copious amounts of watered-down grape juice. It should give you the
fluid required, as well as a sugar lift. You'll feel better. Nice and
slowly now. We don't want you to take a header."

Phoenix did not resist, as he craved liquid. Still a problem with
his motor skills, he climbed the stairs slowly with burned hands and
blistered feet, while Kenny led and Nigel followed. The river breeze
refreshed his already sticky body, but rain clouds threatened and
another torrential downpour was imminent. He felt badly about his
confrontation with Foster and hoped the man would forgive him. The
idea of standing naked in front of Sloane unnerved him, but as a bribe,
he disrobed on command. His actions distorted in his mind, bringing
his best night into another perspective. He relented to the inevitable
without a fight; his phobias bounced back and forth, unable to
distinguish the greater fear.

Quietly watching Baldwin testing the time for cooking the
perfect boiled egg, and Nigel cutting bread into thin strips for dipping
toast, the youngest on board drank the watered-down juice, attempting
to still his head and heart. He remembered the anaconda; he
remembered the aftermath of the attack; but his mind lost the timeline
between the first steps of their walk and the dugout nudging home.
Muddling over his assorted injuries, he tried piecing his sojourn
together; he remembered so little. A suggestion to help Trevor with
his dinner gave Phoenix a task he wanted and could handle, taking him
away from the dreadful day. He needed to see Sloane at full strength;
the way he should be; the way they started.

The three men ate, deciding the soft-boiled eggs, with plenty of
salt and pepper, were the perfect meal for upset stomachs, recurring
headaches, and depleted energy. Phoenix managed the climb down,
and with some doing, affixed a smile on his face, secured the hot
dinner in his hands, and entered the room he usually shared with
Trevor.

The photographer waited patiently, propped up against pillows,
feeling better than he had since descending the vine. With the surprise
attack, the confrontation forced him to face the demons his fear had
enveloped, but only after the crisis ended successfully. He had not
realized the deadly dilemma remained critical for his young friend who
battled an unnerving war to reach safety. The Yanomami finding them
was nothing but luck; and the consequences of Phoenix, left to his own
devices, would never be known. If the young man had regained
consciousness, his quick mind may have hatched an idea, but severe

heatstroke would disable the strongest of men. His heart soared at the sight of the unstable figure entering the room. Phoenix appeared exceedingly tired and severely sunburned, but stood erect with his perfect but blistered lips in a smile.

"You're awake. I have your dinner; it's actually very good. Can you manage on your own while I sit with you?"

"Sure. Hand it over; I'm starving."

Phoenix helped him sit straighter and gave him the bowl. Still tantalizingly hot, Sloane started, moaning with pleasure over every bite of his comfort food.

"Well, kiddo, another experience we won't forget."

"No shit. How are you feeling?"

"I'd be walking around but for these ribs. They hurt like hell."

"The place we just left?"

"The very spot. What about you? You look wasted."

"I can't remember feeling so tired. The day dragged on forever. We've done our share of walking, Trev; bed will feel good tonight."

"No doubt."

"I wish you were lying next to me, not to do what I did, but just to..."

"...I know, baby, and no more apologizing over an act I enjoyed. I wish I could spoon around your sexy little body as well, although both of us would be in agony. I can be glad of this overwhelming heat, however; it will prevent you from wandering around looking for extra warmth."

"I guess. This may upset you, Trev, but please, why didn't you tell me about your fear of snakes? I'm sorry; probably the mention of the word has your heart beating against your sore chest." Phoenix set aside the empty plate handed him and returned his purple gaze toward his friend. Contented that Sloane felt better, recovering from the injuries inflicted by a mental ghost and his own hands, the smaller man relaxed and leaned forward to listen.

"I never thought about it, considering we were in New York. The brain has a wonderful capacity to push an unwelcome memory back into its farthest recesses. It never occurred to me that my experience might have helped you fend off the sporadic reminders that trigger some of your phobic responses." Trevor reached forward to examine the small, burned hands, both the backs and the peeled palms, holding them delicately while gently stroking the tops with his thumbs.

"I'm just glad you came back to me. You can't know how

scared I was and still am."

"I do know, Phoenix, and I'll never forget what you did. You had better have Kenny look at your hands. They must hurt."

"The Yanomami have better recall than I do of this day. My hands are okay, just burns from sliding down the vine too fast; something I do remember. You should rest, Trev. Let me get you comfortable, and I'll sit here until you fall asleep."

"I'm fine for now, but my life would be easier knowing you're safe in bed. You can't keep your violets open, kiddo. Go find the bunk Kenny has prepared for you. I'll see you come morning."

Thornton-Jones eased back onto his aching legs and looked down at his friend who seemed to be drifting off. He leaned down and kissed the soft wrinkle of the man's brow. "Good night, Trev."

"Night, Phoenix. I love you, superman."

"I love you too." Phoenix's hushed whisper went unheard, lost in an unrequited dream of a sleeping man.

Chapter XVIII

On exiting Trevor's quarters, Phoenix bumped into Nigel whose concern warranted further checking on his muscular friend before seeing to everyone else on his short list. With great intentions, the exhausted hero bid the blond botanist good night and gently made his way to a readied cot, while the captain turned to catch Baldwin changing for a respite before spelling off his partner in three hours. Both Englishmen would secure the boat and its passengers whom would be well looked after this unnerving night.

"How are you, TJ?" Kenneth looked up to see the young man clenching a handrail for support.

"Feeling really cold. Hope there's more than a sheet on the bed."

"Thought you might be. You're suffering from two exhausting and upsetting days. Nigel and I set up these cots in the main cabin, so you won't be alone if you need anything. We'll take turns sleeping and keep close watch over you both."

"Thanks, Kenny. Nothing should disturb me tonight. I feel sick I'm so tired."

"And rightly so. I'm surprised you're still standing. Severe sunburn is enough to necessitate several soft sheets plus a light blanket to stop skin shivers." On a last exchange of pleasantries, Phoenix sank into the cot, content to sleep in the warmth of the light coverings that the brunet host tucked around his shocked and burned body.

Foster entered to wish them good night, kissing his partner before Baldwin slipped under a single sheet in his designated cot, only a foot away from their youngest guest. The two guides had just recently learned that Phoenix walked in his sleep. With immediate decisions made, one pair of eyes would remain vigilant in case of the eventuality. The first guard turned to look at both men settling in and smiled wistfully at his responsibilities, before climbing through the hatch to watch for renegade miners. Warned by the Yanomami of night patrols, they had little information on those attacked while anchored in the main tributary, an assumed safe harbor. No mention was made to the weary journalist of the potential danger, only stating Trevor may need assistance if awakened. Nigel felt unnerved, too late to inform his partner of the newly acquired knowledge about the man sleeping next to him. Bad timing for Sloane to reveal the young man's penchant for chilling nightmares; at least the English duo became aware of the night crawler before this day's eventful turn around.

Making a cup of tea and securing his handgun, Foster looked upon the dark waters, expecting a sudden light to beam down upon their unprotected vessel. He would have trouble relaxing until dawn, when they would be away and safe. Several hours passed; and once again, he negotiated his way into the main living compartment to check on the three men. Kenneth laid awake, watching Phoenix toss in his sleep while mumbling a few intelligible words. The captain of the vessel, and the solid force behind an alternative relationship, put his finger to his pursed lips, a signal to ignore his presence while he looked in on Sloane. All seemed quiet, but for the fitful sleep of one. Climbing the stairs once more, he stuck his head out to scan for lights other than their own small lanterns. Silence enveloped the boat, until the sudden shriek from below.

Quickly descending, Nigel found his lover holding a mortified man who breathed heavily, apologized profusely, but still hung on for his life. Trevor had emerged too rapidly, leaning against the frame of his door, barely able to stand and hold down his dinner at the same time. He looked exceedingly concerned, necessitating his blond friend to demand that the photographer return to bed, allowing an opportunity for TJ to seek others to trust. Sloane nodded, groaning in extreme discomfort, as Nigel helped him return to his bunk.

The captain returned to aid his partner who spoke gently to the young man clinging to him like a frightened baby gorilla. With few words and a soft tone, Phoenix responded. A cool cloth to the fevered face calmed him further, while extra blankets were tucked around his fevered but chilled body. The two men had him sleeping in minutes, but troubled over a theory and their realization of the difficulties Trevor dealt with daily over the past several months. They decided not to convey their fears to their friend who had not yet recovered from his own ordeal.

Morning found them safe but tired. Kenneth nudged his skipper to arise, to weigh anchor, and to navigate them downriver, heading for the Amazon. Facing a tedious day of travel down the tributary and across the major river, Foster and Baldwin breathed in relief on leaving their dangerous location. The vessel needed a safe haven; the photographer needed to heal; the journalist needed to release his anxieties over life and death decisions, both past and present. Time for venting, perhaps the youngest passenger would open up to the dire atrocities hidden in his head, but not his body.

Sloane slipped out of bed, an inch at a time, dressed equally as slowly, and emerged to find Phoenix alone and sleeping. Tenderly, he touched the damp forehead; with even greater sensitivity, he pulled up a single sheet to cover the bare scarred shoulders and burned raw skin. Cooler air blew this day on a river breeze laden with the smell of rain, as he emerged through the hatch. Their two days of blistering sun disappeared behind the jungle mist; a difficult and slow trip lay ahead. He looked at his watch and realized how long he had slept. The Amazon grew near.

"Morning, Kenny. Looks like we've been underway a few hours."

"Right you are, mate. How are you feeling? Need a hand?"

"I'm doing quite well; I think. Headache's gone, but I'm still dizzy. Ribs remain painful, just as broken ribs do. The machete slices, however, will take a week or so to scab over, and then you can pull out the stitches. I didn't feel a thing after you injected me with whatever, and for too many times. Man, they hurt worse than the actual cuts."

"Always handy to keep a strong pain killer at the ready. Stitches are better than cauterizing, which scares the dickens out of me and leaves severe scar tissue. You should have TJ's plastic surgeon repair the damage when you get home."

"He certainly knows a few. Sorry we put you through a trial yesterday." Trevor finished his climb to stand tall to help his breathing.

"No need to apologize, for we're also sorry. We allotted you only two days to complete a difficult task, as we were worried about many things in that particular area; all of which you ran into. Unfortunately, failsafe measures collapsed, leaving us in a quandary whether to wait, or chance finding you somewhere close to the river in darkness. A long shot, we created an unnecessary dilemma, never to be repeated."

"Can't turn back time, but we can learn from the unfortunate consequences of one event ruining a good plan." Trevor gently sat down at the table, while rubbing his face to become fully alert.

"We should have known, and our stupidity left a decisively heavy burden on one inexperienced with the jungle."

"He's a survivor, Kenny; the one thing I do know about him."

"He dreamed of alligators, jaguars, snakes, and blond miners for some reason, not too happy about any of them."

"Heatstroke can certainly turn you around. He's suffering from the chills, judging by the extra coverings."

"Fear, shock, over-exertion, and burned lobster red, he's quite a mess. At least you have dark skin, my friend, already turning brown. Here's a coffee. Drink up. Nigel will be happy to see you standing up and erect."

"Don't make me laugh. I could still empty my guts onto your clean deck. Thanks for helping TJ last night. He's a good man and a brave one."

"We have no doubt, but he looked ghastly upon reaching us. He sat in the dugout, stone silent, gazing up with those incredible eyes, with your head in his lap. The lad was so close to passing out and falling into the brink, we had to hurry. Nigel urged him to take one step up the ladder, while my heart broke over the will of the man, an incredible last effort for one who carried such a load. What did he call it? Ah, yes, muscle memory. I'd say it was far more." Kenny looked at the man who had been saved from succumbing to his first brush with snakes.

"Very much so. He fights fear daily. Every word, every vocal inflection, every nuance, you must be so damn careful of them all. What you heard is only a hint of his nervosa. You said he dreamed of our escapade only, nothing more?"

"Nothing either of us detected."

"That makes a huge difference. I wondered how you managed to settle him so quickly. His usual nightmares leave him catatonic for some time. I've stewed over the likelihood of such an occurrence since we left Colorado; I think he has as well."

"He was very frightened; and the last thing we want is a new phobia similar to yours. How do you feel about the attack? I'm surprised you didn't suffer a complete shut down."

"My only chance and I grabbed it. Petrified to stone, I could barely speak to help Phoenix. He did a remarkable job once he started. What a helpless feeling. On any given day, I would have been on my own, a week's dinner for an anaconda. Fuck!" Trevor shook himself, warding off a relapse. Death had come close; a white angel had intervened on his behalf.

Two men sat stock still, mulling over the near miss. The lone photographer took many chances in his life, but caution and nerve rallied him to overcome many a threatening encounter. One eye-opening day brought risk to the forefront. Baldwin and Sloane looked at each other in wide-eyed acknowledgement, both thinking the same thing. They diverted their gaze to the steam rising in their mugs, attempting to sweep death away from their minds. Too close, the friends reflected in silence.

"Trevor! Trevor!"

"It's Phoenix! Shit, I mean TJ! I'm coming, kiddo." Sloane attempted to rise on hearing the plaintive call, but pain aborted his attempted dash down the narrow ladder, leaving him hunched over, holding his fractured ribs and bandaged wounds, unable to progress forward.

"Stay here. I'll tend to him. Anything I should know?"

"Nothing I can think of, but he sounds a little disoriented to me."

The brunet scurried through the hatch to find the journalist lying supine on his cot, disheveled physically and mentally. "Good morning, luv; your mate's up on deck. What's the matter?"

"Where are we? It's still dark and I can't move! Everything burns and hurts. God, I'm so stiff; I can't move anything!"

Baldwin mused to himself over the would-be Atlas. The young man had done more than his share of the work and now suffered for it. "I'm not surprised, considering what your body wrestled with over two days. As to our location, we're underway, almost clear of the tributary; and the darkness I can correct by opening these overhead shutters. We're traveling in a downpour today, cooling us a little, although it remains oppressively muggy. Our journey will be slower due to the heavy rain, but we'll manage. There we go. Now, let's get you on your feet, and we'll rub some liniment into your aching muscles with something that won't sting your burned skin."

A helping hand lifted Phoenix into a sitting position, one that nearly set off a scream of torture. "Shit, life sucks, and this is only the day after! I'll be totally immobilized tomorrow! You and Nigel will need a winch to hoist me out of the damn cot." Phoenix chuckled, knowing exactly how he would feel on the morrow.

"I believe we're capable of lifting you. Let me swing your legs over, and we'll get you standing. Leave your pants and boots for now, until we have you rubbed down. On the count of three." Baldwin smiled in understanding, as he helped a man, in excruciating but understandable pain, stand erect. The groans and uncharacteristic profanity were heard on deck, loud enough for Nigel to yell out his concern. Trevor, being the closest, looked down the hatch, impatiently waiting for an explanation of the young spirit's affliction.

"Okay, luv, hand-over-hand, step-by-step, we'll get you on deck. The more you move; the easier life will be."

"Damn, I can't bend! I can't even lean forward, and my hands! The blisters have broken! Shit, they hurt." Fussing as he struggled with his severe aches and pains, the ailing journalist tried his best to climb the ladder, while Kenneth followed, helping to raise a leg, or move an arm when muscles failed. Phoenix remembered every physiotherapy session that he had endured; progress only came after much time and great suffering. Unfortunately, this was now, giving him an urgency to keep moving. A familiar smile, seen through the hatch opening, gave him encouragement; and he willed himself to crawl, on burned hands and scratched knees, to someone in worse condition. They were both alive and out of trouble, thanks to two people they now considered close friends, not to mention several Yanomami tribesmen and their healer. Left alone to rise this day in the forest, they would have been doomed, survival dim at best.

Trevor sat clutching his chest, watching in sympathy as Phoenix groaned at each muscle manipulation. The small man lay on his stomach stretched out on the table, with body scrapes, hands, and feet bandaged, unable to escape the kneading fingers. Nigel again called out for a briefing, and his partner yelled out his diagnosis. The trip slowed to the pace of ailing men. Once across the main river, the blond navigated their craft deep into a narrow, sheltered rivulet, eliminating any rocking that may upset the passengers who fought dizziness.

Allowing many days for Trevor and Phoenix to regain their senses and stability, the two botanists relaxed as well. Four men chatted in the rain, played cards during the long nights, and laughed over everything as the beer flowed. No need for lookouts, they felt safe enveloped by the forest that protected a small, seldom visited tributary, and its small waterfall. Daylight hours afforded them an opportunity to study, and capture on film, the wildlife that came to drink; even a rare jaguar ignored the boat lights to lap up a refresher. Having anchored the vessel far enough from shore, animals posed little threat; and Phoenix sighed happily with every sighting. His confidence returned slowly, coming out of himself to enjoy the break from the insufferable responsibility he carried about his job and his relationship with Sloane. He and his working partner grew closer, spending time together discussing all, except work, secrets, and two unfathomable encounters of the sexual variety. Their injuries prevented them from touching, but affection shone from both pair of eyes; both men infatuated with the other. Younger muscles loosened over a week; sunstroke and heatstroke subsided enough for the journalist to awaken alert. Sloane gave into his ribs, stifling the pain, hiding his headaches and uncomfortable wounds when he could. They slept apart, Trevor secluded in the forward stateroom, and Phoenix in the second largest, the squeaky door of which remained shut when occupied; any nightmare or walking figure quickly deterred by one of the two sleeping outside the portal. Time drifted, as did the four men, a respite after one terrifying day.

With a clear sky overhead, Trevor gave word to weigh anchor; they were underway. The photographer remained in discomfort, but coped to scan for potential pictures. The first area of interest, on the southern side, proved that the forest did grow back in the poor soil, but with only a fraction of the original species of flora. The short trek in, by Phoenix and Nigel, had an instant impact on the youngest, with validation of the claims against deforestation. The distressed land took more than thirty years to re-establish, resulting in a poor imitation of the original. In a few hundred-years, one would still see the difference between new growth and old.

Further along the same waterway, the boat docked at a large wharf built by a lumber company, one authorized to clear a limited number of hectares. World standards were a non-issue to the workers; only the size of the area under contract concerned them. The idea of selective cutting and replanting seemed unknown to the crew. The four men, however, did find cordial employees to speak with, happy for a diversion from their labors and unafraid of the camera. With Brazilian law on their side, they took pride in the quality of the araucaria they harvested, seldom veering from their targeted objective. Trevor shot what he needed, along with the moment when a single axe connected to an ancient but noncommercial tree for no justifiable reason. The photographer heard a living entity slain on a silent scream; one the world would hear through a picture. A quick glance at Phoenix's countenance, Sloane knew his partner also heard the final lonely cry. Finding sufficient photographic opportunities and journalistic information to tell the story, they readied themselves to depart. The younger man carried the camera equipment and his notepad, as the two men boarded the comfortable vessel to prepare for the next dismal stops: two deforested sections due to fire caused by lightning and man. Devastation awaited their arrival, but with luck, some hope beforehand.

The laboratory of the Pilot Program seemed a feasible project, although not yet operating at maximum. Various scientific minds, zoologists, botanists, and environmentalists, worked in a controlled test area, studying and recording accounts of all flora and fauna that used and bordered the Amazon itself. A daunting task for so few, they also waited for manpower. With money in hand, they wished to recruit new eyes, ears, and insightful thoughts, but few Brazilians wanted to enter the furor, or decipher the odd vision statement set forth by the World Bank and the G8 Nations. As professionals, the small group endeavored to supply their government, and the international naysayers, with alternatives to Brazil's many problems, according to the ponderous explicative document they had to follow. All four men looked at it; all four men were at a loss as to the meaning of the manifesto.

After a week's visit, the vessel veered east and south, and Phoenix's renewed hope dwindled to non-existent. With mouths agape on two men, four stood portside aghast at the charred remains of hectares upon hectares of rainforest. Lightning had struck with fury; its resulting fire unleashed to decimate a wealth of trees, only stopping on one side by the wide tributary, but spreading wildly in the other three directions. Nature wreaked havoc of its own accord; a perfect world this was not.

The journalist could not believe the waste created, before a sudden but saving downpour impeded the fire's further progress. Before him lay ash and dead debris as far as the horizon, without a blade of grass growing, a bird singing, or a monkey screeching its wrath at an uncaring creator. Two years after the fact, it remained a soggy patch of grayness, waiting for strong winds to carry life-giving seeds from the surrounding forest. The eventuality would take years, decades, lifetimes, only to return as a one-dimensional remnant of its former beauty and diversity. An innocent opened his soul to reality; he felt sick.

They traveled for hours, moving very slowly in reverence to the cemetery of primitive ferns, colorful birds, and rare insects that were now forever gone, this one area on the planet having been their only home. Reaching the fringe, Nigel navigated the boat to the opposite side of the river for Sloane's indulgence, and then returned to the bleak landscape where more pictures could be taken. While the photographer found his bearings and focus, Phoenix accompanied the brunet botanist to a hidden test patch, a small section of evenly paced-off land--a monitor for new growth--but not a weed appeared in the marked zone. Seeing proof that the soil was too poor for even a market garden, the youngest of the four men contemplated the devastation, attempting to understand man's interference, burning more land when nature did the deed for you. There seemed no excuse to leave an area for several lifetimes to struggle on its own. After spending days sifting through the waste and exploring the ragged perimeter closest to the river, time came to move on. Further upstream, a man-made fire had taken a lesser toll, but equally problematic.

Weighing anchor, Phoenix sat dejected, his eyes forever forward. He had had enough of a country with no regard for life. He wished to go home, understanding how easy giving up would be. At a juncture in his life, he could willingly bury his head in the sand, imitating an ostrich that felt the same. His glassy stare caught a distant cloud; a black veil hovered close to the river. Deeming it an unnatural occurrence, confirmation was required, and he yelled for the others.

Nigel swore under his breath and immediately changed gears to speed the vessel forward. He saw the dark smoke of smoldering embers, recognizing a controlled fire, as far as one could handle such a volatile element with limited workers. He had seen too many and knew that another four bodies could only play a minor role in stopping the rampage. Meanwhile, Phoenix scurried down from his high perch to stand between Sloane and Baldwin. Blinking his frightened violets, his anger grew in the silence of the others. He would burst if he did not open his mouth. "How do we find it and stop it, if not on the river?"

"The smoke is coming directly toward us, hovering very low over the water, as opposed to spiking into the air. Man-made by the looks of it and controlled for the most part, the fire does appear spent. Deforestation next to water is common, giving new families or businesses an area inaccessible by road. We'll keep going until we find it." Kenneth continued to watch ahead looking for water hazards, but very sure of the fire's location. Unnerved at what the two investigative reporters may see, the botanist knew how easily one could jump to the wrong conclusions, or more likely the right ones. He understood Sloane's quiet way of taking pictures without comment, but the distressed younger man would not take kindly to a calamity in the making. Questions needed asking before erroneous opinions were spouted. Baldwin also worried about the mental frailty displayed on occasion by one who may be incapable of coping with the reality of jungle management.

Thick, dark smoke obscured their sightline, only to open for a moment and close again. The four men donned protective masks, saving their lungs and eyes from flying ash on the rising breeze. One chance opened, and Phoenix spotted a cleared area, still in need of replanting. He pointed the situation out to the captain who continued to steer his vessel down a blind path. "That's the area we planned to show you. Leveled some years ago under the Free Land Policy, the family gave up and returned to the city."

"The new fire appears to butt up against it."

"Very typical, pet. Let's hope they are a creative and agricultural savvy group."

"Why don't they use the land already cleared?"

"Good question, kiddo." Trevor piped in to explain the dilemma of the Free Land Policy. "The first parcel is still legally owned by the original applicants and will be for some time, until the government sees the necessity to expropriate it. The situation occurs throughout Brazil's section of Amazonia, land titles bestowed on those filled with great dreams and expectations, but ill equipped for such a dangerous life. A sad fact, one cannot eke out a living farming cleared jungle. The area may look fertile with its indigenous plants, but it leads to false hope. Some of the free land has been given outright to lumber, mining, and coffee companies, as well as farmers and entrepreneurial groups, all with unqualified promises to conserve while keeping it populated. Unfortunately, they destroy for their own greed, and then leave it in disarray when they are unable to implement their plans. Due to ownership rights, the land remains abandoned. Part of this policy includes the eco-tourist resorts and the buy-waterfront-front-property-in-Arizona entrepreneurs." Trevor explained the policy precisely, leaving Phoenix perplexed over the stupidity of burning and then leaving only ash without regard to replanting.

"The eco-groups should be conserving what they own, Trev."

"No way, for they're smoke and mirrors as well. Eco-tourism makes money on the pretense of conservation, but they track through important jungle, creating crisscrossed paths of human scent that many animals fear as marked territory, entrapping the creatures between the beaten routes. They also exploit the indigenous people, or drive them further into the forest. How many people can afford the luxury of traveling into an area glamorized in magazines and television? Only the wealthy can look forward to a new thrill, or the adventurers who should be using a more conscientious means of exploration. The entrepreneurs, on the other hand, sell land not belonging to them, knowing a die-hard naturalist will fork over dollars to save an acre, or two, or three. A safe bet considering the charitable act, a tax deduction for people who will never venture near. Hell, an individual could sell the same parcel a thousand times over. Many have already been caught, but charlatans continue to prey on the stupid and ignorant."

"So much for the Free Land Policy."

"An idea that blew up in many faces and continues." Trevor coughed out ash, groaning with the action. He returned to silence, easing the pain invoked, but scanning the water where two other vessels docked at a recently built pier. They had arrived too late.

Once on land, Phoenix gaped unbelievingly at a group of people covered with black soot, ones who continued to watch the smoke rise from a fire still smoldering after days of toil to contain the flames. They had succeeded, and a new group of landowners, along with a government representative, had little strength left to greet visitors. Nigel immediately found the official he knew, to clarify any misunderstandings. "Good afternoon, Paulo. Need a hand?"

"A difficult task with the weather fluctuations, but the bordering river and the adjacent cleared property contained the flames. As it remains intensely hot, we'll keep a guarded eye on it for the next week. What are you two doing here? Stirring up trouble, Señor Foster?"

"Always. Can we look around? Our passengers would like to help, or at least see what a fire accomplishes."

"An unlikely story, but go ahead. We used a method of cutting the perimeter first, in this case two sides, felling trees toward the river and the center of the property. The fire then heads for open ground, rather than spreading through the adjacent forest. It takes more effort, but the technique seems well worth it. I'm sure you can agree to at least that, Nigel."

"Better than nothing."

"We're trying, and I hope your guests will see the effects. They're your responsibility if they venture too far. Mine is with these exhausted men. We put up a fight for many days."

"Thanks. So, who are these new owners? Qualified individuals and tough ones I hope."

"The three young men ready to drop over there. Unlike their predecessors, these men have money to back them for farming materials, are educated in agricultural studies, and appear eager to face the dangers and hardships, along with their wives and assorted family members. They have new ideas on potentially failsafe crops for this infertile soil."

"Good luck to them. Kenny and I will pop in occasionally to check on their progress and well-being. If any need medical attention, we'll be here a few hours while our friends look around. We'll see you later." Nigel valiantly held back his contempt, as he lied outright. In his mind, the entire group should be arrested for something, anything, just to get people out of the delicate forest. The scenario, unfortunately, lay in state and federal hands. "Okay, lads, you're free to wander. Be careful of the heat and don't stray too far. If the fire breaks out again, you need an escape route back to the river."

"Thanks, Nigel. Looks like rain, which should quell spontaneous blazing. See you in a few hours. Ready, Passepartout? Are your boots feeling the heat yet? Let me know, and we'll return to the boat immediately."

"I can't feel anything, Trev, still numb from the initial shock. I can't believe they actually burn more land, leaving already cleared areas because of ownership rights. It's ludicrous."

"Life sucks, as you stated before."

"And will forever. How are your ribs? Can you walk any distance?" Phoenix still stood stunned; his thick-soled hiking boots would protect his feet for the allotted two hours. He could only shake his white head, wishing more smoke would obliterate the bleak vista entirely, instead of the ghostly wavering of rising hot steam from the smoldering ashes mixed with sprinkles of rain. A picture of hell awaited his friend the photographer.

"I'm taking very little and should be fine if we walk slowly. Quivering air, an oncoming deluge, man, this should make for some interesting images. Stay close, Phoenix, and keep out of my sightline. Let's go."

The two walked away, disappearing into the pale gray still glittering with orange embers, the first stage of death both would forever remember. Sloane wallowed in the mystical, immediately shooting picture after picture, of which only one or two might capture the essence of a forest no longer able to scream. Nothing survived, entrapped by deadly flames moving toward the river. Using cut trees to guide a controlled fire, the method torched the lower floor first; perimeter trees were felled before becoming flaming arrows to ignite the tops of others. Uniform and precise, the wind had remained calm; the perpetrators of the deed had been lucky the weather held.

Looking back, and then forward, a skilled artist continued clicking, lost in a surrealistic world of gray. A rise turned him around to capture the death of a forest from all directions. Another shot and then another, he continued covering the carnage with each step and picture taken. From another knoll, he pointed his lens at a strange anomaly; a white-haired angel, covered in soot, slowly and delicately came over the lip. Beautiful, perfection in movement and countenance, the sorrowful face searched the ground, looking for something he could relate to as living in his world. The photographer sensed and saw the hopelessness that the wingless one suffered.

Abruptly the figure stopped. Wide eyes appeared shocked; the slight body refused to move. After a moment of fearful trepidation, one foot stepped in the direction the eyes had veered, but again the body came to a sudden halt and waited breathlessly. One more foot forward, another stop, something fell at his feet, causing a terrifying start, and again the hesitation. A back and forth look, the image struggled with indecision, but a sound alerted the soot-covered figure to direct his attention in the opposite direction. A sudden break in the slow motion action, the unearthly creature took several quick steps and picked up a small bundle of a color as distinguishable as the white head against the smoke-filled background. The heat haze distorted the image, but Sloane continued to grab ethereal shot after shot, his subject crying in despair as he examined his cradled golden armful.

The ghost of the forest turned back, taking several steps and placing his treasure down. Unable to see, Sloane moved forward, never taking the camera away from his eye. Left alone in a colorless cloud of death, he continued his search for perfection. The figure moved again with great caution, lifted the bundle, and held it delicately in his arms, as his head dropped back and sorrow shrieked from perfect lips, a perfect mouth. Click after click, Trevor continued, spellbound by the slender ghost; a broken angel covered with the charred remains of a disappearing jungle. A heavy deluge started, pelting the sweet being that stood knee deep in debris, mourning a loss, as the photographer continued unabated, unmindful of the changing weather or his sorry subject, but saving moments of time that only he could see.

"Trevor! Trevor!"

The urgent calls finally echoed in the oblivion of Sloane's mind. Tears cascaded down the dirty face as he zoomed in. His subject filtered through the blinds of his consciousness, finally to recognize the drama unfolding. Thornton-Jones, the love of his life, stood not twenty feet away, crying for help, but his camera came first. Another heartfelt plea for aid penetrated the obsessed photographer's being, a man now able to look through his camera to view the real world. "My God, Phoenix!" Trevor quickly covered his lens and dashed to the confused man's side.

"Trevor! Help me! Help me!" The sobs echoed of desperation; the calls plaintive and exaggerated; the cries broke a heart in their helplessness.

"Okay, kiddo, you have my full attention. What do you have here?"

"A baby. The mother's dead, right here at my feet, with her other cub. Trevor, they burned her and her babies alive! We have to save this one. Maybe there are others." Phoenix stopped babbling, to look in the direction from whence the cub had first appeared, hoping another searched for its mother.

"Unlikely, as cubs stay together when in danger, and they usually have only two or three. This mother bravely saved one, and yet tried again to save her last baby. Let's go; let's get this little one back to Kenny who may have something for burned paws."

"Why didn't you come? What were you doing? I needed your help with the mother! We might have saved her!"

Trevor stared deeply into violet petals awash with holy tears, finally enabling him to distinguish reality from his dream state. He had neglected helping another human because of his obsession: the fleeting moment of a perfect photograph. "Oh, Phoenix, I'm so sorry, but even with my help, it would have been too late. She and her cub died of burns and extreme smoke inhalation. They would have never survived. There's no excuse for my tardiness, except that my subject overwhelms me, and I don't respond appropriately. I'm here now; let me help you." Sloane stepped closer to the shaking body and encircled the small figure and the wild baby in his protective arms. A life needed saving, whether it be the distraught white angel or an injured jaguar cub; this time the award-winning photographer refused to give up on either for the sake of his art. "Let's go and take care of this precious creature you saved. Sounds hungry, hurt, and those little lungs are rattling from smoke. We had better hurry."

"It's too young to feel such pain of injury and loss. These people trapped an innocent jaguar family in a circle of fire; the mother had no knowing of how to escape. She could have taken the river, but she didn't. Instead, she braved the flames with one, and then returned for another that had succumbed. God, Trevor, this is horrible! Why didn't they fan the jungle before setting the blaze? I don't understand why they didn't try to save what lived in the forest!"

"I know, baby, I know. What our society believes is appropriate behavior; others do not. When you live with poverty, animals and trees take second place, as you rightly suggested before venturing on this expedition. We cannot change a different culture's social mores. Consider this: the continents of South America, Africa, and Asia have little regard for wildlife, even abusing their pets and domestic work animals, according to our standards. Just south of our border, in the third country that makes up North America, Mexicans do not understand our penchant for feeding, healing, and nurturing animals, and nothing will change their predetermined mind set. We must not judge them, for who is to say we are right. A strange thing to suggest, western civilization applies human characteristics to animals, making them think and act as we do. Nature doesn't work that way, but the belief and the trying helps us emotionally. Because of our caring hearts, we have become designated saviors of all nature; the only ones who care beyond reason, with the knowledge, resources, and love to help all wildlife. As citizens of the modern world, we can take pride in that."

"I hate this. I hate it. I want to leave. Let's go home and take this cub with us. I don't want to leave it with uncaring people."

"You know that's impossible, but there are many kind people we've met, like the zoologist from the lab. He cared enough to give up his lucrative career in the city to help in the jungle."

"I still won't leave it, not knowing."

"We'll find the cub a good home, but it is a child of the forest, Phoenix; an animal difficult to save at such an important stage in its life. Tell me something. You put the cub down for a second. What were you doing?"

"The mother was still alive. I had to show her that one baby survived. I had no choice."

"She could have mustered the last of her strength to lunge for you."

"I know, but she didn't; she couldn't. We both knew somehow. Her eyes glassed over with the touch and cry of her cub, and then she stopped breathing. I picked it up again, but look at these little paws! I promised the mother I'd help her. I had to!" Phoenix let his tears wash away the soot, as did the rain that neither man had noticed, both intent on the golden bundle and each other.

"We need to save this little thing before attempting to rectify a world gone awry. I'll take your arm to prevent you from slipping and tangling yourself in the debris. Your cargo may be small, but I'm sure it's heavy. Ready?"

"Thanks, Trev; sorry I questioned you. I know better." Phoenix started walking, a strong man guiding his steps and securing his position despite torn stitches, aching ribs, and the necessity to cough from too much smoke.

"You were right. I lose myself in another place I am loath to give up, neglecting the horrible reality of a situation or person I'm photographing. You're probably the only person I'd set down my camera and come to help. One day you'll understand the intensity of my feelings toward you."

Thornton-Jones said nothing, pondering the thought. Trevor Sloane had put up with his problems long enough and he had to reciprocate in a sane fashion. For the meantime, the fate of a jaguar cub lay foremost in his mind; he dared not think of anything or anyone else. The handsome photographer, however, could not be discarded so readily.

As rain cleansed the pair, they returned to the riverbank, both quietly considering their next move. Sloane fondled his obsession hanging around his neck; an item easily replaced or handed to another artist. There were many, but he could never set aside the forlorn figure he supported. A sweet, unnerving young man, as fragile as fine china, as strong as titanium, his love encompassed every horrifying nightmare and whimsical flutter of an eyelash. He could not let the white angel go, nor would he ever again hide behind his camera, ignoring the man's plight. Redeeming himself in those violet eyes was a rest-of-his-lifetime commitment.

Phoenix struggled with his balance and the intangible thoughts of the man assisting him through the rubble. He did love Sloane, and now yearned for him in private, able to relieve himself of the anxiety. One touch had turned him upside down, but only affectionate gestures followed. He wanted more; all he had to do was ask. Returning home, he would gather his courage. Procrastination tripped him up, tears sprang anew, and the rain camouflaged his dire emotions.

Chapter XIX

Upon reaching the river, a regretful photographer and a confused journalist found their comrades speaking with the group of hopefuls. The cordial conversation quickly silenced upon seeing the deeply troubled expressions and the two pair of bright white stunned eyes blinking away smoke and rain. The brunet botanist rushed to his friends' rescue, stretching his arms out to aid the men. "My goodness, luv, what do you have here?"

"It's weak from hunger after so many days of fire. The mother is dead, burned alive along with her other cub. Help me, Kenny; help me save it. It's so small, so very little. God, it was horrible." Feelings of sorrow, anger, and despair poured out of Phoenix, as he cuddled the ailing cub against his dying heart.

"We'll try, and she's a girl. Give her to me for a closer look. She's probably about a month old and lucky to have survived this long, but she's much too young to be showing color. Jaguar cubs are gray until two or three-years old, as camouflage against predators. She's an unusual specimen."

The journalist immediately snapped back, "She's not a specimen! She's a living, grieving baby!"

"Sorry, TJ, but this cub is very unique." Baldwin was mystified over the bizarre golden color of such a young cat, but medical need came before zoological discovery. "Nigel, could you help us please? Let go, lad; give her to me. Come here, little one; we'll cool your tiny paws and feed you. Goodness, you're a sweetie." Safely cradling the coughing cub, the brunet Englishman handed the baby to his partner, before scampering aboard their vessel, where he turned to reach down for the bundle that was unable to open its swollen eyes.

The heavy-hearted journalist, feeling empty without his warm package, watched while others took over. A large hand on his head gave him consolation that all would be well for the orphan. Phoenix turned to thank his friend when the violet eyes spotted the new owners of the land, their workers, and the government official, congratulating each other and laughing loudly after such an arduous task, but ignoring the tragedy they had caused. The fine white hairs bristled on the back of the journalist's neck, anger exploded in an assault of words on the unsuspecting. "You stupid, stupid people, what is the matter with you?

You killed innocent animals today, trapping them without an exit. How many trees of commercial value did you save? I see none. You destroy without thought, believing you can earn a living on non-fertile land. What do you know that your neighbors did not? When will you learn? How much of the jungle will you consume by fire, before understanding the global ramifications and the forest's many uses just as it stands? All you think about is yourselves. You are selfish, arrogant, ignorant, greedy, and did I mention stupid! I'm tired of defending you. You take one step forward and six..."

"...Phoenix, stop! That's enough. Come, we have work to do. Leave these people to try something new. Maybe their ideas will work." Trevor nudged him gently, hoping an international crisis would not erupt because of his partner. Unfortunately, his single touch proved insufficient to calm the man's wrath. A worse tirade ensued, soon stopped by a hand over the mouth calling names. Strong arms lifted another wildcat off the ground and handed him off to a healthier Nigel. Two men secured the ranting whirlwind below deck, while a fourth apologized from the control room, as he navigated to open water and a course downriver.

"Phoenix, stop! Now! What happened to your dreams for our host country? We came to view all sides before making decisions." Sloane stepped clear of the swinging arms and kicking feet, protecting his aching chest from the attack, while Foster held the dynamo from behind, attempting to stay out of danger.

"They're murderers! None of this makes sense! What happened to rational thought and human sensitivity? I heard what you said about cultural differences, but I still don't understand. I want to get the hell out of here. I'm sorry, but I just want to go home!" Phoenix dropped to the floor in a ball; the captain recognized the defeat in the voice.

"Steady on, pet. You've had some miserable experiences while in Brazil; but once you're home, you can deduce fact from your overwrought emotions. Too many shocks, you're having trouble coping."

"It's the jaguar mother, isn't it, Phoenix? You couldn't let her die alone. I understand, kiddo, I do; but your concern does not give you latitude to yell obscenities at others. Now, Kenny needs your help on deck with the cub. Clean yourself up and meet us above."

The two men assisted the smallest onto his feet, found dry clothes and a towel, allowing the young man to change and gather himself alone and in peace. Three men waited in the control room, Foster taking over navigation from Baldwin.

"What was that all about, Trevor?"

"More ghosts, Kenny. He does have an uncontrollable temper when provoked. Sorry, boys, but he is a grown man who we've all been babying. It's time he grew up." Shaken by the unwarranted outburst, Sloane returned to the gathering area with Kenneth. He waited for the white head to emerge through the hatch, as he stroked and subdued another baby hungrily sucking warm milk from a bottle found amongst the remaining emergency supplies. Having changed in the covered galley, he felt drier and more comfortable, but readied himself for another verbal confrontation. For now, he had babysitting chores.

Upon the hour, two pair of hands drummed fingers against the table; a third set tapped the wheel. Unable to control his stress level, Nigel found an anchorage and summoned his partner to assist in securing their water-home for an early stop. Quickly done, the English duo came to rest in the galley, out of the rain and eager for their day to end. Trevor held the sleeping cub close to his heart, keeping it warm with blankets and the soft hum of his baritone growl. No matter the species, a baby needed its siblings and a mother's snuggled presence. Three men attempted to compensate for the wild creature's loss. After burned paws anointed and wrapped, eyes soothed with lotion, and a full tummy rubbed for comfort, the exhausted orphan slept.

Phoenix peeked out of the hatch, wondering who would knock his head off first and deservedly so. The men on deck appeared busy, as he climbed up with a two-page, scribbled letter in hand. "Read this, Trevor, as I'm having difficulty sounding sincere."

"What is it?"

"An apology to those I attacked today. I'm not sorry, but need to restore tranquility for Nigel and Kenny's hazardous position working with these people. I regret causing you strife, guys." Phoenix handed his note to the photographer who in turn placed the twenty-pound baby into Foster's arms. The cub's savior reached out to receive a little purr at a remembered scent and to hear the acceptance of his apology from at least two friends.

"How very adult of you." Trevor squinted over the pages, studying his disquieting friend over the wire frames of his reading glasses.

"What do you mean by that?" Phoenix looked surprised, but the voice indicated more anger.

"You behaved like a spoiled child, embarrassing us all. You had better rein in that temper, before it gets you into deeper trouble."

"I had a righteous cause and still do. Who ate crackers in your bed last night, Sloane? I'm at least attempting to make amends."

"No one, since you came along. As for making amends, I'd suggest you do a rewrite. You're correct; the letter lacks sincerity." The older man returned the note to the shaking hands, which grabbed the flimsy piece of paper, scrunched it into a ball, and tossed it into the garbage.

"Fine. I'll do it again."

"Good."

"Go to hell. I don't think I'll send anything now, considering your shitty attitude, putting me down for no fucking reason."

"Lads! Lads! Please. Our ire is up when we all require calm. Trevor, you attack without listening. TJ, you retaliate with anger initiated by others. Now, shake hands, kiss, and make up, as Nigel and I need time for us. We have incurred an equally upsetting day." Baldwin glared at the two men sparring, unable to determine who was right and who was wrong.

"We're all overwrought; and the only cure, for the two of us, is an hour alone, down below, with the hatch closed. You two do whatever you do in private, but beware, for we do not wish to be interrupted by loud quarrels, men overboard, or bawling babies. Dinner will be prepared at the usual hour. Here is your patient who is tired and frightened, although now full of cream and as content as she can be, considering. We've decided to return to the lab, and with fingers crossed, the zoologist may take her on as a project. Let's go, mi amour." Nigel guided his upset partner to the portal, both men eager to shut out the world for an hour and reconnect in the most intimate of manner. They left the Americans to sort out their problems.

Phoenix cradled the cub, veering away from the photographer's glaring, hurtful eyes. He felt his anger justified; but his ranting at the Brazilians was wrong. No escaping his mistake, he had some explaining to do. The warmth of the cub and its rattled breathing soothed his heart. He had many things to say, and he turned to speak first. "I did react inappropriately, Sloane, calling them names. I don't hate them, only what they were doing and what other's have done in the past."

"You were unkind, and I don't know if I can forgive you for that."

"One error in judgment and I'm condemned for eternity. How exceedingly condescending of you, but I know you felt the same way. Too bad you couldn't see it through the lens of your damn camera, your only way of viewing the real world instead of speaking your mind. I thought I had a problem with reality, but you win first prize as the best fucking bystander."

"So, without our permission, you decided to speak on our behalf. What else do you have to say, before I send you packing and finish the job myself?" Sloane immediately regretted his threat, but remained steadfast for another strike. He had no choice, considering the overtly judgmental accusations iterated by his partner.

"Fine, go right ahead, but answer me this. Do you think so ill of me, Trevor that I come across as a snotty-nosed brat? I do have fathers who spoil me, coddling me like a child, but that's who I am to them and will be forever: a seventeen-year-old kid who couldn't take care of himself for a very long time. That's what parent's do, care for the only baby they'll ever have, and that's me. You don't have that right to criticize any man in such a manner. I also happen to have a feisty grandmother who dotes enough to yell her displeasure, and many ranch friends willing to indulge my flights of madness. They all let me loose occasionally to vent my unhappiness over something, but you tie ropes around my wrists and heart, tugging unmercifully to keep me in line. I can't be your obedient slave or cub; I have emotions and opinions, equally as strong as yours, requiring verbal expression. I don't recall ever hurting you intentionally, Sloane. Why are you playing the son-of-a-bitch with me?" Phoenix slumped down on the bench with his cargo still sleeping in his arms. He doubted his ability to convince the photographer otherwise after his damning outcry, but unabated anger cleared his mind of caring. His only thoughts lay in Colorado, where he could formulate an idea with too much information cluttering his mind.

"Hell, I don't know, but you don't just vent, you go wild: uncontrollably wild." The photographer sighed and closed his eyes to refocus. The journalist was right; he had patronized a grown man that he thought of as a fragile kid and had since they first met. It was also true that he only witnessed the action, the people, the horrors encountered, but refrained from participating in life, choosing to hide behind a camera rather than face the sorrow or respond appropriately to the beauty. Perhaps his confidence was a façade, an act to protect himself from who he was: a single gay male, a quarter breed who discarded his rightful place in two worlds, and a very lonely man with a future dangling too high in the air. "I can't ask anything more of you, kiddo; just be you. Never would I ask you to be my slave, and you're certainly not Sebastian. As for my thoughts of you becoming a diplomat, said positions are appointed to experienced older heads for a reason, people who maintain a calm presence in a world crumbling around them. I may be in the age bracket, but my mouth, like yours, does not serve me well; and just as you suggested, I remain silent. I did attack you without provocation; I do see the world only through my camera; but I'm not sorry for either, Phoenix. We need to regroup, contemplate facts only, before setting our minds on the where-alls and be-alls of our project." Sloane lifted a hand to his head and unconsciously rubbed his right temple.

"I've given you a headache."

"I wouldn't take credit for one of these."

"Feeling sick?"

"Nothing a cup of Nigel's herbal tea wouldn't settle. Are you all right?"

"No." Phoenix felt rattled to the core, his mind whirling from the surrealistically weird day and its aftermath. With trembling hands, he settled the sleeping cub amidst a soft pile of rugs and blankets, and then turned to face a man looking worse than he did after wrestling the anaconda. The journalist was decidedly unclear as to what to think or do, lost in mind with a heart in shreds.

"Get over here and sit beside me. I think we should start this conversation again." The big man extended a hand as an invitation of forgiveness, but whether either could forget was an entirely different story. Someone had to start. "We are an unlikely duo, Mr. Thornton-Jones."

"I wouldn't say that, considering my thoughts today." Swallowing his fear, Phoenix believed an opportunity arose to admit his feelings toward the photographer, with a gap between the asking and the doing.

"What thoughts are those?" Sloane eased the man down next to him, a white head resting on his shoulder and two hands playing with his larger one.

"I can touch myself now, Trev, with some lingering reservations. Although the act is still frightening for me, I do remember what to do and how good it once felt and still does. Thanks for helping me; I've missed so much."

"You're twenty-seven; you have time to make up the loss." Trevor's headache mellowed with the release of a strained, furrowed forehead.

"I'd like to ask you something."

"Go ahead." Life eased further for Sloane when the young man relaxed, scheming schemes and dreaming dreams.

"You said you'd wait for me. Are you still waiting, or have I blown my chances with you after today?"

Brown eyes opened fully; Sloane immediately alerted to the question, believing the answer extremely important to them both. He had to be sure; he had to be correct. "Today is only one day. As far as waiting for you, I will for as long as it takes."

"If you're sure, perhaps, when we get home, to New York that is, we might explore..." Phoenix stumbled, too frightened to go further. A memory of pain and broken bones flooded over him; and Sloane, if truly enraged, was large enough to annihilate him. Perhaps solitude in Colorado was his only future.

"...explore what? Do you want me to guess all sorts of ridiculous scenarios, or can you just blurt it out?" Trevor waited, instinctively understanding what the seventeen-year-old, hiding within the man, wanted to say.

"Life sucks, doesn't it?"

"Sometimes, but I've done that to you already. Do you wish me to repeat the act?"

"Oh brother, did I infer that?"

"You did."

"Maybe one of those innuendoes, but much more, Trev. At least I think I do; I want you to, but this scares me senseless. Would you say it in the nicest way possible?" Phoenix closed his eyes in mortification, fully aware of what he wanted and needed.

"I'd forfeit my soul for one chance to make love to you. If that's your desire, I'll fulfill your dreams without a clock. You give me the subtlest of signals, and I'll woo you like the man you've proven yourself to be." Trevor lifted a trembling chin and kissed the perfect lips. They opened to a sweet sigh, an invitation to continue the simple caress. With the lightest of touches, the older man pulled the small body around, gently adjusting the diminutive figure to sit on his knee, creating a more comfortable position to hold the flighty creature before he flew away. Needy arms encircled the muscled neck, as the opening lips sought out the experienced ones for a third taste. The kiss bewitched them both, growing stronger and more deliberate. Each new sensation released a groan as an enticement for more, particularly when Sloane's tongue entered the honey of youth, exploring a cavern ticklish with desire, one learning how to respond. Time--the older man thought--in time the perfect lips would be his, trained to lavish him with sincere adoration. He pulled away, leaving Phoenix unglued over another wanton but simple seduction.

"You make me crazy, Sloane. I don't know how to describe my feelings when around you, or to anyone else for that matter. Hell, I don't even understand them."

"Let me guess: toes curl, palms itch, mouth dries, genitals harden, sphincter muscles pucker, and you want to squirm out of your skin as nerves run up and tickle your rectum. Am I close?"

"Too close. You forgot sweating and heavy breathing."

"Good. We stop each other's heart."

"Oh yeah, heart palpitations and thoughts bordering on salacious."

"I rather like salacious. Nothing illegal about mutual adoration and expectations." Trevor laughed, tussled the damp hair to coax more waving, and wiped remnants of saliva off the softening smile. "Better pick up the cub for some mothering, before I change my mind about waiting and start here, right on the deck."

Phoenix stood on wobbly legs, reeling after the flirtatious kiss; each caress better than the last. Regaining his balance, he scooped up the gold and gray treasure, secured it against his chest with bandaged paws pointing skyward and sore baby eyes blinking to awaken. He breathed in deeply, regaining his composure enough to settle and coax the cub to open its mouth. With a low, growling whimper from one so small, two men looked at each other and smiled broadly, as the baby successfully took to the bottle. Their second argument had ended with new knowledge of each other and further insights into their own spirits. Hope rekindled the fire within. They sat together for some time, waiting for the crew to untangle themselves from whatever position suited the pair. A private thing for many, the prospects were endless, causing giggles, both on deck and below, to lighten the dreary rain-filled evening sky. An hour into darkness, after a gentle play with a rough little cub and the continual swabbing of the deck, Phoenix carefully disinfected broken scabs, applied ointment, and redressed the wounded chest of the man he had attached himself to with promises. Neither heard the hatch open, lost in thoughts of a new future for them both, one to ebb their mutual loneliness.

"Evening, lads. Glad to see you're both alive and smiling."

"We can see your lustful smile as well, Nigel. I hope Kenny feels as satisfied." Trevor winked at the captain; thankful a cruel day would end happily for all.

"Where's your partner? I'm starving." Phoenix stood, rechecked the new bandages, and helped Trevor don his shirt.

"Directly behind me, but I was led to believe that you're a fine cook yourself. We may just give you a go, TJ, or should that be Phoenix?"

"Oh! Well, let's make it Phoenix, since I'm finding it difficult to go back and forth." The smallest man looked up from underneath fluttering, bashful lashes, accompanied by a silly smile directed at the photographer who was equally confused by the various names.

"Great, now I won't have to worry about what I call you in public."

"I never thought about the difficulty before. The situation seems rather hurtful to Twister and Caly anyway, considering they gave me the extraordinary moniker."

"Right then, Phoenix you are. So, what's for dinner?" Baldwin poked his brunet head out of the hatch and beamed at his young friend who stuttered a response. On the suggestion, the emotionally recovering journalist willingly helped the cook gather the makings for dinner and threw a salad together, the starter before the co-operative spicy chili.

Finding refuge for the cub proved difficult, but Phoenix's innocent pleas touched the soft spot of the zoologist who hesitantly volunteered to raise the cub, to investigate the premature coloration, without any undue pain, and to find a suitable home. With grateful salutations, a wistful young man handed his baby over and walked quickly back to the boat, leaving parental tears hidden from strangers. Trevor remained behind when the zoologist signaled bad news with a subtle shake of his head. Learning the man's reasoning for the forlorn look, the photographer looked away into the forest, hoping for a miracle. The fate of the cub lay in the stars, although the zoologist and the veterinarian would try nurturing it and attempt the arduous task of locating a zoo willing to accept the huge and costly responsibility. Chances of survival, for one so young with lung damage and burns, were astronomical. A hand-raised wild feline needed at least three months with its mother; history had proven younger cubs were prone to mental impairment, making it difficult for them to socialize with either jaguars or humans. Prayers were needed to any god listening, and Trevor returned to the boat shaken. His partner need not hear the news until word came back from those currently loving the endangered little creature.

The back and forth journey took days, but Nigel and Kenneth deposited their two comrades at the terminal at the Manaus port. With stoic good-byes and back pounding hugs, the two Americans waved farewell and walked into the jungle of civilized man. One last job, which they hoped would not prove another risky confrontation, would be their last stop.

Trevor and Phoenix wrapped up their rainforest sojourn with only the road system to review, something they did in a federal government office in the largest city along the Amazon River. The staff members, at the Department of Transport, were exceedingly helpful, a delightful change from the bureaucratic fumbling they ran into at the beginning of their trip. Readily giving the two men detailed maps and information, along with illustrations of the type of roads indicated, the department's officials wished to make foreigners comfortable and safe while traveling throughout Brazil. Of tremendous interest to both Phoenix and Trevor, they learned where four-lane highways changed to two-lane country roads, and then to four-wheel-drive one-vehicle tracks. The road system was extensive in the eastern and southern sections of the country, with super-highways between the major cities, but the number dwindled dramatically as one toured through the network of Amazonia. Little was paved, and vehicles consisted of pollution-reducing ethanol powered trucks for industrial transport and buses for passengers, including tourists and those working in the interior. Sixty percent of all travel was by road, and mostly good roads, surprising both men who believed the waterways and air travel supported the majority of transportation. The large country had grandiose plans, however, to increase the roadways deep into the jungle, ending at planned new cities similar to Brasilia: new, clean, vast, and relentless. The rainforest again lay in peril. With another catastrophe waiting to unfold, there seemed little to do but wait for the inevitable. The giant loomed too large, and any words, dreamed up by a lone inexperienced writer, would be inconsequential to slay the monster.

With quantities of information in hand and stressful emotions behind their blank stares, Trevor and Phoenix flew away from the mighty forest with lasting memories of sorrow and joy. Confusion and disappointment stirred within the journalist; worry and doubt filled the photographer.

Chapter XX

Sloane convinced Phoenix to close his eyes on the journey home; and with little objection, the beautiful violets shut tightly and the small body curled into a ball to sleep sitting up. Rubbing the man's forearm, which rested across his large thighs, the photographer remained alert, as sore ribs and mending cuts would not allow him the comfort of their first class seats. Intensely proud of his partner, he gazed thoughtfully at the still figure, wishing to spoon around the once innocent who had an acute awakening into the reality of civilized and uncivilized man. He wondered himself as to whom fit into each category; the Yanomami certainly acted more in accordance with the meaning of civilized.

After a full day's flight, they arrived late on a cold March evening; winter dawdled, preventing spring breezes from melting the iced-packed snow. Phoenix shivered at the intense change of temperature, as they passed through the gateway and along the covered debarkation ramp. With quick reassurance from Sloane that they could buy warm coats at a store in the International Terminal, they could then depart in comfort for Mott Street. The pair lazily stretched out their aching cramped muscles, while waiting the excruciatingly long time for their luggage. Securing all pieces, two weary travelers walked into the busy terminal. With their backpacks slung over their shoulders and each with their business carry-on bags in a tight grip, they slowly made their way through the throng of night flyers. Bumped and jostled, little regard was given to tired, cold, and injured men who only wished quiet, warmth, and the comfort of home. Their three months of mind-altering experiences had left them with no patience for the cacophonous racket of hundreds of individuals who made up the cramped crowd. Sloane had to stop. "Let's take a break, Phoenix. I need to get my bearings."

"Something wrong?" The smaller man abruptly turned to face his friend who leaned against the closest wall with his eyes shut. "You have another headache. Maybe you should stay here with the bags, while I chase down some jackets and gloves."

Sloane rubbed his temples, attempting to rid himself of the sharp needles stabbing into his forehead from the inside. "I'll be okay, kiddo. Just give me a minute. Seems these migraines are growing worse."

"There's a bar up ahead. Let's sit a moment and get you some water. Something to eat might help."

"Good idea."

Phoenix adjusted his bags, giving him a free hand to guide his friend toward the pink and purple neon lights. Feeling very cold himself, he wished to get them out of the draft wafting through the high-ceiling building, to rest somewhere warm and out of traffic. Together they stepped into the onslaught of humanity (typically heading in the wrong direction), only to have the photographer drop to the ground.

"Trevor!" Phoenix yelled and quickly knelt beside his fallen comrade, attempting unsuccessfully to roll the encumbered body over. Too heavy a weight, only the graying wavy head could be turned. Sloane's eyes were closed. "No, Trev! Come on! Get up! Help! Somebody help me!" The young man yelled as he struggled to his feet in frenzied alarm, looking helplessly for aid, but overwhelmed by too many people who appeared all physically taller than his five-foot seven-inch stature.

"What's the problem, son?" An airport security officer appeared out of nowhere and came to his aid.

"My friend passed out! Please help me! He suffers from migraines. Trevor, wake up! Wake up!" Phoenix again tried to turn the bigger man over but failed. After another attempt, he mumbled a prayer of thanks on hearing the official calling for paramedics over his radiophone.

After an endless time, amidst the suffocating body of onlookers who kept yelling over the ruckus, several men in uniform pushed an opening through the mêlée, reaching the unconscious man and his frightened young friend. "Move aside. Right, cut his backpack off and roll him over. What happened?"

"He just dropped."

"Heart problems?"

"No, I don't think so. He said his head ached, and he was slurring his words. We just arrived back from Brazil. What's wrong with him? Please, help him. His ribs are broken and has machete wounds on his chest." Phoenix abruptly stopped, realizing he had no information about his friend's medical history. Left in torment, he watched nervously as the paramedics checked for vital signs. Unable to rouse the photographer, the experienced personnel quickly raised the deadweight onto a gurney, placed the appropriate bags at the unconscious man's feet, and hustled toward the exit where an ambulance stood ready.

"What are you doing? Where're you taking him?" Phoenix trotted behind with all his gear; his fear continued unabated that they may leave him stranded and unable to find the one he loved. Starting to hyperventilate, he stumbled behind the speeding gurney. "Please wait; I need to be with him."

"There's little room. Are you family?"

"No, his friend."

"Sorry, we must hurry. Is someone meeting you?"

"No, sir."

"Do you know anyone in New York?" The paramedics lifted the gurney, struggling to get the large body into the ambulance, while attempting to appease a distressed young man.

"I'm all he has. Please, we're freezing." Phoenix felt like a piece of lint brushed off onto the snow; but the look on his beautiful face alerted the man in charge.

"Okay, son, jump in front with the driver and stay out of the way."

The bedraggled traveler obeyed the commands, clambered into the front seat, and held on as the ambulance driver switched on the flashing lights and the banshee-screaming siren, while merging into traffic that slowly made a narrow pathway for the life-saving transport. Phoenix heard the men in back, speaking to an unknown person over a radiophone, as they hooked up machines to the still figure. The oxygen tubes upset him further; the electrical currents applied to the forehead scared him to stone. He needed to find help; he wanted his cellular telephone. Beyond rational thought, he sat in silence with his teeth chattering and a heart pounding too fast. *Emergency:* the word flickered in his eyes. They made the trip at speed, and once stopped, a horde of white coats and stethoscopes surrounded them under the pulsating red light. Leaping out, gathering his bags and nerve, he scurried after the men pushing the gurney.

Curtains, hanging on metal rods, instantly blocked his view of Sloane and any recognizable equipment remembered from too many hospital encounters. He could only stand in one place, freezing with a sudden draft of cold air. Drumming his fingers against the wall, he waited in trepidation for someone to explain. More rushing of different doctors, a nurse turned him around, insisting he wait in a chair close to the frenzied opening and closing doors. Another commotion and Sloane's lifeless body was wheeled to an elevator. "Wait! What's wrong? Someone talk to me!"

"Sorry, son, we're taking him upstairs for an MRI. We need you to help the nurse with any information as to a contact person or medical history. We need his family." The resident turned and ran after the moving bed, leaving the young man in shock, frozen to the core, and helplessly alone.

"But I'm his family." Phoenix whispered, while watching in disbelief as strangers rushed his friend away. Having no idea as to his next step, he slumped forward, his hands on his knees, his body ready to collapse from shock. A female voice set off the alarm in his head; and he immediately straightened to attention.

"Come along and tell me what you know. His passport has Denis Grayson as a contact. Do you know him?"

"Yes, he lives in Houston. He's another friend, like me. Can't you tell me where they're taking him?"

"The doctor will speak with you when he returns with the test results. Has Mr. Sloane been a patient of this hospital before?"

"He mentioned something about tests for his migraines. I think he said they were done here over several days."

"Good. Let's see if he's listed on our computer. Yes, here he is. Now, please, find a seat in the waiting room. We'll take care of your friend."

Phoenix returned to the designated area, calming a heart that refused to settle. With no experience on this side of the drawn curtains, he needed help. Asking a passing nurse for a telephone, he received only a point of a finger indicating one hid around the corner. He hoisted his luggage once more and scuttled to find a payphone: he had no American change! Another nurse walked by in haste, but the white-haired youth stopped her progress, growing more hysterical without a familiar presence. The kindly woman, dressed in a shade of pale blue, stopped to calm someone shaken to his boots and accompanied him to the front desk to ask for spare quarters. After a quick checking and a deep digging for coins amongst the staff, she left Phoenix with a pocket full of change to fend for himself with a public telephone he had never used. With stumbling fingers, he punched in the first number that he recalled instinctively, and then his telephone identification card. Confused and in shock, he waited to hear a loving voice.

"Hello, you've reached the TJ Ranch. Twister Jones speaking."

"Dad! Please, Dad, I don't know what to do! Trevor's unconscious; no one is telling me anything! I'm scared and cold. What do I do?"

"Where are you, son?" The honeysuckle voice remained calm, as did the stifled concerns on another line.

"New York, in a hospital. The New York Hospital I think."

"Slow down and take a breath. Are you in Emergency? Are you all right?"

"Yes, maybe this is Trauma. They've taken him upstairs for tests. They said something about an MRI. Is that for brain scans? His headaches are so bad. What can I do? I'm so cold, Dad, I can't think."

The two men, on the other end of the line, deduced their son was far from all right by his babbling and indecisiveness. Immediately on alert, Twister continued talking. "Okay, listen carefully. An MRI is a three-dimensional computer-imaging device; and you've had many of them. The lettering stands for Magnetic Resonance Imaging, nothing to fear. Now, ask the nurse for a blanket, and if you can, keep ringing my cellular. Caly and I are on our way, as soon as Frank can prepare the jet for take-off. Stay calm, mi poco Diablo. Stay at the hospital, and we'll see you come morning."

"Thanks, Dad, I need you and Pops. Please hurry."

"I know, son, I know. While we're in flight, I'll have Granny make some calls. Sit tight; everything will be fine."

Phoenix hung the telephone on its cradle and returned to the nursing station. "Excuse me, ma'am, did you contact Denis Grayson?"

"He is currently unavailable. We'll keep trying."

"But he could be anywhere. Do you have Trevor's... Mr. Sloane's address book? There must be someone else to call."

"No, sir. Please sit down. You must wait with everyone else." The irritated voice shattered all hope for the frazzled man shaking on the other side of the high desk. He turned once more to test the communication device, but a familiar green figure ran out of the opening elevator.

The doctor ignored the plight of an insignificant yet frantic friend, but blurted out the information to an Emergency Nurse. "We're prepping Mr. Sloane for surgery. Have you contacted his family? We can't wait for a signing authority."

The journalist went pale and pulled the resident around to cry out a more fearful question. "What kind of surgery? Is it serious? Is his life..."

"...Who are you?"

"His friend. We work and travel together. You must tell me."

"Wait here."

"No!" Again left alone, Phoenix watched the man run to catch the next elevator going up. "Please, ma'am, I'm all he has." Another plea failed, and a stern nurse pointed a testy finger toward the uncomfortable plastic chairs affixed to the floor. He fumbled for his own listing, walked over to the public telephone, and carefully dialed a number that connected him to an answering machine. "Joey, this is Phoenix. I mean TJ, Trevor Sloane's friend. If you're in New York, Trev's unconscious, going in for surgery at New York Hospital. I need your help. They're not telling me anything. Please, Joey, come if you can."

Hanging up, he looked in his wallet and spotted the card. He fingered it carefully, the number on it already memorized in his head. Although a risk, he had to chance calling those who wielded power. One ring, then two, he vowed he would hang up after four, but on the third, a serious formal greeting rattled him to his toes.

"Agent Kowalski here, Washington Office."

"Sir, this is Phoenix Thornton-Jones."

"Code."

"Mutant."

"Okay, son, where are you and what is your situation?"

"I'm at New York Hospital. Maybe I shouldn't have called, but I need help for my friend. They won't tell me anything, and he has no other family."

"What's his name, Phoenix?"

"Trevor Sloane, the photographer."

"Yes, here it is. You're currently working with him. Have the doctors indicated anything?" The voice remained authoritarian, but exuded warmth and kindness. The young man breathed in deeply; relieved he had done nothing wrong.

"I'm not sure, but I think they're operating. Maybe it's his head. Jesus, I just don't know! I'm alone, Agent Kowalski! Can you help me? I don't know what to do!"

"Let me try, son; we owe you. Stay put while I make a few calls. Ring back if the situation changes."

"Yes, sir. Thank you, sir." The black transmitter clanked against metal; Phoenix could not release the handle. He stood swaying, feeling sick to his stomach, unable to focus on the spinning room.

"TJ! God, it's good to see you! You've scared the hell out of me. Have they told you anything?"

"Joey! I'm so glad you're here." Phoenix flung himself around the former basketball player who immediately hugged and held him tightly.

"I know. I know. Let's see what's happening. Damn, is that all you're wearing?"

"Yeah, I'm so cold. We just got back. Trev collapsed at the airport. He had one of his headaches. They're growing worse, Joey."

The tall man continued to hang on, touching a sweating but cold forehead. "Here, I'll take your luggage and you put on my jacket. You're suffering from a bad case of shock. Why haven't they taken care of you? Shit! Come with me; it's time for action."

Calloway had been unlocking his door when he heard the plaintive message whispered into his answering machine. Immediately alarmed, he left without further information, ran the distance to the nearby medical facility, and entered Emergency looking for a tussle of white hair with pastel highlights. The young man stood at the payphone, barely able to stand, his teeth chattering. With his arm now supporting the extraordinary beauty, he gently guided the disheveled and frightened kid to the Nurses' Station, where two serious looking men in dark suits stood and immediately looked up in surprise.

"Jonathon Tremblay, what are you doing here?" The eldest of the two men dressed in black spoke first.

"Could say the same for you, Agent Burke." A swift look into the violet eyes, and then back to the harsh, cold blue ones, Joey calculated his next move.

"It's been a while, Tremblay. I still haven't figured you out."

"An art dealer for the discriminating few." Joey again glanced at Phoenix, ensuring the distressed man caught the message.

"So you say, but are you the dealer or the thief? We haven't yet apprehended the person responsible for the forgeries, or the one who accomplished the break-ins to replace the originals. In fact, we still can't find the originals, or whom they belong to legally. Quite the well thought-out caper, my hat comes off to one of such brilliance." The agent eyed the tall man and the one clutching his arm.

"I'm sure you will one day."

"A cold case file now, but I must point out that you remain on

our list of suspects. Now, the man beside you must be Phoenix
Thornton-Jones; the reason we're here. We were in the building when
a call came in from the Washington Bureau. Seems you are of
importance to head office. How can we be of service?"

"We need information regarding Trevor Sloane, sir. The staff
seems too busy to help me. I'm sorry, but I had no one else to call."
Phoenix looked from the agent to the man who had changed persona.
Even through the dense fog enveloping him, he understood Calloway's
plight of being several people. He would follow along.

"Hospitals can take regulations too far; I've personally
experienced that as well. We'll make inquiries for you. Are you
involved, Tremblay?" The man in charcoal gray scrutinized both the
small man and the one securing his shoulders. He wondered to whom
he spoke, and why the special consideration toward the youngest who
wore a jacket multiple sizes too large.

"I'm also a friend of Trevor Sloane's, traveling the same circles
in search of art. Phoenix and I have met but once. The only one he
knows in New York, I was lucky to be in town and able to respond
quickly to his cry for help. I'm sure we can straighten this matter out."

"I'm sure you can with your connections. You're not wearing
one of your $5,000 suits. I'm not used to seeing you in denim."

"Midnight sojourns, to help friends in hospitals, do not require
lavish style."

"Glad you have rich and powerful comrades, Mr. Thornton-
Jones, but we did promise to help."

"I find that a difficult notion to get my mind around, Burke."

"Now, now, Mr. Tremblay, we may have a radical reputation on
television and in the movies, but we can certainly sympathize with
someone in duress. Step aside while I talk to Nurse Devlin. Excuse
me, ma'am, can you tell us of Mr. Sloane's condition? This is now
FBI business." The man in the cheap dark suit took over, while
Calloway encircled a frightened innocent within his arms, attempting
to calm a heart racing and to warm a body too cold.

"We also require trauma blankets, Agent Burke. Phoenix seems
to be in shock not yet treated." Having stored the young man's alias in
his mind, Joey eased into his Tremblay persona, looking squarely at his
nemesis to ensure his demand was relayed to the head nurse.

She peered down her nose at them, scanning up and down with
her eyes at the men who surrounded her, unsure of the level of
authority staring her into the ground. "Of course. Dr. Rashman is the

night resident and will return shortly. Dr. Weddrix has been summoned. Currently, Mr. Sloane is in the Surgical Unit, Fourth Floor, Neurology."

"Neurology! Fuck!" Calloway clenched Phoenix fast to his chest, understanding the diminutive man's aggravation and distress, while nervously waiting for word. It was cruel. "Just give us the blankets, and we'll wait for Dr. Weddrix in the waiting room on the fourth floor. Agent Burke, thank you. We may need your assistance, or a flash of your ID, to obtain information from this Dr. Rashman before seeing Weddrix."

"I'll be waiting by the Second Floor's Surgical Unit. One of our agents was shot tonight, but will be okay, once the slug's removed from his leg. Take care of our charge." Burke turned to leave but stopped, twisting his head around to speak, "Mr. Thornton-Jones, I'll contact Agent Kowalski to inform him of your situation. If you require further assistance, while in New York, here is my card and cell number. Good luck, son."

"Thank you." Phoenix responded in his shy way, while comforted by a man who once greened his heart with jealousy.

Red blankets appeared. Joey quickly secured one around the shivering body before he picked up the bags and the extra blanket, finally steering the two-man parade toward the elevator. Concerned about his former lover, his paling young friend, as well as a story to explain Tremblay to the FBI and Calloway to Phoenix, the taller man remained silent during the short ride up. With much to consider, he attempted to focus on the one who refused to let go of his arm. The tight grip reminded him of friendship and loyalty; he mustered his fortitude to display both honestly. Sloane could be dying; Phoenix appeared mentally fragile enough to follow. "Feeling warmer?"

"Yeah, your jacket helps."

"The fourth floor will be more comfortable. Here's our stop. Don't be frightened; hospitals are scary places."

"I know. Look, there's the resident who won't talk to me." The frustrated journalist pointed at the man in green medical attire exiting the Operating Room at the end of the long corridor. Rushing to catch him, two men readied themselves to tackle the elusive creature before he disappeared into another *Staff Only* section.

"Dr. Rashman, tell us everything you know about Trevor Sloane, and stand fast, man, no more running in the opposite direction." Calloway reached out his long arm in case he had to derail the doctor by squeezing his neck.

"I assume you are Mr. Tremblay and Mr. Thornton-Jones. The FBI requested I tell you what I know. Please, come and sit in the waiting room. It's empty--a good place to talk--where Dr. Weddrix will inform you of the treatment necessary." The resident changed his attitude quickly, after unsmiling agents had subtly threatened to tear up his hard-earned credentials and send him into the cold world, never to practice again. Nervously escorting the duo to the warm waiting room, he noticed the blanket color and prepared himself to care for those who appeared as distressed as any close family member would be. "Here we are. This will be more comfortable for you."

"Please, Doctor, we won't keep you, but I need to know what's happening." Phoenix could barely speak, but stuttered out his concerns.

"Yes, of course; I'm sorry for the delay. We were unsure of your status with the patient, but the FBI, as well as your grandmother..."

"...Dr. Rashman, move aside. You must be Phoenix. I just received a startling call from Maddie about your ill treatment at our facilities. Has anyone helped you?"

"And you are?" Joey piped up, annoyed at the interruption by a gray-haired but balding man with a red flushed face.

"I'm Dr. Crowe, one of the hospital's administrators. Your grandmother, Phoenix, is an old friend of mine."

The young man reined in Calloway, taking his hand and standing to meet both doctors towering over him. "I'll be fine, sir, as soon as Dr. Rashman tells us of Mr. Sloane's condition and what's being done. We're anxious for an explanation."

"Of course. Go ahead, Doctor." The agitated Dr. Crowe stepped forward and turned, to stand beside the two men who waited for a diagnosis. He would relay the information to a feisty, angry woman whose power extended beyond Colorado's borders. Her philanthropic endeavors were legendary, donating millions of dollars to every hospital in her home state over a ten-year span. An extraordinary woman, she never gave a reason for her kindness.

"Mr. Sloane has a small anomaly exerting pressure on his brain. Located in the left cerebral cortex, we believe it benign, although the surgeon will clarify the results when completed. Surgery was necessary to relieve the pressure and to determine the cause of the anomaly: tumor, aneurysm, blood vessel malformation or malfunction.

Currently, a blood thinner prevents oxygen deprivation, allowing an opportunity for a successful removal. Due to the unknown nature of the anomaly and the speed of its development, considering Mr. Sloane's clear MRI of less than a year ago, Dr. Weddrix determined invasive surgery was necessary, rather than stereotactic radiation. Although riskier, he can validate his findings, rather than eradicating the problem and waiting for another attack. In the meantime, we expect a full recovery, and depending on the results, medication may or may not be prescribed." Dr. Rashman unclenched his sweating fists; even doctors troubled over words that may impart bad news.

"But he's suffered from migraines his entire life." Phoenix nearly collapsed from the frightening answer to his simple question, but Joey held firm from behind.

"One condition apart from the other, but indistinguishable I'm afraid. Treatment for one often negates finding the other. We must feel lucky his intense pain caused a blackout, necessitating a more acute examination. I have nothing further to offer but these couches to ease the wait. Make yourselves comfortable, and I'll send someone to procure whatever you need. I am sorry to have caused any unnecessary grief." The resident held back, waiting for a stinging blow from one much higher in authority, an official who could fire him without a final paycheck.

"Has he sustained any permanent damage?" Calloway's turn, but the quiver in his voice intensified Phoenix's fright.

"We must wait for the final results. Once Mr. Sloane is conscious, we'll know more. Please be aware that Dr. Weddrix's reputation is noted worldwide. Your friend is in excellent hands."

"Thanks. We'll wait for Dr. Weddrix then." The tallest man muttered the words, recycling the terrible news repeatedly through his head, while helping a cold, rigid body sit down.

"Joey, ask him if..."

"...Steady, Phoenix. Dr. Rashman, can you be more specific as to Mr. Sloane's well being?" Calloway understood his small friend's thoughts; the kid seemed confused over the medical terminology. Speaking for both of them, he hoped for a simple answer to explain a complex procedure.

"He's strong and healthy, Mr. Tremblay; and we found the tumor in an early stage. We have great expectations, but must wait for Mr. Sloane to tell us."

"Thank you." The former basketball player turned his attention to the glassy purple eyes, as the resident disappeared. "Everything will be fine, Phoenix. Sloane has much to live for. Now, let's get these blankets around you. Dr. Crowe, how long do these operations last?"

"Some time, I'm afraid. Could be a few hours, could be many. Here's a friendly face to help us. Good evening, sir. We are in need of hot drinks, more blankets, and a warm wet cloth. I'll tend to the young man personally. He suffers from shock, and I fear from the cold as well, considering his summer attire. Please do not delay, for we have incurred the wrath of someone who could smite us with a point of her bejeweled finger."

The Nursing Aid scampered away to fetch all items requested, plus a few added luxuries to make unhappy men feel closer to the living. While not his particular job, he did endeavor to help those who stood in the shadows. In minutes, he prepared a fresh pot of coffee, ordered soup and sandwiches from an obstinate kitchen worker, and scavenged more blankets for the beautiful young man who everyone hovered over. His thanks came with three attempted smiles. He would stand aside, waiting for a summons.

Hours passed. Crowe paced off his concern after telephoning his long time friend to give her an update, while the other two men ate a little and warmed their shaken spirits with the eldest stroking the white head of the youngest. Calloway had convinced Phoenix to lie down, place his head on his lap, and rest. With his long arms and large hands, he covered the trembling legs and cold feet with many red blankets, and then secured more around the yellow quilted jacket. As independent as his friend the photographer, he had never been the giver of comfort, always somewhere else when tragedy struck down a family member or friend. As terrified as the man he consoled, he could only look down and hope he was helping in some manner.

"Thanks for coming, Joey."

"Not to worry; I'm happy you thought to call me."

"I didn't know what else to do."

"Life comes at us a little too fast sometimes. We forget we're mortal beings." The older man twisted his finger around the baby fine pastels, using the perspiration, caused by trauma, to create ringlets in the longer hair. His own solace came from tender touches to his friend's angel, a young man he prayed would never be hurt by the wandering photographer.

"I guess it's too late to call Twister and Caly. They'll be in the air."

"Rest now. We may be here for some time."

"Yeah, I'm so tired and I can't stop shivering."

"A result of a sudden shock. How are you feeling otherwise?"

"The soup and crackers settled my stomach. I'm okay." Phoenix snuggled unashamedly against the strong thighs and comforting hand, while he kept his eyes on the worried stranger pacing the hallway. He did feel ill from the uncontrollable shaking of his body, a natural reaction to fend off the chills caused by a winter's night, the fear over his friend's surgery, and a possible revelation of a carefully guarded secret to someone clever enough to connect two important words.

"Once your family arrives and Trevor's condition stabilizes, we'll get you back to his apartment. Master Chui has access to turn up the heat, start a fire, and stock food for tomorrow. We'll know something by then."

"Thanks, I'd like that." The journalist breathed deeply; Calloway probably had missed the error made by his grandmother who had miscalculated her old friend and what he may say. The secret remained safe.

"Home, or a good friend's home, feels better than an austere hotel, even for those who can afford the finest. Try to sleep, a difficult request I know."

Phoenix closed his eyes to envision a joyful world of new beginnings with Sloane. Negative thoughts dispersed on a continuous affirmation silently whispered in his head; a lesson learned after many a fitful setback. After five hours of restlessness, for those in the waiting room, Dr. Weddrix emerged with good news. The photographer would recover fully after the successful removal of the benign tumor; the risk of brain damage listed as negligible to non-existent. Fear, of a god and his mighty sword, finally abated; life continued for those who waited. Several hours before dawn, two men bid farewell to a frenzied administrator, shared another pot of fresh coffee, and waited to see their friend in recovery. The clock overhead ticked off the minutes slowly; their nerves and wits stretched beyond endurance; their sanity saved by another doctor who greeted them with a friendlier good morning. He immediately ushered them into a sterile room of monitors and strange noises, where Trevor laid still, his eyes closed, and his head bandaged.

"Currently under heavy sedation, Mr. Sloane should be coming around within the hour. Always best to wake up to happy faces. Talk to him and call me when he moans. He won't be suffering with the painkiller given him through the IV drip."

"Thanks, Doctor, we'll call you when he's conscious. Sit beside him, Phoenix. Should I stay or leave?"

"You can't leave now! He's your friend as well, and I'm the one who panics. Look at him; he's so sick. I needed to ask more questions, but I'm such an idiot, I forgot to ask." The young man tugged at the red blanket slipping off his shoulders and reached down to touch the still hand. Sloane lay precisely in the *Attention* position.

"You did everything right, calling your parents, leaving a message for me; however, rallying the FBI was a surprise. How did you manage that, and the Washington Bureau no less?"

"Oh, man, I'm sorry. I forgot your different connections and could put you in jeopardy; but I wasn't sure if you would get my message, or if you were even in New York."

"I saw your acknowledgement of my perilous situation in just a blink of your eyes. Thanks for not exposing Tremblay or Calloway to Burke. So, who in your family works for the Federal Bureau of Investigation to spur such swift action?"

"No one. I just helped them once."

"I thought as much, a secret like so many of mine."

"Probably very unlike yours. I wonder if they checked Trevor's ribs and cuts." Phoenix shifted thoughts, knowing too much of one Calloway character and feeling extremely insecure of his own.

"You didn't tell me he was injured!" The taller man also veered course, disturbed over the run-in with Burke and confused over the young journalist's involvement with the notorious investigative body. One seldom touched the human side of an agent, let alone many.

"An anaconda crushed his chest; and I sure didn't help cutting the damn thing off with a machete."

"Shit! A fucking snake! I don't believe it!"

"I was there, man; it happened. Most people can identify one or two worst days of their lives; I seem to experience one after another, interspersed with a rare good day."

"We'll light candles to make sure this is a good day, with Sloane waking up and smiling at us; nonetheless, I am surprised he survived the terror. I can't even envision you chopping up a snake! That takes guts, man." Calloway cringed at the notion, wondering if he could accomplish the same feat without freezing with his own strange phobia brought on by any reptilian. He shook himself, deciding the younger man had sufficient courage to handle any kind of trouble if left on his own accord.

"Scared me shitless. Only the Yanomami know what happened. Trevor and I were too far-gone to grasp the danger. Hey, Trevor, wake up and tell Joey the story of our adventure." A shaking, hesitant hand reached for the unconscious man's cheek, but immediately pulled back before the caress.

"I'll leave you two alone for a few minutes. You must have a few words to plant in his psyche that will stir him to awaken." Calloway started for the door on seeing the affection the youngest had for his former lover.

"Thanks, Joey; thanks for being here."

"I'll be right outside if you need me. Give me your father's cell number, and I'll try to reach your parents. You'll feel better once your folks have arrived."

Phoenix scribbled down the number. He did need Twister and Caly, but while he waited, their loving words to him, upon coming out of an anesthetic, would be tried; words forever imbedded in his subconscious mind, his fathers always gave him something to look forward to. As Calloway departed Intensive Care, Phoenix leaned forward and brushed his lips against the still ones. "I love you, Trevor Sloane; and I'll prove it, if you open your eyes and kiss me."

Chapter XXI

Phoenix rambled his yearnings to an unconscious man. He disclosed every feeling he had, some very real, while others unhinged him with the utterance. Expressing and describing the most lurid of acts, he wondered if he could fulfill his promises. He gently stroked the muscled arm and serene face, attempting to awaken the man with promised loving aspirations. On a twitch of a finger, a soft mutter, his heart skipped several beats, stopping his monologue to call, "I'm here, Trevor. I'm waiting for you. Wake up."

"Phoen..."

"Yeah, man, I'm right beside you. How do you feel?"

"Strange... Hurts to breathe."

"Probably your broken ribs. Do you remember?"

"Yeah. Think so. What happened? Where... where are we?" The dark fringes fluttered, but the eyes did not fully open.

"At the hospital. I'm supposed to fetch the doctor as soon as you moan." Phoenix felt the man vainly attempt to squeeze his hand; and he responded, giving a stronger squeeze to circulate warmth into the large, cold one.

"Tell me, kiddo... Tell me first..."

"...I'm still unsure of what they did or what happened to you, so I really can't tell you anything."

"No, tell me what... what you said. I heard some of it, like... like I was sitting too far away." The photographer finally opened his warm brown eyes, blinking a drugged gaze at his partner's tired violet orbs. His young friend looked dreadful, so very gaunt and weary, as if arising from the dead.

"Oh, that! I guess I was telling you how much... how much I need you. I've fallen for you, Trevor Sloane; at least as far as I understand the meaning."

"I love you too, kiddo. Guess I better hear the doctor's story first, before listening to more of your sweet murmurings."

"I'll find him, but I'll stay close. While you speak with the doctor, I'll take a quick break. You have no idea how glad I am to hear your voice." Phoenix leaned over and kissed Sloane on the mouth, receiving a real moan of pleasure that made the younger man chuckle.

"You better start doing that more often, as well as giggling."

"I hope I can make you happy, Trev, but stay patient a little longer. Rest now and I'll return after the doctor is finished with you." Phoenix hesitated, nervously fingering the heavy zipper on Joey's ski jacket.

"Something wrong?"

"No, but... this sounds so pathetic... please, don't scramble my head and heart if I don't know what to do or get scared." Phoenix bit down on his perfect lower lip; a gesture seldom seen by the photographer, but one that always made him smile at the cuteness.

"We'll discuss many things beforehand. I'll never rush you. Besides, I think your instincts have sparked to life." Trevor grinned painfully, causing his forehead to wrinkle slightly. He opened his eyes fully to see his guardian angel bite harder on his lip, blinking white eyelashes, and blatantly flirting with a man who had no escape from his charms. On a silly wave, Phoenix disappeared out the door to summon the person who could explain the procedure performed. With the doctor checking on his patient, Thornton-Jones returned to the waiting room for solace from Calloway.

"Phoenix!" Twister immediately rose to his feet.

"Sugarhead, are you all right?" Caly raced toward his son, bear-hugging him tightly and bringing the white head around for a paternal kiss.

"Yeah, I'm fine, Pops. I'm sorry I alarmed you, but I feel so much better now that you and Dad are here. I'm still shaking in my boots, but Joey helped. Again I'm sorry; I called the FBI!" Phoenix released his grip to welcome Twister's embrace.

"Good to see you, mi poco Diablo. There's no reason for worry in that regard. The FBI gave you that card for such an emergency. Now, how's Trevor?" The tallest father lifted his son off the ground for another nurturing hug and set him back down on legs a little too weak.

"He's awake, sounding like Trevor. God, I've missed you both."

"Fear gave you the impetus to call us, and we're glad you did. Now, we met your friend here, who explained some of what happened. We brought your winter duds, so let's get you changed and feeling better. Go with Caly, while I rustle up some food. You and Joey must be hungry." Twister took over from the two men who had held vigil for one long night. Both looked drawn and shaken; fear oozed from their pores. Time to rally the troops; Phoenix's Dad would care for them all.

"Why didn't you tell me your father's were fathers?" Calloway had been delighted, but confused, on seeing two cowboys exit the elevator, taking charge at the Nurses' Station to find their son. He liked them at once.

"I didn't think about it, considering you're gay."

"Oh, that explains everything. Try again." The tall man, with the mysterious career, chuckled, also relieved to see the bright smile on his young friend's face; a signal his old friend had survived another crisis.

"Enough chat, boys. Come along, Phoenix. The medical staff kindly offered their locker room for you to shower and change. You're very cold to the touch; a hot shower will rid you of some of your chill. We don't want you falling ill. If you two will excuse us, we'll return in minutes for further conversation, as well as looking for sustenance, Mr. Jones." On the subtle command from one partner to the other, Caly pulled his son by the arm and playfully shoved him toward a *No Admittance* area.

Showered clean, dressed warmly, an exhausted Phoenix emerged, kept in a straight line by the strong arms of a bull rider. The two men laughed aloud upon seeing Twister pull out his wallet to pay the New York delivery girl who stared in awe, drooling over the handsome cowboy from boots to Stetson. Although in his fifties, the man was still an attraction wherever he walked. The pretty, little thing finally departed with a large tip, but not before Calloway had checked the four breakfast containers to ensure the temperature and quantity of pancakes, sausages, and toast, with all the right condiments. Four men needed nourishment: two had flown all night in their executive jet, while the other two had waited a never-ending night after their own grueling day. They all ate with gusto, medical worries abated, and the mentally fragile glowed from within. Three experienced men exchanged glances and winks, knowing the youngest enjoyed a secret of the heart, ready to explode from the chest for the telling. All wished to take him aside and ask particulars, but time would come for a revelation when Phoenix felt safe.

Each man spent time with Sloane, while together they listened intently to Dr. Weddrix. The surgeon in charge had rousted early to check on the famous photographer who had friends flashing FBI identification. Albeit daunting to work under such scrutiny, he expressed his happiness over the results of the operation and ensured everyone that his patient could return home within the week, but warned them that regular checkups would be required over the next few. With life on course, each man bid his bandaged friend farewell with a promise to return that evening. Calloway also said good-bye to the cowboys and their son, wishing them a pleasant stay in New York. In return, the family invited him to dine several days hence, at the only restaurant where Phoenix felt comfortable. With everything done and said, Twister and Caly toted two backpacks, an over-the-shoulder bag full of papers, and one important camera case, following their son safari-style to a waiting limousine. They headed for Mott Street, looking forward to comfort and the quiet warmth of a fire.

After greeting and informing Master Chui of the goings-on, the Thornton-Jones family slumped into the soft, man-sized furniture, put their feet up, and flipped a coin as to who would pour the freshly brewed coffee. Phoenix lost and happily, so; a sense of domesticity swept him into a peaceful grace, feeling he belonged in the apartment, inviting his fathers to visit his own home. An odd thought, he reveled at the opportunity to show Twister and Caly he had taken another leap through the dreaded portal of real life. His confidence soared, as did the sheepish grin stretching his lips upward.

"We're proud of you, Phoenix. You handled yourself extremely well through Trevor's crisis. You've also had an astounding trip to Brazil, met some interesting people, made new friends, and experienced many wild adventures, ones your Dad and I would run from, but we certainly enjoyed reading your few emails. What are your future plans?" Caly accepted the mug of java handed him and rested comfortably against his partner who also appreciated the pick-me-up.

"Wait for Trevor to heal, I guess. He'll want to process the many images he took, but Dr. Weddrix believes the fumes may initiate some of his headaches. I hope I can get him to rest, while I attempt the impossible, sorting through tons of information and formulating my thoughts on paper. Shit! I forgot to call Mr. Graham!" Phoenix had taken the chair by the telephone and quickly pressed the single number programmed to connect him with the publisher. The call was relayed quickly to the important individual who wanted to know every detail. After a short summary, the young journalist also emphasized his need for sleep, which Graham understood and indicated he would visit his old friend after work. Upon a farewell, Phoenix hung up the telephone, returned his attention to his fathers, and smiled broadly for the first time in hours. "I'm so relieved you're here. Man, what an unexpected turn after a long trip."

"You're tired, son. Perhaps we should all take a timely nap."

"I'm feeling rather excited, Dad. I don't think I can sleep with so much to tell; we barely scratched the surface over breakfast. By the way, you and Pops can sleep in the room I occupied before running away, while I take..." Phoenix stopped, embarrassed at the giddy feeling running through his body at the thought of a name.

"...take Trevor's room?" Caly finished the obvious thought and winked at the young man he adored, unnerving the blushing innocent further.

"Do you have something to tell us, Diablo?" Twister grinned mischievously, turning the tanned face a brighter crimson.

"I suppose. I don't know; but you're my fathers. I'm not sure if you want to hear this, or if I'm supposed to tell you."

Caly chuckled, as did Twister, but the smaller cowboy played the sweet interrogator. "I'm sure we'll enjoy hearing whatever you have to say. Can I bluntly suggest that Mr. Sloane has something to do with your excitement?"

"An easy guess, hunh?"

"We're gay, Phoenix, able to understand your feelings, as well as the difficulties, unless they involve an anaconda." Twister joined the chuckling, bringing more sparkle into the dancing purple eyes.

"Okay, I'll try. I've been sleeping with Trevor for some time, but not in a carnal fashion. Even in the heat of a Brazilian summer, I sleepwalk, always finding his bed, as I used to do with you guys. He finally just accepted the fact and insisted I start the night beside him. I didn't think anything of it, except feeling rather awkward. I'm used to older men who platonically love me, like the ranch hands, and of course paternally, like yourselves, but this is so different." Phoenix stumbled, unsure of a sexual act and the ramifications for one's parents.

"Sounds very caring, but also suggests it may have led to something else. Don't be shy. Who wants to see you happy, Sugarhead?"

"You and Dad; but this is extremely awkward and embarrassing." Phoenix sat forward, resting his elbows on his knees, while wringing his sweaty palms and gathering his will to speak freely and openly. "The first night we spent alone in the jungle, before the snake incident, I heard a sound I didn't recognize. Thinking it some night prowling creature with teeth, I called to Sloane who groaned and told me... Well, he was jerking off, which upset me to the point of anger. Really stupid, hunh?"

"No, not at all. You've been isolated your entire adult life. How could you know? Your normal instincts were crushed beyond anything we could mend." Caly reached out his arms, inviting a newly invigorated man to sit with his two fathers.

The invitation was accepted, and Phoenix slithered between the two, each holding a clammy hand. "Trevor retaliated by daring me to do something you don't even know about. The phrase *sexual aversion* came up often with my therapists, and I clarified the terminology with *sexually inert*. The meaning sounded less intense than the real condition suffered; something I discovered when I could use one finger to poke at a keyboard. I couldn't face or accept the idea I could be so scared, so I hid the phobia from everyone. I didn't need the hassle from psychiatrists who told me: *'use it or lose it'*. Anyway, the condition started with a wet dream while recuperating from the initial injuries. Unfortunately, the pain was so excruciating, I would do anything and everything to prevent my cock from getting hard. I swore never to let it happen again."

"You probably still had stitches, Phoenix. Of course it would have hurt, and as for your psychiatrists, you better tell me which of them said such a stupid thing." Twister squeezed his partner's hand; both fathers cringed at the thought of their son's misfortune and the insensitivity of doctors who should have known better.

"They all said it, and I'll never forgive them for their useless advice. They didn't help me with any of my phobias. As for my wet dream, I did still have stitches; but the act hurt more mentally and has continued until..." Again, hesitation stifled his words. Phoenix could not release his mortification in front of his fathers.

"Did Trevor touch you inappropriately?" Caly suddenly grew serious, troubled over another possible travesty suffered.

"Oh, no. No, of course not. Well, maybe. Sort of. No he didn't, not until later. Shit, what am I trying to say?" Phoenix heard the concern and wondered why he had started the conversation with two overly protective men. Growing more upset, his lower lip quivered, alerting Twister to rescue his son from his uncertainty.

"Easy, Diablo; you too, Caly. Let the boy finish."

"This wasn't my best idea. Maybe you've heard enough."

"You're our son. If you've had a sexual awakening, please tell us. We'd be more than happy to hear the details of your coming out, not just as gay, but from a condition we could not correct for you." Jones affectionately ruffled the white hair, which needed a trim, while squinting adversely at his nervous partner to still his overwrought concern and potential misconceptions.

Phoenix looked from one man to the other, feeling very uncomfortable. "Trevor forced me to touch myself; something I've been unable to do since the *accident*. I can't even urinate in a public washroom for God's sake, considering I've never touched that part of my body in ten years."

"I didn't know that, did you, Twister?"

The biggest man of the three shook his head, equally surprised as his partner. "How did you manage at school?"

"Gas stations and small cafes, with one toilet bathrooms, and holding myself up with whatever was handy."

"Good lord, why didn't you tell us?"

"I couldn't, Dad. I felt so out of place, and my scars made it worse. They still do." Phoenix grew closer to tears, rehashing memories he wished to banish.

"We're sorry; we're making this hard for you. Your Pops and I will relax our questioning, so you can tell us how Trevor forced... maybe the word should be *persuaded*. Would that sound better?"

"Nice try, Dad, but forced seems more appropriate. Although unaware of his remarks, he made me feel ashamed of my inadequacies, which I tried to rectify by listening to the instructions he gave. I reached down and held my hands over my hard-on, that he noticed bulging under my shorts. When I couldn't lower my hands, he reached over and forced them down against me. He never really touched me, but I screamed and started to--well, you know how weird I get when scared shitless--I went into a meltdown, knowing I couldn't stop myself from coming, but readying myself to endure the pain. Trevor whipped my briefs off and took me orally. His actions created a tidal wave of terrorizing shock; I couldn't deal with the overwhelming emotion at the time."

"Did he hurt you? What did you do?" Caly sounded bent on killing Sloane over the wanton lust over his son.

"No! No! He made the act easy for me; pulling me from the hell I've put myself through. I felt wonderful, floating on the softest cloud, but I thought he was angry with me. All the next day, we walked in silence. Unsure of our changing relationship, I remained euphoric the entire day, but unable to tell him, and then we got back to the boat... Shit!" Again, Phoenix hesitated and uttered a profanity. How was he to explain his wanton lust and resulting action to his fathers? He had never been in such a situation.

"What happened? Did he say something to embarrass you, to tease you?"

"Easy, buckaroo." Twister laid a hand on his partner's shoulder as his son sat forward, unable to face his fathers to confess a sin experienced only once.

"I was so distressed when we got back, confused over his silence; I finally asked him why he was so hostile. It never occurred to me he was upset and worried over his handling of my predicament. I started to cry so hard, I couldn't think." The young man put his face in his hands to stop another monumental downpour that could flood his best friend's living room.

"But you don't cry, or very seldom do."

"I've become very good at it recently, Dad, since meeting Sloane. I fall apart with any affectionate gesture, either from excitement or from terror. The line seems so thin."

"Crying isn't a bad thing; and he must have recognized your radiant afterglow. You had just conquered something of immense importance, learning that you're sexually normal. Twister and I are ecstatic over your recovery." Caly pulled the young man back into protective arms, squeezing love into his son who appeared shattered rather than joyous.

"Trevor helped me so much with his words. I tried to respond accordingly, but I messed it up so badly. Never in my wildest dreams would I repeat the act I perpetrated on him, jumping on him and rubbing myself against him. It was so intense; man, I came in my pants! I wanted to die right there, but he held on; he held me so tightly, I could barely breathe; and then he walked me through the humiliation I couldn't face alone. How many *Hail Mary's* do I have to say for something so disgusting?"

"Absolutely none, considering you're not Catholic, and there's nothing disgusting about any sexual act if enjoyed by both participants. Rubbing genitalia together is part of sex for both gays and straights. How many times do you think I've dampened your Dad when he carries me? We love the playful intimacy; it's a part of our existence. Thank heavens Mr. Levis Straus created denim that doesn't show stains as readily as other fabrics do. You did nothing wrong."

"I think your actions would have endeared you to him, Diablo. The experience was appropriate under the circumstances, and dare I say, very cute."

"Hardly cute, more like horny as hell. Dad, Poppy, I love him, I think, and have told him, but I'm fucking afraid of sex... afraid of the pain! I can pleasure myself on occasion now, which takes my entire will; but how can I break through completely without such crudity? I'm scared stupid. He loves me, says he'll wait; but I'm still not sure. What do I do?" Phoenix again pulled himself forward, his hands hiding his tortured face. With his excitement dashed with the truth, he wondered how to redeem himself after his miscues and statements to Sloane.

"We're here for you, Phoenix, and always will be. You love Trevor and that's all that matters, as is the recognition of an emotion we hoped for you. He's a decent, caring man who has helped you already. I don't expect him to change. You'll work this out together, slowly and patiently. You're a virgin, Sugarhead, never able to experience the first time like the rest of us. Be seventeen again, wishing for a hero to whisk you away. Trevor seems a very good start and may be the finish. Take the risk. You've come so far since you met." Caly switched gears, thankful for the clarification before shooting Sloane. He rubbed his son's back, while Twister wiped a tear from his own eye. Both men held back feelings of joy and concern. Their son had announced an affair of the heart they never thought possible, but the sorry spirit could crack under the mountain he bore on his shoulders.

"I'm totally bewildered over all the unknown feelings and physical reactions I'm having. What have I done?" Phoenix scrubbed his face with his hands and sat back, looking from one father to the other.

"You've taken several monstrous steps while overwrought, overtired, and overcome with renewed feelings, particularly after this taxing forty-eight hour day. Life is full of challenges, all impossible to predict. Ease your way into the relationship, never take anything for granted, and just keep your sweet, loving heart open for the pleasures and potential troubles ahead. No one is immune to either. Now, I suggest Caly help you into bed, while I gather bags and find the guest room. Up you get, and we'll keep our conversation secret when we visit Trevor tonight." Twister had his son on his feet, along with his partner, and gently pushed them in the direction of Phoenix's gaze.

"Thanks, Dad. I don't know what I'd do without you guys. Man, I'm ready to drop. Your room is on the left, up those few..." The youngest man stopped abruptly, listening intently. "What was that? Did you hear something?"

"Sounded like a cat. Oh, I am sorry, Phoenix."

"It's okay, Pops; I can say the word now without going catatonic. It must be Bogart." Walking to the roof garden door, the youngest man confidently bent down and unlatched the small opening to allow the chilly feline entry. "Hey, Bogie, do you remember me from one scary night?" Reaching for the purring cat, he picked it up and snuggled his face into the cold fur.

"I don't believe this!" Caly looked at Twister who shrugged his shoulders in equal surprise.

"After the mother jaguar died at my feet, her one cub desperate for a friend, and Trevor's subtle manipulations in a conversation about wildcats, the phobia disappeared quietly, although I remember the event that caused it. I didn't realize the fact until I heard Bogie scratch at his door. Trevor once suggested this critter would stop my sleepwalking like Snow and Sky. I think we'll try it. What do you say, Bogart?" Phoenix sweetly rubbed the silver silk, receiving a contented purr and a little nose-to-nose sign of affection. "Wake me if I oversleep. I've really missed you. Please stay in New York awhile."

"For as long as you need us. The jet sits at a private airport, the crew is on standby, and the limo rented for a week. Since we were unsure of the seriousness of Trevor's condition, or what may transpire, the easiest form of transport seemed warranted. We can bring your new love home in luxury."

"My new love, hunh? You mean my first."

"I think he's your second, Diablo."

"Oh, yeah, good old Rory, he'll be happy to hear the news, if it's news at all. Thanks, Dad. I can settle myself, Pops. You guys get some rest. Bogie and I will see you in a few hours." Phoenix kissed Caly, and then repeated the family tenderness with Twister. While carrying the happy furry bundle, he left his fathers befuddled over the dramatic changes in their son, who closed the door of the master suite and wistfully sighed. The legendary photographer lived here; Sloane's scent wafted over the love-struck young man when he opened the closet full of expensive suits and travel attire. This was what he wanted, and he would fight his fears to grasp a piece of happiness, no matter the duration of his sweetest dreams and wickedest thoughts.

Chapter XXII

After four days of watchful treatment, Sloane returned to his New York home to a houseful of joyful friends. Wolfe hugged him, Sebastian kissed him, and relieved smiles winked about the room. Greeted with flowers, books, and erotic gifts, his eyes never diverted from Phoenix who shone unearthly bright amongst the *gay* periphery of larger, stronger men. The legendary photographer's face beamed with less furrows in the brow; his chronic pain reduced to nil on taking the hand of his white angel.

Family members departed after seeing the Broadway lights and New York sights, sharing lost months of day-to-day activities, and ensuring their son was functioning in his normal off-centered state. Many words of wisdom came from enthusiastic fathers, in private and without a negative word. Phoenix waved good-bye from street level, blinked his eyes repeatedly to stop the tears, and then climbed the long stairs to a quiet apartment full of important work.

Trevor watched the young man scribble page after page, and then trash page after page. Seeing the struggle within his partner, he puzzled over the journalist's dilemma, and he too went to work, ignoring the objections of the troubled one. The darkroom exterior light glared red for many days, but when the processing required a waiting period, Sloane spent those hours comforting an irreconcilable young man who tried too hard. The photographer could only sympathize. After another frustrating day, Phoenix viciously assaulted a plastic button on his keyboard and shut down the publishing program, accompanied by a few unkind profanities. With no words to fill in the gaps of data, he raised his hands in surrender, defeated before drafting the first paragraph. At the highest moment of the younger man's anxiety, Trevor exited the darkroom carrying a fat folder. "Hey, kiddo, how's it going?"

"Not. What about you?" Phoenix sat in front of the monitor, elbows on the desk, his head in his hands, ignoring the streaming video of an X-men cartoon, blasting their mutant talents at the bad guys.

"Better than you from your demeanor. I've been thinking about your writer's block." Trevor tussled the white tresses playfully, while pulling back the chair on rollers. He received no objection when he leaned down, encircled his arms about the dejected man's chest, and kissed the clean cheek from behind.

"I'm stuck, Trev; trapped in a world I don't understand. Facts and figures are not my forte." Phoenix whined slightly, but bit his lip to prevent further grief for his friend.

"So, don't use them." The bigger man hoisted him out of the chair and guided him over to the window to gaze upon a bright sunny day.

"How can I avoid them?"

"Easy, because most are inaccurate. For instance, you analyzed the world's population statistics and what did you find regarding Brazil?"

"They use two figures: a census number and an estimated one. Each of their largest cities has a discrepancy of several million people, and when added together, plus those living in remote areas, favelas, and the overwhelming number of street orphans, hell..." Phoenix sighed heavily and paused to regroup his thinking.

"...precisely. In other words, you can't rely on either figure as factual, not even close. The same goes for any statistic associated with growing or declining populations. Rates we've looked at and discussed include: mortality, literacy, economic growth, education, religion, and ethnic makeup. Looking at each country logistically, most claims are bogus on either side of the scale; the one exception being national debt, which is carefully monitored by both lenders and borrowers." Trevor swayed slightly, rocking the young man from behind, as both contemplated the problem while studying the street below. Standing quietly, the eldest prayed for a cosmic breakthrough for his unnerved partner: the deadline grew closer.

"What else can I do?" Phoenix turned to face Sloane; his thoughts focused on the smiling lips. His partner no longer wore bandages, allowing the dark hair to spring forth. The younger man resisted no longer and raised his hands to stroke the bristly head.

"Before you distract me with a first time signal, or rather a second seduction, do you remember the article you wrote to land this unmerciful job? You had no data, no rules, no pressure, and no photographer to say *aye or nay*. You had only my pictures and this." Trevor poked at the smaller chest, tapping at the heart. "They're all you need, kiddo. Now, let's look at the images. You have a ton to sort through, and many good ones, at least to my discerning eyes. The task won't be easy, but picking out the right images for the article may start the creative flow." Sloane escorted the journalist to the office area, located in the main living quarters, to sit together at the large layout table. Phoenix took a stool and opened the folder, with the vigilant photographer ready to comment or assist.

"Man, these are awesome!" Immediately filled with renewed enthusiasm, the former aerialist flew once more, while scrutinizing each photograph before turning it over for another surprise. Countless images of the surreal, of magic, of light and shadow, none disappointed his artistic eye. "They're so good, Trev, all of them. How do we decide? Wow, look at this one!" He lifted the picture for both to see.

"I rather like that one myself, but it's up to you. Perhaps, for your first job, select one photo from each set I've marked, and then reduce the number to accommodate the pages we've been allotted."

"This one seems a likely start for the article, placed across two full pages with only the title, which hasn't come to me either." Rubbing his eyes and focusing on a vista near impossible to capture on film, the smaller man remembered the day and the night before. Sloane had seized his euphoric moment in a photograph. "Liquid gold lies at the end of the rainbow, between tree and lake, wildflower and mountain. A waterfall spills its wealth into a rainforest of life..." The tenor voice, with the underlying rattle, faded like an ending to a sad song. Phoenix blinked his velvet violets in embarrassment. "Well, you get the gist. Too stupid? It's the first thing that came to mind." Phoenix again bit his lip when he met the approving gaze and upturned mouth.

"You're on your way, kiddo; allow the poet to emerge. I'll leave you to it, but you must use one of the last set, as a favor to me." Trevor walked away, calming his arousal from the gesture made by the perfect mouth and leaving his partner to make his own exciting discoveries.

"But these are of me!" Shocked, rather than embarrassed, the subject in the photograph certainly expressed a point, but the journalist had no thoughts of incorporating himself within the article.

"You represent the ghost of the forest, carrying away and mourning the last remnants of life."

Storing the line in his head for reference, Phoenix looked at the image in a new light, while recalling each step taken through the black smoke, the hot embers, and then the pouring rain and scalding steam. Sloane had enhanced his sorrow through haunting colored photographs in grayscale. A ghostly shot rendered a slender figure emerging from the colorless haze; in the second still, the soot covered man held a bundle of gold; the third zoomed in on purple eyes filled with rain and a cub crying as hard as its savior. With his senses and emotions unleashed, Phoenix began to write.

Two twenty-hour days later, a weary man stood, staggered over to his friend, and handed his first draft to an eager recipient. "I've numbered the pictures to keep them straight, but before laying out the article, the text requires scrutiny. The ending is very dicey, needs copious amounts of work, but we're getting there. We should make the deadline."

"We only have a week. Are you sure about this? Takes time to produce a clean layout."

"I'll sleep tonight, after a large dinner I plan to eat with you. Tomorrow I'll rewrite the ending, and the next day, simplify and cutback the entire article. The layout I can do electronically, with the images photo-scanned. Should take me a day, and the Graphics Department need only follow my example."

"Okay then. I'll order food, while you shower and relax your stiffened posture. After dinner, I'll sit in a corner to read, and maybe you should go to bed. You are a wonder, kiddo."

"As are you, Mr. Sloane. On seeing myself in your pictures, I do understand you better. You fall into your work--seeing, observing, but not participating--an admirable quality of non-interference in the events surrounding you. I selfishly thought you cold when you ignored my calls for help, but I was so wrong. You can't separate yourself emotionally from what you see from what you know; if that makes sense."

"Perhaps the heartless part of the equation. I do find difficulty in seeing my pictures as real, although that is photography: real life, real people, real happenings. By losing myself behind the lens, I separate myself from the sorrow, the beauty, the pain, the majesty, the terror, and then seeing the apparitions become real when transferred onto paper. My heart then bleeds."

"You're an artist, Trev, one who remains true to a proven method. Your work is perfection; and I guess I'm feeling rather inconsequential writing about those feelings."

"You were there, Passepartout, standing beside me with every shot. You felt and participated in my magical world."

Violet eyes blinked a bashful thank you, and two men settled in for a quiet evening. One read while the other returned to his computer to catch up on email and the news. Trevor's attention immediately peaked in the weaving of poetic words that described an unsolvable mystery. His pictures could stand alone; but Phoenix's talent would pull a reader into the intense world two men had experienced together. The ending required work, now just a rough cataloguing of ideas to finalize on the morrow; only a hint of approval from the photographer seemed a requirement before finishing. For a fourth time, the photographer reread a token layman's conclusion.

Draft Ending 1

With no words to accurately describe emotions felt during our journey, we revert to standard terminology: anger, joy, relief, disbelief, frustration, anticipation, distain, and back to anger. The Amazon experience puts man into perspective amidst the vastness of such a primitive kingdom. We must place ourselves within the landscape; and in so doing, become miniscule army ants, equally as small, equally as destructive in our march to conquer. An unfortunate global attitude, the political world seems to care little of consequences rendered and has learned nothing from past lessons. Laden with conflicting information, can the international community justify its arrogance or its benevolence toward Brazil, considering the country's indecision to act expeditiously to save itself and others? No one nation stands as a good example.

The rainforest extends beyond Brazil's borders; the saving of this woodland rests on more shoulders than one. Concern over global warming requires swift action, but we have run out of convincing words. If the jungle is lost in its primordial form (nature's stabilizer of carbon dioxide pollutants), weather problems will undoubtedly escalate with worse torrential rains, blizzards, hurricanes, blistering heat, droughts, floods, and now, the recent discovery of the Arctic lakes disappearing, and the parched earth of Africa increasing. The jewel of our star system, our beautiful blue and green planet, as remembered from twenty years ago, is vanishing.

Recorded history of land clearing is shown in ancient writings and wall paintings. Man must accept responsibility for the damage done from the beginning of our appearance on the planet. We cannot discount our involvement in environmental change, starting with the ancient forests lost in antiquity, and possibly, the decimation of one many believe to be the first: the Garden of Eden. Was the fertile oasis eroded by man's unjustified self-interest to cut down and start again, using lesser crops and livestock that we, as ignorant humans, believe more advantageous to our food supply? A ridiculous notion in theory, as we are earth-made beings given everything we require by nature's abundance before the destruction. We are all at fault, wanting more-and-more, with greed running amuck.

The Amazon River System stretches beyond our perception of a horizon and remains the logical means of transportation for the development of environmentally friendly industries. Naturalists will shake their heads in despair, if we look at the jungle as having other purposes besides sustaining world temperatures, and one of them is not to supply us with luxury wooden flooring material. The use of its natural resources requires extensive planning for selective harvesting of currently recognizable vital plant products found only in the rainforest. Supplying food supplements and medicines alone could increase Brazil's economy, if properly administered and without the waste.

I offer a suggestion, one of a simple man with simple ideas. First, the Brazilian Government reclaims all free land holdings: no more man-made fires, no more land left barren, no more clearing for lumber or livestock. Agricultural development can be an alternative in the jungle, but only using the waste left by lightning-created fires and not spreading beyond the current areas already decimated. By constructing learning centers specifically applicable to the forest, its well-being, and the multitude of natural products, Amazonia could attract a newly skilled labor force, a highly paid governmental work force. Look to the cities' poor and the rural unemployed as that resource, one to educate in new ways of harvesting, how to cut and replant the correct indigenous flora, how to live harmoniously with the wildlife, and how to minimize the dangers the new inhabitants will encounter.

Once these individuals are trained and knowledgeable, small planned settlements would spring up along a few of the more promising tributaries. These communities would restrict their population growth; adhere to all regulations regarding size and number of plants taken in a specified area, while conserving both plant and animal life for many generations to come. Formally educated personnel, including scientists, researchers, teachers, doctors, the list is endless, would finally be convinced to assist a thriving population living within the forest. Not a place for aggressive entrepreneurs and developers, only those industries, willing to save the woodland as it stands, could seek approval of the products they wish to harvest, their bank accounts funding Brazil's new work force, while a devoted environmentally aware country monitors the limits set.

A strong middle class would develop, needing transportation and goods for the dangerously isolated locations in which they will settle. This means new industries for Brazil, in cities and villages already situated on the river and along the coast, while older companies flourish anew. Boat building would become immensely important, from the redesigning and construction of family-sized high-speed cruisers to immense cargo vessels, all environmentally friendly to the surrounding jungle and the ecosystem of the massive river system: no pollution, no noise, no blades in the water, and no further infiltration of a vast road system.

Looking at their resources, Brazil would become

a world power and its savior, based on the riches of the woodland they are currently decimating. With poverty on the decline, wealth redistributed, the slums cleared, old and new industries developed, the jungle could be maintained in its primitive form and the inevitable destruction of our planet by man postponed. In this non-professional's opinion, the rainbow's end is a pot of gold in Brazil... the rainforest and its river system the key to man's survival, if only for a short while.

The End

"Phoenix, you're still looking at that damn computer. I thought you were tired."

"I am, but wanted your opinion." The weary journalist clicked a few buttons, continuing to stare at the monitor with an odd squint and an open mouth.

"The article itself is beautiful; you require little editing. The ending is too long and very sketchy at present, as you stated, but your ideas are sound. I too believe the river system a likely means of saving the forest and redistributing the population, which Brazil feels necessary for economic progress. Solidify your intent, word it as poetically as the body, and you've adhered to Graham's vision statement. I'm surprised there's no blame or pointing of fingers toward Brazil, considering the last part of our trip." Trevor set the pages down, removed his reading glasses, and rested his head against the back of the couch, contemplating the sudden nervous agitation in Thornton-Jones.

"Blame could easily be placed on Brazil; unless the international community is baiting them to retaliate against sound advice. I think any power would be antsy if berated to such a degree. We can't hold back, however, as too much depends on a sane outcome. The whole scenario seems irreconcilable, however, considering the many problems: new governments with different attitudes, changing advice instead of following a set mandate, different people involved from day-to-day. One change in the political arena could disrupt further open discussions and leave the fate of the rainforest to those incapable of rational thought."

"Very true. I noticed you said nothing about the Hidrovia

Project."

"Maybe in another story, one regarding man-made changes and their results on natural habitats. An investigation into the history of the Saint Lawrence Seaway, which created a lake covering 40,000 square hectares of fertile ground, would be prudent. The Aswan Dam flooded the entire country of Nubia and cut off the natural floodwaters essential for Egyptian agriculture. In addition, the one we're most aware of, the levees of the Mississippi have created a destructive force costing millions of dollars every year due to unnatural flooding further upriver; and they require immediate upgrading. After the last hurricane, perhaps the latter problem will be corrected. Adding our inconclusive findings and a potential solution would make the piece too long."

"Agreed, but did you come up with anything we could pass on to Señor Vianna?"

"Too many variables, considering the five countries involved. My mind is already beyond repair over the forest." Phoenix chuckled lightly, but his eyes remained fixated on the monitor. Something had caught his attention. Suddenly, with great ferocity, he could no longer rein in his contempt over what he had just re-read for a fourth time. "Jesus! I don't believe this! They're out of their goddamn minds!" The smile disappeared instantly, replaced by a threatening growl and a grim face filled with anger. He pushed back his chair hard enough to send it tumbling backward, crashing it violently against the wooden floor.

"What in hell!"

"Trevor, read these articles I've bookmarked and note the dates. Hand me my ending you just read. I'm about to give it a drastic overhaul, changing my erroneous opinions that Brazil is a culturally aware society. It's bullshit! Nothing but fucking bullshit! They're up to their armpits in corruption and issuing misleading statements to their own people and the world!" The snarl returned Sloane to a cold city street and the thugs Thornton-Jones could have obliterated in the same frenzied fury exhibited at that moment. The photographer jumped toward the computer, sat down, rested his glasses on his nose, and read each fact and figure, while Phoenix scribbled a second draft of his ending. Shaking his head in disbelief and disappointment, Sloane waited nervously for the results of his partner's outrage. The conclusions had been too easy.

"Here, Trev, try this; a corrected ending to be edited when I'm less angry. We'll submit something testier with your amazing images, considering one picture no longer exists. The line has been crossed."

The big man, with the deep furrows in his worried forehead, took the handwritten pages of a much shorter ending to a beautiful article. He understood completely and read it only once, while Phoenix tried to calm his ire by painfully abusing the strings on his guitar.

Draft Ending 2

Attempting to ingratiate oneself socially, morally, and politically lies in diplomacy, as a friend once told me. Today is not the day, and I am not a diplomat. I had finished this article feeling upbeat and confident Brazil could and would be the planet's savior from one cause of global warming, our pot of gold at the end of the rainbow.

Reading the news today (news I had missed while away) has destroyed my positive attitude with the reporting of the latest statistics of deforestation from the malignant ooze seeping out of a rancid country. The Brazilian people are not at fault, deliberately left ignorant by their government and the handful of wealthy that control all decisions. Unequivocally, in the most insidious example of greed, less than a handful of individuals approved the escalation of rainforest eradication, already at astronomical proportions. Within the last month, one state government ordered the leveling of an area the size of Wales, and for what: cattle and soybeans!

The world has been brought to its knees; and we have no more words to convince, coax, cajole, or beg. We were there, and we know the exact location of the lands destroyed. At the rate of current destruction, the Brazilian forests will no longer exist in 50 years--a fact--just as the photograph captured the last living picture of one area. The jaguar sipping at the water's edge is no more, the surrounding foliage is in ashes, the tributary has been bulldozed out of existence for irrigation purposes, and the waterfall no longer empties into a pool of gold to feed the mighty Amazon.

We must step through the fiery gates of hell and eliminate further aggression against our planet's greatest gifts: clean air and pure water. If it takes armed force, I raise my hand to bear arms against those bordering on insanity. We do it now, or we all die. Do we allow a handful of the too rich, too greedy, to continue filling their bank accounts in Switzerland, while we implement the building of biospheres to generate clean air to breathe and artificial sunlight for good health? Do our grandchildren don oxygen masks to play outdoors, never to feel fluffy snow on their eyelashes, spring breezes in their hair, sparkling sunshine on their skin, or soft rain washing them clean? No! People of the world must attack the source, confiscating and protecting all remaining rainforests for humanity, forcing the issue now, demanding all governments and global associations work faster and harder for a solution, or lose Earth for a handful of soybeans.

The End

"You've said it all, partner, and man, did you say it! Fucking dynamite! Remember those bullets I warned you about?"

Phoenix changed the inflamed flamenco beat of his guitar to a dirge, giving him solace after an emotional battle over the awesome photographs, the discouraging news, and his ongoing concern of promises made to a man still recovering. The delay of the latter affected his mental attitude toward the job, but on the other hand, it gave him time to prepare psychologically. A night of uninterrupted sleep, beside Sloane, might clear his mind to solve at least one of his conundrums. "How much trouble am I in?"

"I'd say you've declared outright war; one of the few righteous ones I'm convinced about. This is about saving our planet, our lives, not a philosophical battle of linguistics and ideologies, but one of global significance--air and water--we have to protect both for everyone and share them equally. South America, Brazil in particular, had better step forward with a valid plan to rectify this one catastrophe. I can't believe the highest official of this particular state increased his holdings by destroying 300,000 acres of jungle; that's 6% of half of the remaining world's rainforests in just a few months. I'd call that a conflict of interest: the man should be impeached, his land holdings divided, and his arse kicked out of the ballpark. He's building his own empire, as are his cohorts, all of them exceedingly wealthy landowners who can sway, order, or bribe government officials to sanction such activity, while they obliterate the rainforest and the small farms that are no longer considered economically viable. This last archival article makes the Brazilian government look completely hypocritical and incompetent, stating that deforestation has dramatically decreased over the past several years. How could they miss this one cataclysmic event, proven by photographs of red, barren earth recently dug up by bulldozers? Someone has to stop the lunacy; and if we're assassinated for saying so... well, kiddo... I'm right beside you."

"Thanks. I can't believe the Brazilian Ministry of the Environment has the nerve to come out with that last article either, and then to say nothing about the blatant misconduct of one individual. Who has the right to hold that much land? His ranch is now bigger than Massachusetts, for Christ's sake. Can you imagine the uproar if we turned that New England state into a lake or burn it down. Topping off this Senator's complacency toward the crimes he has committed, his flagrant mishandling of the news media will backfire in his face, telling the world that only large holdings can place Brazil as the biggest exporter of agricultural products. Making matters worse, he openly hires illegal immigrants, rather than seeking out some of the millions of poor living on mountains of garbage. Man, this is so fucked up!"

"This story has been difficult, but seeing one of my pictures for the first time, and then finding it no longer exists, chills me straight through. With a few modifications to the ending, you could have people from all over the world setting aside their differences and invading South America armed to the hilt, as the entire Northern Hemisphere is suffering." Sloane sat back dumbfounded by the harshness, but he too felt horrified at the latest statistics and blatant political corruption.

"We have to protect the forest at all costs, Trev. It's imperative we instigate some action, considering the slow speed of correcting other man-made disasters that have escalated the greenhouse effect.

The world's educated populace is equally aware of the crime, but we're moving at a sloth's pace. The G8 nations, at least seven of them, are trying, but they praise Brazil, accepting their input on the use of ethanol gas, yet saying shit upon learning of the mass cuttings of the rainforest in the past year. Canada has come up with an even better solution for making a non-pollutant gas, which the international community has yet to discuss. Perhaps currently under patent laws, it will eventually allow all countries to use their agriculture waste material to refine their own clean gas, without destroying anything. Other alternative fuel sources require an even greater threat: the growing of crops strictly for fuel, forgetting said crops are required to feed people! Moreover, after a summit of the G8, four countries including the US have formed another group of would-be saviors for pollution control. No two countries can agree on anything! It doesn't make sense! Who's covering whose arse here anyway?" Phoenix continued to storm, all the fire alarms in his head going off simultaneously, his agitation taking a huge toll on his exhausted mind and body. Real life was beyond his comprehension.

"I know, kiddo; the task is daunting. We'll submit the article, with your pointed ending, and travel the journey wherever it takes us."

Chapter XXIII

Calming the journalist's ire, with a cup of hot cocoa laced with
Sambuca and a few of the young man's favorite cookies, Sloane
basked in watching the white lashes flutter. They created an opening
in the vapors of the hot treat to reveal violets of soft velvet, just as the
jungle mist parted for a rare sighting of something beautiful. After the
comfort drink, Trevor rose to his feet, yawned, stretched, and extended
a hand to his partner who had him charmed with his wild mood
fluctuations. "You're exceedingly tired, Mr. Thornton-Jones, and still
somewhat antsy. Ready for bed?"

"Yeah, I'm wasted. Grab and pull. I don't think my legs will
move. Dinner was delicious, but the liqueur has finished me off."

"Right then. Up you get and I'll carry you piggyback to your
waiting bed." The larger man had him standing before he could think.

"No way; you're still a sick man. Besides, I want to sleep with
you, in your bed that is, like always." The younger man took words so
literally; one would never consider a poet lurked inside.

"You do, do you?"

"You know what I mean."

"Mi cama, tu cama."

"Oh, good one, Sloane, but you're still recovering. What about
your ribs?"

"I feel 400% better than I have in years, and my ribs can handle
a workout. Now, climb aboard." Sloane assumed a position easily
mountable by an able body. Cautiously, Phoenix moved forward, put
his arms around the broad shoulders and strong neck, while raising one
knee for an arm to encircle. Once held tightly, the younger man felt
himself lifted and naturally swung his other leg around the hips.
Trevor secured the slender male thighs in the crook of his elbows
without effort, while his passenger straddled his waist.

"Are you sure about this? I feel really stupid." Phoenix thought
it ill advised to admit that he had reveled in racing piggyback astride
Rory. Often a game played after a full day of training on the slopes, he
and his teammates would release the intensity of their hard work with
laughter and frivolity in the freshest snow they could find. No one
knew, and only Rory would chortle at the hardening sensation felt
against him. Fun when he was sixteen, Phoenix now felt awkward

with a man who tempted him more than his first taste of puppy love.

"Too bad, as I'm rather enjoying myself, considering the dangerous position we may be in once the story breaks."

"So much for freedom of speech. Now our conservative consciences impede us. We're too damn nice when we should be nasty, and vice versa."

"You'll make the same points tomorrow, perhaps subtler, perhaps not. We should just bite the bullet and go with it, kiddo."

"Now, that is a saying I understand the meaning of, and where it came from. I agree with that expression."

"Okay, let's get you balanced. Hang on." The former football player jostled his cargo as he would a backpack and chuckled happily.

"What are you doing?"

"You're such a lightweight physically and just the right size to play with. I must confess wanting to chance this maneuver, ever since two men played the game for the cover of *The Advocat*. They appeared to be the happiest, most delightful couple I've ever seen. It's one of my favorite images, and I want to feel the same glee they experienced when the picture was snapped."

"Great, now we're *Advocat* pin-up boys, which should be newsworthy once we've handed our time bomb off to Mr. Graham."

"Don't spoil my fun with morbid thoughts. Now, these men did look like model types, but the look on their faces--I'm telling you, kiddo--their toes were definitely curling."

"Is that what's supposed to happen?"

"Would you relax and have some fun." Trevor's grin widened, while thinking wicked thoughts.

"By all means. Fun, fun, fun, if I can keep my eyes open and my head from unraveling. What have we done, Sloane?"

"Expressed an average man's point of view from the little factual information doled out to the public, nothing more, nothing less. Rid your mind of everything and relax. Duck going through the door."

"I'm glad your ceilings are high." The younger man's smile could not be seen, as he mused to himself. Riding on the tall man in such a position, his eyes barely saw over the bristly head.

Trevor delighted in the sensation felt against his lower back; a soft pouch, even through jeans, teased the older man. Upon reaching the bed, he turned, sat down, and dumped his weary baggage onto the feather-filled duvet. "Are you smiling yet?" He heard Phoenix giggle and turned to look at his partner who had suddenly become very giddy:

precisely what he had hoped.

"You can be so weird at the oddest times, Mr. Sloane."

"So, why are you laughing?" The older man loved sweet, intimate games of seduction, even when they led nowhere, or meant nothing to the object of his attention.

"After ranting my wrath on corruption and those who live by it, I'm so bagged, I'm getting silly." Phoenix continued to snicker softly, stretching to full length and attempting to yawn through his huge smile.

"Bed then. Did I ever mention how much I appreciate those tight jeans of yours?"

"No, why? What's so important about my denims?"

"As if you weren't aware of your perky derriere and slim legs, amongst other parts of..."

"...heard enough, thank you very much. Maybe I am out of fashion and should update my look into something befitting my age."

"Not a chance. I hate those ill-fitting clothes your peers wear, hiding everything, including their masculinity. They don't look good on anyone."

"Good, I'll stay in my usual gear then. I hate tripping over the crotch of my pants; and that's exactly what I do in street-smart clothes."

"Fine with me, because those faded blues are sexier than hell."

"Don't start, Sloane."

"Who's starting anything? Now, can you undress in your weariness, especially pulling off those pasted on Levis, or do I get the pleasure?" Disrobing down to his shorts, Trevor gave the supine man a daring smirk, avoiding further conversation of the dramatic conclusion of their exposé.

"I can manage thank you very much." The smaller man moved only his arms to tug at his two sweaters; the under one needed loosening from the overly snug denims. Once released, he closed his eyes and rested, not wishing to over stimulate even an eyelid muscle.

"Looks like it's up to me then."

"Oh no!"

"Oh yes." Trevor laughed and started at the most innocuous of apparel: sneakers and socks. A lunge for the metal button, fastening the waistband of the overly tight jeans, received an instant yelp. Phoenix's speed seemed unimpeded by his fatigue, and he twisted away from the playful assault, to roll onto his stomach and grasp the duvet, attempting to crawl out of the reach of a man with arms the length of a giant octopus. On his knees, the sprite's tiny buttocks stirred more lust in the photographer who could no longer resist such a delicacy when wriggled before him. The bigger man tackled his helpless prey around the waist, pinned him to the mattress, and immediately rolled them both over.

Phoenix laughingly fought off the attack, legs moving in search of an advantage to extricate his body from arms too strong. Giggling harder than Trevor had ever heard him, the young man squirmed madly, his fists unable to connect with the large target crushing him from behind and fumbling with an inconsiderate zipper. "God, Trevor, let me up. I need to piss."

The older man released his hold, his own laughter following the diminutive, flying-figure into the bathroom. Not a bad start, the reaction proved better than anticipated. He pulled back the expensive covering, while waiting for his comrade, and slipped into the comfort of his enormous bed, deciding on his next move. A long dry spell, without a single score since Joey, Sloane needed this night. Need, however, did not justify force, particularly upon a man having difficulty sharing his desires and the understanding of them. He would wait until asked.

The bashful man emerged, unable to erase his twisted silly grin that such playfulness inspired. After placing his clothes neatly on a nearby chair, he sidled up to the bed in his sleepwear and looked down at the inviting nest.

"Take off that damn oversized T-shirt, and I'll give you a massage, a full body massage." Trevor fiendishly smirked, creating more wariness in his partner.

"A massage; just a massage, right?" The University of Southern Colorado T-shirt came off, and Trevor tried not to shiver at the scars revealed on the back of the man's shoulders, when the garment was tossed on top of the rest of the small-sized apparel. He had seen the horrific reminders many times, but tonight he would dare touch them. "Just a massage, kiddo. You're too tired for much else."

"Such as?" Phoenix alerted to the innuendo that he thought he heard. Unable to ask the ultimate question, he wished Sloane would take the initiative. Fear stopped him from his normal jump onto the bed, where a favorite resting place waited on his best friend's bare shoulder. If the larger man did have intentions, he had no physical defenses to fight him off, and mentally the idea had him almost catatonic before the actual start of anything. Now perspiring with unbridled apprehension, Phoenix's wishes conflicted with his memories.

"There are many types of massages besides what you're imagining. I could indulge your fancy with a therapeutic massage, a penetrating rubdown, an aromatherapy massage... What's the matter?" Sloane recognized the expression of panic that crossed the perfect face when experiencing a reminder of *the accident*. "Come to bed. I'll knead your sore back. You're very tense after two days of continual work on your computer." He patted the bed beside him in a friendly, good-humored gesture, while he discarded his plans A through Y leaving only Z: just a massage.

Phoenix climbed in and laid on his stomach, while he gazed left and up at Sloane's handsome profile. The aging lines around the eyes, and those running down the hollows of the cheeks, held him spellbound. The straight, slim, but masculine nose fit proportionately with the high cheekbones, large laughing lips, and bedroom eyes half closing in the light, now being dimmed by a remote held in a large hand. Even without his long, silver-sprinkled hair, the muscular fifty-five year old was an attractive man, perhaps the descendent of a Cherokee warrior, legendarily as tall and sleek. The straight white teeth, with a slight overbite, flashed at him; the mouth, perfect for kissing and being taken by, exhaled a warm breath to lull him. Phoenix shook so hard, the tremor nearly tossed the bigger man off the bed.

"You okay, Phoenix?"

"Yeah, just thinking."

"Good thoughts I hope."

"More often now. I'm ready for that massage, if just a massage. I'll reciprocate the pleasure tomorrow night." The smaller man pushed the pillow away to lie flat. A good rubdown always made him feel better after any type of workout; a two-day writing marathon qualified as such. He closed his eyes; waited for a movement from the man he adored; and thanked one god, whatever god, that his weariness would prevent an embarrassment.

"I have a fragrant oil to use. Any trainer or therapist these days uses a combination of scents to achieve different results. I'm not sure what this one does, since I haven't read the labels on these presents from Wolfe and Sebastian. Smells nice though." While he spoke, Trevor carefully selected one vial of oil out of the many given to him by the bear/cub duo. Giving no indication of its purpose to Phoenix, he would test the man for scent appreciation and response. Once on his knees, he straddled his partner, poured sufficient oil into a cupped hand, and rubbed both together. He breathed in once, very deeply; the aroma certainly aroused his own senses, right down to his independently thinking organ that was secured within his shorts. The petit figure stretched before him, a temptation thwarted by the fine-line scars running up both arms and ringing his elbows. They would heal, becoming invisible over time, but the harsher remnants of *the accident* made Sloane swallow hard to stop from choking on an imagined cause that he had conjured up in his head. A much deeper gouge required cosmetic attention on the right shoulder, where a dent in the muscle structure needed filling, as did the right thigh. Future surgeries numbered too high for the photographer; painful, exhaustive operations eliminated the naturally smooth skin on a soul etched with reminders. Sucking in his sorrow, the larger man commenced.

The atlas region of the neck succumbed to kneading thumbs. Delicate, manipulative motions coaxed the slender body to relax and enjoy the sensation offered. Large hands slipped over the shoulders and down the arms, while the scent of rain, ferns, and freshly mown grass wafted into Phoenix's olfactory system. Peace settled over the younger man, when the wilderness perfume drizzled along his spine, and the giant hands returned to his knotted shoulders. A soft sigh of contentment floated him away to another place, one free of nightmares, day terrors, and death.

Sloane smiled wistfully at the shy man, as he felt the lingering intake and exhale of air. The massage would be innocent; time simply spent caring for the sprite he regularly slept with, one who supported him through a hot, humid jungle to reach safety. He recalled only snippets of their dramatic quest for the river, an outstanding feat for one not half his size.

The pastel highlighted head turned in the opposite direction, eyes remained closed, and the perfect lips softened to the will of finger-pads pressing gently down his spine. They extended to his lower back, slipping under the waistband of his briefs only an inch. Pleasure replaced worry.

Trevor moved closer to the bottom of the bed, which the younger man could not reach with his toes. Starting with the ticklish digits, he rubbed them with the fragrant lubricant, contemplating their size while playing with each. On an impulse, he lifted one foot and sucked the largest toe, preparing himself for a kick to his face. Receiving a quiet giggle from Phoenix as encouragement, he laid the leg flat and confidently spread both slim appendages enough to allow room for his hands to slip up each. Reaching the edge of the longer-legged underwear--he stopped--willing himself to desist before making himself crazy with temptation, but his squeeze of each thigh produced a movement. The lower back arched, raising the perky backside in expectation of something greater. Having silently promised to behave, Sloane again tightened his long fingers around the thighs; the body before him responded once more. Growing bolder, he nonchalantly slid his powerful hands under the legs of the shorts. Not far, he waited for the complaint. A refusal was not forthcoming. Returning to the waistband, he gently pulled it down slightly further, on the pretense of stroking the lower back before encountering the round buttocks. A groan from Phoenix instantly halted his progress.

"Why did you stop?"

"Your briefs are in the way."

"Take them off then. Take them off!" The beautiful face scrunched up, losing a battle against an erection that struggled between the hungry body and the thick mattress.

"Lift up and ease back onto your knees. Sit erect, baby."

"Trev, I... Oh God, I can't."

"Yes you can. Lean back against my chest." Sloane assisted the lift, bringing the agitated figure to a kneeling position, while hurriedly pushing the confining shorts far enough down to let loose the twitching arousal. After two nights of innocent seduction with this particular virgin, he knew a single touch would result in a premature ejaculation. "Hold on, kiddo. Can I help?"

"Yes! No! God, yes!" Phoenix felt every sensation described as love, from his asshole puckering to his toes curling. Deep inside his lower torso, he tensed those muscles to squelch the exploding rapid-fire nerve endings surging up his rectum. The action created more need, and his back arched dramatically, involuntarily exposing his most profound body parts that required immediate attention.

Trevor reached around the twitching hips to take the elusive prize in his hand. Only his touch, just one touch, he captured cool cream in his free hand, while gyrating hips bucked to climax. The younger body, satiated and sweating, collapsed backward against a pounding heart; the virgin took short gasps of air as fast as his last few jerks. Sloane felt the tension ease within the shaken spirit and held fast to the damp, silken chest. After the man's breathing calmed, he settled Phoenix on the coolness of the sheet and rolled him over to gaze into the dewy violets. "Are we still okay, kiddo?" A nod of the white head did not abate the anxiety seen in the eyes, nor felt under a touch to the heaving chest. "Slow down. What do you wish of me, Phoenix?" Trevor waited, believing the damaged angel needed only a comforting paternal embrace to recover from his sexual fear.

"I don't know. I just don't know."

"Sit up for me. That's my boy." Sloane helped his partner into a sitting position, bringing him into his warm chest. Two hearts slowed after time, while beating against the other. "Feeling better?"

"Feel stupid."

"Well, you're not. You had a decade to develop a defensive behavioral pattern, which may take years to resolve."

"No, now; I want it resolved now! Right now!" Phoenix pushed away to stare into the surprised eyes and quiet face.

"You can't push back fear on command." Attentively stroking the white head, Trevor attempted to eradicate the doubt in a frightened virgin.

"You did with the snake."

"Making love is hardly a *'do or die'* situation." A serene smile attempted to sooth the rising anxiety of his inexperienced partner.

"It is for me."

The comment stunned the older man, remembering the revelation of living on borrowed time. Speeding up his thinking, he returned to plan Z. "Let's finish the massage. I believe you're enjoying the pampering. Whatever you wish me to do, I'll do; and conversely, will stop when you've had enough." Trevor lowered Phoenix to a supine position in the soft bedding and carefully removed the underwear entrapping the man's knees, scared to stone at what he may see and how he would react to further evidence of damage.

"No! Don't look. Please, don't look! You say my scars don't bother you, but I'm a freak! I should be in a sideshow!" Phoenix lamented his mutilated body, just as someone opened the impenetrable door to normalcy for him to walk through. He couldn't cope.

"You've said that before, and it's nonsense. Your cock is a beautiful color, and as it swells, the texture of veins adds a wonderful shade of purple. The small white lines contrast with the deeper color your pecker becomes, and their slight texture, along with the protruding blood-carriers, is a tongue's delight. Besides, over time, these minute scars will disappear, like the ones that once existed around your handsome face and under your hair." Trevor came through, shining his brightest when such sadness cloaked itself in purple mist hovering on the edge of a cloudburst.

"Don't you care what caused them?"

"Very much so, but my ignorance of the matter does not overshadow my penchant for sucking the twitchiest part of you. Having lost your body hair, touching you almost seems scandalous. You have an amazing piece of equipment between your legs, and I won't have you degrading such a beautiful part of you, one that could entertain me forever, along with your backside. You have nothing to be ashamed of, or to worry about. Go with whatever makes you feel good, Phoenix."

"What I want and what I say get tangled in my head. I'm scared of intimacy, but more frightened to lose the chance. Is confusion a part of sex?" The youth's breathing continued in short gasps with the natural exertion, but a little chitchat, over things he knew nothing about, slowed his excitement minimally to regain some composure.

"You bet it is. The person performing the act must rely on signals from his lover, and every partner is different. Roll onto your stomach, and we'll suffocate you with more of this oil. Over you get." Helping the anxious sprite into a comfortable position, Sloane reached for the bottle and again poured sufficient quantity into his hand. Upon another deep inhalation of the seductive fragrance, he knew he should have switched scents to one less intoxicating.

"It does smell nice, outdoorsy like a hike through a cool, rain-drenched forest."

"How does that make you feel?"

"Rather contented actually, considering what I just did and admitted to."

"Still hard for you, isn't baby? I do understand you have a deeply rooted fear, and I respect your reasons for taking your time."

"I'm sorry I'm at odds with myself, not knowing what to do or how to do it. First, I want you to touch me, but the next moment--hell--the next moment I'm fighting for my life. It makes no sense."

"Love and sex (not interchangeable by the way) follow no rational path. Now, enough of your paradox, let's talk about this fragrant oil. Does the aroma heighten other senses?" Trevor continued the easy conversation of sundry things, diverting the young man's attention from his fear-driven inexperience. His hope rested on simple words, including the recognition of the scars he felt with his fingers. He expressed no judgment, only unperturbed vocalization of their existence. The briefs had hidden secrets of further travesties inflicted upon one too young. Phoenix had not survived an accident, but something more dire. The photographer could not imagine the horrors his partner endured, or for how long.

Lines of relatively new pink skin contrasted with the alabaster complexion of an area safeguarded from the sun's reach. They radiated from the anus; protected by tight, yet baby soft cheeks. Nothing short of a violent rape could cause such markings, although meticulously mended. The hipbones screamed of more torture, with remnants of compound fractures that once pierced the thin skin and still required correction. Horrendous to feel, as was the scars running from the waist and deep into each cheek, Sloane recalled the fractured pelvis mentioned and veered his sight away from the repaired mutilations; his touch told the tale. Continuing, as if not sickened by the freakish injuries, he moved his hands down the back to the buttocks and over the grisly marks, believing the man, under his manipulation, could only experience numbness. Another movement belied his theory; the back of an aerialist arched gracefully; and the cheeks of the tiny derriere again contracted in excitement, or perhaps an instinctive refusal of entry. "Can I continue, Phoenix?"

The young man spoke nary a word, but moaned into the mattress and wriggled slightly. A positive signal allowed Trevor to place his thumbs cautiously at the upper most part of the crease. Taking much time, he ventured along the shadowed crack, while pushing and separating each smoothly reconstructed gluteus muscle. Moans grew more frequent and the legs quivered with goose bumps. Unsure of further action, the older man finished the massage.

"Feel more relaxed?"

"No! Do it! Please, Trev." The panted plea of excitement left the photographer in a quandary of indecision. Could the delicate body handle more, and would old injuries disallow entry?

"Do what? I need to know for sure."

"I can't... I can't say it."

"Yes you can. Roll over and face me."

Phoenix struggled to comply, his second arousal flipping independently over his lower abdomen. Desperate for more than an ejaculation, he reached up to encircle the broad neck, as he uttered a stunning demand from one suffering from a sexual phobia. "Penetrate me! I need you inside me! Jesus, just fuck me!"

Sloane embraced the strained body, holding the head steady to kiss the perfect lips. "Are you sure, baby?"

"Yeah. No. I hope so. Just take me and ignore any objections. Just do it!"

The pleading subsided when the bigger man teased the whimpering mouth to remain open with a flick of his tongue. More pressure of lips upon lips had mouths opening to taste the other, as two tongues battled for position. The kiss melted icy fear, and the younger man secured his trembling body against the larger one, while strong hands petted him from white head to twitching hips. Soft and delicious turned into harsh and volatile, as two men tempted the Furies, lavishing their lust and adoration on the other. Excitement heightened, exhaustion dissipated, and Trevor laid his life's desire on the mattress. "I want you, Phoenix."

"I want you too." With short, clipped breaths of anxious anticipation, the younger man spread his knees nervously. "Do it! Hurry, do it now!"

Trevor lifted the slim thighs, which were the size of his own bulging biceps, and pushed them forward enough to dare a touch, to dare a look at the purple center of the spider's web. A squeal urged him to press firmly upon the tight opening that puckered and released to the sporadic breathing between pants and words of objection.

"Wider, Phoenix, spread your legs wider and hold them." With gentle nudges, the thin limbs opened and rose, feet danced in the air, and the virgin hole felt the touch of the warm air current coming from the heater vent. More taunting of the hungry orifice, one etched with white lines and running deep inside, Trevor had his young lover tensing and relaxing, until ready for a partial entry. Only an oily finger to begin with, the experienced man felt the guardians of virtue nearly crush his longest digit on the right hand. Pushing gently passed the grip, which loosened on a moment of exhaled air, Sloane tried again. An unusually tight orifice, even for a virgin, he stopped to wait for the unaccommodating muscles. "Relax, kiddo."

The forcible player of the act eyed the arousal squirming upward for attention. While licking his lips to moisten winter-dried cracks, he adjusted his position and engulfed the straining serpent, ready to relieve his confused partner a second time. Again, life-creating cream spluttered in moments of pleasure, after the experienced tongue danced about the swollen cock ready to burst its veins.

Phoenix gasped on the release of painful pressure and struggled for needed air. "More, Trev. My insides are burning! Fuck me; fuck me now!"

Upon finding the condom, which always lay ready under his pillow, Sloane expertly manipulated the latex over his hard arousal for an attempt he felt impossible to complete. Whatever Phoenix could handle, he would try, but ready to pull out if a panic attack arose suddenly. With the orifice unprepared for a serious assault, he snuggled the head of his elongated organ at the entry of so many delights, to force his way carefully between the strong protectors of unknown treasures. "Easy, baby, this will hurt a little the first time."

"But I want you in there! It doesn't matter!"

"Okay, deep breath, relax. Help me out here, Phoenix. Another breath and then try to relax completely."

The smaller man tried, and tried again, willing his muscles to give way; muscles that had been ripped and bones that had been broken while he screamed for help. Objects too large had been rammed up his rectum, forced without care into a body incapable of accommodating a pencil. He felt a hot, smooth ball instead; the head of his friend's enraged viper searched for a hot cavern to spill its venom. A little more pressure, he breathed deeply and relaxed, his clenched sphincter muscles releasing enough for further penetration. Repeatedly, a hard stick attempted to enter gently, while setting sensitive nerves aflame. In the throes of rapture and fear, Phoenix allowed the larger than average shaft to continue to ravish him, the extended tool withdrawing slightly, only to lunge at a faster rate. He screamed his objections, as he did years ago, when his muscles were severed and skin was torn.

"Sorry, baby, relax if you can." Trevor also grew increasingly frightful, feeling the strain of his lover to protect the once abused anus. Unlike anything he had experienced, his hard rod rubbed against inner scar tissue, a pronounced prostate, and an unusually rough, heated urethra, all pushing against the outside wall of the canal. The guardian muscles were not his only difficulty; his swollen organ broke open ten-year-old scars that only soft stools could be excreted without pain. Carefully, he commenced thrusting to satisfy his own need, while comforting a lover attempting to fend off the intruder, but paradoxically clenching to hold firm, forcing the shaft further up to squelch the burn. Lunge, withdraw, lunge, withdraw, slowly, delicately, and deliberately, Sloane smoothed the rhythm with the aid of the lubricated condom, which enabled him to fill the extraordinarily deep cave. "Man, you're steaming hot and beautiful. You are a piece of heaven."

With the sweet endearments and easing of his twitching, aching rectum, Phoenix let go of his remembered torturous experience, allowing himself the pleasure upon which he set his dreams. In and out, his every nerve exploded upward, making his neck arch and his mouth search for anything to kiss or suck. He raised his head, his lips captured by a mouth tasting of his own fluid mixed with the exotic flavor uniquely belonging to his champion. The caress intensified with every driving thrust, the pleasure too much to bear, and the tears cascaded from his eyes in relief. His smaller than average body bucked in want of more, but his hips were stilled by large gentle hands, calming his frenzy to finally enjoy each wondrous stroke tickling his insides to ignite, as did the fireworks displayed in the darkness behind his tightly clenched eyes. A vibration shook him with such intensity, he screamed as he spurted cum onto his lover who chuckled at the third coming, while endeavoring to make sex fun, sweet, and endearing for one who misunderstood every carnal action. Sloane continued to satisfy them both, kissing the closing purple eyes of a bashful kid who finally let go of his past, to allow one man to envelop his happy heart with the deepest form of affection and desire.

The larger man groaned, losing himself in a moment of pleasure never thought possible. He made an impassioned seduction of another whom he loved, releasing his own lust into a powerful opening of mystery. With a last series of quick jerks, Trevor came inside the virgin who trembled and shrieked his pleasure, both finally falling limp with exhaustion. Satisfied, Sloane gave his soul and life to the scarred and frightened man; and he slipped out for this night, hearing the receiver of his gift sigh in appreciation.

Phoenix moaned and whimpered at the loss of the uncontrollable weapon; he panted in raspy, sobbing breaths, while wiping away the sweat and tears coursing down his face. Satiated but sore, he rested, slowing his breathing, calming his ravished heart, and feeling the shimmering afterglow. He had come three times, while relieving the twitching nerves running up his arse that seemed to end at the back of his throat. A gentle giant, in an oversized bed, had appeased his ten years of torment.

"You were outstanding, Mr. Thornton-Jones, but those violets are leaking again."

"Are they? Did I do it right? Are you as happy as I feel?" The gravelly voice cracked several times, while Phoenix attempted to conjure up a demeanor appropriate for the occasion, but a post-sex dialogue had no meaning to him. The significance of lighting up a cigarette became profoundly clear.

"Definitely satisfied, kiddo; and there is no wrong way. We better check that awesome little derriere of yours, considering you were too excited for proper penetration; and I am somewhat larger than average." Trevor rolled onto his side of the bed, bringing an exhausted man with him.

"You are? I didn't see it. Am I normal, or too small like the rest of me?" Phoenix alerted to a new fright he had not thought to ask of anyone.

"I'd say you were perfectly beautiful and more than adequate for my needs. Besides, height has nothing to do with pecker size. Having seen all my giant-sized friends in locker rooms, except for Sebastian, you're all shaped slightly differently but similar in size. As for you being small physically, I rather like tiny. You're a lot more fun to play piggyback with." Trevor laughed and tickled the surprised man into a lingering kiss, his favorite after sex treat.

"Tiny?"

"Most people are to me, considering my height. You are amazing, Phoenix."

"Thanks, but you're making me blush. Do you think the next time will be easier?" The extraordinary purple eyes gazed down into the emotion-filled darker ones.

"The next time? The next time I'll make it more comfortable for you, with gentleness instead of speed. You've waited a long time, and I wanted to make your first encounter special, but you're a needy little devil."

"For a reason."

"I'm sure of it; but I sincerely hope you can put that far off memory to rest permanently." The photographer ruffled the soft hair, which was very much askew and sweat drenched, making Phoenix look cuter and even younger than his twenty-seven years. His broad smile of encouragement comforted the younger man who was coming to terms of need versus fear.

"I'll risk anything to have you seduce me again. Teach me everything that turns you on, so I can return all the feelings currently stuck in the back of my throat."

"Just be you: sweet, bashful, a hellion in bed once started, and a creative mind in all arenas. You'll learn on your own. Tonight was a wonderful surprise, and I feel fantastic. You are a delight, kiddo; I hope you stick around for a very long time. I'll be your slave, your lover, and most importantly, your friend."

"For as long as you want me, and if I am to go, please dismiss me without breaking my heart. I love you, Sloane."

"And I've loved you since we rode down that god-awful elevator together."

Chapter XXIV

Daybreak filtered through the tall obelisks of Manhattan, heralding the awakening of a once disturbed young man. Life began again, and the seventeen-year-old within blossomed to enslave an older heart. The article layout came together magnificently--the text--two men's honest opinion. Phoenix ventured up the glass elevator alone to deliver the package and disappeared without seeing the publisher. Neither Thornton-Jones nor Sloane relished waiting for someone to scrutinize their work. Opinions stated could make or break the magazine, which now stood behind a militant demand for leadership change in at least one Brazilian state, the immediate sanctification of the forest for humanity, and stronger actions by the United Nations, the G8 countries, and the World Bank in all matters relating to global warming. Measures would include asking for aid and withdrawing the money held in trust, boycotting all agricultural exports, and possibly mobilizing armed forces against any nation not abiding by environmental laws to be set down by year's end. Many other problems added to the growing greenhouse effect; nonetheless, earthlings needed to gather resources quickly and to intervene immediately to contain one gigantic problem first. It would be hard, but so would any stoppage of intentional planetary destruction. Developers in all nations had to cease their activities that ignored the environment for greed; examples displayed themselves throughout the world. No one was exempt from stupidity. Man's compulsion to destroy would ultimately obliterate the planet, never to heal.

The two men, postulating the attack on a world gone awry, forgot the wrath that may target them in the future. Their only recourse was to keep hope in their heart for the earth's stabilization, while tending and nurturing their own life commitment of trust and affection. Continually gazing at each other with dream-filled eyes, stroking intimately with tender hands, they laughed aloud until bursting and played piggyback until they fell asleep satiated with the other. Endearing terms grew bolder, eroticism and romance entwined, the partnership sealed with every seductive touch, smell, and taste. Gestures of men in love became the norm and excitedly accepted by their friends. Phoenix, being so much smaller, had no qualms sitting on Trevor's knee, his smaller thighs and arms encircling the muscular torso. Whenever they shared a moment, a white head rested on a broader shoulder while reading whatever page Sloane turned to in the *New York Times.* Now mid-April, their interest turned to the sports section, the Stanley Cup playoffs for Phoenix, baseball's spring training camps for Trevor. A promise to be kept, the couple would visit Twister and Caly before the older partner left to check his property in New Mexico, where Phoenix would join him after a longer stay with his fathers and ranch friends. Before their departure for Colorado, one crucial decision needed explaining by Trevor to his young amour, as well as to Warren Graham.

Sloane started with Phoenix, breaking the news gently. His lover understood, although the young man's dreams of paying back his fathers and grandmother quickly derailed. After much consoling and rational thought, the photographer made him fully aware that his family did not hold a marker for their kindness and extraordinary generosity. Nothing was owed but a son's never-ending love. An heir to three large fortunes, plus a possible fourth on Sloane's demise, the young man need not work another minute, but the thought of anyone's death turned Phoenix around, causing an anxiety attack of the highest rating. Once he had settled his lover's concerns, Trevor had other decisions to make, for day-to-day both men required something to do, in their own time and in their own way. A night of tenderness and promises rebuilt the esteem of the mentally fragile; one who first thought the photographer's decision discarded him from the important man's life.

Over one major hurdle, without knocking it completely over, Trevor entered the frightening fishbowl alone and with trepidation. The wooden office and cappuccino awaited, along with a man eager to see his old friend glowing with renewed health. Time had sped away since seeing the bandaged head in the hospital.

"Morning, Gina. How's everything?"

"First addition is currently being compiled, as per your partner's beautiful layout and explosive text. Once again, your photographs are outstanding, Mr. Sloane. We're all very excited."

"Thanks, and after all these years, can't you call me Trevor? We're friends, aren't we?"

"I certainly hope so, Trevor." The beautiful women smiled at him, knowing just how long she had been so formal with the icon in the photographic world.

"Is our lord and master in?"

"Yes. I buzzed him the moment you exited the elevator."

"So that's what it's called. I hate the damn thing."

"Afraid of heights, are we?"

"No, just uncontrollable free-falling in a see-through Tupperware container."

"We're glad Mr. Thornton-Jones likes it, or we'd have never received your work."

"He's funny that way. Can you believe he presses his nose against the outer glass? I think I'll buy him a parachute before he breaks through and jumps."

"You are fun. By the way, Mr. Graham believes he has conquered the cappuccino machine, which I am sure is steaming as we speak. Take care, Trevor."

"That sounds ominous."

Graham's assistant laughed and walked Trevor down the hall. Left alone to announce his arrival, he inhaled deeply and entered on the command.

"Sloane, you look great. How are you feeling?"

"One hundred percent. How about you?"

"Marvelous, absolutely fucking marvelous. The Thornton-Jones' article and your images are precisely what I wanted and expected, but what a scorcher of an ending. Of all the conclusions I thought he may come up with, declaring war on the world was not even on the list!"

"You wouldn't recognize any of his drafts as the finished ending. A news release ignited his fire, leaving no one safe, not even a cat. I did manage to calm some of his ire to prevent something that catastrophic. We're waiting for the first bullet to whiz passed." Sloane was certainly afflicted with anxiety regarding the final ending, although no longer a declaration of outright war.

"We're nervous about the release of the story as well, along with the outcry, having already spoken with our attorneys regarding the fallout and freedom of speech act."

"Good God, he really nailed our coffins shut!"

"When the issue hits the streets, I'd suggest you both stay hidden for a time. Nonetheless, we would like your permission to enter your pictures and Phoenix's explosive article for several awards; they're that good. Ask him if he'd do some regular captions for your pictures. You know the drill."

"Oh brother, the target on my back is growing larger, which

makes my decision somewhat easier."

"So, my friend, what's next?"

"This last trip started me thinking, and now your words, deeply resonating of a risk to Phoenix, have made up my mind."

"You two have become very close. Is love in the air this spring?"

"Damn right, and I have you to thank. His commitment to me came even after I broke his sorry little heart. I'm retiring, Warren, slowing down to enjoy something I've never had: a domestic life with someone I would die for, a large unorthodox family, and time for whatever pursuits that interest the two of us." Trevor slumped into one of the large comfortable chairs, ready to accept an infamous cup of bitter coffee with foamy cream and a sprinkling of cinnamon. Unfortunately, his beverage was set down next to the machine, as the stocky publisher whipped around gulping like a goldfish.

"You can't! Not now! You're going down in history with these latest pictures." Crimson color rose from the neck, hitting the cheeks, until blood vessels popped out on the sweating forehead, unconsciously dabbed away with a tissue.

"We'll do the occasional piece for you, just not a regular job. Far too hard on both Phoenix and myself mentally, and it takes very little to push him into a frenzy. When something strikes us as important, we'll head out to investigate and present you with something befitting your vision statement. Instead of two articles per year, you may get one, if we're up to it."

"Great! That's just fucking great! When you're up to it! I gather you'll be up for more important things."

"He's my lover, Warren; and I'll ignore your remark. Phoenix still wants to write, and I wish to continue taking pictures. If you're not prepared to back our stories, we'll remix the text in some fashion to interest someone else." Sloane sat forward in his thinking position. Announcing his retirement to Graham was painful; they had been friends for too many years in a cutthroat business. The man's words made his decision seem premature, considering the publisher's ire, which may be justifiable concern for his new magazine.

"Of course, I'll take whatever you have. You were my star photographer for every cover. My God, we chose our first one out of the many possibilities your partner gave us. The picture of Thornton-Jones' full image emerging from the smoke and holding the cub... Damn, it's powerful."

"A fire-damaged angel caring for the last of the forest's living." Trevor leaned back into the chair, his mind and heart on the violet-eyed innocent who would break millions of hearts as the poster boy for the *PlanetTerra Journals*.

"Okay, Sloane, I doubt if I can convince you otherwise, but one story a year I'll settle for, on a consignment basis."

"One story if you're lucky. How about that cappuccino now?"

The old friends regrouped over coffee. Trevor reclaimed his freelancer's prerogative of choice; and Graham's magazine held firm as the primary publication for the photographs and stories of the soon-to-be notorious team of Sloane and Thornton-Jones. After a handshake, a man-to-man hug, with the compulsory thumping of each other's back, the bigger man made his exit, to descend on a few invisible wires of hope. Phoenix waited in the restaurant at the bottom of the glass joyride, their packed bags next to him, and Bogart sleeping in his carrying case on the bench. All were ready for a trip to the country.

"Sorry I took so long. Have you ordered?"

"I was waiting for you. How did Graham take the news?"

"Professionally. It's done, kiddo; and we're free to explore at will. I'm looking forward to starting anew, particularly with you. Just seeing you sitting here made my heart miss a few beats. I feel like the luckiest man alive on our precarious planet, right down to my curling toes." The large hand covered his left pectoral muscle for emphasize, courting a sheepish smile from the younger man. Both ordered brunch, planning to have a leisurely travel day. A flight left late afternoon, arriving close to the same time in Colorado, leaping over two time zones. They had time to relax over the obscure ingredients of an eco-friendly omelet and copious amounts of organic Kenyan coffee.

"Did you confirm we're on schedule with your fathers?"

"Not yet. I should do that now." Phoenix set his cup down and dug for his cellular telephone hidden in his fanny pack, always handy for any emergency, particularly in airport terminals. "Hi, Pops, we're heading for La Guardia in twenty minutes. Everything's a go at this end... Pardon me... Oh no! I forgot... Of course, I think so, but I should discuss it with... Yes, I know... All right... Pops, this is awkward to ask, but do you mind if I sleep with Trevor? His room has a bigger bed, and we're bringing Bogie... Really! Thanks. I hope it's not an imposition for you and Dad... Now, you're making fun of me... I love you too. See you soon." The small hands closed the call with a click of the lid, but the flutter of lashes hinted at bad news, finally exposing the worrisome truth expressed in the purple eyes.

"What's the matter? I'm sure our sleeping together is not the problem." Sloane reached his long arm across the table to lift the quivering chin.

"No, they're delighted and are fully aware of our status. I neglected to tell you something. Shit, I can't believe I forgot."

"Something important?" The hand remained; the thumb stroked the paling cheek.

"It is for me, but the timing's so wrong. Dr. Bradford is flying in next week to fix my hips. I totally forgot, and we can't cancel. The hospital in Colorado Springs will be setting up for it. Damn, this will ruin our plans. This is so bad." Phoenix clasped the hand holding his chin and squeezed his fear through his fingers. Another surgery planned long ago, now his affair of the heart became a deterrent. Real life blocked his forward momentum.

"What are you having done? Is it serious? How painful will the recovery be?" Sloane tensed. He knew many more operations were required for the young man's complete mental recovery, but having formed a lifetime bond, there seemed no need to continue the cosmetics. A quick shake of the shaggy head brought fact into focus. Being twenty-eight years younger, Phoenix could have a second opportunity with another; perhaps, many more chances, but the ghastly reminders would once again stand in his way. The raspy tenor voice broke his wanderings.

"It will take too long, Trev. Please don't leave me." The aqueducts started overflowing to drown the violets.

"Never. Now, tell me everything. I'll be at your side throughout, along with Twister and Caly."

"Dr. Bradford plans to smooth some of the scars, opening them again if necessary. The first operation rectified the femur fractures, the hip joints, and the three breaks to my pelvic bones. They only wished to save me and mend what they could, never believing I'd live through the first day. You've seen their initial handiwork. This time they'll smooth both frontal areas, possibly do a skin graft, which will hurt like hell for only a short time; but, if they reopen, I'll have difficulty walking and bending at the waist until the stitches come out. Just when I was starting to feel good about myself, and with you, the horror story begins again. I have to face reality, Trev; I'll never be free."

"I don't know why you're bound to the future you keep referring to without an explanation. You don't have to continue erasing scars just for me, particularly if the procedure causes more pain." Sloane unashamedly clasped the two smaller hands drumming an offbeat tune on the tabletop.

"I once told Dad and Pops that the only thing of meaning to me was to look normal. They continue to grant my wish, but then you came along. I'm being vain, and you don't care."

"I most certainly do care, about many things. Remember, I'm much older than you and will assuredly die while you're still in your prime. I don't want scars getting in your way, disabling you from finding another man who loves you, straight through to your plastic and metal plated bones."

"You're not going to die, Sloane, not for a very long time. I could be killed by a yellow taxi as readily, if I use your method of hailing one."

"Very funny. I'll get the doorman at Macy's to teach you the proper method."

"Gee, thanks."

"Come on. Enough of this. If the operation is something you feel necessary, we'll get through it. I'll be in New Mexico for several meetings with my ranch staff and accountants, but I can race back and forth readily."

"My fathers will arrange the ranch jet for your use. You can come and go within an hour, if you're so inclined."

"Very much inclined. It's settled; we better get moving. I'll take the heavier bags; you take the smaller two and Bogie. He likes dogs, but I wonder who'll end up sleeping with us: Snow and Sky, my cat, or all three."

"All three."

The new couple laid another difficulty to rest and made the short journey to Denver where they boarded a commuter flight to Pueblo. Two familiar dark felt Stetsons were spotted, and the cowboys welcomed them on arrival with bear hugs and crooked grins. Family time began when Granny excitedly met them at the sprawling home. A fiery evening sky blazed bright, as the sun set through the aspens and firs. The ranch shone in the afterglow, with tulips of red, poppies of orange, daffodils of yellow, and lilacs and violets in every shade found in Phoenix's dancing eyes. Love took a different twist in the home of one's parents, but it blossomed equally as beautifully as the surrounding flora. The scent of lilacs, caught on fresh morning breezes, heightened their awareness of all things, allowing the two lovers to awaken early for dawn delights before starting their day. Every sighting of the other brought large smiles, and their newly found excitement continued until one afternoon's drive back to the city.

Phoenix packed a small bag in silence, watched intently by a nervous Sloane. Their last night, before a long dry stretch, went awry with too much worry; the young man was distressed over losing time with his partner, sending him spinning in the wrong direction, unable to fend off returning nightmares. Trevor, on the other hand, troubled over his young love's sullenness and the operation itself. Further details came from the fathers; the cowboys had watched many a slow recovery that disrupted Phoenix's life mentally and physically. All hope rested on Sloane to keep their son from falling into another pit of hell; the photographer's participation was vital. With great care and tender good nights, three men left a bedraggled young man in the hands of knowing, caring, private nurses who would remain steadfast by their patient until early morning preparation for the surgeon's knife.

Sitting alone by his fire on a Colorado night, Sloane came to a decision. He had a very early morning rising and a long drive with an entourage of family and friends, to wait the undisclosed hours of the multi-faceted operation. Meanwhile, he contemplated the flames, composing the question in his mind, with two dogs and a cat standing by. He decided to wait until after the surgery, but then he would find out. It was imperative.

A lover, two fathers, a grandmother, plus Jazz, Eagleclaws, and Grant, bit their nails, drummed fingers, or quietly conversed on trivial matters. The Arapaho elder tended all with coffee, pastries, soup, and sandwiches, as the day dragged endlessly until Dr. Bradford entered the tense waiting room. Not a life threatening operation, nonetheless, concern levels remained high; the small group readily stood for word.

"Gentlemen, Mrs. Russell, Phoenix is in recovery and will awaken within the hour. We did several procedures, thus the lengthy surgery. His complaint of numbness needed addressing, along with the cosmetic aspect and replacement of the last metal plate with a latest plastic one."

Six men attempted to stand tall, while a staunch grandmother held them all together as they listened to the doctor. Sloane stood quietly, his fingers twitched with nervousness, understanding most of the medical terminology, however, only one word echoed in his head: *Russell*. He had his first clue to follow. With a question from someone, his attention quickly shifted to the man raking his head on the removal of the green head covering.

The operation had gone well, although the medical experts reopened the frontal hip scars to stimulate the nerves electronically. Besides the plastic plate secured to his pelvis, they also inserted permanent filler into missing muscle mass and stretched the skin smooth. Trevor questioned everything and received the answers. Phoenix's numbness would disappear for the short while, but many sessions of therapy were required to generate feeling in the damaged areas. The largest man volunteered to learn the method. The filler was a non-toxic substance used in common facial enhancements, such as cheek implants, which would not interfere with the already strong muscles. All seemed in order, with stitches in four places in both the front and back. Phoenix's prognosis was excellent, and a future cosmetic sanding would remove the resulting devastation of raised surgical scars caused by dislocated hip joints, pelvic breaks, and femur compound fractures. His worst physical scars were diminishing to normal human wear and tear.

The three ranch hands returned home to spread the tidings of success, while the other three and an elderly woman worried as to whose face Phoenix wished to see first. Dr. Bradford made their decision simple, allowing the fathers, the grandmother, and the lover to hold vigil bedside. They waited tentatively, every murmur a hope. The first groan, they all stood, each with a hand on an arm or the pale cringing face.

"Trev?"

"I'm here, kiddo. Open your eyes. We're waiting for you." Sloane swept the longer hair off the sweating forehead.

"Where's Dad and Pops? I feel..."

"We're right here and know exactly how you feel, son. The anesthesia always makes you sick. Hold onto your stomach a moment." Twister rubbed the left shoulder, as Caly found a tin kidney dish and gently shoved the photographer aside. David easily convinced Goliath to move, while the taller father raised his son slightly, and the smaller one cupped the forehead for the patient to pitch up nothing but a little mucus. Delicately returned to his pillow, Phoenix murmured a thank you for the assistance and the warm wet towel Twister wiped over his face.

"Feeling better?" Caly clutched the hand without the intravenous drip, as he put aside the revolting metal container.

"Yeah, thanks. I heard Trev. Where..."

"Right beside you, as is Granny." Caly continued while Twister stepped aside for the tiny woman.

"Hey, Granny, what did they do to me this time?"

"Hey, yourself. They did many things to make you feel better, child. Now, you rest with Trevor in attendance. Your fathers will return in fifteen minutes, and then I'll take over to lull you back to sleep. Rest now. You're doing very well and the doctors are pleased. We're all here for you, Phoenix, and love you so much. Sweet respite, my darling." Granny leaned over and kissed the damp forehead, as the journalist's purple eyes closed in contentment.

The family members left the room, and Sloane brushed the dry lips so gently, the small man barely felt the whispered touch. Nothing anyone could do but quietly converse in a one-way conversation, as Trevor's white angel lay unmoving, looking too small, too pale, too ill. The big man choked back his admiration along with his worry. Only time would heal his lover, enabling him to stand erect, spread his legs, and feel large hands on parts now too sore to touch. He would love the man eternally, with only affectionate gestures and words if necessary, but for now, he relinquished his spot to Caly. An important telephone call would be next, and in private.

"Hi Joey, it's Sloane."

"Hey, is the surgery over? How's Phoenix? Everyone's been calling."

"Thank them for their concern and let them know he'll be recovering at the Colorado ranch for the meantime. We'll be able to take him home tonight. He seems fine, but I hear a little tension in his voice when speaking."

"Follow Twister and Caly's lead. They've been through this many times. Will he be up for company? Sebie's ready to fly out, as soon as a request is made."

"Probably by the end of the week, although he'll have trouble sitting for awhile. They reopened both hips in front and the pelvic area to replace the metal plate with a better one. He'll be sore, but Sebastian can spell off the fathers while I'm in New Mexico next Monday and Tuesday."

"I'll arrange something."

"Great. Can you help me with a little research, or are you heading out soon to do whatever it is you do?"

"Nothing I can't postpone. What's up?"

"This stays between you and me, Calloway."

"Of course."

"Scan Colorado newspapers dated nine to eleven years ago, using the keyword *Russell*. Search for an accident or criminal activity involving someone related to that name, possibly ending in a legal situation. I'm not sure what else to tell you, except it would be major, revolving around a boy of sixteen or seventeen."

"No problem. I'm on it. What do I do with the information?"

"Call me as soon as you find something."

"Phoenix, hunh? Shit, that reminds me of a name Dr. Crowe mentioned. What was it? He called Phoenix's grandmother something. Maddie! He called her Maddie."

"Fantastic, add it to your keywords, but this stays between you and me, baby, just you and me. Talk to you soon. Thanks." Trevor ended his call and returned to sit with Mrs. Maddie Russell; her identity now unveiled after the mistake of two doctors.

Three men bundled a drugged young man into the family van equipped for such important cargo. Having brought their incapacitated son back and forth on many a hospital run, and from various types of surgeries, Twister and Caly had refurbished the vehicle to accommodate a bed and the paraphernalia required for any condition plaguing their treasured patient. They quietly and slowly drove home through the Colorado darkness.

Back sleeping alone in separate rooms, Phoenix grew agitated with everything and everyone, although understanding his specially built hospital bed allowed doctors, nurses, and his fathers to tend his needs from either side, until he could stand easily. Time came for Trevor to leave the sad figure to his family for a few days, to attend to his own boring but important business. On the day before his departure, his cellular telephone sprang to life with the haunting piece of music that Phoenix had composed. Calloway's number appeared. "Hi, Joey. Did you find anything?"

"Maybe. Nine years ago, the *Denver Post* ran a small article on a closed court case. No details were reported, and the records were sealed for a decade; however, the file is labeled Kevin Russell Braxton."

"Kevin Russell Braxton--could be possible--if the middle name indicates an honor to the maternal side of the family. No public information makes me wonder. What could have happened to this Kevin person?"

"I can't say for sure, but we know Phoenix is under FBI protection for some reason; his name changed by his adoptive fathers. Whatever the incident, it had to be huge, considering the attention he receives."

"Possibly as a witness?"

"Possibly, or... I hate to say this, but considering what you've told me of his physical and mental problems, he may be a survivor."

"Christ, Joey, a survivor or victim of what? Attempted murder, rape?"

"I stopped when I discovered the small news item, but I could go back further to see if anything humongous happened. Another six or seven months, the court transcripts will be released, unless the Bureau clamps the lid down for another ten years. It's possible."

"Thanks, but I think it's time to confront those who know. Shit, this sounds out of whack somehow."

"It certainly does, considering the prominence of one Mrs. Madeline Russell. Get this! She was the *crème de la crème* of Colorado society, but ten years ago she disappeared from the social scene due to a family tragedy--the death of her grandson--who..."

"...who could be Phoenix, since they pronounced him or whomever dead, to take on a new name and family."

"The woman's a bastion of power, worth millions, is now highly reclusive, but donates vast sums to various needy hospitals throughout her home state. Interesting to note, most of her donations buy medical evacuation helicopters and positioned throughout the Rocky Mountains. Considering the horrific automobile accidents, potential avalanches, and severe skiing mishaps that could happen, it seems more than a coincidence, linking Kevin to Phoenix as one in the same."

"Sounds like something Granny would do for him, thinking of the sport he participated in, and he did mention being airlifted from his accident. This grows more intriguing all the time. Did you find a picture of Mrs. Russell?"

"Yes, but you don't need one. She looks like Francesca Annis with white hair and purple eyes."

"That's Phoenix's grandmother all right."

"I'll leave you to it. Oh, have you heard today's news?"

"No, I've been at the hospital all day."

"He's dead, man; the Thai police brought your terrorist down, along with a half-dozen others in a raid on his domicile in Bangkok. I would suggest that Interpol found him, discovered his other illegal activities, and leaked the information of his whereabouts to those who could initiate such an attack. Thailand's officials were pulled into the mêlée upon researching their records and finding a woman's allegations of kidnapping and marketing of young Caucasian females by this zealot. He put up a fight; and they killed him in the foray. Apparently, those he abducted knew of his terrorist activities, and are now willing to pull the plug on the son-of-a-bitch. Such a backlash would bode unfavorably with the al-Qaeda fundamental belief in Islamic law. Instead of the martyrdom received by most terrorists killed in action, the Islamic radicals will cast him as a freewheeling capitalist. Very cunning on someone's part, but we'll never know who actually set him up."

"I killed him, Joey."

"No you didn't. As Muslim law states: *an eye for an eye*. He should have died several hundred times over. It's justice, man, pure and simple. Now, get a hold of yourself and return to your sprite's side. Good luck, Trevor. Don't forget to call Sebie. I'm sure your little darling is getting bored, considering he's semi-mobile."

"Damn right about that. In a few days, the stitches will be removed, and he can start walking with more confidence. He hurts like hell without painkillers, to which he is immune. Seb may spark a little life into him."

"Give him my love. I'm heading for London, so I'll meet up with you two when I get back. Take care."

"Thanks, Joey. We'll look forward to your return." Sloane ended the call and immediately rubbed his temples to subdue a normal migraine caused by more information than he needed. A terrorist had been slain because of his work; a diplomat, playing both sides, would soon be exposed; and without detailed information on the former, the latter could have set up the al-Qaeda kingpin and not Interpol. The problem seemed far away and out of sight, along with the new couple's militant stand against those countries unwilling to participate in the planet's struggle to survive. Closer at hand, hidden documents, concerning his partner, lay in a guarded vault. He knew Phoenix and Kevin Braxton were one in the same: only the fathers could explain *the accident*.

Chapter XXV

On Trevor's last night, dinner was a quiet affair. Granny had returned to Denver early, hating to see her grandchild struggle through more pain. Phoenix could now sit at the table, rather uncomfortably and irreconcilable over his lover's upcoming departure. Twister and Caly hovered over their son, willing him to smile over the arrival of Sebastian the following day. Nothing worked to erase the frown, except for Trevor's presence on entering the enormous suite, to sit beside and hold the small hand of a hapless patient who lay in an adjustable hospital-styled bed with the foot raised.

"I'll only be gone a few days, kiddo. Enjoy your time with Seb."

"Sorry I'm not in the game tonight. I'll miss you, Trev. Are you taking Bogie with you?"

"Not if you wish him to stay."

"If you don't mind. He likes sleeping on my bed; and since Snow and Sky can't without hurting me, it's nice to have his hot little belly on my feet."

"Sounds perfect. Now, get some sleep, because you have a busy day tomorrow. Bogie's already toasting your tootsies, and I'll be in cell range whenever you wish to call. Make it anytime, kiddo; anytime you feel as blue as you do tonight."

"I really miss sleeping with you. Man, this sucks."

"Not much longer. When I return, your stitches will be gone, and you'll be in my arms. Say good night, Phoenix."

"Good night, Phoenix."

"You are your dad's Diablo all right." Trevor kissed the perfect lips, swept his fingers through the soft white hair (freshly cut and highlighted with the strange pastels), and left his partner to fall away with a powerful potion brewed by Eagleclaws. He closed the door quietly behind him and walked down the long hall to find Mr. Jones. The question would be put forth this night.

"Did you settle him, Trevor?"

"He seems rather dejected. I wish I could stay, but I've neglected my own business dealings for over a year. The IRS will be after me soon."

"Phoenix understands. Our boy always has a down period while recovering. Boredom and frustration bounce around in his head. He'll be fine by the time you get back, and the constricting stitches are out. Caly and I would like to thank you again for all you've done and will continue to do. We're very pleased you found each other. It's cute how nervous he was, bringing a first time lover home, even though we've known for some time. We never expected such a roller-coaster ride with a gay son. He's our greatest joy, and I must admit, our favorite entertainment: the highs and the lows."

"I'm sure of it, because he's also mine. I never thought, at my age, that I would find someone I wished to share my life. He took his time rescuing me."

"He's saved us all in the strangest way. Caly and I can't be more honored that he accepted us as fathers."

"Where is your partner?"

"Went to check on Dancing on Diamonds with Jack and Grant. The filly's getting older, and we'll start weaning her soon, using the gradual method. A little wild for her mother at times, a forced separation could cause DD undue stress. She's quite an impish bundle as you've witnessed." Twister folded his newspaper and pushed himself out of the comfort of his chair to pour them each a scotch.

"She's all that and an extraordinary beauty. I've also witnessed Eagleclaws' tenderness toward Grant. They've grown very close. Nice to see them both smiling and healthy."

"Grant needs the inspirational words of our Arapaho wise man, while Jack requires the company. They have become good friends, finding each other, as one grows elderly, and the other... Well, they have each other for the moment."

"Hopefully the moment will last many years. I have something to ask you, something very important." Sloane accepted the drink, and the two men sat across from each other, nervously swirling the liquid amber in the crystal to catch the evening firelight, wondering who should start.

"I assume it's regarding Phoenix." The lanky cowboy opened the door first.

"I must know what happened to him. If I am unaware of anything that could trigger a setback, I need more information. Please, Twister, he hedges around the so-called *accident*, as if unable to voice his fears and the reasons for them."

"Caly and I have discussed this at length. Of course you must be told, but how was the question. We decided that if our son did not reveal his secret while on your long sojourn into the rainforest, and if your interest in him continued, we would show you. Unfortunately, your surgery left us all too fragile to deal with more. Now seems an opportune time. In the left-hand bottom drawer, of the large desk in the office, you'll find eight DVDs mastered by the FBI from a series of camcorder tapes. Underneath is a copy of the court transcripts, all priceless items to be sure. Pack everything in a case you can carry on the plane, and for God's sake, do not lose any of them. View them privately in New Mexico and bring them in like manner when you return to us. Be prepared for one shock after another. I would suggest you have a friend close by for aid. Since Sebastian will be here, perhaps Wolfe would be a strong supporter. You'll need someone, Trevor." The cowboy studied the face growing paler, knowing the big man already knew of one act perpetrated upon his son.

"Jesus, that bad?"

"A very mild term for the actuality. There are no words to describe what took place. I shudder and feel sickened as certain images assault my head when I least expect them. Caly displays symptoms of severe anxiety on recollection and awakens with nightmares to this day. He needs my protection to keep him from losing his mind over the ghastly mess we stumbled upon. Only court officials, the jury, a single FBI agent, and one police officer, plus Caly and me, have seen these films. The doctors allowed Phoenix and Granny to view a few minutes of the first disc to identify himself and those involved, as they were extremely concerned of adding visuals to his memories. We can only hope you can tolerate the answer to your request, without similar troublesome repercussions hurting you and passing them on to our boy. Can you promise me that?"

"Of course. I can promise blindly, for he is now part of me. From his scars, I gathered he was raped and viciously."

"Many times over, and perhaps the least traumatic of his injuries. Please take care. Return the tapes to me, and we'll destroy them when... We'll take care of them in three months time." Jones left the statement hanging. The photographer would discover the family's last troubling episode soon enough.

"Thanks, I'll call Wolfe immediately. I'm sure he'll accompany Sebastian tomorrow and rearrange his stay to accommodate a flight to Santa Fe. I'll take care of business first, before watching the trial."

"These are not court tapes, Trevor." Again, the cowboy eyed the large man who compulsively sat forward, his elbows on his knees, rubbing his palmed fingers against his lips.

Sloane said nothing further, now visibly rattled. With his request granted, he had to face a fearful unknown. New questions came to mind, pertinent ones, ones of dramatic consequence. Should he view the DVDs, or remain ignorant of Phoenix's nightmare; a young man scared to phobic proportions over too many things? If anguish filled two tough rodeo competitors over memories spanning a decade, what would witnessing the assault on the one he loved do to him? Would viewing the man's torment turn him around, preventing him from touching the innocent victim of the Furies? Nonetheless, he needed to know; curiosity ruled his head but broke his heart. Every detail of a youngster's changed pathway lay hidden in the left-hand bottom drawer.

Excusing himself from further conversation, a distraught man went into the office, found an expensive briefcase waiting for his use, and opened the designated drawer with trepidation. Innocuous enough in their plastic containers, the DVDs numbered one to eight. He reached down and hesitantly picked them up. Filled with doubt, Trevor calculated the footage of each, while contemplating their content. If they were not court files, the assailants must have videotaped the unknown deed, using copious amounts of film. The photographer would rely heavily on his dispassionate eye to watch the action. With a lump in his throat, he telephoned Wolfe who rallied to support his upset friend.

Travel arrangements were changed; the TJ Ranch executive jet would transport them to New Mexico quicker, more comfortably, and in their own time. After endearing kisses to their respective partners, they winged away to a private airport close to the cozy Southwest-influenced ranch. Swiftly managing his business affairs, Trevor readied himself to spend a day witnessing Phoenix's secrets. Wolfe stood firm; he refused to leave his friend alone during the predicted torturous task. Ensuring they had sufficient coffee, along with a few numbing beverages, the giant-sized men sat side-by-side in the locked study. The first DVD commenced; and they saw a handsome teenager, with wavy light-brown hair tied in a ponytail hanging down his back. Enthralled at the first look of the original model, they watched the boy enter a friendly living space, to enjoy a gathering of businessmen in ski sweaters. Kevin Braxton beamed happily; familiar purple eyes danced with each cordial greeting from a guest. The signature eyes disturbed the two men watching, knowing exactly who the teenager was.

The atmosphere seemed jovial, and the young man readily accepted a bottle of German brew and took a sip. He appeared to look around as if searching for friends. Another swallow of the liquid, a slight stagger forward, he fell to the ground, disoriented, and dazed. Violets startled wide open; the pupils dilated to obliterate the wondrous color. The host and another man consoled him, taking a few minutes to ensure the drug had taken affect, before carrying him up a flight of stairs and into a room furnished with one large bed, dozens of cameras, and many unrecognizable devices. Wolfe and Trevor sat forward, both had hands over their mouths, as the frightened teenager lay unmoving, unable to fend off those who secured his hands and feet to the four bedposts and cut off his clothing. Only the eyes showed terror: Kevin Braxton was immobilized, but his mind and senses remained alert to all else.

A redheaded woman attacked first, along with a nasty looking tabby feline. Dressed in stiletto-heeled boots to the thigh, a bustier, and a garter belt, the cheap looking she-devil climbed upon the boy, attempting to raise his limp cock with flagrant heterosexual oral sex. Unsuccessful, she bashed the young face with her fist, twisted off her prey, and placed her cat upon the boy's genitals. The virgin penis was used as a scratching post and the first agonizing scream escaped.

Moment by moment, the horrified men watched helplessly as the torture mounted, from gang banging to objects too large (for even the most ardently kinky gay) forced into a torn rectum. A pair of rough hands inserted a glass tube into a stretched bruised penis, only to smash the fragile item into bits within. Bones were broken, joints dislocated, the jaw unhinged grotesquely and used for sordid oral copulation, preventing the chance of teeth trimming the penetrating weapons. The blood, the screams, the sadism continued for hours; and still the young man lived. Laughing with fiendish glee, seven men wrapped the distorted figure, of one once human, and drove to an isolated area as the night sky lightened with the approach of dawn. Dumped in a predetermined location, another camcorder captured the broken angel, lying in fresh white snow slowly turning pink, as the purple dying eyes closed on the rising sun.

Five minutes after the green van departed, two cowboys stopped and jumped out of an expensive truck pulling a loaded horse trailer. Much excitement had one racing for the body, while yelling orders at his smaller friend to stay away, to contact the police, and to summon a medical airlift team. Riotous confusion commenced ten minutes after the call. The two men in Stetson's, however, had come to the dying boy's assistance, gently covering the broken body with warm horse blankets straight off the animals' heated backs, and as they waited, spoke to the deaf ears with the sweetness of grieving fathers. A helicopter landed on the road; ten police cars, three fire engines, and dozens of paramedics blocked the area. One horror-struck police officer found the last camcorder mounted on a fence post and handed it to his captain who asked the rewinding of the tape immediately.

At the end of the second last DVD, two men sat silent; both sick mentally and physically. Sloane could not move in his shock, his worst fears had not prepared him for such sadistic brutality. His friend, however, inserted the last disc and hit play, while reading the court transcripts. Wolfe watched the conclusion of the drama, following the trial along with the parts missed on the DVD. Eighteen relatives painfully identified loved ones from a still taken upon being greeted in the same manner as Kevin. On the tap of the gavel, the family member exited, and the jury was shown the disturbing photograph of the final demise of the lost spirit. All but three bodies had been found and identified, thanks to the FBI's findings of all the locations owned by the sinister group, as well as the discovery of the decayed remains by various police departments around the country. Their autopsies identified them all.

More salty droplets coursed down Trevor's face, still sitting silently, still unable to move as he listened to Twister's testimony, then Caly's stress filled statements, and then Mrs. Russell who identified her grandson in a picture showing the important cross tattooed on the finger holding a beer bottle. The finale pushed Sloane over the edge. Two armed guards, a doctor, and a nurse rolled in a gurney with a man lying supine, unable to speak. With weak squeezes of his fingers and little choking sobs, he answered the gentle questions put forward by the District Attorney and the accusations thrown at him from the defense team, which were quickly hushed by the judge. A poignant moment came when Granny tearfully stepped to the bandaged man's side, whispered loving words, and exposed the tiny tattoo.

Two hearts no longer beat in the locked study. Both Trevor and Wolfe sat disbelieving at the torment perpetrated on one who had already endured more than any man could. Kevin Braxton was removed from the courtroom and away from the finally silent defense team. The trial ended six months after Twister and Caly found the near dead body. Two months later, after sentences were decreed and the highest appellate court refused to grant a retrial or separate trials; the last victim was pronounced dead after medical complications. Phoenix Thornton-Jones rose from the ashes.

Wolfe finally stood and removed the disc, carefully placing in its case and back into the carrier. Turning, he slowly bent down in front of a mentally destroyed man who fell into his arms and clung for his life weeping. "Trevor, listen to me. He survived. You must dwell on that fact alone. This group of psychopathic killers had Phoenix marked as their nineteenth victim. These DVDs encompass every detail of a snuff movie; the original tapes then edited into a two-hour format and his torturers' faces eliminated. According to the transcripts, the police captain identified the host of the party immediately upon seeing the influential personage help discard the body. The police and FBI were on them immediately. I remember something about this hideous crime; the aftermath was enormous considering who the monsters were and the extent of their carnage. Phoenix or Kevin identified every one of the bastards, which in turn, along with the edited movies and original tapes found of the other eighteen murders, proved their guilt and sent them all to death row. Only parts of the extraordinary story were released to the news to protect the survivor. Are you listening to me, Trevor? The perpetrators are all dead, but one; all quietly terminated under Colorado Penal Law and FBI security. Each man's execution hit the headlines, and not even the believers fighting to eradicate the death penalty dared picket the prison in protest over such horrendous crimes. Seven men and one woman made up this group of serial killers who had tortured and killed young men for pleasure, for sport, and for money. The FBI had spent years hunting them, after their undercover agents discovered the first two movies made and sold via the Internet, and eighteen ungodly murders were solved through confiscated tapes found in the man's ski lodge. Phoenix pointed a finger at them all, laying them to waste, while helping the relatives of the other victims find and bury their missing sons. The only survivor, thanks to Twister and Caly, spoke out for those who could not. Come on, Sloane, you need fresh air, and I need a drink. It's over, and now you know. Kevin Braxton is dead, and you must let go of your horror, to enjoy a loving relationship with Phoenix Thornton-Jones. He needs you, my friend; he needs you more than his life." Wolfe helped steady the man on weak legs and led him through the darkness into the patio garden. With shaking hands, he lit candles in the stillness and returned to hold onto his friend; Trevor had not said a word in hours.

A choir of crickets' night-call filled the air, as two men sat, neither hungry, neither thirsty. In shock, sweating but shivering, Sloane finally cleared his throat and attempted to rub some feeling into his sorrow-filled face. The brown eyes had darkened in fury, wishing Phoenix's attackers had paid with similar vile treatment, and he uttered an oath of profanity. Never had he imagined the enormity of *the accident*, and he remembered every shiver and tremor the young man experienced whenever touched. Even after weeks of lovemaking, the involuntary movements continued; he now knew why. Trevor felt equally responsible for his fragile lover's nightmares, having attempted to ease the phobias, but possibly creating others. Unable to think rationally, he started forming wrong conclusions in his fevered head. With his senses ravished, his sight blurred, his listening impaired, he felt alone with no idea as to his next step. He needed Phoenix, but could not separate his partner from the grotesque figure being tortured.

"I think you need to rest, Trevor. It's been a hellish day, probably the worst one of my life." Wolfe played with his glass, having difficulty swallowing a liquid to distort the images he had viewed for hours.

"I have things to think about." The baritone voice cracked, and a hand came up to wipe the smoldering eyes overflowing with holy tears.

"There's nothing to think about. We'll leave early in the morning to see delighted smiles on our lovers' sweet faces." The crystal whiskey glass was set aside and large nervous hands wrung together.

"I'm not returning, Wolfe."

"Yes you are. Phoenix can't come here, not yet anyway." A squint of puzzlement, laced with anger, stared Sloane down.

"I must leave him, man. How can I touch him after the hell those psychopaths forced upon him? He's so very tiny, so very frightened, so very..."

"...I don't believe this. He loves you, and you love him. What do you plan to do--send him a note--lie to him? You can't tell him that we saw his attack, and he now revolts you. That's it, isn't it? He's no longer a beautiful angel, but a scarred leftover used by others. Jesus, Sloane, you're worse than those who tossed him aside."

"No! No, of course not. Hurting him now will be easier on him. Never seeing me again, disappearing from his life, he will be upset and angry at first, but it will be swift. Just as he rides the fences, not searching for breaks but for fucking camcorders, he will find away to forget me. I can't look at him, Wolfe, because I'll never forget seeing him twisted... oh, god, what he went through, I just..." Trevor shook his head and covered his gaunt, gray face with his hands. He only saw the atrocity inflicted upon one no longer human. His future had died, even though the innocent had not. Freeing his troubled partner was his only choice; releasing the young man to chance love with someone unknowing of *the accident*.

"Think, Sloane. The assault was demonic, but the boy on those DVDs was Kevin Braxton, not the man we know as Phoenix Thornton-Jones. They don't look alike, and after ten years and what has transpired since, they can't possibly think alike. Separate them, and love the one you know: a survivor, a man of courage, a man who saved your life twice over, a man who is perfect for you. Don't throw him away; you'll lose everything." The big man, with plaited hair hanging down his back, arose and took one pace toward his friend. He had a decision to make.

"They have the same eyes. God, he lived through it all and remembers every detail. I don't want to remember; but those images will haunt me forever." Trevor also stood, turning away from a cobra's stare before it struck. The hand on his shoulder was not kind as it twisted him around. He felt a whistle of air before the black fist came out of nowhere. Falling backward, he had no chance when the large hands grabbed him by the neck and hauled him to his feet. He tasted blood; he felt the pain; he deserved more.

"You selfish son-of-a-bitch, I'm fed up with your conclusions and will leave as soon as I drag the pilot out of bed. Are you coming with me, or are you going to sit here feeling sorry for yourself and hurting Phoenix further?"

"No, I'm sorry, Wolfe, but please, return the DVDs to Twister."

"The hell I will; they're your responsibility." The larger man dropped the photographer and shoved him into the expensive furnishings. The young man, with the purple eyes, would have loved the reclusive, beautiful home and surrounding lands, but one bad decision by Sloane would nullify Phoenix's chances of ever seeing the oasis hideaway. Wolfe could not believe the anger rising through his soul, wanting to beat his old comrade senseless.

Trevor rubbed his head after wiping the blood from his swelling lip. A coyote howl sent goose bumps up his spine, making him shiver;

the strange melody programmed on his cellular telephone scared him to his grave. "Jesus, it's Phoenix. I can't speak to him."

"You can and you must. It's very late, and he's calling for you." Wolfe pulled his feelings inward and reached out, tipping Sloane's hand up toward his ear. The time came for the photographer to pull himself out of the past and into a young man's future, a crucial moment for the new couple and for the one standing by.

"Trevor? Are you there?"

"Hey, kiddo. How are you feeling?"

"Missing you. Can't wait for your return. I called a few times, but you're phone wasn't working."

"I put my cell in my pocket, and by habit, shut it off."

"That can happen."

"What have you and Sebastian been doing today?"

"Went for a walk this afternoon. I'm healing fast, Trev, now that the stitches aren't pulling at me. Seb and Jazz just left my suite. We had a late night and some fun."

"I'm happy to hear that. You need company of your own age."

"I just need you. Is something wrong? Your voice quivered."

"Just tired."

"Oh, I'm sorry. Did I wake you?"

"No, Wolfe and I are having a very late night as well."

"You need company of your own age, Mr. Sloane." A giggle opened a door for both, and the older man feigned a chuckle.

"I guess I do."

"Tell me a story, Trev. Talk about anything. I want to hear your voice whispering in my ear. How about something lurid and sultry?" The beautiful tenor voice grew raspier in its seduction, unfortunately it now sounded artificial to the photographer; he only heard a voice created by surgeons. Trevor could no longer identify what was human and what was manufactured.

"Phone sex? I don't think so."

"Spoil sport. Tell me about your Cherokee heritage then, or your grandmother. You must have plenty of stories from your travels." Phoenix's instincts honed in on the strained idle chatter of clipped sentences and alerted to something not right.

"From sex to grandmothers, where is your head tonight, Phoenix?"

"You sound stressed; and I thought a diversion would make you feel better. Are you sure everything's okay? I'm really looking forward to seeing you tomorrow."

"About tomorrow..." Trevor held back the gagging sensation, unable to say the words.

"Do you have further business to take care of? I hope not, since I miss you like crazy, and so does Bogie."

"No, Phoenix, I won't..." The soft baritone voice broke again, but heard on a vibration of a telephone wire. Sloane knew the young man held his breath; he had to speak the truth. "I'm not returning to Colorado."

"What? Why not? Should I come there?"

"No, kiddo, that wouldn't be wise."

"I don't understand. When will I see you again?"

"Not for some time. I'm going away for a while, Phoenix. I have things to think about."

"How long will you be gone, and what is there to think about?"

"I don't know, but I need time. Something has come up, and I'm honestly confused and upset. Please take the opportunity to explore your options, now that you have experienced a taste of real life. You keep Bogie. He needs a good friend." Trevor wiped his eyes, controlling the stinging emotions of saying good-bye. Looking up, he watched Wolfe turn away and leave.

"You're kidding me. You wouldn't break an oath, or leave me alone to defend our views on the rainforest. You're the only man I trust; there won't be anyone else. What are you thinking? What's happened? We're partners; I love you and thought you loved me." The frightened voice rose to a higher pitch; spitting sounds of sobs made the words almost unintelligible.

"I do, but you're young. Life stretches before you, to change on a breeze or a final whisper. Eternity lies elsewhere for me, and I must follow that road." Trevor stifled his breathing to prevent choking on his broken promises. Hurting someone, already suffering from woes beyond reason, had not been his plan. An instant decision, he could say no more.

"It sounds like you're never coming back. I don't understand. What will I do? Please don't leave me, Trevor. God, say something. What has happened since you left? What have I done? What about our plans, our work? Tell me something, anything. You'd never be this cruel." The truth hit hard, and Phoenix stiffened in his shock. His life in the real world crashed down on shoulders too frail.

"Good-bye, kiddo."

"No! Please, no. No." The little whimpers sounded exactly

like the pleas of Kevin Braxton as the drug wore off and before the jaw was brutally dislocated. Sloane could not deal with the memory and clicked off his telephone, dropping it on the cushion next to him. Covering his face with his hands, he understood every phobia of the troubled heart and needed time to adjust his raging fury and disgust after witnessing the horrible secret. His mind whirled with images too powerful to dismiss. How did his partner survive a night of torture: every bone broken twice over, his face smashed to pulp, a larynx nearly severed through, the small chest mutilated, and his genitals and rectum damaged almost beyond repair? Trevor shivered violently. His diminutive lover was stronger than any man he knew. Phoenix lived to tell the story, sending seven men, one woman, and a cat to their deaths for eighteen murders, eighteen snuff movies, and one unsuccessful attempt. The damaged white angel was a hero he had to set free, but Trevor Sloane wished only ignorance and sobbed like a child into his cupped hands, without a friend, a family, or a lover to console him.

Phoenix remained as stone, frozen in a moment to last his remaining days. With his beautiful mind and heart shattered, his purple violets no longer danced, and he slipped out of bed, to stand alone on knees unwilling to lock. His only thoughts fixated on Trevor Sloane; all his dreams fell into disarray. He limped slowly and carefully down the cold wooden hallway, fear of the dark making him shake and wanting to run; but he kept moving, needing to find the bedroom he had shared with a legend. The bed drew him in, to slip under the sheets for a moment in search of a familiar scent. A heady aroma of musk and fern fragrant soap set a mind in motion. Tears would never fall again, now fully and finally satiated by one man. He needed no other. Nothing left for him to do, he clasped his sore hips and slowly walked away from life, exiting the front door in navy blue flannel, his cowboy boots, an oversized green Arctic parka (just for the memory), and two white dogs and a silver-coated cat following closely behind. The sky grew lighter just before dawn; he would walk east, to fall into the sun like the firebird he was named after. With no sense of feeling or a final glance backward, he and his band of comrades would finish the job started ten years earlier.

End of Volume I

Author Biography

Raven Davies attended university in the faculties of Fine Arts and Interior Design, unfortunately ending up in the corporate world. The well paying job gave this author the means to travel much of the world and to live in other countries. When a 9 to 5 job became too distressing for an artist's mind, Davies discarded the security and started an in-house business, designing and hand-painting ceramic tile, as well as becoming a spiritual guide for seekers of ancient wisdom. Albeit rewarding artistically, spiritually, and mentally, the monetary challenges grew too great, and Davies started writing epic Slash tales under the name 'Ravin' to ease the strain.

A storyteller by nature, Raven creates character-driven fiction to challenge a reader's thoughts, whether it be spiritually, politically, or socially. On a rash decision, and having had overwhelming success as a Slash fan fiction writer of five novels, this Canadian renegade packed up a small U-haul, purchased a broken down jeep, and left all behind. While residing in Mexico, Davies wrote two gay novels: *Between Here & There*, a published paperback, and the *PlanetTerra Journals Volume I: WET SEASON,* now available in both eBook and paperback formats, as well as contributing to two hardcover anthologies. Having returned to Canada, Raven Davies is hard at work with four new stories, plus a series of sequels to the *PlanetTerra Journals.* You will find what currently is available, plus a free Slash read based on *The Magnificent Seven*, the television series, at www.frictionfiction books.com, the home page of Raven Davies.

Other Publishing Credits

"Between Here & There":   currently published by Llumina Press, but is being re-edited and published as an eBook and a paperback with Friction Fiction Books (this version should be available by late 2012), but in the meantime, the original paperback is available from Llumina. See Raven's website for information: www.frictionfictionbooks.com

"When David and Ted meet the Mistress they embark on a whirling adventure through spiritual realms and earthly lusts that transforms them both and enthralls the reader. 'Between Here & There', by Raven Davies is a sweeping, glorious gay love story like no other you've ever encountered. By turns comic and heartwarming, Between Here & There is a story to engage the heart, mind and soul. Be warned: Once you begin it, you won't be able to put it down." Ralph Higgins (reviewer for *Wayves Magazine).*

"Raven Davies is one of the most original literary artists working today. Davies is successfully bridging the gulf between traditional fiction and the new, exciting world of Internet 'Slash' writing. With tremendous assurance and with great panache, Davies is giving readers an entirely fresh and fascinating reading experience. At this time of crossover literary technologies, Davies is emerging as a singular creative voice. This breathless, altogether remarkable storytelling makes for compelling reading." Joseph Dispenza (author): *'The Way of the Traveler', 'The House of Alarcon', and 'Religion without a God'.*

"Raven Davies brings unusual and exhilarating life to a unique work with a poetic style, imagination, and a keen eye for what lies beneath the surface of the human condition." Warren Redman (award winning author): *"Achieving Personal Success", 'Listening Power', 'Portfolios for Development, 'Counseling Your Staff', 'Facilitation Skills for Team Development', 'Working Towards Independence', 'Finding Your Own Support',* and *'Creative Training'.*

*"**Between Here and There** is a well-crafted novel, combining romance, mystery, mysticism, and adventure. The writer takes us inside the character's emotions, showing an intensely complex range of fear, anger, love, need, desire, human curiosity, and so much more. The power of male love, shown through sex and intrigue, is blended together not only in the world as we know it, but the spirit realm as well. This makes for a thought provoking and interesting tale, which still has me reeling and thinking. The story is exciting, mature, and erotic, with a climax as surprising as any you will find. Truly an engaging, wildly imaginative story, I recommend this book highly."* Reviewer (a reader from Tennessee, USA).

"Sexy and well written, a thought provoking novel. Constructed to make a coherent, powerful, and unusual statement. Found it intellectually stimulating, spiritually provocative, and entertaining to read." Reviewer (a reader from San Miguel de Allende, Gto, Mexico).

Contributor of the essay *'**The Slash Fanfiction Connection to Bi Men'** for the anthology: *'Bi Men: Coming Out Every Which Way'.* Editors - Ron Suresha and Pete Chvany; Published by Haworth Press.

Contributor of excerpt from *'**Between Here & There'** entitled *'**Unleashing Deranged Snakes'** for the anthology: *'Bi Guys: Firsthand fiction for Bisexual Men and Their Admirers'.* Editor - Ron Suresha; Published by Harrington Park Press, 2005

*"...The literary tone and styles vary. There are polished pieces by famous writers like Felice Picano and Pat Califia, grittier accounts by relative newcomers ...Myself, a traditionalist, I most enjoyed Larry Lawton's prison story, Simon Sheppard's encounter between two college boys, **Raven Davies' depiction of two closeted actors**, and Felice Picano's variation on a perennial favorite ...These stimulating stories will satisfy the erotic needs of pretty much all readers. As Ron Suresha explains...the stories are meant to instruct as well as excite.*

First and foremost, the collection wants to overcome shame...Whatever the specifics, all stories insist that bisexuality is an authentic human experience, to be pursued without shame.

"We can all then be grateful to Editor Ron Suresha and his writers for this collection. Their stories are not only entertaining and stimulating; they introduce to a wide readership a range of bisexual issues and emotions not normally treated in literature, straight or gay. And they deal with these issues positively - with the seriousness and clarity they deserve..." Review by David Van Leer in the *'Journal Edition of BI MEN 2006'*

Both anthologies are available online at http://www.haworthpress.com/web/JB © 2005 by The Haworth Press, Inc. All rights reserved. They also appear in *'The Haworth Journal of Bisexuality'*, vol. 5, nos. 2-3, December 2005.

For further information on *'Between Here & There'* and a Slash free read, please go to Raven Davies' website:
www.frictionfictionbooks.com

www.ingramcontent.com/pod-product-compliance
Lightning Source LLC
Chambersburg PA
CBHW020604270326
41927CB00005B/168